D1681037

90 0411074 1

This book is to be returned on
or before the date stamped below

WITHDRAWN
FR
UNIVERSI

BURIAL IN MEDIEVAL IRELAND

Burial in Medieval Ireland, 900–1500

A Review of the Written Sources

SUSAN LEIGH FRY

FOUR COURTS PRESS

Set in 10.5 on 12 point Bembo for
FOUR COURTS PRESS
Fumbally Lane, Dublin 8, Ireland
e-mail: info@four-courts-press.ie
and in North America
FOUR COURTS PRESS
c/o ISBS, 5804 N.E. Hassalo Street, Portland, OR 97213.

© Susan Leigh Fry 1999

A catalogue record for this title
is available from the British Library.

ISBN 1–85182–309–3

All rights reserved. No part of this publication may be
reproduced, stored in or introduced into a retrieval
system, or transmitted, in any form or by any means
(electronic, mechanical, photocopying, recording or
otherwise), without the prior written permission of both
the copyright owner and the publisher of this book.

UNIVERSITY OF PLYMOUTH
LIBRARY SERVICES

Item No.	411074 1
Class No.	393 FRY
Contl No.	✓

Printed in Great Britain
by MPG Books, Bodmin, Cornwall.

For my mother,
Martella Graves Fry
and my fathers,
John Robert Mitsch (1916–1962)
and
George Blanchard Fry (1911–1997)

And what you thought you came for
Is only a shell, a husk of meaning
From which the purpose breaks only when it is fulfilled
If at all. Either you had no purpose
Or the purpose is beyond the end you figured
And is altered in fulfillment

T.S. Eliot, 'Little Gidding'

Contents

Contents

Abbreviations of Sources Cited

AClon	*Annals of Clonmacnoise*, ed. Dennis Murphy
AConn	*Annals of Connacht*, ed. & trans. A. Martin Freeman
AFM	*The Annals of the Kingdom of Ireland by the Four Masters*, ed. & trans. John O'Donovan
AI	*Annals of Inisfallen*, ed. & trans. Seán MacAirt
ALC	*Annals of Loch Cé*, ed. & trans. W.M. Hennessy
AMacF	'Annals of Ireland from the year 1443 ... translated by ... Dudley mac Firbisse', ed. John O'Donovan
Ann. Mon. Beata	*'Annales monasterii Beata Marie Viriginis, juxta Dublin'*, (Annals of St Mary's Abbey, Dublin), ed. J.T. Gilbert
AU	*Annals of Ulster*, ed. & trans. Seán MacAirt & Gearóid MacNiocaill
Bk Fe.	*Book of Fenagh*, ed. & trans. William Hennessy
Caithr. Th.	*Caithréim Thoirdhealbhaigh*
Cal. Pap. Reg.	*Calendar of entries in the papal registers relating to Great Britain and Ireland (letters)*, eds. W.H. Bliss, et al.
Chart. St Mary's	*Charters of St. Mary's Abbey, Dublin ... and the annals of Ireland, 1162–1370*, ed. & trans. J.T. Gilbert
Clyn & Dowling	*Annals of Ireland by Friar John Clyn and Thady Dowling*, ed. R. Butler
FAII	*Fragmentary Annals of Ireland*, ed. & trans. Joan N. Radner
Félire	*Félire Oengussa Céli Dé* (Martyrology of Oengus the Culdee) ed. & trans. W. Stokes
JRSAI	*Journal of the Royal Society of Antiquaries, Ireland*
Lives	Charles Plummer, *Lives of the Irish Saints* (*Bethada Náem nÉrenn*)
Met. Dind.	*Metrical Dindsenchas* ed. & trans. Edward Gwynn
Mon. Hib.	Mervyn Archdall, *Monasticum Hibernicum*
OED	*Oxford dictionary of the English language*
PRIA	*Proceedings of the Royal Irish Academy*
Reg. Mon. Athenry	*'Regestum monasterii fratrum praedicatorum de Athenry'*, ed. Ambrose Coleman
RIA Dict.	*Contributions to a dictionary of the Irish language* (Royal Irish Academy)
RSAI	Royal Society of Antiquaries of Ireland
SG	*Silva Gadelica*, ed. & trans. S.H. O'Grady
Stat. Scot.	*Statutes of the Scottish Church 1225–1559*
UJA	*Ulster Journal of Archaeology*

Preface

My object in producing this work has been to find what information exists in the historical sources regarding burial in Ireland between 900 and 1500, organize it by subject-matter and make some preliminary observations about it. Ireland is in the enviable position of having rich and widely diverse source for this period, and while I have the examined the majority of these, time has not permitted me to fully exhaust the supply. For this reason I have subtitled this study 'a review of the written sources' rather than a 'survey', and included a full biography to allow readers to see exactly what has been consulted.

While I researched and wrote this book, many people asked why I chose to study burial. The answer is simple: no one gets out of life alive. Death is one of life's few common experiences, and while death does not always inevitably lead to burial, for people who died in western Europe during the Middle Ages, the odds were overwhelming that it did. Burial, then, functions as a sort of 'control' which offers insights into the religious practices and social structures of a society – a sort of magic window which allows us to view the religious practices and social structures of a medieval European society.

Burial has also proven to be a sort 'Pandora's box'. Almost as soon as I started working on medieval Irish burial, a huge, diverse, an seemingly ever-expanding number of subjects began emanating from it, including civil law, early Christian liturgical history, architecture, medicine, geography, cartography, comparative anthropology, and many more.[1]

Surely, many historians have been astonished by the breadth and diversity of their subjects and have found it necessary to narrow their focus. But limiting the scope of my inquiry was problematical; my goal was to sift out and organize all information about burial contained in the source – and a single reference often touched on a myriad of topics

It was, therefore, extremely helpful to find Philippe Ariès' introduction to his seminal history of death in France. In it, Ariès has explained why he decided to

[1] Because Christianity was adopted gradually as the majority religion by European populations, the usefulness of the term 'early Christian' continues to be the subject of scholarly debate. I take the view that these objections have some validity; however until another term comes into general usage, I have chosen to use 'early Christian' to refer generally to the period of roughly the late fifth through late eighth centuries.

incorporate such a wide range of evidence into his study. He has stated that his original intention was fairly simple: to study the piety of the French, who he had observed coming to visit cemeteries each November. However, as Ariès conducted his research, the scope if his work began expanding exponentially, a situation that is parallels with my own experience studying medieval Irish burial. As he tells us,

> I decided to take a closer look. Imprudent curiosity! … There was no turning back. I had lost all freedom; from now on I was totally caught up in a search that constantly expanded. I would gladly have limited my attention to choice of burial in wills. But how could I resist all this other fascinating evidence, so varied beneath its deceptive appearance of sameness?[2]

In the end, Ariès' study of piety as demonstrated by visits to French cemeteries grew into a survey of burial in France over the period of one thousand years.

When I read this, I began to think that if Ariès – a fine historian who surely appreciated the need for scholarly discipline and limiting one's research to one's area of expertise – had determined that he needed to consider information provided by enormously disparate sources and disciplines, perhaps I could also take a broadly based approach. In no way do I mean to compare my work with that of Ariès. But his courage in considering such an enormous amount of evidence, and his ability to synthesize it into an immensely readable volume, provided a valuable and encouraging precedent.

That burial has proved to be a vast subject is not surprising given the number of western Europeans who have participated in it throughout the centuries. The enormous popularity of burial (not to mention the high probability that anyone reading this will have personal experience with it at some point) has encouraged me to make the information in this book as accessible as possible to all readers, regardless of their level of familiarity with Ireland's geography, medieval history or literature. To this end, I have supplied copious references in the belief that the additional detail they provide may prove useful and time-saving to some readers. Where Irish-placenames occur, I have noted the counties in which they are located, endeavored to include their modern names, and when indicated, the best information available as to their location. Irish surnames can be daunting, so in numerous cases I have provided their modern anglicized spellings, as well as English translations for quotations and inscriptions originally written in Irish or Latin. I have also done my best to list dates of composition for sources whenever it seemed that such information would be helpful. While some readers may find these practices tedious, I hope that they will appre-

2 Ariès, *The hour*, p. xv.

ciate that they are attempts to repay the debt which I owe to scholars who so greatly assisted me by including this kind of information in their own works.

I have been greatly assisted in this work work by a number of generous people, foremost among whom are Dr Katharine Simms of Trinity College, Dublin and Professor David Dumville of Cambridge University. When Dr Simms agreed to be my supervisor, I was given a great gift. Her passion for medieval Irish history, and her wide-ranging knowledge of its myriad facets are inspiring; her generosity in sharing her knowledge and her enthusiastic interest in my work and its publication have been enormously motivating. Professor Dumville first surprised me by agreeing to look over a part of this work, then stunned me by reviewing the entire manuscript. The attempt I make here to express my gratitude to both of them is woefully inadequate.

Professor Gearóid Mac Niocaill of University College, Galway, and Dr Seán Duffy of Trinity College, Dublin, read my dissertation and gifted me with their expert criticism. Professor Geoffrey Koziol of the University of California, Berkeley, and Professor Jim Mallory and Dr Finbar McCormick, both of Queen's University, Belfast, were kind enough to review sections of this manuscript prior to publication.

Sincere thanks are also due to Dr Joan Keefe of the University of California, Berkeley; and to Professor J.F. Lydon and Dr Bernadette Williams, both of Trinity College, Dublin, for their support and assistance. Loyal friends and true whose help was of critical importance include Dr Tina Hellmuth; Dr Ruth Johnson; my sister, Ann Simonson; Norman Mongan; Dr Micheál Beausang and Aïsha Beausang.

Dr Sylvain Louboutin invested countless hours in this project; Michael Adams, Ronan Gallagher and Martin Fanning of Four Courts Press have made it possible for me to share my work with a greater audience.

The encouragement which I received from both Professor Alfred Smyth of the University of Kent and Professor Dan Melia of the University of California, Berkeley, when I was tentatively exploring the possibility of doing research in medieval history is remembered and gratefully acknowledged. Special thanks to the helpful staff of the Berkeley Library at Trinity College Dublin, who made my long days spent there brighter: Iris Bedford, Eileen Birch, Harry Bovenizer, Tony Carey, Mary Higgins, Shane Mawe, Veronica Morrow, Donncha O'Donnchadha, Jimmy O'Keeffe, Jimmy Wall, Anne Walsh.

CHAPTER I

Introduction

Much scholarly research has been done on attitudes to death and dying, including the ways in which individuals and communities have prepared for death and responded to it. This book, however, is concerned only with burial itself and is a study of the events, actions and physical artifacts which relate specifically to burial in medieval Ireland.

METHODS

The 600-year period examined in this book is an exceptionally long one for a historical study, though not without precedent in cultural history. In the introduction to *The hour of our death*, his ground-breaking study of death in France, Philippe Ariès explained his rationale for the very great period of time which he chose to consider.

> If [the historian] confines himself to too short a time span, although it may seem long according to the classical historical method, he runs the risk of attributing originality to phenomena that are really much older. The historian of death must not be afraid to embrace the centuries until they run into a millennium.[1]

The period AD 900 to AD 1500 has been chosen for this study for a number of reasons, the first of which is that burial is a conservative social practice which changes slowly.[2] Because of this, a long period of time must be considered for changes to be detected in burial customs. The six centuries which are the focus of this study encompass major events in Irish medieval history, including the Gregorian reform of the Church, the introduction of the Continental monastic orders to Ireland (beginning in 1142), and the arrival of the Anglo-French in 1169. At first, I considered a study of the somewhat 'tidier' 500-year period of 1000 to 1500. However, because so few Irish annalistic entries relating to burial occur prior

---

1 Ibid., pp xvi–xvii. 2 See, for example, P. Brown, *Cult of the saints*, p. 24: 'Burial customs are among the most notoriously stable aspects of most cultures'.

to 'Anglo-Norman' involvement Ireland, starting this study at the millennium would have required me to eliminate tenth-century entries which contain uniquely interesting information. The reader will also find that I have occasionally overstepped the stated time-boundaries when I felt that presenting earlier or later evidence would help illuminate burial practices between 900 and 1500.

Ariès described the methods which he employed in researching *The hour of our death* as being 'more intuitive and subjective, but perhaps more comprehensive' than a 'quantitative analysis of homogeneous documentary series'. Using his method, 'the observer scans a chaotic mass of documents and tries to decipher, beyond the intentions of the writers or artists, the unconscious expression of the sensibility of the age'.[3]

My original intention was to produce just such a 'quantitative analysis of homogeneous documentary series' – an analysis of the information in the Irish chronicles which relates to burial. However, it soon became obvious that such a study would not be nearly as informative as I had originally hoped. To begin with, I discovered that the number of Irish-chronicle entries relating to burial is smaller than I had anticipated and, with a few notable exceptions, they tend to be fairly formulaic and lacking in detail. This group of sources also reflects various geographical and political biases, and each focuses on particular regions and kindreds. It became clear that, because of these factors, a quantitative analysis of burial information in Irish chronicles would not provide an accurate 'overview' of burial practice in medieval Ireland. This would be true even with the inclusion of evidence from the 'Anglo-Irish' chronicles, since the Anglo-Irish entries also pertain to a narrow – albeit different – segment of Irish society.

To find information on as much of the Irish population as possible, it was necessary to consult many different types of sources, since any source was as likely as the next to contain information about burial. For example, I had not initially expected to survey the *Calendar of papal letters*, yet this source supplied some unique and valuable details, just as an eighteenth-century travel-journal yielded striking testimony regarding the disposition of skulls and bones. In the end, Ariès' 'chaotic mass of documents' proved impossible to resist, and I eagerly consulted sources of all types.

RATIONALE FOR THIS STUDY

Most of the work done to date in later medieval Irish history has been in the areas of political and economic history; far less consideration has been given to social and cultural history. It is a lack which needs to be addressed, and that need

---

3 Ariès, *The hour*, p. xvii.

has been noted by leading scholars of the medieval British Isles, specializing in a variety of disciplines.

A strong case can be made that the 'Anglo-Norman' conquest of Ireland was the most important event to occur in Ireland during the Middle Ages. Yet R.R. Davies, the noted historian of medieval Wales, has argued that an alien, invading population's success in subjugating a native population depends not only on military and economic conquest, but on cultural conquest as well.[4] Therefore, we might suspect that any conquest would also affect the conquered country's most important religious and social rituals.

In 1978, the influential historian F.S.L. Lyons pointed out the urgent need to study Irish cultural history. Expanding on E. Estyn Evans' view that Irish historical studies needed to co-operate more closely with geographers and anthropologists,[5] Lyons stated

> When we look … to social history, cultural history, the history of ideas, the poverty of what we have to offer is deeply disturbing … Not only have historians too often disregarded the physical evidence around them, they have not even fully explored their literary evidence to give us a rounded view of our society.[6]

In the same year, R.D. Edwards, another great Irish historian, also cautioned that 'the archaeological and anthropological evidence linking Ireland historically to Europe and Asia must be studied further …'[7] Studying traditional social institutions in order to assess changes in social and cultural practices is an obvious place to look for such links, and as one of the most conservative of social practices, burial provides an excellent opportunity to do this.[8]

Archaeologists agree that burials can provide a great deal of information. J.P. Mallory, for example, has noted that 'there is basically a rough hierarchy of evidence that ranks burials as among the more significant evidence for migration and intrusion, closely followed by changes in architecture, ceramics and economy …'.[9] Tania Dickinson and others have written that, as a subject, burial has the potential to contribute information on an extremely diverse range of topics.[10] Archaeologist Susan Hirst has stated[11] 'the Anglo-Saxon cemetery … ought by now to have been recognized as an unwritten form of historical document roughly equivalent (though at once broader in scope and less exact) to the parish register of later times, and investigated as such.'

In his famous Hunter Marshall lectures of 1968, Charles Thomas' comments about his own discipline of archaeology seemed to echo the statements by Lyons,

---

4 R.R. Davies, *Domination*, pp 19–24. **5** Lyons, 'The burden', p. 92. **6** Ibid. **7** Edwards, 'An agenda', p. 59. **8** Ariès, *The hour*, p. xvi. **9** Mallory, *In search of the Indo-Europeans*, p. 165. **10** Dickinson, 'The present state', p. 21. **11** Hirst, 'Some aspects', p. 239.

Edwards and Estyn Evans quoted above: 'an excavated church is, when all is said and done, no more than an excavated church; there is a limit beyond which inference, however cunningly deployed, cannot legitimately wander.'[12] More recently, archaeologist Richard Bradley has also appealed for greater integration between disciplines, pointing out that

> historical archaeology does need a coherent methodology but this must be one which uses *all* the material … By the late Saxon period the combination of artifacts and written sources might even permit us to calibrate the archaeological record. This would be a fundamental advance towards an integrated discipline.[13]

Of the state of the study of medieval European history at the close of the twentieth century, medieval historian Patrick Geary has written:

> More and more, historians look at structures, long-term processes, and other issues previously the domain of ethnography and anthropology. As a result, we are increasingly aware of the limits of our written sources and also that, for much of our work, archaeology is indispensable. The time has come when we can and must work together.[14]

Happily, in the recent work of insular archaeologists, especially Heather James and Elizabeth O'Brien, we are starting to see a movement in Irish archaeology towards just the kind of integrated approach which Bradley has championed.[15] Yet this 'calibration of the archaeological record' for burial in medieval Ireland will only be accomplished if the information available from *all* extant written sources for the period is considered.

In spite of the fact that an enormous number of written Irish sources have survived from the Middle Ages, Elizabeth O'Brien's work remains the first deliberate effort to analyze them specifically for burial information; however it does not consider Irish sources written after *c.*700. Virtually no study has been undertaken – historical, archaeological, or anthropological – of Irish burial in the Middle Ages. This is true in spite of the fact that these were the turbulent centuries during which both Vikings and 'Anglo-Normans' invaded Ireland (which was then a country with a highly localized polity), and ultimately (by 1650) effected the transformation of the island into one political and economic unit ruled from England. In consequence, the study of native medieval Irish social institutions certainly seems worthwhile.

12 C. Thomas, *The early Christian archaeology*, p. 3.   13 Bradley, 'Anglo-Saxon cemeteries', p. 175.   14 Geary, *Living with the dead*, p. 45.   15 James, 'Early medieval cemeteries in Wales'; 'The cult of St David in the Middle Ages'; O'Brien, 'Late prehistoric/early historic Ireland: the burial evidence reviewed' and 'A re-assessment of the "great sepulchral mound"', to name just some of their work.

Kathleen Hughes argued that written accounts of Irish saints' lives – long thought to be of little use to historians – can yield useful historical information if one is willing to learn the genre, and thus become able to distinguish literary convention from what is probably genuine historical detail. Similarly, Katharine Simms' work with Irish bardic poetry is proving that this genre – also formerly regarded as being of little use for historical study – has much to offer.

In advocating the consideration of a wide range of sources for the study of medieval Irish burial, I echo the views of the scholars quoted above. However, it is useful to point to R.D. Edwards' cautionary observation that in choosing an interdisciplinary approach 'one is not underestimating the difficulties of assessment'.[16] Edwards was commenting specifically on the literary material, but the same may be said for virtually all of the sources I have consulted.

The large quantity of extant Irish medieval written sources, their diversity, the wide-ranging nature of their themes, and the limited amount of time available to complete this study have precluded in-depth analysis of the information which they contain on burial. Many of the subjects touched upon would benefit greatly from further exploration by experts in the various specialized disciplines, as well as from a more thorough search for comparative material from other western European countries. I hope others will take up the challenges outlined here.

In addition to providing an overview of the burial-related information contained in Irish medieval sources, I have considered the question of what medieval Ireland's cultural relationships were with her closest neighbors in western Europe. As an island located off an island, Ireland is geographically isolated from the European continent. This isolation, coupled with the fact that Ireland was not conquered by the Romans, has for centuries fostered the view – certainly the popular view – that Ireland was also *culturally* isolated and remained largely 'outside the mainstream' of the romanized culture which so profoundly affected her neighbors to the east, both Insular and Continental.

The view of Ireland as an uncivilized backwater with very different social customs from those of England and continental Europe was already prevalent in the late twelfth century when Giraldus Cambrensis wrote his *Topography of Ireland*, a work which further popularized this idea. Indeed, the view that the Irish were barbarians running amok who needed to be dragged into line with the practices of reformed Continental churches was partly used to justify the 'Anglo-Norman' invasion and the subjection of Ireland to English rule.[17]

It is indisputable fact that some customs of the Gaelic Irish churches differed significantly from those of Continental churches, and the writings of the highly

16 Edwards, 'An agenda', p. 60. **17** The accuracy of the terms 'Anglo-Norman' and 'Anglo-Norman invasion' are hotly debated; because they have been widely used in previous works on the history of medieval Ireland, I have chosen to use them, but to place them in quotation marks.

politicized Giraldus and others record these writers' perceptions of the ways in which the Irish themselves were different. However, the question of how different the social customs of the native Irish and their English and continental European contemporaries were in reality is an important one. More complete use of all existing written sources can yield valuable information. For example, the written evidence regarding burial which I present and discuss in this book touches on subjects as diverse as Irish law, the court system, transport, concepts of territoriality, the importance of the physical body, the role of the Church, art history, and the social status of women and other social groups. Taken as a whole, this burial evidence shows that the practices of the medieval Irish were very similar to those of their western European neighbors.

PUBLISHED WORK ON BURIAL IN MEDIEVAL IRELAND

No cultural history of burial in Ireland has been written. The work which comes closest is a chapter on Irish burial practice written by P.W. Joyce in his popular work *A social history of ancient Ireland*, published in 1903.[18] As the book's title indicates, much of its discussion is given over to prehistoric burial practices. The sources used include nineteenth-century archaeology, medieval stories and poems relating to the prehistoric heroic period, notably the Ossianic cycle and *Táin bó Cuailnge*.

A study of Irish wills by Margaret Murphy was published in 1987.[19] Unfortunately, few medieval Irish wills have survived. Only 98 Dublin wills exist, all but 24 of which are preserved in one register and date from 1457 to 1493, which is the last half-century considered in this study.

The study of Irish funerary art has benefitted from many years of detailed investigation by George Petrie, R.A.S. Macalister, John Hunt, Françoise Henry, F.A. Greenhill, Helen Roe, and others. Five works in particular are indispensable for burial in medieval Ireland: Macalister's *Clonmacnoise memorial slabs* (1909), and his *Corpus inscriptionum insularum celticarum* (1949; reprinted 1997), which cover the memorial stones of early Christian and pre-Conquest Ireland. The third is Hunt's *Irish medieval figure sculpture*, which examines the period 1200–1600. Greenhill's *Incised effigial grave slabs: 1100–1700* considers all of western Europe, but lists a total of just fifteen examples for Ireland. Pádraig Lionard's long and detailed survey, 'Early Irish graveslabs' is excellent, but as the title indicates, it focuses on an earlier period.

Despite the fine work done on Irish slabs, crosses and effigies, it has not often been possible to positively identify these artifacts with the actual people they were created to commemorate. For example, in *Clonmacnoise memorial slabs*,

18 Joyce, *A social history*, i, pp 533–79.   **19** M. Murphy, 'The high cost of dying'.

Macalister was able to identify only thirty-one slabs with historical figures, and the degree of certainty which he offered varies widely from instance to instance. Hunt listed 110 graveslabs and effigies datable to the period of this study, yet for only ten examples can certain identification be made. Despite the difficulties in associating graveslabs with specific historical figures, these art-historical studies provide invaluable information regarding the advents of particular styles of Irish memorials, and the artistic traditions from which they borrowed. Two frequently cited art-historical works relating to the period under study, *Death in the Middle Ages* by T.S.R. Boase, and *Tomb sculpture* by Erwin Panofsky, do not offer information specific to Ireland.

Irish wake-customs, the burial of children, and other burial customs were discussed by Seán Ó Suilleabháin. However, Ó Suilleabháin was a folklorist, not a historian, and his studies concern twentieth-century burial practices.[20] While one may suspect that many of the beliefs and practices which Ó Suilleabháin discussed were current in the Middle Ages, it is useless to speculate further until we have a clearer understanding of what constituted Irish medieval burial practice, based on written, archaeological and artifactual evidence.

Much of the most popular and most-cited work in 'burial studies' is concerned with death, rather than with the activities related to burial. However, both French and English burial practices have been the subject of excellent social histories. *The hour of our death* by Philippe Ariès (1977), has already been mentioned. In this work, Ariès traced the change in the French attitude towards death as it evolved from one which generally regarded death as a part of life and the dead as ever-present members of the community, to one which feared death and sought to privatize it. The range of subjects which Ariès has discussed and the methods which he employed have proved helpful in formulating the themes and structure of this book.

Clare Gittings' social history, *Death, burial and the individual in early modern England*, has been of great value. Gittings has sought to determine whether Ariès' observations about the evolution of burial in France are also applicable to England. Although Gittings' study focuses on a period later than the one considered here, her opening chapter covers the medieval background to burial in modern England, and her work has been a useful source for comparative material. Christopher Daniell's fine study, *Death and burial in medieval England*, was published in 1997. It is unfortunate that the thesis on which this book is based had already been filed when it appeared. His volume touches on many of the themes addressed in this work, and it could have saved me many hours spent ferreting out English comparisons.

R.C. Finucane has written about many aspects of early Christian and medieval Continental burial ritual including the wake, embalming, and the translation of

---

20 Ó Suilleabháin, *Irish wake amusements*.

relics.[21] Other articles which have been helpful on various aspects of medieval European burial ritual at large are cited in the text.

THE ARCHAEOLOGY OF MEDIEVAL IRISH BURIAL

Julia Barrow has used the word 'elusive' to describe urban graveyards of the later Middle Ages, citing the small number of archaeological excavations of urban cemeteries and the fact that most properly surveyed city maps postdate the medieval period.[22] The situation which she has described is also recognizable in Ireland, where the evidence for medieval burial – urban or rural – is disappointingly meager.

Áine Brosnan has recently written the following summary of the situation in Ireland:

> ... in Early Medieval Ireland ... there are just a handful of sites that have produced any evidence for mortuary practices ... This area of study is even less represented in the Later Medieval period (1200–1600), from which few ecclesiastical sites have been excavated ... Many of the excavations have been quite limited in extent, and have focused on the investigation of the standing architectural remains ... until recently, even the sampling of the human remains which were recovered was not normal practice. In some cases, the research objectives seem to have almost completely ignored the potential of burial records, which were rarely scientifically excavated, and often the human remains were immediately reinterred, without any record of them being made ... a limited amount of information is available on the form of burial and commemoration in Ireland from the Early Medieval era up to and including the Post-Medieval period. However, the accompanying ritual and the insight that can be gained from this is an area in Irish archaeology which has been given very little attention.[23]

To clarify the situation further, it might be added that interments are still being made in many important medieval Irish cemeteries which are, therefore, regarded as unsuitable for excavation. Also, many graves which are quite possibly of medieval date have been disturbed by later burials or by architectural alterations, thus making accurate dating and analysis extremely difficult. Materials which are commonly analyzed to provide close dating – notably wood and fabric

---

21 Finucane, *Miracles and pilgrims*, especially pp 25–38; also 'Sacred corpse'. 22 Barrow, 'Urban cemetery location in the high Middle Ages', pp 78–9. 23 Brosnan, 'Mortuary practices', pp 22–3.

– often have not survived because of adverse soil conditions. Excavated human bones have seldom been tested to provide close dating, with the result that burials have often been assigned to a time-period with a range of two or three hundred years. Clearly, such a range is too broad to be of much use to the historian. There also seems to be something of a predisposition to assign to the early Christian period burials which have not been closely dated. This problem may be circular and self-perpetuating; that is, with so little Irish burial evidence reliably dated to the Middle Ages, archaeologists may be more comfortable assigning early Christian dates to burials for which conclusive evidence for the date of interment has not been found.

In the quotation cited above, Brosnan has noted that the archaeology of the central and later Middle Ages has not thus far been given the level of support in Ireland which that of earlier periods has received. It may be that the number of excavations of sites dating to the prehistoric and early Christian periods, and the artifacts which they have recovered, has kept the focus and funding away from later medieval (i.e. post-early Christian) archaeology.

Archaeological techniques have progressed rapidly in the second half of the twentieth century. Formerly focused primarily on the collection, analysis and classification of artifacts (including human remains), new procedures can now provide a much wider range of information on subjects as diverse as average life-expectancy, diet, and genetic and social relationships. Major long-term excavations have been conducted in Anglo-Saxon cemeteries in England, and also in French cemeteries dating to the Merovingian and Carolingian periods. Subsequent detailed analysis of these excavated burials has contributed significantly to the understanding of early medieval English and French populations and their cultures. The same kind of expertise now needs to be applied to Irish burial-grounds.

No study of burial in the British Isles should overlook the Hunter Marshall Lectures given by the archaeologist Charles Thomas at the University of Glasgow in 1968.[24] His seminal work on the archaeology of burial in Great Britain and Ireland utilized hagiography and other early written sources. While his focus was the early Christian period, his work contains important information on the development of cemeteries, graves, and memorial art in Ireland which is invaluable for the period which is considered in this book.

In the field of archaeology, I have already mentioned the review of the Irish archaeological burial evidence by Elizabeth O'Brien, who has considered it in the light of the written evidence dating AD 400 to AD 800.[25] Áine Brosnan's analysis of the medieval burials found at Ardfert cathedral, Co. Kerry, opens with

---

24 Published under the title *The early Christian archaeology of North Britain.* **25** O'Brien's study 'Late prehistoric/early historic Ireland' excludes the Irish chronicles, presumably because of their limited number of references to burial for this period.

an excellent consideration of medieval burial practice, touching on a number of subjects – notably the use of coffins and sarcophagi – discussed in this study. Additionally, Seán Ó Donnabháin, in reporting on his scientific analysis of the human remains recovered from Tintern abbey, Co. Wexford, has sought to place those burials in a wider social context.[26] Recent reports on excavations of medieval sites in Waterford and central Dublin have carefully considered interments, expanding the amount of data for the period.[27] Heather King's recent work on burials at Clonmacnoise will prove of great interest.

SOURCES FOR THIS STUDY

Sources extremely varied in type, provenance and origin have been used in this study. I hope to have consulted most, if not all, of the written evidence concerning Ireland from 900 to 1500, although the time allotted for completion of this study has made it impossible to ensure that the survey has exhausted all of the Irish medieval sources, let alone all possible sources, which would include works that are not necessarily medieval or Irish. The great majority of the information relates to the burial of the upper or élite classes, since little information was recorded relating to the burial of the far more numerous members of the lower classes. Even so, the amount of information is not great for any social class, rich or poor.

Written sources for medieval Ireland are filled with obituaries, yet most of the obituary notices in them do not mention burial. While we may assume that there were instances where the place in which a person is said to have died is also the site of burial, this cannot be known with certainty, and it would be unwise to make such assumptions. For example, on reading of the death of a bishop or abbot of a given church, one might easily assume that he was also buried there. However, the chronicles contain a number of examples where this clearly was not the case. For these and other reasons, in this study I rely *only* on annalistic entries and excerpts which *specifically and explicitly* mention burial; obits that do not give this information have not been included. In cases where the obit of the same person is recorded in more than one chronicle, but one or more source does not include information about burial, only the entries which contain this detail have been cited. Therefore, some of the references which I have noted as being unique to a particular source can also be found elsewhere as mere obits.

The types of sources consulted and used for this study include chronicles, ecclesiastical records (cartularies, papal letters etc.), secular administrative records,

---

26 Ó Donnabháin, 'A study'.   **27** For example, Simpson, 'The excavations'; Power, 'Human skeletal remains'.

hagiographical material, and a wide range of other literary texts. Each primary source surveyed for this study is listed in the bibliography (sources which do not include information about burial – such as the 'Annals of Roscrea' and the *Dignitas decani* – are included along with those that do, in order to show which sources have been consulted). A brief discussion of these different types of sources and the specific ones which have proved most valuable for this study is presented below.

Native Irish chronicles
Irish chronicles provide the obvious starting point for any historical study of native Irish society in the Middle Ages. D.A. Binchy stated that they provide 'the most copious and reliable sources for the history of native Ireland for over a thousand years',[28] and F.X. Martin has written that

> the quantity and quality of the [Irish] annals are formidable … as far as annals are concerned, Ireland has an *embarrasse de richesse*. Few European countries, if any, can claim a similar body of literature on a national scale.[29]

Taken as a whole, Irish chronicles provide the largest number of names of individuals and their places of burial; however, the individual annals vary considerably in origin, accuracy, the time period covered, and the information provided.

While some annalistic burial entries provide fascinating details about ritual and social practices, in a large majority of instances only date, name, social position, and place of interment are noted. Despite this, it would be dangerous to presume that the relatively small amount of information on burial means that burial was not of much importance to the annalists. We would do well to remember that Irish annalists were essentially writing for themselves and their own religious communities in an era when the population of Ireland was small, and Irish society was highly localized and clan-based. In the Middle Ages, the cemeteries where each Irish kin-group traditionally buried its dead would have been as well known as the names and lineages of the kings and high-ranking clerics whose lives and deaths the annalists recorded. Given that this was the case, it seems possible – and even likely – that when the Irish annalists do mention a burial, they do so because there was something unusual or noteworthy about it.

Despite the fact that the Irish annalists recorded events which related to or affected the religious foundations where they were written, Irish annalistic entries recording burial are not necessarily narrowly focused from a geographical perspective. For example, in the fifteenth century, the 'Annals of Connacht' (*AConn*)

---

28 Binchy, 'Lawyers and chroniclers', p. 59. **29** F.X. Martin, in the opinion of Mac Niocaill, 'The medieval Irish annals', p. 5

contain records of burial in places as diverse as Sligo in the northwest of Ireland (1402), Trim in Co. Meath north of Dublin (1419), Cavan in the north midlands (1460), and at Tralee in Co. Kerry, in the west (1488).

I offer now a brief overview of each of the chronicles and the burial information contained within them, arranged in descending order according to the amount of information on burial that they contain, along with some quantitative information. The caveat has already been given that, due to the relatively limited amount of burial information in the Irish chronicles, a quantitative survey of these entries will not provide a reliable assessment of medieval Irish burial.

The so-called 'Annals of the Four Masters' (*AFM*) record events for the whole of the period under study and contain by far the largest number of entries regarding burial in Ireland of any of the sources consulted. This chronicle was compiled in 1636 by four Franciscan brothers of Donegal who provided an extensive list of their sources down to the year 1227. O'Donovan, in his introduction to the *AFM* told that

> The old books they collected were the Annals of Clonmacnoise ... the Annals of the Island of the Saints, on the Lake of Rive [Loch Ree]; the Annals of Senat Mac Magnus, on the Lake of Erne (now called the Ulster Annals); the Annals of the O'Maolconary's, the Annals of Kilronan, compiled by the Duigenans. The antiquarians had also procured the Annals of Lacan [Book of Lecan] compiled by the Mac Firbisses ... the Annals of Clonmacnoise and those of the Island of Saints, come down no further than the year of our Lord 1227 ...

O'Donovan reported that the Franciscan 'four masters' described the manuscripts that they used to compile the chronicle as

> the greater part of O'Maolconary's book, ending with the year 1505; the book of the O'Duigenans aforesaid, from the year 900 to 1563; the book of Senate MacMagnus, ending with 1532; a part also of the book of Cucogry, the son of Dermot O'Clery from the year 1281 to 1537.

AFM preserve more entries that relate specifically to burial than any other chronicle, Irish or 'Anglo-Irish'. The most frequently noted burials are of people named O'Connor, MacDermott, O'Donnell, O'Farrell, O'Hanley, and O'Rourke.[30] In descending order, the most commonly mentioned sites of burial are Boyle, Co. Roscommon; Armagh, Co. Armagh; and Clonmacnoise, Co. Offaly. Ardcarne in Co. Roscommon is the only place of interment mentioned in this chronicle which is not noted in other chronicles.

---

30 The O'Connors are mentioned in eleven instances; the O'Farrells, O'Hanleys and O'Rourkes each receive three mentions.

'Annals of Connacht' (*AConn*) provide the second largest number of entries regarding burial, and record more burials that are not listed in any other chronicle. *AConn* span the period 1224–1562, with gaps occurring 1184–92, 1263–1306, and 1315–98. *AConn* provide a more complete version of the chronicles used to compile the 'Annals of Loch Cé', and may have used the 'Annals of Boyle' (see below) as a source.[31] The chronicle seems to have been written contemporaneously at Loch Cé in Co. Roscommon from 1224, which is the first year under which events are recorded. The names of sixty individuals and their place of burial are provided, and twenty-nine of these entries are unique to this chronicle. The most commonly mentioned names are Ua Conchobair (O'Connor), Mac Diarmada (MacDermott), Maoilchonaire (Mulconry), Ua Ruairc (O'Rourke), Ua Fergail (O'Farrell) and Mac Donnchada (Mac Donough).[32] The most commonly recorded places of burial (given in descending order) are Roscommon and Boyle, both in Co. Roscommon; Sligo, Co. Sligo; and Lara (Abbeylara), Co. Cavan. Seven places of burial are mentioned in *AConn* which do not appear in other Irish annals. These are Abbeyderg, Co. Longford; Clare Island, Co. Mayo; Cluain Lis Beg;[33] Kilmacallan, Co. Sligo; Coole, Co. Cork; Ballyboggan, Co. Galway;[34] and Rossreilly, Co. Galway.

The 'Annals of Ulster' (*AU*) contain entries for the entire period of this study. The chronicle is thought to be contemporaneous by the tenth century, with interpolations made before it was transcribed in the fifteenth and sixteenth centuries.[35] Aubrey Gwynn and Gearóid Mac Niocaill argued that from the mid-thirteenth century the chronicle was written at Armagh.[36] The earliest text of *AU* which survives was compiled by Ruaidhrí Ó Luinín, who was the scribe of this primary manuscript for the entries down to 1489. From 1461 onwards, at the latest, *AU* records events which were contemporary with the writing of this primary manuscript. Kathryn Grabowski has pointed out that *AU* pay particular attention to Uí Néill (O'Neill) and 'have by far the largest geographical coverage and especially as regards the northern half of the country'.[37] By the opening of the tenth century, when the present study begins, the principal source-chronicle was being kept in Meath, perhaps at Clonard. The most commonly mentioned kin-groups are Mag Uidhir (Maguire); Ó Raighilligh (O'Reilly); and Mac Mathghamhna (MacMahon). The most commonly men-

---

31 O'Dwyer, 'The Annals of Connacht', pp 83–85.   **32** These are names for which three or more burials are recorded.   **33** Edmund Hogan identified this as a site in Anghaile (Annaly), in the province of Connaght (see *Onomasticon Goedelicum* [Dublin, 1910; reprinted Dublin 1993], p. 266); no place with this name appears in Donnelly's *Index to the townlands*.   **34** There was an Augustinian priory at Ballyboggan, Co. Meath, but one of the two townlands called 'Ballyboggan' in the barony of Kilconnell, Co. Galway, seems more likely. See Donnelly's *Index to the townlands*, p. 62; also A. Gwynn & Hadcock, *Medieval Religious Houses*, p. 159.   **35** Hughes, *Early Christian Ireland*, p. 150; Smyth, 'The earliest Irish annals', p. 34.   **36** Mac Niocaill, *The medieval Irish annals*, p. 37.   **37** Grabowski & Dumville, *Chronicles and annals*, p. 3.

tioned places of burial are Lisgoole, Co. Fermanagh; Cavan, and Armagh. Burial locations unique to *AU* include Louth, and Aghalurcher, Co. Fermanagh.

The entries in the 'Annals of Loch Cé' (*ALC*) commence in 1014 and continue past the end-date of this study. Until 1180, the chronicle contains information also found in AU, after which time it appears to reflect other sources, including the 'Annals of Boyle'. It provides the names of thirty-four people whose burial places are also given. Of these, five are unique entries. The most commonly mentioned surnames are O'Connor, O'Donnell, and MacDermott. The most commonly mentioned site of burial is Boyle, Co. Roscommon, followed by Loch Cé, Co. Roscommon, and Derry, Co. Londonderry. There are no unique mentions of burial sites.

The 'Annals of Inisfallen' (*AI*) begin in Antiquity and end at 1450, with a lacuna beginning at 1130 and extending almost to the end of 1159. Entries from 1159 to the middle of 1214, and between 1285–95 are missing; and the pages for 1274–77 and 1321–24 are blank.[38] *AI* is the earliest surviving native Irish chronicle, dating from the final decade of the eleventh century, and is centered on Munster, the southernmost province of Ireland.[39] Gearóid Mac Niocaill has stated that it is based on a text 'of the Clonmacnoise type'.[40] Grabowski's analysis has led her to conclude that up to 911, the entries in *AI* are based on the same source that was used to compile the *AU*, after which time several Munster-based sources appear to have been incorporated into the earlier entries. Grabowski has identified what she thinks is a ninth-century strata from Lismore, Co. Waterford, and a group of entries centered around Emly, Co. Tipperary and Killaloe, Co. Clare, that end before the 1080s. This has led her to suggest the possibility that from the second half of the 1060s through the middle of the 1080s the *AI* was at Killaloe, which had strong connections with the O'Brien kings of Munster.[41] After this, the chronicle was moved again, probably to Lismore, before ultimately arriving at Inisfallen, Co. Kerry, deep in the heart of MacCarthy territory.[42] Burials of MacCarthys and O'Briens are the most frequently noted, and Cork is by far the most frequently mentioned place of burial. This is the only chronicle to record burial at Inisfallen, and at Abbeymahon, Co. Cork.

The 'Annals of Duald MacFirbisse' (*ADF*) survive only in a seventeenth-century English translation. They constitute an extensive record for 1443–68, and mention seventeen burials between 1444 and 1464. These entries mention burials of people with ten different surnames (four are burials of O'Connors) and ten locations. *ADF* contain the only mention in the Irish chronicles of burial at Tulsk, Co. Roscommon.

The 'Annals of Nenagh' (*ANen*) are essentially obituary notices kept for the Franciscan abbey of the same name in Co. Tipperary; and contain entries dated

---

38 Mac Airt, *Annals of Inisfallen*, p. xiii. **39** Ibid. **40** Mac Niocaill, *The medieval Irish annals*, pp 24–5. **41** Grabowski and Dumville, *Chronicles and annals*, p. 93. **42** Mac Niocaill, *The medieval Irish annals*, pp 24–5.

from 1336 to 1528. Twelve entries which specifically mention burial are recorded from 1345 to 1429, and three of these are female burials. All of these entries
are unique, with the exception of the one for Joanna de Burgo, 'Contissa Kildare',
whose burial in Kildare is recorded *s.a.* 1359.[43] Burials at Ennis, Co. Clare;[44]
Ardfert, Co. Kerry; Kilkenny, and Armagh are noted, along with burials at
Nenagh.

The 'Annals of Clonmacnoise' (*AClon*) begin in Antiquity but were kept contemporaneously from 1224 to 1408. These survive only in the idiosyncratic
Hiberno-English translation by Conell Mageoghagan completed in 1627. The
source from which he worked is unknown, and his autograph manuscript has
yet to be discovered. This chronicle should not be confused with the now-lost
'Clonmacnoise Chronicle' created in the tenth century, of which it is derivative.
Down to the middle of the tenth century, the burial information in this source
is essentially identical with that contained in *AU* and *AT*. In the thirteenth century, a Meath element is evident in this chronicle. However, based on the fact
that the entries for the later thirteenth and the entire fourteenth centuries are
essentially identical with *AConn*, Mac Niocaill has argued that these two chronicles derive from a common source, which *AClon* preserves in a version closer
(except in language) to the original. *AClon* is the only chronicle to mention
burial at Mullingar, Co. Westmeath; and Clonfert, Co. Galway, between 900 and
1500. Unique entries include the burial at Clonfert of Donnell O'Duffy, archbishop of Connaught *s.a.* 1136; and those of 'Gillernew' O'Farrell at Boyle *s.a.*
1274, Aedh O'Connor (Felim's son) at Boyle, *s.a.* 1274, the 'bishop of Meath' at
Mullingar *s.a.* 1282, and Cathal O'Kelly at Clonmacnoise Co. Offaly, *s.a.* 1283.
The geographical range of burial entries is relatively wide, extending as far south
as Athassel in Co. Tipperary, north to Derry, and east to Mullingar, Co. Westmeath.
The families of O'Connor and O'Kelly take 'pride of place', while the sites of
Boyle and Clonmacnoise receive the most mentions.

'Mac Carthaigh's Book' and two annalistic fragments[45] were collected and
published by Séamus Ó hInnse in one volume in 1947. These entries extend
from 1114 to 1437(?) and the chronicle has lacunae for the periods 1184–1192,
1263–1306, and 1315–98. The location where it was composed is unknown,
although Mac Niocaill has noted that its entries relate mainly to Munster, with
an element from the South Ulster/Oriel area. For the thirteenth century, there
is a close relationship between 'Mac Carthaigh's Book' and *AI*.[46] The first
Rawlinson fragment comprises short annals related to *AConn*; the second
Rawlinson fragment was begun by Aughuistín Magraidhín, an Augustinian canon

---

43 Her burial is recorded *s.a.* 1357 in the 'Annals of St Mary's Abbey, Dublin', p. 393.   **44** 'Inis-
cluan-ruada' is another name for Ennis, see Gwynn & Hadcock, *Medieval Religious*, p. 430.   **45**
Oxford, Bodleian Library, MS. Rawlinson B.488.   **46** Mac Niocaill, *The Medieval Irish annals*,
p. 26.

of Saints' Island in Lough Ree, Co. Galway, and his work was continued by other members of his community.

'Mac Carthaigh's Book' contains seven references to burial from 1119 to 1402, including the burial at Killaloe in 1119 of Muirchertach Ua Briain (Murtough O'Brian) over-king of Ireland (also found in *AT*), and five references are unique to this source. This chronicle contains a detailed account of the burial of Amláib Ua Donnchada (Aulay O'Donough), 'high king' of Eóghanachta Locha Léin, at Aghadoe, Co. Kerry, *s.a.* 1158, the only annalistic mention of burial at Aghadoe. It also records that Aed, grandson of Amláib, was buried in 'the old monastery of Uí Mhathghamhna' in 1231.[47] The burial of Toirrdelbach Ua Briain (Turough O'Brian), king of Thomond, at Ennis, Co. Clare, is recorded *s.a.* 1306. This source also relates that the body of William de Burgo was transported from England for burial at Athassel, Co. Tipperary, and notes the death and burial of Maolsheachlainn Ua Ceallaigh (Melachlin O'Kelly), 'high king of all Uí Mhaine,' at Knockmoy, Co. Galway, *s.a.* 1402.

The 'Annals of Boyle' (*AB*) are of north Connaught origin. The chronicle begins in prehistory and continues to 1257. The latter part is contemporary with the events recorded. Lacunae occur at 1201–24 and 1238–51. This chronicle appears to have been written at Boyle, Co. Roscommon, until towards the end of the last entry *s.a.* 1228, after which time it was continued at the monastery of the Holy Trinity on the shores of Loch Cé, also in Co. Roscommon. It seems certain that this chronicle was used as a source for both *ALC* and *AConn*, and it is closely associated with the MacDermotts (*Carraig Locha Cé* was the stronghold of the MacDermotts). *AB* contains information about the burial in 1014 of Brian Bóruma, as well as those of Diarmait Mac Gilla Charraig, a priest of Tibohine, Co. Roscommon, who was buried at Loch Cé in 1229; Gilla Comded Mac Uilin, father of Clarus of Elphin, buried in the same church *s.a.* 1235; Aedh Ó Gibellán of canon at Holy Trinity who was buried there in 1236; and the interment of Clarus himself at Loch Cé *s.a.* 1251.[48]

The 'Annals of Tigernach' (*AT*) record events from Antiquity to 1178, with lacunae at 766–974 and 1003–1118. This is a recension of the now lost 'Clonmacnoise Chronicle'. This chronicle takes its name from Tigernach Ua Braen, abbot of Clonmacnoise, Co. Offaly (d. 1088), who was once supposed to have been its original author. Tigernach was of Síl Muiredaigh, the family which counted the over-kings of Connaught among its members. Gearóid Mac Niocaill has noted that in the twelfth century, the chronicle was clearly being continued by an annalist with strong Ua Conchobair (O'Connor) loyalties, and that material from Connaught, as well as Leinster and Clonmacnoise, is also included. This chronicle records five twelfth-century burials and contains unique records of the burials of Gilla na naem Húa

---

47 The territory of Uí Mhathghamhna was located in the barony of Kinalmeaky, Co. Cork, *AI*, p. 564.   48 *AB*, §280 (1014); §390 (1229); §398 (1236); §401 (1251).

Birnn (O'Byrne) at Roscommon in 1133; Gilla na nóeb Húa Fergail (O'Farrell) at Inchcleraun, Co. Longford, in 1141; and King Toirrdelbach Ua Conchóbair (Turlough O'Connor) at Clonmacnoise, Co. Offaly, in 1156.

The so-called 'Fragmentary Annals of Ireland' (*FAII*) end *s.a.* 914. As Joan Radner, who edited *FAII* notes, there is 'some dating confusion throughout the text',[49] and there are numerous small breaks in the text, the one which occurs at 873–906 being relevant to the period of this study.[50] Before the end of the eleventh century, and perhaps even later, *FAII* is the only extant chronicle to focus specifically on events in the southeast of Ireland. Radner noted that the kingdom of Osraige is the focus of the narrative portions which chronicle events in 849–73 and 906–14 and has argued that its source was a now lost 'Osraige chronicle' which seems to have been assembled during the Viking Age, and which may have been kept at Kildare for a considerable period of time.[51] This work presents unusual problems because it contains literary material, and Radner has suggested that *FAII* may have originated as a saga of Cerball Mac Dúnlainge, king of Osraige, and his descendants.[52] *FAII* tell of two royal burials from the early tenth century: one at Dísert Diarmata (Castledermot), Co. Kildare, the other at Naas, Co. Kildare. While it is just possible that these events may not strictly be historical, the entries are rich in incidental detail relating to contemporary Irish society and culture.

'Chronicum Scotorum' (*CS*) appears to be a seventeenth-century derivative (by An Dubhaltach Mac Fhirbhisigh) of the now-lost tenth-century 'Clonmacnoise Chronicle', which has been described as 'for the most part an abbreviated version of the "T" ['Annals of Tigernach'] text itself'.[53] *AT* begins in Antiquity and continues to 1150. Lacunae occur throughout the text, with the most important occurring between 719 and 863. Both Mac Niocaill and David Dumville have written of the clear similarities between *CS* and *AT*,[54] and Dumville has stated his agreement with Hennessy, who edited *AT*, that this chronicle had its medieval origin at Clonmacnoise.[55] Mac Niocaill has argued that from at least the late eleventh century on, *AT* contains a Meath or Leinster element.[56] *CS* reports two eleventh-century burials at Clonmacnoise. The first is the theft of the head of Conchobar Ua Maelshechlainn (Connor O'McLoughlin) from Clonmacnoise and its recovery from Kincora in 1070; the second is the burial *s.a.* 1096 of Gilla na Naemh O'hEidhin (O'Heyne). Both of these burials are recorded in *AT*; the latter is also found in the *AI*.

Anglo-Irish chronicles

These sources begin recording events in Ireland after the 'Anglo-Norman' invasions of the late twelfth century. Like the native Irish chronicles, they are the

---

49 *FAII*, p. vii, n. 3. **50** Ibid., p. xi. **51** *FAII*, p. xvii. **52** Ibid., p. xxv. **53** Mac Niocaill, *The medieval Irish*, p. 23. **54** Ibid., p. 22; Grabowski & Dumville, *Chronicles and annals*, p. 6. **55** Grabowski & Dumville, *Chronicles and annals*, p. 156. **56** Mac Niocaill, *The medieval Irish annals*, p. 27.

product of religious foundations, but their entries concentrate on the activities of members of the 'Anglo-Norman' (which becomes the Anglo-Irish) community and on events taking place in England. Geographically, the chronicle focuses on the areas where English power was greatest, particularly the counties of Dublin and Kilkenny.

The earlier entries in these chronicles tend to be heavily derivative of other English chronicles and histories, including those of Henry of Huntingdon, Ranulph Higden and Giraldus Cambrensis. Burial entries are extremely 'Anglocentric', with almost no attention given to the native Irish. The information recorded in these sources is different from the bare and formulaic entries regarding burial recorded in the native Irish chronicles; the Anglo-Irish annalists wrote more freely and included more detail than their Irish counterparts.

Of the Anglo-Irish chronicles, 'Grace's Annals' contain the largest number of references to burial. The first occurs *s.a.* 1074 and concerns Ua Dúnain, bishop of Dublin; the final entry concerns Thomas Butler, the seventh earl of Ormonde. This chronicle is thought to have been compiled *c.*1538, supposedly by 'Jacobus Grace', a Prior of St John in Kilkenny, although it is doubtful whether such a person ever existed. 'Grace's Annals' begin with Noah and the Flood, and the chronicle proper ends at 1370; it continues with a list of obits for the families of de Lacy, Burke, Butler, and the Geraldines. From 1162 to 1370 it agrees in subject matter with the fourteenth-century chronicle known as 'Pembridge's Annals', and it seems likely that they were both compiled from a common source. The chronicle is Anglo-Irish and aristocratic in its orientation, with the exception of an entry regarding the burial of the Scottish nobles who fought for Edward Bruce in his unsuccessful attempt to conquer Ireland. 'Grace's Annals' are wide-ranging regarding places of burial, although, predictably, references are limited to centers of colonial power.

Two chronicles, one written by Thady Clyn, the other by John Dowling, were published together in 1849 in one volume as *The Annals of Ireland by Friar John Clyn and Thady Dowling*, and therefore tend to be considered together although they are not related in any other way. John Clyn was a Franciscan friar of Kilkenny. His chronicle continues to 1480, and includes seven Irish burial entries from 1321 to 1347. These entries are contemporary with Clyn's life and concern the consecration of the Friary's new cemetery, as well as three burials and three Anglo-Irish funerals. They mention burial in the town of Kilkenny, at Gowran, Co, Kilkenny; Drogheda, Co. Louth; and London. The chronicle of Thady Dowling, chancellor of Leighlin, Co. Carlow, begins in prehistory and the last entry is dated with the year 1600. It provides six references to burial beginning with the death of Strongbow in 1173 and with the last entry *s.a.* 1420, all concerning 'Anglo-Normans'. Some information regarding wills, bequests, and debts of deceased persons is also included.

Records of the diocese of Dublin are contained in the *Liber niger* ('Black Book') and *Liber albus* ('White Book') of Christ Church. Records in *Liber niger* span the period 1186–1585, and those in *Liber albus* cover 1169–1338. *Liber albus* is a collection of miscellaneous tracts bound together and thought to have been compiled 1504 x 1517.[57] The only mention of burial found in H.J. Lawlor's calendar of the *Liber albus* is that of James Butler, earl of Ormond, who was interred in the abbey of the Blessed Virgin Mary, Dublin, in 1452. Aubrey Gwynn has suggested that *Liber niger* was recorded by a person living in England who was involved in the diplomatic activities of King Edward I. The margins and blank spaces of the book were later used to 'enter various documents and records of interest to the Christ Church community'. *Liber niger* is thought to have been brought to Dublin in or around the year 1300. Some of the entries regarding the fourteenth century may have been made by Henry La Warr, an Augustinian canon of Bristol, who came to Dublin as prior of Christ Church in the winter of 1300–1. Four of the burials noted in *Liber niger* concern the early prelates of Dublin and come from the 'second narrative of the foundation of Christ Church' which were written in a hand of the later fourteenth or early fifteenth century.[58]

The 'Annals of St Mary's abbey, Dublin' begin with the birth of Christ and continue to 1405 with many gaps, the longest of which are 1181–92, 1221–1307 and 1309–14. The 'Annals of St Mary's Abbey', a fragment of another Anglo-Irish chronicle, and 'Pembridge's annals' were all edited by John T. Gilbert and published in 1884 in two volumes which also contain the cartularies of the abbey of St Mary in Dublin and Dunbrody abbey, Co. Wexford. The first portion of this chronicle is almost identical with a fragment of the *Liber niger* of Christ Church, and the writer obviously had access to other historical works, for example, those of Henry of Huntingdon and Eadmer of Canterbury. In his introduction to this chronicle, Gilbert did not suggest a date for its composition, or comment on the date of the manuscript, except to say that it was owned by Sir James Ware in the reign of Charles I. This chronicle seems to have been given its name by Ware, but as Gilbert pointed out, Ware's reason for choosing to call it *Annales monasterii Beatae Mariae Virginis juxta Dublin* is unknown.[59] The 'Annals of St Mary's, Dublin' contain numerous entries regarding burial of both 'Anglo-Norman'/Anglo-Irish nobles, prelates and English kings spanning the twelfth through the fifteenth centuries. Some of these notices have been taken from other sources. Information on the consecration of cemeteries, bequests and wills is also included.

The annalistic fragment included in the same volume records events for 1308–17. It was written in the fourteenth century, on evidence of the sole sur-

---

57 Lawlor, 'A Calendar of the Liber niger and Liber albus', p. 2. **58** A. Gwynn, 'Some unpublished texts', pp 283–5. **59** *Chart. St Mary's*, II, pp cxii–cxiii.

viving manuscript. 'Pembridge's annals' are written in a fifteenth-century hand
and contain entries for 1162–1370. In the initial parts, the writer appears to have
had source-materials identical with those used by the compiler of the 'Annals
of St Mary's, Dublin'. No information about the original compiler, transcriber,
or owner of this chronicle is known. Later chronicles – including Flattisbury's,
Campion's, and Camden's – contain extracts from this one, and 'Grace's Annals'
also borrows heavily from it.[60] 'Pembridge's Annals' also contain fourteen burial
entries relating to Ireland from 1117 to 1337, all regarding the 'Anglo-Normans'
or Anglo-Irish.

   Liber primus Kilkenniensis includes a series of annals, a large percentage of
whose entries comprise obituary notices. A later scribe added a note to Richard
Marshal's obit under 1233 which records his burial in Kilkenny. A record of the
'Anglo-Norman' invasion of Ireland, and burial information on William, Isabel,
and Walter Marshal (none of whom was buried in Ireland), were also added at
a later date.

Non-Irish annalistic sources

Of the non-Irish chronicles which I have consulted, *Cronica regum Mannie et
Insularum* was the only one which proved particularly useful. It records the buri-
als in Co. Down of three important non-Irish people. These include Affreca de
Courcy (daughter of the Manx king Godred, and wife of John de Courcy), who
was buried in Grey abbey, as well as the interments of two bishops of the Isle of
Man, both natives of Galloway in Scotland, at Bangor, Co. Down.

Ecclesiastical records

Most of the ecclesiastical sources which I have consulted contain at least some
reference to burial, whether in the form of a will expressing the desire of the
testator for burial in a stated foundation, or the granting of the right to free burial
in the cemetery. However, most of the sources contain only one or two references and generally do not contribute information which is particularly illu-
minating in relation to burial. The sources which contain useful information I
have briefly discussed below.

   The ecclesiastical source which preserves the greatest amount of information is the register of the Dominican friary at Athenry, Co. Galway (*Regestum
monasterii fratrum praedicatorum de Athenry*). The first part of this register is a chronicle of the de Bermingham family, the founders and great benefactors of the
friary at Athenry. The writing of the register has been assigned to the mid-fifteenth century.[61] The entries begin with the founding of the abbey (in 1241; the
date is not given in the register), and continue to the mid-sixteenth century. This
register contains a large amount of detailed information regarding social aspects

---

60 Ibid., pp cxiv–cxvi. **61** *Reg. Mon. Athenry*, p. 201.

of burial, in particular, groupings of burials and their locations within the church. It also presents some difficulties due to the fact that some burials have been omitted, while others are incorrect.

The registers of the archbishops of Armagh, particularly those of Milo Sweteman and John Mey, contain various types of documents which preserve unique details regarding burial, along with pertinent observations noted contemporaneously during the 'visitations' of the diocese. For example, entries in the 'Register of Archbishop Sweteman' (archiepiscopate 1361–80) indicate that cemeteries were used for important meetings and record public displeasure at animals being allowed to feed in the cemetery. The 'Register of Archbishop Mey' (archiepiscopate 1443–56) records the burial of John Prene, interred in the choir of the parish church at Termonfeckin, Co. Louth, in 1443, and the existence of a charnel house at Kilmore, Co. Cavan, in 1449.

The *Liber Niger Alani* is named for Archbishop Alen of Christ Church cathedral in Dublin, who held the office from 1528–34. It contains documents dating from 1172 to 1553, and a good deal of information regarding funeral oblations and the duties of the coroner (two burial-related topics outside the scope of this study). The late fourteenth-century visitation-records of Primate Colton include information on the reconciliation of cemeteries, and the sixteenth-century register of Archbishop Cromer, who acceded to the archbishopric in 1521, tells of penance being performed in cemeteries.

The 'Obits of Kilcormick' record the fifteenth-century burials of three members of the O'Molloy family at Kilcormick (now Frankfort, Co. Offaly), which are not recorded elsewhere.

The bulk of the entries in the *Liber ruber* of Ossory seem to have been written in 1360 x 1396, probably towards the early part of this period. It is likely that the book itself was written as a record of memorable occurrences in the diocese of Ossory in the second quarter of the fourteenth century, when Richard Ledred (died *c.*1361) was bishop.[62] This source preserves a provincial constitution made by the archbishop of Dublin in 1518 which, though later than the period under study here, is the only reference known to me which proves that people were allowed to reside in cemeteries on a temporary basis.

The 'Register of St Saviour's Chantry, Waterford' is thought to be the only surviving register of an Irish chantry. It contains documents from the second half of the fifteenth century and seems to have been written in 1482 x 1484. Gearóid Mac Niocaill, who edited the register, has considered it possible that the main scribe was John Collyn, who founded the chantry, was appointed dean of Holy Trinity in Waterford in 1441, and figures in a number of the documents in the register.[63] This register contains numerous charters with detailed descrip-

---

62 Gwynn & Hadcock, *Medieval religious*, p. 85. **63** *Registrum cantariae S. Salvatoris Waterfordensis*, pp 137–8.

tions of the location of property in relation to the cemetery, which offer hints about the social uses to which the cemetery was put.

The 'Deeds of the parish of St Werburgh, Dublin', while technically later than the time-span of this study (the first entry relating to burial is dated 1547), are of interest for the information which they contain regarding a dwelling bordering the cemetery of the church.

Collectio canonum Hibernensis and the so-called 'Canons of the second synod of St Patrick' are collections of early ecclesiastical laws relating to the Irish Church. Ludwig Bieler has suggested 457 for the date of the synod, while the 'collectio' is thought to date from the first half of the eighth century. These laws provide important background information for the period under consideration.[64] One of the penances described in this work includes spending three nights in the grave with a corpse.[65] The canons also show that the propriety of burying men and women together was being debated at that time.[66]

'The Martyrology of Oengus the Culdee' (*Félire Oengussa Céli Dé*) is an early source which contains references to embalming. The work, which was previously thought datable 797 x 808, has recently been re-dated by Pádraig Ó Riain to between 828 and 833, although this has proved controversial. The commentary on 'The Martyrology of Oengus' was composed probably in the eleventh century, and certainly by the late twelfth century.[67]

The *Calendar of papal registers (letters)* relating to England and Ireland provide valuable and unusual examples of problems relating to burial in Ireland and comparative information from Great Britain, including what appears to be unique written evidence for fifteenth-century field burials.

The ecclesiastical decretals and statutes printed in the *Councils and synods* of England and *Statutes of the Scottish Church* provide comparative information regarding medieval Scottish and English cemeteries and record the continuing efforts made by the Church to eradicate them. Comparative information about the burial ritual for monks is found in two English works, 'The monastic constitutions of Lanfranc' written at Canterbury in the late eleventh century, and the *Regularis Concordia*, written perhaps at Winchester in the second half of the tenth. Additional comparative English material has been drawn from the 'Cartulary of St Mary's abbey, Clerkenwell' in London, and the *Records from the heresy trials in the diocese of Norwich*.

Administrative and legal sources
As is generally true for each group of sources (with the exception of the native Irish chronicles and a couple of the Anglo-Irish ones), Irish administrative and

64 Kenney, *The Sources*, pp 245–7. **65** Bieler, *The Irish Penitentials*, p. 165. **66** Ibid., p. 189, cf. 'Canons of the alleged second synod of St Patrick' §XI. **67** Ó Riain, 'The Tallaght martyrologies redated', pp 25, 37–8.

legal sources contain few references to burial, although some of these are highly revealing. Based on linguistic evidence, it is known that many of the Irish law texts were originally written in the seventh and eighth centuries, and exist today in manuscripts produced mainly in the fourteenth through sixteenth centuries.[68] These have been published as *The ancient laws of Ireland* (1865–1901) and *Corpus iuris hibernici* (1978). The 'Anglo-Normans' brought their administrative and judicial systems to Ireland in the late twelfth century, and these relied heavily upon written documentation. From the 1170s onwards, a large corpus of written documents relating to Ireland is available, including charters, leases, judicial records, and documents regarding taxes and liberties. These documents provide diverse bits of burial information: for example, the *Senchus mór* decrees that a tomb must be built for a chief, while the *Calendar of documents relating to Ireland* and the *Justiciary rolls* tell of violent acts committed in cemeteries and record that felons sometimes dwelt in sanctuary lands for as long as four weeks.

Hagiography

The dating of Irish hagiographical texts continues to be a highly topical subject. The lives of Irish saints fall into two categories: the '*uitae*', (or 'Latin "lives"') and (generally earlier) 'lives' written in Irish. For some of the Latin '*lives*', Richard Sharpe has suggested a composition date of the early ninth century or earlier. The view that the Latin 'lives' have survived in versions which were redacted in the late twelfth or early thirteenth century has often been expressed, but the issue is still debated.[69] James Kenney suggested that the 'lives' and their revisions were completed locally, but Sharpe has disagreed.[70] Issues of dating aside, the Latin 'lives' were generally originally produced in one of the principal foundations of the patron concerned and appear to have been revised over a lengthy period of time from the eighth to the fourteenth century.

In addition to their dating, other issues make these hagiographical sources problematical. Their purpose (at least partially) was to strengthen the power of the local churches by linking them with a saint from the local ruling dynasty. The information they include on burial – for example, the accounts of the sun not setting during the wake of a saint – is often formulaic, literary convention which has been borrowed from other sources used as exemplars. While one must be cautious about presuming that details regarding burial contained in these sources are historical, they are not valueless to the social historian. Charles Thomas and Kathleen Hughes both noted the historical and archaeological usefulness of the incidental detail included in these tales.[71] The lives of these local saints were

---

68 Kelly, *A Guide to Early Irish Law* (1988), p. 225.   **69** Kenney, *The Sources*, p. 294; Hughes, *Early Christian Ireland*, pp 22–3.   **70** Ibid., pp 392, 422; cf Sharpe, *Medieval Irish saints' Lives*, pp 363–4.   **71** Hughes, *Introduction to the sources*, p. 220, 246; Hughes, *The sources of history*, p. 220; C. Thomas, 'Early Christian', p. 206.

to some extent popular tales regarding 'local heroes', and therefore some of
the details which they contain – especially when of a more incidental nature
and not obviously fabulous or borrowed from literary convention – are probably useful insights into daily life which would have been recognizable to the
general population which these tales were created to edify. For example, passages stating that it was regarded as an honor to be the first corpse interred in
a saint's cemetery, probably reflect a genuine belief. Likewise, descriptions of the
activities which were part of the wake of a saint (prayers, psalms, for example)
either reflect actual events, or at least indicate the kind of ritual which the local
populace would have thought should rightly be accorded to a person of great
local stature.

The most useful hagiographical texts for this study were the Irish 'lives' of St
Ciarán of Saighir, St Brendan of Clonfert, St Berach, St Lasair, and the story of
the 'Expulsion of St Mochuda from Rahen'. The 'Book of Fenagh', a work
regarding the life of St Caillin, contains information about burial fees and the
importance of burial in the territorial church which has been quite useful for
this study. Adamnán's 'Life of Columba', though pre-dating the period under
study, also contains valuable comparative information.

Vernacular literature
The bulk of the information on burial which is included in medieval Irish literature and poetry refers to artifacts, such as pillarstones, monumental stones,
and tombs. Four literary sources proved to be particularly useful for this study.
The first is the 'Metrical dindsenchas', a collection of tales and poems recount-
ing how Irish places acquired their names. These tales survive in two recensions,
the earlier of which is preserved in the 'Book of Leinster', written in the second
half of the twelfth century. As Edward Gwynn stated in his introduction, 'there
is no means of fixing with precision the date at which the collection was first
formed',[72] but the collection known as the 'L-Dindsenchas' seems to date from
*c.*1079,[73] and many of these *dinnshenchas* poems are considered to date from the
ninth and tenth centuries. The poem *Ailech II* is known to have been written
by Maelcholuim of Derry in 1036 x 1056; '*Lecht oenfhir Aife*' is thought to have
been written before the eleventh century; and the language of '*Mag Femin* II'
indicates that it may date from about 1000.

Duanaire Finn is a seventeenth-century collection of poems, at least the roots
of which are extremely old. The poems tell of the exploits of the Irish champi-
on Fionn and his band of soldiers (*na fianna*) during the pre-Christian period.
According to Eoin MacNeill, one of the editors of the printed collection, these
poems started to be written down in the ninth century and were continuously
reworked over the centuries.[74] Determining how much revision the poems

72 E. Gwynn, *Met. Dind.*, p. 91.   73 Ibid., p. 111.   74 *Duanaire Finn*, ed. & trans. MacNeill, i,

underwent between their initial writing and the seventeenth century transcription of them made at Louvain is extremely difficult.[75]

Caithréim Thoirdhealbhaigh ('The Triumphs of Turlough') is an account of the battles fought by the O'Briens in Co. Clare in the early fourteenth century. It is a nearly contemporary account which contains detailed information on the burial of soldiers, and the author may have witnessed the events described.[76]

In this study I cite a number of other literary sources, and the dates which are currently accepted for their composition are noted in the texts when I thought they would be helpful.

p. xxvii. **75** Ibid., pp xxi, xliii. **76** Flower, intro. to *Caithr. Thoirdh*, ed. O'Grady, i, p. xiv; K. Simms, *From kings to warlords*, p. 7.

CHAPTER 2

The medieval Irish cemetery

Many questions remain about when and how the transition from pre-Christian to Christian burial practice was effected in Ireland. It is clear that, from the early Christian period onwards, certain sites were understood by the local populace to be set aside for the burial of baptized Christians; however, it is not known at what date burial in formally consecrated Christian cemeteries became the standard practice in Ireland. Investigations into how closely these Irish cemeteries of the early Christian period resemble Irish cemeteries of the central and later Middle Ages and how standardized (or diversified) burial practices may have been during the period of this study are still in their infancy.

THE BACKGROUND TO CHRISTIAN BURIAL IN IRELAND

Inhumation of the dead had become standard practice throughout Britain and Ireland by the fourth and early fifth centuries AD (with the exception of some evidence for cremation among the Picts of northern Scotland).[1]

Early medieval Irish texts indicate that existing ('pre-Christian') burial sites were often appropriated for Christian burial. Bieler has noted that incidents in the lives of Patrick written in the seventh and eighth centuries by Tírechán and Muirchú indicate that 'burial in non-Christian, possibly family or tribal cemeteries was still commonplace'.[3] The 'Tripartite Life of St Patrick' tells how the saint revived a man who had been buried for a hundred years in what was clearly a pagan tumulus.[4]

The body of King Niall of the Nine Hostages, progenitor of Uí Néill, was recorded as having been disinterred and reburied by St Cainnech, 'so that it was Tuilén's (Dulane, Co. Meath) first corpse'.[5] 'The Colloquy of the Ancients'

1 C. Thomas, *The early Christian*, p. 47. 3 Bieler, *The Patrician texts*, p. 60. 4 *Bethu Phátraic*, ed. Mulchrone, p. 123. 5 *Félire Oengussa* (hereafter *Félire*), ed. & trans. Stokes, p. 245. As we have it, this is a text of the twelfth century, but it was probably first compiled in the ninth or tenth centuries from sources of varying ages.

(*Acallam na Senórach*) tells of a prophecy which foretold that a burial ground of the prehistoric warrior-band of Finn mac Cumaill will be taken over by the *familia* ('community') of St Maedóg[6] and also describes how St Patrick blessed 'the hill of the kings' turning it into a burial ground.[7] In the 'Life' of St Lasrair, a place called *Ard na Marbh* ('height of the dead') becomes known as *Achadh Bethadh* ('field of life'), indicating its consecration sometime after the twelfth century.[8] It is regrettable that conclusive dating is not available for the early Christian interments excavated at the very important religious sites at Reask and Valencia Island in Co. Kerry, as they might add significantly to our understanding of when Christian-style burial was adopted in Ireland.[9]

Territorial churches held great power over the kindreds associated with them, which were considered to be subject by law to the head of their territorial church.[10] Thomas Charles-Edwards has written:

> The place of burial was a matter of concern, partly because of the strong interest of kinsmen in the dead members of their lineages, an interest which descended from the pre-Christian period when the graves of the dead stood guard at the boundary of the kindred's land … a man was normally buried where he father was buried so that the solidarity of kindred might be expressed … [the church] depended upon [the kindred's] fortune and continuity … [the kin group perceived] contemporary reality and its validity as a bequest from dead ancestors, so the pressure on their church to care for those ancestors was very strong.[11]

Given this situation, it is interesting to note that although numerous passages regarding burial may be found in the various 'Lives' of St Patrick, and 'The Rule of St Patrick' (*Riagail Phátraic*, which dates from the late seventh or early eighth century) tells of the churches' obligations to perform baptism, give communion and sing psalms and prayers for the dead, it does not mention any obligation to *bury* them.[13] Elizabeth O'Brien's survey of the Irish literary and archaeological evidence for early Christian burial in Ireland led her to the conclusion that 'many Christians were still being buried in tribal or family burial places, rather than in Christian cemeteries, perhaps as late as the eighth century, when the canons were completed'.[14] This 'lag' between the coming of Christianity and the abandonment of traditional burial grounds was also common in continen-

---

6 'Colloquy of the Ancients', *Silva Gadelica* (hereafter *SG*), II, p. 168. 7 Ibid., p. 132. 8 *Beatha Lasrach*, ed. & trans. L. Gwynn, p. 73. 9 Fanning . 'Excavation of an early Christian', especially p. 151. M.J. Kelly, 'Church Island', especially pp 87 and 118. 10 Charles-Edwards 'The pastoral role', n. 74, p. 76, commenting on *Hib. 1* ('*De reliquiis in deserto humatis*'). 11 Ibid., p. 76. 13 'The rule of Patrick', ed. and trans. O'Keeffe, §§5–8, §12; Charles-Edwards, 'The pastoral role' pp 69–70. 14 O'Brien, 'Late prehistoric–early historic Ireland', pp 50, 54–6.

tal western Europe. The first British graves that can confidently be said to contain ordinary Christians date to the eighth and ninth century, and thus coincide with the advent of churchyard burial.[15]

Various dates are offered for when cemeteries began to be located in churchyards. The first 'explicit mention of the consecration or benediction' of a cemetery occurs in Gregory of Tours' *Liber in gloria confessorum* written *c.* 587.[16] Philippe Ariès stated that the cemetery first appeared around French churches after the seventh century, but gave examples of places in France – such Châtenay and Guiry – where the church cemetery was used alternately with cemeteries in open fields. He noted that as a general rule, interment around the churches became normal during the eighth century or later.[17] Bertram Puckle stated that burial in and around churches became common in the eighth century, but concluded that 'it was not till the ninth century that the consecration of cemeteries became common'.[18] The earliest extant instructions for the ceremony of consecration of the cemetery date from the tenth century.[19] The main features of the current Roman Catholic rite for cemetery-consecration also date from this period, albeit with thirteenth-century additions.[20]

Ariès has concluded that in the Middle Ages, the ancient custom of interment in private graves was considered 'unacceptable'.[21] It would seem, however, that it was only the Church which found it unacceptable, and that the practice continued throughout the Middle Ages. In Carolingian Germany, the population had to be forced to abandon traditional burial mounds with the order 'that the bodies of Christian Saxons be taken to church cemeteries and not to pagan burial grounds'.[22] In the ninth century, we find a bishop (Ionas of Orléans) still giving permission to bury the dead *in agris suis* (on their own land) – for a charge.[23] This practice has never completely been eradicated; the Roman Catholic Church still permits burial on private property, although it is not a common practice.

Despite these official efforts to force burials into Christian cemeteries, several hundred burial barrows constructed between the years 450 and 1000 have been identified in various parts of England and Germany. Scottish barrow-burials dating from the early Middle Ages, previously thought to exist only in the Pictish areas of northern Scotland, have now been found in southern Scotland and in Wales.[25] It has recently been suggested that in Germany, the erection of

15 Bassett, Dyer & Holt, eds, *Death in Towns*, p. 4.   **16** Gyug, 'Consecration of cemeteries', p. 540.   **17** Ariès, *The hour*, pp 37–8.   **18** Puckle, *Funeral customs*, p. 140.   **19** Gyug., 'Consecration of cemeteries', pp 540-1.   **20** Podhradsky, *New dictionary of the liturgy*, p. 52.   **21** Ariès, *The hour*, p. 53.   **22** Ibid., p. 38, quoting *Monumenta Germaniae historica* (Hanover, 1875–89), Leges 5, Capitula de partibus Saxoniae, sub anno 777, p. 43; *Capitulio de partibus Saxoniae*; cf. van de Noort, 'Early medieval barrows' pp 29–34.   **23** Ariès, *The hour*, p. 39, quoting Lesne, *Histoire de la propriété ecclésiastique*, (Lille, 1936), iii, pp 122–9.   **25** Etheridge, 'Some aspects'. p. 48.

these medieval burial barrows may have been an effort by the older, local élite to re-assert their traditional power in defiance of the new Christian ideology and socio-political structure which emerged under the Carolingian empire.[26]

The question of who would have control over places of burial continued to be a source of friction throughout the Middle Ages. Records of the Church's insistence that Christians be buried apart from non-Christians can also be found an ecclesiastical law, which forbade the consecration of churches in places where bodies had previously been buried.[27] This effort to end burial in traditional (that is, 'pagan') graveyards that had not been consecrated as Christian cemeteries, as well as such practices as burial *in agris suis* would have aided efforts to consolidate the important religious, social and political associations of burial in sites where the Church would be able to control it – and the substantial income that it generated.

In France in the late twelfth century the Waldenesians, an early Protestant sect, asserted that the place of burial or consecration of the grave made no difference. This view was later echoed by John Wyclif and his followers in England in the second half of the fourteenth century, and by the Hussites in Bohemia in the first half of the fifteenth century.[28]

The persistence of burial in non-Christian graveyards

In the light of the various laws and decrees that were made in an effort to standardize Christian burial and the continuing resistance they encountered in Continental Europe in the ninth century, it would be unwise to presume that burial in traditional, non-Christian sites and non-Christian burial practices (or at least practices which deviated from 'standard' Christian burial practices) could not have survived in Ireland to some extent into the tenth century and later, especially in the more remote and inaccessible areas of the island. It is known, for example, that in Northumberland, England, unconsecrated altars and cemeteries became a problem, perhaps as a legacy of the disruptions that occurred during the Viking invasions, which certainly also wreaked havoc in Ireland.[29]

26 van de Noort, 'Early medieval barrows', p. 34. A similar reaction occurred at the time of the Reformation, when Irish Roman Catholics, took to re-using old, long-abandoned sites, 'sometimes for worship but more often for burial because the parish churches and graveyards were under the control of the established church'. See Ó Súilleabháin, *Irish Wake Amusements*, p. 46. On the burial of unbaptized children in abandoned burial grounds, see Manning, 'The excavation of the early Christian enclosure at Killederdadrum'; especially p. 262. **27** 'If bodies have been buried before the church has been consecrated, let it not be consecrated.' 'Nullo tumulorum vestigio apparente, ecclesiae reventia conserveretur. Ubi vero hoc pro multitudine cadaverum difficile este facere, locus ille coemeterium et polyandrium habeatur, ablato inde altare, et constituto sacrificium Deo valeat offeri,' Ariès, *The hour*, p. 51, n. 57, cited by Auguste J. Bernard, 'La sepulture en droit Canonique', law thesis, Paris, 1933, pp 20–1, n. 7. **28** Ibid., p. 41. **29** Butler, 'The churchyard in Eastern England,' p. 385.

Giraldus Cambrensis, the famous Cambro-Norman commentator on early colonial Ireland, wrote *c.*1185 of his own visit to Ireland, reporting that 'although all this time the Faith has grown up, so to speak, in the country, nevertheless in some corners of it there are many even still who are not baptized, and who ... have not yet heard of the teaching of the Faith'.[30] He went on to recount a meeting with some sailors who told of having met two men in a small skiff who 'were from some part of Connacht, and spoke the Irish language ... When asked if they were Christians and baptized, they replied that they had as yet heard nothing of Christ and knew nothing about him'.[31]

That Giraldus had his own agenda (part of which was to point out the laxity of the Church in Ireland) is well known, and there is little doubt that he included this tale to support his own views. If we choose to accept the veracity of the story – that is, that the group of Connaught people among whom these sailors lived were ignorant of Christianity – then we also accept their ignorance of Christian burial. While such naïveté may have been highly unusual – Gerald certainly seems to have found it so – it is unlikely that it was unique.

There is additional evidence from both Ireland and Britain to support the view that non-Christian burial was being practiced in Ireland as late as Giraldus' time, and even for centuries after it. Papal letters record the granting of permission to consecrate more than sixty new cemeteries from 1396 to 1503. The letters are remarkably similar: they cite the need for a new cemetery (generally to be located at an existing local chapel), complain of the long and inconvenient distance to the parish-church (generally one to two miles away), and protest that during the rainy season flooding and muddiness delay the transportation of corpses to the parish church's cemetery for burial.

It is notable that of these more than sixty Insular requests for burial rights, only two relate to Ireland. The first concerns the chapel of Loughans (*de Locanis*) which belonged to the Premonstratensian abbey of 'St Mary's Urburne' (Woodburn) in the diocese of Connor, Co. Londonderry, which was granted permission for burial in 1412.[32] The second dates from 1475 when 'John de Geraldinis, knight of Kerry of the diocese of Ardfert', granted some of his land for a cemetery.[33]

The situation in England, where parish-churches were often located a mile or two from other small settlements, would probably also have been common

30 Giraldus Cambrensis, *Topographia Hiberniae*, pp 90.   **31** Ibid., pp 94–5.   **32** *Calendar of entries in the Papal Registers for Great Britain and Ireland, Letters* (hereafter: *Cal. Pap. Reg.*), VI, 2 John XXIII, 6 Id. March 1412, p. 310. Loughans is located in the barony of Iveagh (Upper) and the parish of Tullylish (*Index to Townlands*, p. 672). Also, a Scottish supplication to Rome which seems to date from the first half of the fifteenth century which emanated from parish of Strageith (now Blackford) in the diocese of Dunblane, Perthshire, records that a great number of the parishioners lived 'ten or eight or six or five Italian miles' from the church and that 'many of them ... are utterly ignorant of the divine office and the mandates of the church'. *Calendar of Scottish supplications* (no rubric), Florence, 8 Id. Sept., anno. 130, 233v.   **33** *Cal. Pap. Reg.*, XIII, 4 Sixtus IV, 15 Kal. May 1475, p. 433.

in Ireland and thus presented the same problems regarding transportation for burial. What then accounts for the discrepancy in the number of Irish and English requests to consecrate new cemeteries? There would seem to be two likely explanations: either the Irish bore their inconvenience without complaining or they buried their dead in places which had not been consecrated for Christian burial, without first consulting the Church.

The written record proves that in 1412 the latter solution was chosen by the people in the neighborhood of the chapel of Loughans. Their letter to the pope complained that divine offices had not been held in their chapel for twelve years and of the 'many parishioners who have died without ... sacraments and have been buried in the fields'.[34] If such burials were found today, their east-west orientation, lack of grave-goods and interment in places which provide no indication of ever having been the site of a Christian church or cemetery-enclosure could easily lead to the deduction that they date from the early Christian period, when the definitions between Christian and 'pagan' burial were still blurred. Yet the testimony of the people of Loughans, as preserved in their letter to the pope, shows that it is possible that burials found with these features could be of late medieval date.

Some graves uncovered in the last century provide examples of the kind of evidence which might benefit from re-evaluation. In 1916, R.A.S. Macalister published an article regarding 'an ancient cemetery' in Mooretown, Ardee, near the border of Co. Meath. A total of eleven graves was found, which he described as being 'shallow trenches, 2 ft, 6 inches below ground level, lined on each side for their lower 10 or 12 inches with slabs on edge, supporting horizontal cover-slabs'.[35] Some of the graves were aligned 'approximately east/west' and no grave-goods were found. The 'total absence of any trace or tradition of a Christian church or other consecrated site' led Macalister to conclude that these graves were pre-Christian. In view of the situation that is known to have existed in Loughans in 1412, the absence of any trace of a church or consecrated site does not seem adequate to prove that the burials at Mooretown were not Christian.

An excavation conducted at Ballinlough, Co. Laois, in 1962 may also be worth reconsidering. It uncovered what was clearly a skull-burial with three human rib-parts and a human hip-bone neatly placed around it. This was a re-burial, with the body tentatively identified as a female. Etienne Rynne, who led the excavation, pointed out that the east-west orientation of the burial alone could not conclusively date it to the Christian period. He concluded that 'the shallowness of the graves, the apparently deliberate skull-burial, the nature of the site, and the presence of a Christian graveyard of long-standing at Kilteale, within a few hundred metres of the site, all hint at a pre-Christian date for these particular buri-

---

34 *Cal. Pap. Reg.*, VI, 2 John XXIII, 6 Id. March 1412, p. 310.   **35** Macalister, 'An ancient cemetery, Mooretown', p. 61.

als'.[36] I have already noted that many Christian cemeteries were consecrated at or near the sites of pre-Christian burial-grounds, as well as the reluctance of native populations to abandon these traditional sites. Therefore, in the absence of other evidence, the presence of a Christian cemetery near a burial would not seem to offer enough evidence to conclude that the burial is pre-Christian.

Archaeologist J.P. Mallory has written that distinguishing between Irish pagan and Irish early Christian medieval inhumations can be 'enormously difficult':

> For example, 'The Táin' regularly suggests that the deceased were buried *where* they died and there is no trace of the Early Medieval cemetery, i.e. single burials are presumed to be pagan. Unfortunately, this cannot be demonstrated by any other independent evidence, i.e. it cannot be excluded that Christians may have also been buried independent of a cemetery or other formal Christian mortuary structure.[37]

This view is further supported by passages from written sources which document the separate burial of heads by Christians throughout the Middle Ages. For example, Hugh de Lacy's head and body were buried separately in 1198,[38] and *Caithréim Thoirdhealbhaigh* reports that in 1312 Melachlainn MacNamara was beheaded, and his head and body were not left together: 'The good chieftain was beheaded and, for fear lest his friends might recover him, he also was not left both head and body in one place.'[39] Unfortunately, we cannot go back to the burials documented by Macalister and Rynne and make the tests which would be needed to establish a more accurate date of burial.

The existence of medieval Irish field-burials is given additional credibility by similar evidence from Norfolk, England, which postdates the letter from Loughans by eighteen years. In 1430, John Reeve, a glover in Beccles in north-east Suffolk, was accused of (and confessed to) having 'held, believed and affirmed' that:

> … it is as meritorie and as medful and as profitable to all Cristis peple to be byryed in myddynges, medues or in the wilde feldes as it is to be byryed in churches or churcheyerdes.[40]

---

36 Rynne, 'Ancient burials', pp 430–3. 37 Mallory, 'The world of Cú Chulainn', p. 130. 38 *Annals of St Mary's Abbey, Dublin*, II, pp 221, 276, 307. 39 *Caithréim Thoirdhealbhaigh* (hereafter *Caithr. Th.*), ed. and trans. O'Grady & Flower, II, p. 56; Irish, I, p. 59: '… agus tugatar na bloidig bás Póil phortuaine pennchorcra paiderghlain ar Lochlainn ar in láthair sin .i. a chenn do bádhad iarna bhuain dá cholainn tré chelgfelltaib ua mBloid trénnaimdide … agus do díchennad go dianláidir in degflaith, agus nír fágbad ar egla a fhaghbála dá fhírcháirdib i néninad é itir chenn agus chaomcholainn.' 40 *Heresy trials in the diocese of Norwich, 1428–31*, ed. Tanner, p. 112. In Modern English: 'It is as meritorious and suitable and beneficial to all Christ's people to be buried in middens, meadows or in the wild fields as it is to be buried in churches or churchyards.'

This testimony was given by a 'Lollard', that is, a follower of the English religious dissenter, John Wyclif, who protested against the enormous power priests had because they controlled the administration of sacramental rites. Wyclif's chief centres of support were the cities of London, Oxford, Leicester, and Coventry, and the dioceses of Hereford and Worcester, and later, Norfolk.[41] The complaints of the Lollards must have been known in Ireland, and the same inconveniences involved in transporting corpses to duly consecrated burial grounds would have been experienced by the Irish, who lived in a similarly rainy climate. What is certainly known is that burial in unconsecrated and seemingly 'pagan' locations was taking place in the British Isles during the fifteenth century and this practice was not limited to the 'wildernesses' of Ireland. Undoubtedly a more thorough search of medieval records from Great Britain and France would uncover additional examples.

The historical evidence certainly indicates that there is reason to consider a far wider range of dates for medieval interments in Ireland and to reassess what should constitute acceptable evidence for 'pagan' or 'Christian' burial.

THE SOCIAL USES OF THE CEMETERY IN MEDIEVAL IRELAND

In medieval western Europe, the realities of illness and death were ubiquitous and unavoidable, and the community of the dead was accepted as a part of the community of the living and integrated into it. In a time when houses were tiny and crowded and streets were narrow, muddy and filthy, the cemetery served as the town's public space. The cemetery – rather than being removed from the daily life of the living community – was at its centre.[42] The remainder of this chapter will be devoted to the various functions of the Irish cemetery which are identifiable from the historical record in the light of what is known about cemeteries in other parts of the British Isles and in France.

Philippe Ariès has observed that the medieval French cemetery served as

> Marketplace; place for announcements, auctions, proclamations, sentences; scene of community gatherings; promenade; athletic field; haven for illicit encounters and dubious professions … it was the public place *par excellence*, the center of collective life … for a very long time, before it was isolated from the church, the cemetery was the public square.[43]

Clare Gittings has recorded that in England during the early modern period churchyards were not reserved entirely for graves, and she has noted that bishops:

---

41 Urquhart, 'Lollards'.　**42** Ariès, *The hour*, p. 62.　**43** Ibid., p. 70.

had to issue injunctions against the feeding of cattle in churchyards, the
playing of games, depositing dung, the emptying of chamberpots or 'easing
of nature', fighting, performing plays and hanging out washing to dry.
This list of activities suggests a closeness between the living and the dead
almost unknown today.[44]

If the difficulties associated with the process of standardizing burial were common
to Ireland and other countries of western Europe, then we may well ask about
the similarities between the social uses of cemeteries in Ireland and in those countries.

Achieving a clear picture of the uses to which Irish cemeteries were put during
the Middle Ages is necessarily limited if we rely on the material available in the
written sources. Our view is also clouded by the terminology used. Historical
sources written in Irish use the word *reilg* (or *relig*) for a Christian graveyard, and
nemed for sanctuary, thus clearly distinguishing between the two. However, ecclesiastical and secular administrative sources written in Latin use the word *cimiterium*, which can mean either the burial-ground or the churchyard, that is, the larger
sanctuary lands surrounding the church. (This land would, of course, always include
any burial-ground attached to the church.) Therefore, when an activity is described
as taking place in the *cimiterium*, it is not always possible to be certain that this
refers specifically to the site where bodies were buried. Ariès has given examples
of medieval French cemeteries that were *sub priori immunitatis* (primarily for sanctuary) or *ad refugium tantum vivorum, non ad sepulturam mortuorum* (for the refuge
of the living, not for the burial of the dead),[45] though he does not say whether
these sites had previously been used for burial. However, since no reference has
been found which uses these phrases in connection with Irish cemeteries, it may
be that this practice never existed in Ireland, and that in medieval Irish sources
the word *cimiterium* always refers specifically to the graveyard.

Despite ambiguities in terminology, the information available indicates that
the sanctified enclosure surrounding the church – which included the graveyard – was the focus of a wide range of secular activities which were also found
in similar circumstances on the Continent in the same period, a number of which
date from 'pre-Christian' times.

The cemetery as fair- or market-site
Many of the activities noted above as having been associated with French and
English cemeteries are also identifiable in the Irish medieval record. For example, D.A. Binchy's description of the activities which took place at the famous
burial-ground *cum* fair-ground of Teltown, Co. Meath, bears striking similarity
to the description above:

44 Gittings, *Death, burial*, p. 140. **45** Ariès, *The hour*, p. 63.

(Tailtiu was) an old burial place and the site of an old *óenach* … How far this tradition goes back is not easy to determine. It probably dates from pre-Goidelic times … The site of the fair was normally an ancient burial ground; indeed the tradition reflected in many poems and sagas that the *óenach* originated in the funeral games held for kings and heroes may have a kernel of truth. At such gatherings, besides the exchange of goods and the holding of games, horse-racing and various athletic competitions, the 'public' business of the *túath*, including important law suits between different kindreds and the issue of special ordinances was transacted (marriage alliances, too) …[46]

Teltown was a famous site in pre-Christian Ireland, which remained important in Gaelic culture well into the Middle Ages; the last recorded occurrence of the *óenach* at Teltown is found in *AFM, s.a.* 1168.

In Ireland, this linking of cemetery and fair was not unique to Teltown. A *dinnshenchas*-verse in the tale *Lecht Oen-Fhir Áife* links the burial site of a boy with a fair-site:

> Thereafter Chuchulain bore him
> to the *óenach* at Airbi Rofhir:
> Airbe Rofhir, whence comes the name
> but the hewing of his grave-stone?[47]

Similarly, another tale tells that in the fifth century, Amhalghaidh, the son of Fiachra Ealgach, 'raised Carn Amhalgaidh to serve as a place of fairs and great meetings; and it was in it that Amhalgaidh himself was interred'.[48] Irish law-tracts list together the offenses of stripping the dead and disturbing the fair-site, prescribing the same penalty for both.[49] Another tale tells how 'Drithliu the magician is slaughtered on the banks of *Finnloch*, whence *aenach Drithliud* or 'Drithliu's green' has its name … '[50] The 'Death of Crimthann' relates how the body of Eogan Béul, the mid-sixth-century king of Connaught, was stolen by the Ulstermen who re-buried it at the cemetery of *Aonach Locha Gile* in Co. Sligo.[51] Fair and cemetery are linked again in the text called 'History of the

---

46 Binchy, 'The fair', pp 123–4. *Óenach* means 'fair' or 'public gathering', and *túath* means 'tribe' or petty kingdom. 47 'Rosfuc Cúchulaind airsin/co hóenach Airbi Rofhir:/Airbe Rofhir, cid diatá/acht a hairbe i lechtáin-sa?' from *Lect Oen-Fir Aife*', *Met. Dind.*, IV, p. 133. 48 O'Donovan, 'Genealogy of the Hy-Fiachrach of the Moy', p. 101. The death of Amhalghaidh, king of Connaught, is recorded in *AFM s.a.* 449. See O'Rahilly, *Early Irish history*, p. 398–400. 49 *Ancient laws and institutes of Ireland*, ed. Atkinson, et al., I, p. 175. 50 'Death of Crimthann,' *SG*, II, p. 376; I, p. 333: 'martar diu Drithliu drái for brú fionnlocha conid uad ainmnigter aenach nDrithluid'. Crimthainn maic Fidaig's death is recorded in *AFM s.a.* 378. Myles Dillon stated that the tale belonged perhaps to the eleventh century. Dillon, *Cycles*, p. 30. 51 O'Donovan, *Tribes and Customs*, ed. & trans. O'Donovan, p. 471.

Cemeteries (*Senchus na Relec*)', which lists the names of the chief cemeteries of Ireland before the introduction of Christianity as *Croghan, Brugh, Tailltenn, Luachair Ailbe, Oenach Ailbe, Oenach Culi, Oenach Comain* and *Temair Erann*. P.W. Joyce, in his *Social History of Ireland*, written in the late nineteenth century, noted also that fairs commemorating the dead were held at each of these sites, a fact preserved in the *óenach* names of three of them.[52]

A poem attributed to the tenth-century poet Torna Éigeas tells that the body of King Dathí was buried in the middle of *Aonach na Cruachna*, where, according to Duald MacFirbis, it was marked by the red-stone pillar of *Dairrithe Dearg*.[53] Similarly, the seventeenth-century compilation of poetry known as *Duanaire Finn* relates how 'the stone *Aonach Cairn mhic Táil* wert left skilfuly [*sic*] above Cróinfhinne's coffin'.[54] *Aonach Cairn mhic Táil* means 'the Fair of the Monument of the Son of Tál', 'cairn' usually meaning a burial mound or memorial to the dead.[55] Thus, this phrase appears to record that the stone which was located at the site of the fair which had once been held at the funeral monument of the son of Tál, had been moved to become the marker over Cróinfhinne's grave.

This connection of burial sites with fairs and markets continued well into the Middle Ages in Ireland and also in England, Scotland, and France. The presence of pillarstones at the site calls to mind the medieval 'mercat cross'. August Bernard wrote that, in France, the medieval cemetery was 'the noisiest, busiest, most boisterous, and most commercial place in the rural or urban community'.[56] Roberta Gilchrist and Robert Morris have suggested that in England, the likelihood is high that monasteries sold their surplus foodstuffs, along with other necessities, such as nails, tools, pottery, etc. Thus, before the twelfth century, monasteries would have had a function equivalent to that of small market towns.[57] The practice of locating merchant's stalls within, or next to, the cemetery was a common western European practice, and one which was supported by sound financial reasoning since, as part of the sanctuary lands of the Church, cemeteries were beyond the reach of the long and taxing arm of the law. Ariès has commented that in France, 'Undoubtedly it was the appearance of the market

---

52 Joyce, *A social history of Ireland*, II, p. 555. Joyce also noted that the fairs were 'at or beside' the cemetery, ibid., p. 560. **53** *Tribes and customs of the Hy-Fiachrach*, ed. & trans. O'Donovan, p. 25. Of the tale of Dathí (or 'Nathí'), F.J. Byrne has written, 'this story is a characteristic farrago of the etymological ingenuities and misplaced learning of the medieval antiquaries': *Irish kings*, pp 77–8. Still, the tale's connection of burial with the *aonach* seems to conform to established Irish tradition. *Oénach* and *aonach* are variant spellings – medieval and modern – of the same word. **54** *Duanaire Finn*, iii, ed. G. Murphy, poem XLII, st. 101. Murphy entered the caveat that he was uncertain about translating *chiste* as 'coffin'; however, the glossary in Egerton 158 defines *comhra* as *cisde na marbh*. See 'Contributions to a dictionary' (hereafter, *RIA Dict.*) under *comrar*. **55** See *RIA Dict.* The entry is under the spelling *carn* and notes that in the literature these mounds are sometimes connected with the making of agreements. **56** Ariès, *The hour*, p. 64; cf. Bernard, *Sépulture en droit canonique*, p. 60. **57** Gilchrist & Morris, 'Monasteries as settlements', p. 117.

in the twelfth and thirteenth centuries that brought about the enlargement of some cemeteries'.[58] A twelfth-century English charter of the earl of Northampton, granted to the prior of St Andrew's the profits 'of the fair held … in the church and churchyard of All Saints'.[59] Statutes from Ely and Wells dating to the mid thirteenth century forbade the holding of markets in sacred places (*in locis sacris*)'.[60] Similarly, the Statutes of the Scottish Church decree that 'there be no bargaining done in sacred places'.[61] The diocese of Worcester approved a statute in 1240 which linked the market held in the cemetery with the drawing of blood;[62] and the diocese of Canterbury passed a statute forbidding markets in the church and the cemetery.[63] Despite all of these statutes, King Edward II found it necessary in 1308 to forbid the holding of fairs or markets in churchyards in England and Ireland 'for honour of Holy Church'.[64] Yet a papal letter of 1398 reports that the inhabitants of the town of 'Byriton' in the diocese of York seized 'a certain place situate within the wales [*sic*] of the cemetery … to use it for a public market and traffic, please, [*sic*] … and to cause mutilations and homicides to be committed there'.[65]

The information which exists for Dublin does not allow as clear an assessment. In Viking-age Dublin, the market seems to have been located inside the western wall, near what became 'Gormond's Gate'. In later medieval Dublin, a fair-green is known to have been located outside the city-walls, on the southwest side, and does not seem to have had any connection with a cemetery.[66] Charters from Dublin and Waterford provide detailed descriptions of the location of market-stalls, but the records which have survived describe them as being located adjacent to cemeteries, rather than inside them, much as the modern shopping areas of many great European cities encircle great urban squares.[67] A

---

58 Ariès, *The hour*, p. 70. See also J. Barrow, 'Urban cemetery location', p. 93.   **59** Moore, *The fairs*, p. 21, quoting H. Cam, 'Northampton Borough' in *Victoria history of the County of Northampton*, ed. William Page (London, 1930), iii, p. 23.   **60** *Councils & synods*, 'Statutes of Ely Diocese', I, p. 519, No. 21; 'Statutes of Wells', I, p. 601, No. 19.   **61** 'Ecclesiastical statutes of the 13th c.', *Stat. Scot.*, (hereafter *Stat. Scot.*), p. 56, No. 108. It is not known whether this as a provincial or synodal statute: p. 50.   **62** 'Ad servandam quoque tam cimiterii quam ecclesie reventiam prohibemus ne in cimiteriis vel aliis locis sacratis vel etiam alibi diebus dominicis mercata teneantur vel sanguinis cause tractentur … ', 'Statutes of Worcester', eds Powicke, et al., III, *Councils & synods*, II, p. 297, No. 5.   **63** 'So-called statutes of R. Winchelsey' (1295 x 1313), ibid., II, p. 1388.   **64** *Early statutes of Ireland*, ed. Berry, I Edward II (1308) No. VI, p. 257: 'given at Winchester, the 8th day of Oct. in the thirteenth year of the King's reign … And the King commands and forbids that from henceforth, for the honour of Holy Church, fairs or or markets be held in church-yards.' Note 1 adds that 'the statute was ordered to be observed in Ireland by the ordinance made at Westminster, 17th March, 1308'.   **65** *Cal. Pap. Reg.* (ltrs), XLIV, 9 Boniface IX, Non. Aug. 1398, pp 89–90.   **66** See the map *Viking settlement in medieval Dubin* (no named author), p. 24; *Map of medieval Dublin, c.840–1540*, and McCullough, *Dublin: an urban history*. The fair-green encompassed the Iveagh Market, stretching from Thomas Street down to Nicholas Place, and was bordered on the west side by Francis Street.   **67** '*Registrum cantariae S Salvatoris Waterfordensis*', No. 55: 'Sciant presentes et futuri quod ego Willelmus Lyncoll

rental from Waterford, dated 1427, documents payment to one 'Thomas Okkebourne' for '*celdis suis ex opposito cimiterii Sancti Petri* (his stall opposite St Peter's cemetery).[68] A large oval cemetery existed in medieval Dublin, and present-day Dublin's 'Glover's Lane' on the west side of St Stephen's Green continues to bear witness to the commerce which clung to its walls.[69]

James Mills, writing at the beginning of the nineteenth century, informed us that 'In medieval times the crypt [of Christchurch Cathedral, Dublin] was leased to stall-holders who held markets there. As late as the seventeenth century it housed taverns, a practice which was neither new nor unique to Ireland.'[70]

E.W. Moore's study of the large cloth-fairs of medieval England indicates that these were not located in cemeteries.[71] It may be, however, that these fairs were far larger than most and do not reflect the locations of the more numerous smaller fairs. As the capital city of Ireland, Dublin's fairs also presumably would have attracted larger numbers of people than fairs held in less populous locations. A fair of such great size had to be well regulated and kept at a 'fair distance' from the walled town in order to minimize dangers to the town commonly associated with fair, such as fire. Given the historical Irish link between fairs and cemeteries, and the fact that this link also existed in medieval England, it seems likely that smaller Irish fairs and markets were conducted in cemeteries. This is especially true for the first half of the period under study, when trading was not yet as regular or regulated as it later became. It is also well to remember that the information about life in Ireland which found its way into Irish

civis civitatis Waterford' dedi concessi … duas seldas cum suis ortis de sanctuario ecclesie sancti Michaelis in suburbio dicte civitatis et in parochia dicte ecclesie sancti Michaelis … '(1470); also, Deed No. 56:' … unam seldam cum parva (small) vacua terra de sanctuario ecclesie sancti Michaelis in suburbio dicte civitatis et in parochia dicte ecclesie sancti Michaelis … ' (1470); also, Deed No. 70:' … in capella sancti Salvatoris iuxta ecclesiam cathedralem sancte Trinitatis dicte civitatis situata unam seldam cum coquina et orto de sanctuario ecclesie Sancti Michaelis in suburbio dicte civitatis … ' (1471). **68** White, *Irish monastic and episcopal deeds*, p. 106. **69** The cemetery was 'near the church of St Andrew's (St Andrew's Street), a parallel route (today's Nassau Street) led around the Black Pool towards the oval cemetery', McCullough, *Dublin: an urban history*, n. 48. In terms of the geography of contemporary Dublin, the cemetery ran more or less by Stephen Street on the north down to Digges Street, and extended east from Mercer Street Lower (just west of St Stephen's Green) to Whitefriar's Street. The priory of St Mary's (founded 1274), St Peter's parish-church and St Stephen's hospital were all located within its walls. See *Map of medieval Dublin*. **70** Mills, 'Sixteenth century notices of chapels', cf. Christ Church deeds no. 740, 886, 983, 1633, etc. For example, St Mary Colechurch in London stood on vaults over a tavern. See D. Keene & V. Harding, *Historical Gazeteer of London before the Great Fire, I, Cheapside* (Chadwyck-Healey microfiche, 1987, nos 105/0, 105/18). **71** Moore, *The fairs*. It should be noted that Moore's research on the locations of English wool fairs – most of which pertains to the thirteenth century – shows them to have been located in prescribed areas of the town, and aside from the charter mentioned above (n. 48), she made no mention of these fairs ever having been located in the churchyard. Perhaps the fairs had been located in the churchyard at an earlier time, and the custom was waning.

medieval records was always limited, and that only a small percentage of these records survive. Because of this, whatever view we can glimpse from the records of the relationship between medieval Irish markets and cemeteries will necessarily be distorted to some greater or lesser extent.

The cemetery as a place for making contracts and swearing oaths

The linking of human remains (in the form of 'holy relics') with legal functions was already long-established in western Europe by the central Middle Ages.[72] Written sources show that this was also true for Ireland, where burial grounds had long been associated with the swearing of oaths and other legal matters. The connection between burial grounds and *óenach*-sites has been noted in the section on fairs and marketplaces above. The medieval Irish word *óenach* means 'fair' and signifies a general gathering or community meeting, where the business of the community – both commercial and legal – was conducted.

Native Irish law-texts contain two passages linking cemeteries with legal activities:

> He proffers seven *cumals* for reception (into the tribe), and each *cumal* has the force of an oath; if connexion is acknowledged and he proffers it, (i.e. his oath) at seven cemeteries ... every oath respecting trespass must be taken at three cemeteries, every oath respecting contract and covenant at a single cemetery; but if there be in the place three separate relics, they have the force of three cemeteries; and there is no need for other relics to be on the tomb, but if there are such, they are to have the force of cemeteries ... the stranger must go to seven cemeteries to proffer his oath ...[73]

The same source stipulates that, in making judgements, the (wooden) coffin of a patron saint may be used,[74] and also mentions the transfer of another type of property in 'the case of a child who is given back to his father's tribe over the grave of the dead mother'.[75] Native Welsh law-texts, which date from the twelfth century and later, also link places of judgement with cemeteries when they state that the dimension of the court or council is 'a legal *erw*, and that in compass; and that is also the size of a church-yard burial-ground'.[76]

In his description of the social functions at the *óenach* of Teltown, D.A. Binchy mentioned that the site was also used for 'the 'public' business of the *túath*, including important law-suits between 'different kindreds and the issue of special ordi-

72 Geary, *Furta Sacra*, p. 29.   **73** Plummer, 'Notes on some passages in the brehon laws III', p. 114.   **74** Ancient laws, eds Atkinson et al., V, p. 473.   **75** Ibid., p. 201.   **76** 'The measure of the burying-ground is a legal "erw" in length, with its end to the churchyard; and that, circling the church-yard, is to be its compass.' *Ancient laws and institutions of Wales*, I, ed. Aneurin, p. 67, §8. Ibid., note 'a': 'The "erw" appears to have contained about 4,320 square yards'.

nances'.[77] The eleventh- or twelfth-century commentary on the *Martyrology of Oengus* relates that

> the union of Columcille and Cianán was made thus, i.e. Colum Cille's
> hand (thrust) in through the southern side of the tomb even to the half,
> and Cianán's hand (thrust) even to the half side, and then they make the
> union.[78]

'Teigue mac Cein's Adventure' tells of 'royal youths' who entered into a pact with the leader of their warrior band by striking their hands in his 'upon a *tulach*' or burial mound.[79] In the Irish poem 'The Birth of Aedán mac Gabrain', in a manuscript of 1120, the mother of Aedán swears 'by the most potent flagstone in Scotland'.[80] The 'Book of Fenagh', which was compiled no later than 1300,[81] dips back into tribal lore to tell of the cemetery located on the plain of Magh Réin, where 'nineteen kings who possessed the sovreignty of Ireland' are buried under the tombstone of the kings (*Lec-na-Righ*) and that 'the men of Ireland used to come unitedly to that plain, during the time of Conaing, to arrange their covenants, and to pay their tributes, and their rents.'[82] In a passage from the 'Life of St Bairre', thought to date from the late eleventh or early twelfth century, an ordination is performed in the cemetery rather than in the church: 'the Lord himself read [the service of] episcopal orders over him at the cross in front of the church where his remains were afterwards buried'.[83] Unfortunately, the wording of this sentence does not make clear whether the burial was made at the cross in front of the church, or in the church itself.

Sanctuary status exempted Church-lands from the jurisdiction of civil law, and the 'king's writ' held no authority inside the cemetery. The 'Constitutions of the Diocese of Ossory' of 1317 prohibited laymen from carrying out 'judgments or attachments in churches, cemeteries or sanctuaries' as well as the violent removal 'of persons accused of crime who have fled for refuge to churches, cemeteries, or cloisters'; the penalty for such behavior was excommunication.[84] The Irish connection of cemeteries with legal activities may have created problems after the arrival of the of the 'Anglo-Normans', and such decrees may have

---

77 Binchy, 'The fair', pp 123–4. **78** *Félire*, p. 246. **79** *SG*, ed. Stokes, I, p. 356; II, p. 399: 'Ocus ó rángadar na rígmacáim sin co Tadg dorónsat a cura ocus a muinnteras fris. ocus tucsat a láma i láim Taidg ar in tulach. ocus tucsomh ratha tar nach ticthe dona tréinferaib im ríge thíre …' **80** 'The birth of Aedán mac Gabráin', ed. & trans. M.A. O'Brien, st. 48, p. 170. In Irish: 'dar in leicc is treisse thair is meisse, a meic, do mathair', ibid., p. 165. **81** *The Book of Fenagh* (hereafter *Bk Fen.*), ed. & trans. Hennessy & Kelly, p. vii. **82** Ibid., p. 253. This is Conaing *Beg eaglach*. He is recorded as 'king of Ireland' in *AFM*, and mentioned under A.M. 4357, 4369, 4388. **83** *Lives*, II, p. 17. *Beatha Bharra*, as recorded in the 'early vernacular life', as been argued to have been composed between 1196 and 1201: *Beatha Bharra*, ed. & trans. Ó Riain, §33, pp 74–5; for dating, see pp 30–3. **84** 'Calendar of the *liber ruber*', ed. H.J. Lawlor, pp 166–7, no. 14.

been issued in an attempt to sever the connection between law and the cemetery and center legal activities in the courts.

Despite sanctuary status and the Church's attempts to shield its lands from secular law, the cemetery continued to serve as an important site for making pacts and oaths, contracting business and holding important meetings throughout the late Middle Ages. Ariès has stated that French medieval cemeteries were a 'place for announcements ... proclamations, sentences; scene of community gatherings ...' It is worth noting, for example, that the ecclesiastical court which tried Joan of Arc to death was held in the cemetery of Saint-Ouen.

The fact that the Scottish church felt it necessary to decree in the thirteenth century that 'there be no bargaining done in sacred places; that the cemeteries be enclosed ... that secular courts not be held in sacred places' makes it clear that old customs were difficult to alter.[85]

Evidence that English cemeteries saw the same use has previously been cited in the example from Byriton, York, where in 1398 a place within the cemetery was seized and used for a public market and 'please' (pleas).[86] In 1411, a papal letter concerning Westminster-without-the-walls in London describes the 'great concourse of advocates, proctors, lawyers and of serjeants, apprentices and attorneys for divers law business' found 'situate about the cemetery of the city'.[87] Knowledge of the exact sites, not just the towns or cities, at which medieval courts were held remains elusive. In his study of English medieval county-courts, R.C. Palmer stated that county sessions were held in a variety of locations. Prior to the fourteenth century, the county-sessions might have met out of doors, and he noted that the *Summa magna* tells of sessions being held in forests and fields. The dampness of English weather would not have made these locations very conducive to the writing of records, but the need to handle 'special business' in areas where there was no other practical option may have made it necessary to hold sessions outdoors.

In the twelfth century it appears that county sessions were held indoors. Documents tell of English county-courts being held in venues as diverse as castles, monasteries, houses, and interestingly, the crypt of York minster. By the thirteenth century, English 'county sessions were typically held ... in churches, castle halls, or halls specially built for the county court'. Indoor meetings seem to have become usual in England once county courts began meeting 'more than twice a year in a regular session and at a specific place', and 'by the middle of the thirteenth century at latest, outdoor sessions must have been uncommon'. However, even as late as the seventeenth century, Middlesex county court held a special session in an open area.[88]

---

85 Ecclesiastical statutes of the 13th c.', *Stat. Scot.*, p. 56, no. 108. **86** *Cal. Pap. Reg.* XLIV, 9 Boniface IX, Mon. Aug. 1398, pp 89–90. **87** *Cal. Pap. Reg.*, VI, 1 John XXII, 1411, Id. Jan., p. 217. **88** Palmer, *The county courts*, pp 18–21.

The Irish court-system was created by the 'Anglo-Normans' and was based on their judicial system; yet it would be unwise to presume that Irish courts were held in venues which exactly mirrored those of English courts, since their location may have been influenced by earlier native Irish traditions. Ireland had significantly fewer towns than England, especially in the twelfth and early thirteenth centuries, and documents record that courts were held in many locations where it is not known what kind of buildings would have been available for the sessions. Palmer himself makes it quite clear that standardization was slow in England, where there was also great regional diversity in court venues. Given the unsettled nature of much of Ireland during this period of conquest and subinfeudation, it could hardly have been faster or easier to standardize the court system in Ireland. The Anglo-Norman judiciary system was foreign to Irish society; it took time for it to develop and become efficient. Richardson and Sayles' research shows that the office which evolved into Keeper of Rolls and Writs in the common bench appears to have originated in 1232, and that

> it is doubtful, indeed, whether in the later twelfth century and the early years of the thirteenth there were any courts of law other than local courts even within those parts of Ireland John directly controlled.[89]

The court of common law – which was used a great deal by merchants – was not developed until shortly after Edward I took the throne of England (1272), with significant development occurring between 1285 and 1291. Additionally, the office of the exchequer can be traced back no further than 1232, and no chancellor of the exchequer is known before Thomas of Chedworth was given the title at an unassignable date sometime before Easter 1270.[90]

Even after a system of courts had been put into operation by the 'Anglo-Normans', it seems unlikely that people generally would have used such a formal institution to make agreements or 'deals' which were local, small in scale, or of a personal nature. The question naturally arises as to where such agreements were being made from the beginning of the tenth century until the middle of the thirteenth century when the Anglo-Irish court-system was developed. If a court-system designed to serve merchants was not functional until the end of the thirteenth century, where were agreements being made in the century between the 'Anglo-Norman' invasion and its development?

Legal documents show that by the end of the thirteenth century it was common for business transactions to be handled by the exchequer. But again, what of business arrangements between people before 1232, or those made at a later date between people who were not professional merchants and whose transactions did not involve large amounts of goods or capital? And what of the vast

---

89 Richardson & Sayles, *The administration of Ireland*, especially pp 38–47. **90** Ibid., p. 27.

population of native Irish who did not have the right to English law or did not live in areas under English domination? Fairs and cemeteries would seem the most likely venues for courts, especially considering the historical links between the two.

A survey of the extant published Irish records has uncovered no specific information about where medieval Irish courts were convened. James Mills, who edited *The calendar of justiciary rolls* for Ireland, wrote in his preface only that the court sat in the 'King's hall of pleas' when it was in Dublin, which, he felt, was 'no doubt an apartment in the Castle'. The castle, or a public building or hall would be the obvious and logical site in which to hold a court in any of the larger towns of the period, such as Waterford, Limerick and Drogheda. But the justiciary rolls show that courts were also held in small towns and villages. In 1295, for example, courts were held at Clonmel in Co. Tipperary, in Tralee and Ardfert in Co. Kerry, and at Stradbally, Co. Waterford; in 1297 at Mullingar in Co. Westmeath, Nenagh in Co. Tipperary, and Kells in Co. Meath.[91]

Let us consider the case of Stradbally, which was a manorial town (the *caput* of the fitzAnthony lordship).[92] Stradbally had no motte-and-bailey castle, but we do know that by 1307, its church was important: the taxation list for that year shows that, of the eighty-nine churches in the diocese of Lismore, Stradbally was the fourth richest.[93] If the church was already in existence when the court was held in 1297, and presuming that it was not held inside the church, the most likely location would seem to have been the open air. Given the importance of the church at Stradbally, its *cimiterium* would appear to have been its most likely location.

A memorandum of 1366, preserved in the register of the archbishop of Armagh suggests that, even in fourteenth-century Ireland, the cemetery continued to be a place where important meetings were held and where decisions were made. The document records that when the bishop, the proctor, and the whole clergy of Kilmore, Co. Roscommon, met to discuss the important matter of the completion of the archdiocesan visitation by 'Master Peter O kerbyllan', the place which they chose for their meeting was 'in the cemetery towards the east part of the said church'.[94] The careful inclusion of this information and the precision of its detail indicates that the place of the meeting (and not just its outcome) was significant. There would seem to be only two likely reasons for this: either the meeting-place was unusual, or the writer wanted to show that the business had been conducted in the proper and correct place. Since we know that there was an earlier Irish tradition of conducting business and making agreements in cemeteries, the latter would seem more probable.

---

91 *Calendar of justiciary rolls, Ireland* (hereafter, *CJI*). **92** Empey ,'County Waterford', pp 137–8. **93** *CJI, 1302–1307,* p. 300. **94** 'A calendar of the register of Archbishop Sweteman', ed. Lawlor, No. 69, p. 239.

The cemetery as a place for penance

Penance was also often performed in the cemetery, and sometimes it even involved the remains of the dead. The *Canones Hibernensis*, perhaps of the eighth-century, offered the commutation of a year to penitents who would spend three days with a dead saint

> …in one tomb without food and drink, without sleep, clad in one's garment, with the singing of psalms, and the praying of the hours after confession of sins to a priest and after a vow'.[95]

An undated extract from 'The Life of S Magnenn' preserves similar information. It speaks of Finnchú, son of Finnlogh, of Brigown in Fermoy, Co. Cork. Finnchú lived in the time of Comgall of Bangor (*d.* 601 or 602), and it is written that he ' … for the first night used to lie in the grave with every corpse that was buried in churchyard'.[96] The same story is also preserved in the eleventh- or twelfth-century commentary on 'The Martyrology of Oengus':

> Now this was Findchu's custom; every corpse that was brought to the church, to lie with it the first night. And this was the *guerdon* he asked therefore, that the Devil should not vanquish any person who should beseech him at death, and that such a person should not go to hell.[97]

The 'Register of Archbishop Cromer' of Armagh also contains a reference linking the cemetery with penance. It records that the penance assigned to two men for 'their recent contention in the church' included walking 'around the graveyard, dressed in linen on two different feast days'.[98] While this entry is dated 1520, the custom itself probably has far earlier origins.

The cemetery as a place of habitation

During the Middle Ages, the sanctuary status of the cemetery was valuable not only for merchants but also for people in need of a safe place to reside. Among these were people seeking shelter from the atrocities of war, as illustrated by a decree issued in 1080 by a Norman council, which ordered that 'the refugees be expelled [from the cemetery] after the end of the war:' *de atrio exire cogantur*.[99]

Of the situation in France, Ariès has written:

---

95 *The Irish penitentials*, ed. & trans. Bieler & Binchy, p. 165. 96 'Translation of Extracts', *SG*, II, p. 510; Irish text, p. 465: 'is é no luigedh in aonadhnacol la gach marb no hadhnaicthea ina chill in chédoiche.' 97 *Félire*, p. 247. 98 *Archbishop Cromer's register*, ed. Murray & A. Gwynn, No. 66, p. 179. 99 Ariès, *The hour*, p. 64, cf. Lesne, *Histoire de la propriété ecclésiastique*, III, pp 122–9.

the function of sanctuary transformed the cemetery, sometimes into a place of residence ... Sometimes the refugees who asked for asylum in the cemetery settled there and refused to leave. Some were content with rooms over the charnels. Others built houses ... It sometimes happened that the inhabited island invaded the area of the cemetery to the point where there was no more room for graves.[100]

A French document from the early thirteenth century debates whether the Church will allow lords of the manor to demand census, customs, *et alia seruitia* from the inhabitants of the cemetery, and at least one example exists (from the thirteenth century) of inhabitants of the cemetery being granted immunity.[101] In French cemeteries, dwellings were sometimes built on top of the arches in the outer wall of the church where bones from the cemetery were placed after exhumation to make room for newer bones. These were known as the charnels, and 'some were inhabited by priests, others rented to laymen'.[102]

English cemeteries were inhabited, too, a practice which may have owed something to Norman custom. Two different sets of statutes, adopted at Worcester in 1229 and 1240, state that there are not to be any buildings in the cemetery, except 'in times of hostility',[103] and also call for the ejection from the cemetery of what may have been workshops of some kind.[104] Similar statutes were adopted at Norwich, Salisbury, Wells and London at about the same time.[105] The acts of the council held at London and Lambeth in 1309 speaks of buildings located in cemeteries. A statute adopted at Winchester *c.*1247 requires that huts and dwellings of the laity (*domus laicorum*) be removed from the cemetery, in order to stop the fornication taking place there.[106] The account rolls of 1361 for the abbey of Durham record the amount of money paid for the transportation of materials for roofing the 'house in the cemetery'.[107] In Westminster in 1411, there were 'thirty and sometimes more in number, dwelling within the cemetery of the said church dedicated to St Paul and situate about the centre of the city'.[108]

---

100 Ibid., p. 64.   101 Ibid., n. 101, cf. *Cartulaire Saint-Vincent*, No. 153.   102 Ibid., p. 64   103 '... sit nisi tempore hostilitatis', *Councils & synods*, ed. Powicke & Cheney, I, p.172, No. 5; and 'Nec in cymiteriis edificia nisi forsan hoc tempus hostilitatis exegerit nulla fiant ...', ibid., p. 297, No. 5.   104 Ibid., II, p. 174, no. 22.   105 *Councils & synods*, ed. Powicke & Cheney, I, p. 379, §31; p. 601, §19; p. 649, §73. Daniell has suggested that the similarity of many statutes may mean that copies of earlier sets of statutes used as exemplars were copied, but that even so, they still 'throw light on the concerns of the bishops': *Death and burial*, pp 110, 112–13.   106 Ibid., I: p. 413, §67; also ibid., p. 193, §73; p. 413, §67; p. 708, §34; II: 1008, §13.   107 '... in coopertura domus in cimiterio, cum calce, lattes, et sclatstan, cum cariagio, 61s.': *Extracts from the Account rolls of the Abbey of Durham*, ed. Fowler, II, p. 385. It could be that this building was not used for habitation, since the Latin word *domus* also had the meaning of 'room, workshop, out-house'. See Latham, *Revised medieval Latin word-list*, p. 142. Could it have been a charnel-house?   108 *Cal. Pap. Reg.*, I John XXIII, Id. Jan., p. 217.

Irish records suggest that cemeteries were inhabited later than the period covered by this study and, although it cannot be said how common the practice was, records reveal that churchyards or cemeteries were often resorted to by the 'less desirable' segments of Irish society in their attempts to elude justice or escape persecution.[109] Irish canons of the seventh century contain the following quotation in which 'Origen' recorded the types of 'undesirables' who could commonly be found in cemeteries: '... it cannot be called a holy place in which murderers with their plunder and thieves with their loot and perjurers and lawyers, jesters and prostitutes are accustomed to enter'.[110] Later medieval court-records from Dublin document instances of felons fleeing to the sanctuary of the church and living there for as long as four weeks.[111] It may be that these people were living in the churchyard rather than in the church itself, but again, this cannot be discerned from the records.

It seems obvious from a provisional constitution of the archbishop of Dublin that as late as 1518 Irish cemeteries were being used as places of habitation. This document states that 'if temporary persons do not pay the half part of the obventions of their houses in cemeteries, their goods and persons, being in the said cemeteries or the churches, shall have no ecclesiastical immunity'.[112]

Mervyn Archdall reported that at Clonagh, Co. Kildare, at the time of the general suppression in the sixteenth century, there was a religious house or chapel bordered by two tenements, which 'was a burial-place of note; in war-time the circumjacent inhabitants were exempt from all the customary burdens of the country'.[113] In this we perhaps hear an echo of the provisions of the aforementioned Norman document of 1080, and its reference to the use of cemeteries as dwelling places during times of war.[114]

Other documents also seem to suggest the existence of dwellings in cemeteries. A mid sixteenth-century deed from Dublin granted a private citizen a fifty-one year lease for 'the churche yarde of St George's for terme of fifty-one years'. The deed forbids the lessee from harming the walls or taking away the stones lying within the churchyard. However, a provision is included whereby the lease will be void and the ground will be 'converted to the old use' if the church should be rebuilt. This suggests that the lands may not have been used for religious purposes for some time.[115] The 'Register of St Saviour's Chantry'

---

109 'Laics shall not execute secular judgments or attachments in churches or cemeteries or on the ground (solum) of the church. Penalty, excommunication', *Calendar of the liber ruber*, ed. H.J. Lawlor, 'Provincial constitutions of Archbishop Alexander de Bicknor', No. 17 (19), p. 173. 1317 x 1349. **110** See Doherty 'The monastic town', pp 45–76, p. 58. **111** See the cases of 'David Obronan' in Dublin, *CJI*, 33–35 Edw. I, 7 Jan. 1306, p. 489; Stephen le Waleys in Cork, 3–7 Edw. II, 12 March 1311, pp 197–8; and David Barbedor in Kildare, 3–35, Edward I, 3 Feb. 1307, p. 515. **112** 'Calendar of the *Liber Ruber*', ed, H.J. Lawlor, p. 165, no. 13. **113** Archdall, *Monasticon Hibernicum* (hereafter *Mon. Hib.*), II, p. 256. **114** See this chapter, n. 101. **115** *Calendar of ancient records*, ed. Gilbert & Gilbert, II, 'Dublin Assembly Roll', 1564; pp 36–7.

in Waterford contains a deed of 1469 by which John Collin acquired vacant land in the east part of the cemetery of the aforesaid church. Unfortunately, it does not reveal for what purpose the land had previously been used, and the ambiguity of the word *cimiterium* does not make clear whether this land was located within the church-yard or specifically within its burial ground.[116]

An interesting series of deeds from the parish of St Werburgh in Dublin, traces the two-hundred-year history of a small dwelling. Built in 1454, it was situated over the churchyard-wall, with the upper story extending over the wall and into the cemetery.[117] It was located on 'a waste place of said church, with the appurtenances lying between the door of said church, on the south, and the house of St Mary del Dam', and is described as 'a chamber of oak covered with oak wood boards'.[118] In 1547, eighty-three years later, the building is recorded as 'a house or messuage on the south side of the said church door, 11 yards in length, 4 yards in breadth, with a small room over the entry going into said church'.[119]

If this property was not in the graveyard itself, it was in such close proximity to it that there was concern that it could impede transportation of corpses into the churchyard. In 1598, the new lessor of the property was required 'to keep the under room of said chamber as a way to the churchyard; and not to let [hinder] the passage thereof'.[120] In 1651, it is again described in detail, much as it was in 1547,[121] and by 1674 this land no longer seems to have been connected with the church.[122]

The lessors of the property may supply clues about its use. Of the three men to whom this property was deeded between 1547 and 1598, one was a goldsmith, and two were bakers, suggesting that this house may also have been used as a shop, or perhaps was chosen because of its location convenient to the site of the shops which clustered around the cemeteries, as previously discussed.[123] That two bakers occupied it may also be meaningful: records reveal that in medieval France bread was not only sold in stalls located in the cemetery, but the bread was actually baked in ovens which were located next to open graves.[124]

116 'Sciant presentes et futuri quod ego Jacobus Rice civis civitatis Waterford dedi concessi et hac presenti carta mea confirmavi domini Johanni Collyn capellano ac civi civitatis predicte vacuam terram que est in orientali parte cimiterii dicte ecclesie …', *Registrum cantariae St Salvatoris Waterfordensis*', ed. Mac Niocaill, No. 47; p. 173. **117** The 'medieval Dublin' map published by the Irish Office of Public Works in 1978 is 'laid over' a modern map which notes a 'disused cemetery' adjacent to the parish-house of St Werburgh's (east side), and at the south end of St Martin's Lane, bordered on the east by Castle Street. Perhaps this is also the location of the fifteenth-century cemetery. **118** Indenture dated 10 August, 1454. 'Some Ancient Deeds of the Parish of St Werburgh', ed. Twiss, No. 24, p. 288. **119** Ibid., No. 41, 10 June, Edward VI (1547), pp 292–3. **120** Ibid., No. 45, Indenture, 15 July, 1598, p. 293. **121** Ibid., No. 49, 19th Oct. 1651, p. 295. **122** Ibid., No. 53. Indenture, 2. Feb., 1674, p. 297. **123** See this chapter, n. 67. **124** Ariès, *The hour*, p. 68.

The cemetery as a site for dancing, games and contests

Allowing dancing or contests within a cemetery greatly increased the danger of desecration, yet dancing and games have a long historical connection with Irish cemeteries and Irish funeral ritual.

The alleged pre-Christian connection of Tailtiu with funeral games has been noted above.[125] 'The colloquy of the ancients' (*Acallam na Senórach*), a version of which was in existence in the last quarter of the twelfth century,[126] tells that when four hundred of the legendary warrior Finn's people were buried, 'over them their names were written in Ogham and their funeral games held'.[127] That these 'funeral games' were still common in medieval Irish cemeteries is proved by a decree issued by a Dublin diocesan council held in 1366/7 which outlawed 'wrestling matches, dances and other *ludi teatrales* [theatrical plays, pageants] within the churches or cemeteries of the province'.[128] Well into the twentieth century a variety of games and sporting events was a central feature of the Irish 'wake'.[129]

Again, these activities were neither unique nor new, but merely the continuation of a long tradition found throughout the British Isles as well as France. 'Contests and competitions' are recorded as having taken place in the cemetery of Bury St Edmunds in England in 1197,[130] and a number of thirteenth-century documents mention them. A decree made by the Council of Rouen in 1231 prohibited 'dancing in the cemetery or in the church under pain of excommunication'.[131] Statutes adopted in Canterbury between 1295 and 1313 outlawed entertainments in both church and cemetery. The 'Mandates of Robert Grosseteste', bishop of Lincoln, dating from *c.*1235 mention entertainments in the cemetery,[132] as do the thirteenth-century statutes from London, Salisbury, Winchester, Wells, and Worcester.[133] Statutes adopted at Canterbury between 1295 and 1313 also outlawed entertainments in both church and cemetery. The Scottish diocese of Aberdeen echoed the general mood; its synodal statutes of the thirteenth century also prohibit singing and dancing to take place 'at funerals and exequies of deceased lay persons', and continue by stating:

> we also think it well to add that at no festivals shall wrestlings and games be hereafter permitted to take place within churches or churchyards ...

125 See above, n. 46.   **126** Dillon, *Early Irish literature*, p. 36.   **127** *SG*, II, p. 174.   **128** The council probably met in Kilkenny, under the presidency of the archbishop, Thomas Minot (1363–75) either before or after the sessions of Duke Lionel's parliament (of Feb. 1366/7)', A. Gwynn, 'Provincial and diocesan decrees', pp 37–8.   **129** These were catalogued by Ó Suilleabháin, *Irish wake amusements*.   **130** *Chronicle of the abbey of Bury St Edmunds*, ed. Greenway & Sayers, p. 82.   **131** Ariès, *The hour*, p. 69.   **132** Ab ecclesiis autem et cimiteriis omnes huiusmodi ludos commonitione premissa arceri faciatis ecclesiastica censura ...', 'Mandates of Robert Grosseteste', *Councils & synods*, I, ed. Powicke & Cheney, p. 204 (iv).   **133** Ibid., I, 'Statutes of London II' §73; p. 649; ibid., 'Statutes of Salisbury II', §31, p. 379; ibid., 'Statutes of Wells', I, §19, p. 601; ibid., II, 'Statutes of Winchester III', §35, p. 708–9; ibid., 'Statutes of Worcester III' §5, p. 297.

[and that] the Feast of Fools be utterly put an end to … that there be no games … in sacred places.[134]

Puckle noted that in 1367 the council of York expressly forbade 'those guilty games and follies, and all those perverse customs which transformed a house of tears and prayers into a house of laughing and excess'.[135] The fourteenth-century synodal statutes of St Andrews forbid, under pain of excommunication

> any one from daring in the future to have dances, or to hold wrestling matches, or to hold or engage in any other kind of unseemly sports in churches or in churchyards at any festivals or seasons whatsoever, since the occasion of profaning churches or churchyards has been wont to arise from such occasions.[136]

It would appear that the proscription of dancing and contests arose not from some 'Puritan' streak within the medieval Church but from a concern that these activities increased the likelihood that the cemetery would be desecrated. The fourteenth-century Synodal Statutes of St Andrews warn of the profaning of the churchyard 'by the shedding of blood or sexual seed'.[137] The potential for spilling blood during wrestling or fighting matches is obvious; presumably dances were dangerous due to the possibility of fights arising between rival suitors or of the amorous activities to which dancing might give rise.

'Bully's Acre', a cemetery which is located on the western edge of the ground of the Royal Hospital at Kilmainham, Dublin, served as one of Dublin's major cemeteries until the mid-nineteenth century, and may have been used for Christian interment as early as the seventh century. The history of 'Bully's Acre' was long associated with midsummer-revels connected with the nearby well of St John. It is not known when these festivities first began at the site, but they seem to have had a lengthy history when Sir John Trail testified in the mid-eighteenth century that 'the whole situation was generally productive of riot and debauchery, due to the vast crowds attracted to the graveyard and the well'.[138] These revels grew increasingly riotous and uncontrollable until the cemetery was closed in 1832.[139]

It has been suggested that the common name of the cemetery at Kilmainham – 'Bully's Acre' – refers to the fact that this site was a popular trysting place for

---

134 *Stat. Scot.*, p. 56.   **135** Puckle, *Funeral customs*, p. 63 (no source cited).   **136** *Stat. Scot.*, p. 42.   **137** Ibid., pp 76–7.   **138** S. Murphy, *Bully's Acre*, p. 8, quoting Trail's testimony in 'Minutes of the Royal Hospital Kilmainham, 1684–1929', VII, pp 111–15. (National Archives).   **139** See also: G.L. Barrow, 'Knights Hospitallers', pp 108–12. While these 'revels' were regarded as a significant problem, they were not responsible for the closure of the cemetery, which occurred when its capacity was deemed to have been exceeded during the cholera epidemic which swept through Dublin in the nineteenth century.

lovers, or, alternatively, to the fighting matches which took place there.[140] Both of these derivations seem to provide tantalizing hints of activities in this cemetery. Unfortunately, because the earliest maps of Dublin belong to the sixteenth century, and do not extend as far west as 'Bully's Acre', it is not known when the name was first applied to the site. However, the word 'bully' did not come to mean either 'lover' or a brawling, intimidating kind of man until after the end of the Middle Ages,[141] and documents from the 'Register of Kilmainham' suggest a quite different origin for the cemetery's name. In them we find references to the castle located in Kilmainham, including its wall and drawbridge, the inner, outer and main gates and the 'great eastern tower'. 'Bailey' is the medieval word for the external wall of a castle or any circuit of walls surrounding a keep,[142] and according to the *Oxford English Dictionary*, one of the earliest meanings for 'acre' was 'a churchyard'.[143] Thus, it seems that 'Bully's Acre' may be a corruption of 'Bailey's Acre'. If so, the name would have no connection at all with lovers, prize-fighters, or even the jurisdiction of the bailiff of the Priory of St John over the cemetery, but instead means 'the castle-wall cemetery', thus preserving in its name the cemetery's historic situation relative to the long-gone walls of Kilmainham castle.[144]

   The concerns noted in this section about the propriety of allowing activities which had traditionally been associated with cemeteries to continue may mark the beginning of an important change in attitude that ultimately resulted in the separation of the 'community of the living' from the 'community of the dead'. For many centuries, the Christian dead had been 'included' in daily activities. As the central Middle Ages progressed, the dead were increasingly separated from the living. Eventually, the living stopped experiencing the dead as a daily presence in their lives, death stopped being regarded as an integral part of life, and came to be perceived as an extremely private matter.

The cemetery as storage-place
There is no doubt that many valuables were stored inside churches during the Middle Ages,[145] however, due to their sanctuary status, cemeteries were also used

---

140 S. Murphy, *Bully's Acre*, p. 7; also G.L. Barrow, 'Knights Hospitallers of St John of Jerusalem at Kilmainham', pp 108–12. **141** *Oxford English Dictionary*, II, p. 645. **142** Ibid., I, p. 887. **143** Ibid., I, p. 117, I.a. 'obsolete, except in "God's Acre" (from mod Germ.) a churchyard.' **144** The same idea is preserved in the name of the medieval London church known as 'Westminster-without-the-walls'. See n. 87 above. **145** Indeed, the modern 'safe deposit' box seems to have had its protype in the coffers or chests kept in the church, where members of the congregation stored their valuables; the *CJI* contains numerous references to the robberies of such coffers. In 1311, chests kept in the church of Tristledermot stored goods including silver, woollen web, bacon, beans, a pair of trews, thread and sheets: *CJI*, 3–7 Edward II (14 Dec. 1311), p. 227. It is not, however, clear when this practice began: large conclusions have unwisely been drawn from it about the intentions of raiders who attacked churches in the Viking age.

for this purpose. Two Irish sources record that food was stored in cemeteries. A record from the priory of Holy Trinity, Dublin, reports that in 1346 the tithes of Glasnevin were carried 'from the cemetery into the manor' on two occasions.[146] The 'Annals of Loch Cé' preserve an account of a raid by MacWilliam in 1236, after which 'not a stack of seed or corn of all that was in the great *relig* of *Magh-Eó*, or in the *relig* of the church of Michael the Archangel, was left ...'[147] The use here of the unambiguous word *relig* makes it clear that the goods were stored in the burial ground of the church, and not just in its churchyard.

THE MEDIEVAL IRISH AND 'RESPECT FOR THE DEAD'

In the Middle Ages, the prevalence of hunger, war, and disease translated into early and high mortality rates. The life of the average person was short by today's standards, and after death, the bodies of most people ceased to be of concern.

Death was seen as the ultimate liberation from the body which was tormented by diseases and corrupted by sin.[148] J.G. Davies has pointed out that the medieval liturgy 'is conscious rather of sin and death, purgatory and judgment, thinking of the soul's destiny, rather than the body's'.[149] The development of the *Dies irae* chant, created early in the Church's history, and a central part of its funeral liturgy, indicates that death was regarded as joyous, hopeful and 'looked forward to the resurrection of the body and entrance into God's kingdom'.[150] Ariès noted that 'by the beginning of the Middle Ages, the tomb has become anonymous and unimportant. What matters is the public and enclosed space for the graves'.[151]

When the ecclesiastical site at Church Island, Co. Kerry, was excavated, it was discovered that the walls of the little stone church or 'oratory' (which has been assigned dates ranging from the mid-eighth to the late twelfth century) had been built directly over thirty-three burials. Michael Kelly, who led the excavation, expressed his wonder that, although the builders must have been aware of the existence of these interments, the burials were 'not allowed to impede progress' in constructing the buildings.[152] Despite Kelly's surprise, this is completely consonant with medieval thought. It reflects the belief of the Irish – and western European Christians in general – that the bones of powerful people (which would, of course, include saints and important clerics) were imbued with special protective powers.[153] It is also consonant with what is known about the development of basilicas and 'developed cemeteries',[154] as well as the ubiquitous

146 *Account roll of the priory of the Holy Trinity, Dublin*, p. 120. **147** *ALC, s.a.* 1236. *Maigh-Eó* is Mayo, Co. Mayo. **148** Reynolds, 'Death and burial, in Europe', p. 119; le Goff, *Medieval civilisation*, pp 35–6. **149** J.G. Davies, *A dictionary of liturgy*, p. 98. **150** Ibid. **151** Ariès, *The hour*, p. 53. **152** Kelly, 'Church Island', p. 112. **153** See Geary, *Furta Sacra*, pp 33–4; Finucane, *Miracles*, p. 26. **154** See Doherty, 'The basilica'.

practice that continued for centuries, of burying élite members of the community under the the the church – either under the flooring tiles, or in a crypt.

Adomnan's 'Life of St Columba' tells how St Odhrán was buried in the foundations of the church of Iona, probably because it was believed that the presence of his body there would protect the building from harm. Although the oldest extant version of this story dates to the twelfth century, it may have an earlier origin.[155] The excavations at the early Christian site at Reask, Co. Kerry, found postholes that revealed that the church had been built directly over existing graves.[156] This appears to have perplexed the archaeologists on the site, though it seems consonant with what is known regarding the development of cemeteries and churches in Ireland, i.e. that cemeteries came first, and wooden churches were later built over a focal burial or burials.[157]

The practice of interring the deceased in the foundations or walls of the church survived into quite recent times. As late as 1860, a meeting was held in St Paul's parish in Dublin to 'denounce and stop the present system of intramural interment'. One of the complaints voiced was that 'in one instance two coffins had been dug up to make room for one to be buried, that skulls and human bones were at a distance of 18 inches from the surface, and that such had actually been sold at some bone-yards in the city'.[158] While it should be presumed that these intramural burials were carried out because of a belief that burial inside the church-wall was more beneficial to the soul of the deceased (and/or enhanced the status of the deceased's family), the practice may also have links to far earlier (and presumably long-forgotten) beliefs that burials could provide protection.[159]

The care of the remains of the dead, graves and cemeteries
The difference between modern and medieval western European attitudes towards human remains is enormous. The skeletons and graves of the general, non-élite populace were of little concern in medieval Ireland, and it is not surprising that all of the evidence I have uncovered about care of the remains of the dead and respect for graves relate to the élite classes (ecclesiastics and nobility). It may be that the general lack of evidence for the non-élite population explains this. However, evidence from England and France offers very explicit examples of how the remains of the average, non-élite person were treated after

---

155 *Adomnán of Iona*, ed. Sharpe, p. 360, §365; also, Máire Herbert, *Iona*, p. 261.   **156** Fanning, 'Excavation of an early Christian cemetery', p. 150.   **157** C. Thomas, *The early Christian archaeology*, pp 48–90; Bitel, *Isle of the Saints*, pp 48–66.   **158** 'Intramural interment, St Paul's parish', *Dublin Builder*, 1 June 1860, p. 284. '…Those opposed to ending intramural burial charged that the complaints were being made "to injure the rector by depriving him of part of his emoluments".' The article does not say whether intramural burial was outlawed.   **159** This subject is explored further in the sections 'Disinterment and multiple burial of remains' in Chapter 3, and 'Defensive Burial' in Chapter 5 of this work.

death. It seems imprudent to assume that the same attitudes did not prevail in Ireland, given the parallelism that exists between these countries regarding other aspects of burial practice. By the late Middle Ages, indifference to the remains of the dead was changing and by the end of the Victorian period, attitudes had changed completely.[160]

Irish literature – especially that of the early Middle Ages – reveals a strong tradition of awareness and respect concerning the burial places of the noble classes. For example, the 'Colloquy of the ancients' tells of the superstition which surrounded graves and the respect which was accorded to them: 'Caeilte said: "I remember, saintly Patrick, that for dread of the *Tuatha Dé Danann* nor crowd nor host had dared sit upon these *tulachs*."'[161] In *Lebor Gabála* contains a great deal of information about burial places, including royal ones.[162] One of the ancient prohibitions against the king of Connaught found in *Leabhar na Cert*, a text created in the early twelfth century, prohibits anyone 'to sit on the sepulchre of the wife of Maine'.[163] The rule of the monastery of Tallaght, first written in the ninth century, extols the merits of 'spare diet, short slumber, early rising, frequent obeisance, and gaze fixed on the friends that lie in the churchyard beneath thy feet'.[164] This caution to remember one's final end – and the judgment of God – is markedly Christian.

Rules and regulations for the protection of the dead – and also the living – existed in medieval Irish society. 'The Martyrology of Tallaght' also forbids monks to eat a meal with a dead man in the house, perhaps reflecting the fear of ritual pollution. It may also reveal a superstitious fear of the dead, or have served as a means of ensuring that the dead were buried in a timely fashion (that is, the residents of the monastery went hungry until the required duties were completed).[165]

Other sources indicate that care was given to the layout and organization of graves. The poem 'The Battle of the Sheaves', which Gerard Murphy dated to *c.*1200, includes the lines: 'Rise up, my friend, without fault, fix the coffin without stain, straighten its front to the wall …'[166] A picture of a tidy, well kept and well-ordered cemetery is offered by the fourteenth-century work *Caithréim Thoirdhealbhaigh*. It describes the Franciscan abbey of Ennis in Co. Clare, in 1305,

---

160 Ariès, *The hour*, and Gittings, *Death, burial* provide excellent analyses of this subject. **161** 'The Colloquy', *SG*, I, p. 114: 'Imthecht againn budes[a] ar Cáilte. gá conair sin Pátraic. is cumain lemsa a naemPátraic nach lémdáis sluag náit sochaide suide ar na trí tulchaibse le ceisd tuaithe dé danann'; English trans: *SG*, II, pp 124–5. **162** See especially '*Fíanna Bá ar i nEmain*', '*Cineaéd Huá Artacáin*', '*Gilla na Naem Hua Duind cecinit*', and '*Lecht Cormaic Meic Culennáin*'. **163** *Leabhar na g-Ceart*, ed. & trans. O'Donovan, p. 5. O'Donovan hypothesized that his location might possibly be Tuaim-mna (Toomna) near Boyle, Co. Roscommon. **164** A. Gwynn & Purton, 'The Monastery of Tallaght', p. 119. **165** Ibid., p. 153, §65. **166** 'Eirgid a cáirde gan cair. coirgid in ccomraid gan ail dírgid a hadort go fraig leabad ar ccarat claoidter', 'The Battle of the Sheaves', *Duanaire Finn*, III, pp cxvi, 47–8.

specifically noting its 'well-kept graves, homes of the noble dead'.[167] However, evidence from Ireland, Britain and the Continent exists which provides a sharply contrasting picture, in which cemeteries of the central Middle Ages and later are shown to be in appallingly unkempt states.

A window which used to grace the sacristy of Saint-Denis in Paris clearly illustrates the point. The sacristy was built in 1388, and the window (no longer extant) illustrated the merciful works of Saint Louis, one of which was giving burial to the dead. However, the window did not depict the digging of graves or the laying of corpses in the grave; rather, it showed St Louis gathering scattered skulls and bones. The artist did not ignore the grim sensory realities of the task: those who carried the sack into which the bones were deposited were shown holding their hands over their noses and mouths.[168]

Even much later, Shakespeare's play, *Hamlet*, depicts the prince walking through a typical medieval cemetery. It is littered with skulls, yet here is no hint that Hamlet is either disgusted by the sight or afraid of it – quite the opposite, in fact. He merely picks up one of the skulls which the grave-digger has disinterred and inquires whose it is. Upon being told that it is that of Yorick, he considers it calmly and states simply that the man had been well known to him. A modern reader might easily assume that Shakespeare wrote this scene to show that Hamlet was not of sound mind. Yet a cemetery littered with bones and skulls, and Hamlet's calm acceptance of the realities of death and decay, would have been familiar to an Elizabethan audience – just as it would have been to any person living in Ireland during the Middle Ages – and much later, to judge from eyewitness accounts. Samuel Molyneux visited Aughrim, Co. Galway, in 1704, and noted that 'a few dead men's sckulls scattered in ye fields yet remains of yet battle there fought in ye troubles';[169] in the mid-nineteenth century, William Thackeray observed that the abbey in Dundalk, Co. Louth, 'skulls lie in clusters amongst the nettle-beds'.[170]

Charnel houses, ossuaries and mortuary houses

In parts of France (as in other parts of the Continent, notably Italy) it was common practice to leave the corpse buried for the period of time needed for the soft tissues to decay; after this process had been completed, the bare bones were disinterred. According to Ariès, the use of ossuaries – areas where human bones were stacked and stored after disinterment – became widespread in non-Mediterranean France in the fourteenth and fifteenth centuries, a time when urban development had peaked and the cemeteries were at their capacity.[171] In time, they began to be displayed artistically.[172] In fourteenth-century France the bones were often placed

167 *Caithr. Th.*, p. 32. **168** Ariès, *The hour*, pp 58–9. **169** Molyneux, 'Journey to Connaught', ed. Smith, p. 164. The battle of Aughrim was fought in 1691. **170** Thackeray, *Irish sketch book*, p. 294. **171** Ariès, pp 58–9. **172** An example of this tradition may still be seen in the Capuchin

above arches (or 'charnels') which were purposely built into the exterior fabric of the church. In her research on burial in late medieval London, Vanessa Harding has verified that, in addition to the great charnel at St Paul's, 'at least seven parish churches – and possibly many more – had charnels or charnel houses, though the precise manner in which they were used is not clear'.[173]

Evidence shows that ossuaries and charnel houses were also used in medieval Ireland, and that this practice was not regional but general. In 1263, Thomas O'Kelly, bishop of Clonfert had the bones of his father removed and placed in an *arcuationem*, presumably a vault.[174] The 'Register of John Mey', archbishop of Armagh, records that in 1449 the perpetual vicar of Kilmore, Co. Cavan, encountered resistance when he tried to remove the remains of those buried in the church of Kilmore to a charnel-house erected within the bounds of the cemetery. It is interesting – and perplexing – to note that it was not the removal of the burials from the church which was considered objectionable, but rather the vicar's proposal to locate the charnel-house within the bounds of the cemetery. The entry goes on to state that the situation was resolved by the vicar who 'now proposes to build the charnel-house outside but near to the cemetery'.[175] The passage gives no clue as to why the parishioners would have allowed – let alone preferred – the vicar to remove the bones of those once interred in the consecrated ground of the church cemetery (for which burial dues would have been paid) to the unhallowed ground outside the cemetery.

John O'Hanlon, writing in the later nineteenth century of Mohill, Co. Leitrim (where St Manchán allegedly erected a monastery *c*.608), relates that 'the present site is occupied by a Protestant church, and its graveyard is one yet much frequented. There are no remains of the monastery visible, except an old skull-house.'[176]

Evidence for Dublin consists of two leases of 1676, preserved in the records of St Werburgh's church. They record the presence of a 'new charnel house' which

church on the Via Veneto in Rome, which I visited in 1994. The vaults of the church are open to the public and feature cells in which the robed, standing skeletons of deceased monks are arranged in *tableaux* with the bones of other monks arranged in patterns (rather similar to plasterwork) on the ceilings and walls. Much of this work was completed in the eighteenth century. In Brittany, it was not uncommon into the twentieth century for a home to contain a small box-shrine with a window in it, through which the bones of the deceased member of the family contained therein could be viewed (Ariès, *The hour*, pp 60–1). **173** Harding, 'Burial choice', p. 128–29. She also notes records of payments made for the removal of large amounts of earth from urban London cemeteries in the early sixteenth century which she has argued 'very probably' reflect the removal of bones from some of these charnel houses to unspecified sites. **174** '… Dominus Thomas o Kellay episcopus Clonfertensis qui fecit arcuationem prope magnum altare in parte boriali et fecit cariari ossamenta patris sui ad dictam arcuationem et multa bona contulit fratribus juxta quem jacet dominus Gilbertus de Wale et Diruayl uxor ejus.' *Reg. Mon. Athenry*, pp 212–13. **175** *The register of John Mey*, pp lxxxi–ii, No. 189, 10 Nov. 1449. **176** O'Hanlon, *Lives of the Irish saints*, II, p. 522.

had been 'lately made in the churchyard', as well as the fact that it had recently been 'arched over'. The language seems to suggest that this was not the first charnel house in the cemetery; perhaps the previous one was full or decrepit.[177]

For Connaught, we have Samuel Molyneux's unusual eyewitness account of his visit in 1709 to the old Franciscan abbey of Kilconnell in Co. Galway, where he discovered that 'their churchyard is surrounded by a wall of dead men's sckulls [sic] and bones'. He used his walking stick to measure the wall and reported that it was about eighty-eight feet long, four feet high, and five feet, four inches broad. From these measurements he reckoned 'that there may be possibly here to the number of 5000 sckulls'. Molyneux made no comment regarding the age of this 'wall'. However, he stated that 'within they shew you Lord Gallways' and other great men's heads kill'd at Aghrim'.[178] At the battle of Aughrim, fought near Kilconnell in 1691, more than 7000 footsoldiers fighting on the Jacobite side were killed by the Williamite cavalry. Perhaps it was their remains which were gathered and displayed in this wall.[179] The Irish belief in the ability of the dead to defend or protect territorial lands also comes to mind.

Whatever the date of the wall, Molyneux's account provides unique and valuable evidence for the continuity of burial practices over a long period of time, and their ability to survive enormous social changes. It seems that the tradition of charnel houses was still extant in Buttevant, Co. Cork, in the late eighteenth century, since Archdall noted that 'In the crypt is an immense collection of bones and skulls, which are popularly supposed to be the remains of those who fell in the sanguinary battle of Knockninoss on the 13th of Nov. 1647 ...'[180]

The existence of special 'mortuary houses' has also been noted in Ireland. O'Hanlon's record of the life of St Fanchea records an incident in which she conducted a young man to 'the chamber of the dead' in which a dead sister was lying.[181] Writing of Teach Molaga (Timoleague) in Co. Cork, O'Hanlon noted a building called the 'Labba Molaga' (*Leaba Molaig*, meaning 'bed or grave of

---

177 Some ancient deeds', ed. & trans. Twiss, pp 297–8. **178** Molyneux, *Journey to Connaught*, p. 168. Nearly two centuries later, in 1902, F.J. Bigger updated Molyneux's account: 'At Killconnell [sic] these skulls and bones lay about in heaps until thirty or forty years ago, when Lord Clonbrock and some local gentlemen got some sort of decency brought about, which if not resisted, was barely tolerated by the peasantry'. He adds that 'This custom of exposing skulls is a very common one in Ireland. I have seen windows and niches in old churches in every western county in Ireland adorned with skulls ... I may say that I have been forced to the conclusion that the Irish as a race have little, or no reverence for the dead. I have striven against this conclusion, but it has been forced upon me by close, constant, and varied observation': Bigger, 'Kilconnell Abbey', p. 13. Another account dated 1651 records how beeseiged Irish Confederate forces warded off enemy attack by 'hurling at them stones and the bones and skulls of the dead': ibid., p. 12. **179** B. Fitzpatrick, *Seventeenth-century Ireland*, p. 254. **180** *Mon. Hib.*, I, p. 101, n. 9, cf. the story about the battle of Aughrim in the previous paragraph. **181** St Fanchea is alleged to have died c.480 after establishing a religious foundation on Lough Erne, not far from Enniskillen: Livingston, *The Fermanagh story*, pp 10–11. Neither O'Hanlon or Livingstone give a source for this information.

Moling') which sounds as if it could possibly have filled a mortuary function. O'Hanlon described it as:

> ... [a] small building said to date back to the seventh century ... internal measurement of this building is 13' by 9' ... inside, a kind of a kist, consisting of a large flagstone, resting on low side-stones and leaving an open space beneath, said to have been St Molaga's bed. (It lies to the south side of the chamber and is nearly wide enough to permit a person to stretch on the ground, but in immediate contact with the covering flagstones.) Pilgrims who resort there, afflicted with various diseases, are said to have been completely restored ...[182]

At Banagher and Boveragh, both in Co. Londonderry, and at Saul, Co. Down, are small stone-built structures which seem to date from the first half of the twelfth century and which are thought to have been 'mortuary houses'. According to Waterman, the one at Boveragh was 'designed to accommodate a body', while the precise function of the mortuary house at Banagher could not be determined.[183] The *Eaglais Beag* ('small church') at the famous ecclesiastical complex of Clonmacnois, Co. Offaly, is also thought to have functioned as a mortuary chapel for 'laying out' purposes,[184] and an architectural reconstruction of Duiske Abbey, Co. Kilkenny, shows the existence of a special chamber which appears to date from the early thirteenth century. The chamber, thought to have been the morgue, is located next to the chapter-house, measures 24 ft by 19 ft, and has direct access to the cemetery.[185] Waterman also called attention to a passage from Bede, which tells that St Chad had been buried in 'a wooden tomb [located in Lichfield, Staffordshire] made in the form of a little house with an aperture in the wall through which those who visit it out of devotion may insert their hand and take out some of the dust'.[186] It is, of course, highly unlikely that any tombs or mortuary house constructed from wood before Bede's time would have survived this long – here again, we may hope that archaeological evidence can be found to shed light on these long-vanished structures.

Some of the written evidence presented above post-dates the period under study, yet because burial is one of the most conservative and slowly evolving aspects of social behaviour, it is a valuable indication of the practices that were current at the close of the Middle Ages, and perhaps far earlier. The tradition of removing bones to charnel houses has its roots in the Middle Ages, and to find it mentioned in 1676 could hardly suggest that it was a recently adopted custom.

---

182 O'Hanlon, *Lives of the Irish saints*, I, pp 336, 342. The Irish word 'leaba' means both 'bed' and 'grave'. **183** Waterman, 'Banagher church', pp 25, 35–7. For related passage from 'Martyrology of Oengus', see below, Chapter 4, 'Artifacts', n. 41. **184** Kehnel, 'S. Ciarán's church and his lands', p. 34. **185** 'Charters of the Cistercian', ed. Butler & Bernard, p. 169. **186** Bede, *A history of the English church and people* (London, 1979), p. 212.

It would stretch even credulity to suggest that using skulls and bones as the building material for the cemetery wall at Kilconnell was an eighteenth-century innovation. This is especially true since the deposition of human bones in a charnel house reflects an earlier, more egalitarian and 'communal' attitude towards burial than was prevalent in the seventeenth century, by which time the rise of the merchant class had caused a pronounced shift to burial rituals which were less communal, class- and status-conscious, and more private.[187]

The 'keeper' of the cemetery

A petition dating from 1182, found in a later register of an archbishop of Dublin, states that the cemetery must not only be enclosed (which was a requirement from early Christian times, and also a continuing problem, as we shall see) but must also have 'a keeper'.[188] Current canon law states that Roman Catholic cemeteries should be enclosed and have a custodian, a rule which is held to date from the early thirteenth century.[189]

It would have been logical to appoint or hire someone to watch over the cemetery since, as I have discussed above, cemeteries served as store-houses for tithes and provided access to churches and the chests used to store valuables inside the churches.[190] The bones of the deceased were often considered to be valuable for political or religious reasons (or because they could be passed off as relics and sold), as was the cemetery itself, since it generated income for the church in the form of burial dues and oblations.

The existence of ecclesiastical families (whose heads might be known as 'erenagh' and 'comarb', or 'cowarb', 'coarb') which were attached to the territorial churches of their kin-group, and whose duties and privileges were hereditary, is well documented. A number of these families continued in their traditional role until the dissolution of the monasteries in the sixteenth century.[191] In the vernacular 'Life of St Brendan' a man named Paul tells the saint that he has 'charge of the cemetery of the brethren', and digging graves is one of his duties.[192] The possibility that the Irish 'keeper of the cemetery' may have some sort of hereditary status is certainly suggested in a letter of 1182 from the pope to the archbishop of Dublin which stipulates that 'churchyards and ecclesiastical benefices are not to be held as inheritances'.[193]

The 'Dublin merchant-roll' contains the names of four men with the surname 'Cemetarius', all of which appear before 1222.[194] Surnames in English

---

187 Ariès, *The hour*, pp xiv, xv; also Gittings, *Death, burial*, pp 33–5. **188** *Calendar of Archbp. Alen's register*, 13 April 1182, pp 9–10. **189** Podhradsky, *New dictionary of the liturgy*; p. 52. **190** See section above, 'The Irish cemetery as storage place'. **191** Watt, 'Gaelic polity', pp 336–40; Bradshaw, *The dissolution*, pp 35, 154, 174; *Acts of Archbishop Colton*, ed. Reeves, pp 4–6, n. 'k', p. 7, n. 'n', pp 9–10, n. 'q'. **192** 'Life of St Brendan', *Lives of the Irish saints* (hereafter *Lives*), ed. Plummer, p. 63. **193** *Calendar liber niger Alani*, ed. Stokes, p. 9, 1182, April 13: Lucius III. **194** *Dublin Merchant Roll*, ed. Connolly & Martin, pp 17, 30, 39. Their Christian names were

Ireland were just beginning to develop at this time, and such medieval surnames tended to reflect either the place of the individual's or family's origin or an associated occupation. Therefore, the surname 'Cemetarius' indicates that these men had some close relationship with a cemetery; possibly they were living (or had recently lived) in a cemetery or in close proximity to one. Alternatively, they (or their ancestors) may have been engaged in some activity relating to a cemetery. The pope's letter to the archbishop of Dublin in 1182 may have been precipitated by issues concerning men like these. Thirteenth-century English records from Reading abbey also contain the surname 'de Cimiterio'[195] – again suggesting similarities in social practice relating to cemeteries in both countries, although we can only speculate as to what these might have been.

The potential benefits of controlling a medieval cemetery are made obvious in a papal letter of 1492 regarding an incident in the Irish diocese of Tuam. It records that 'Bernard Ocearnay ... (who) holds perpetual vicarage of the parish church of Chyllmeorbych ... has arranged with those who wished the bodies of their dead to be buried in that church that they should pay him, in each case, a certain sum of money ... thereby committing simony'.[196]

The desecration and reconsecration of cemeteries
Although cemeteries received additional protection because of their sanctuary status, were supposed to be enclosed and have the benefit of a 'keeper', the desecration of graves was an omnipresent problem. There may be many reasons why a cemetery was to be enclosed, ranging from the wish to delimit sacred space to a desire to recreate the 'city of God',[197] but the most utilitarian reason must have been the need to keep out animals which would uproot corpses. The fear that animals would devour or disinter corpses is found in hagiography and other

Robertus, Johannes, Radulfus and 'Magister' Rogerus. Reference is also made to 'Ricardus Cementarius' (p. 40) and 'Jordanus Cementarius' (p. 26), but 'cementarius' means 'mason': du Cange, *Glossarium Mediae et Infimae Latinitatis* (Niort, 1993), II, p. 15; J.H. Baxter & Charles Johnson, *Medieval Latin word list* (Oxford, 1934), pp 72. I am grateful to Patricia Becker for her assistance in locating these names in the index to the Dublin Merchant Rolls which she prepared as a database for her MPhil dissertation at Trinity College, Dublin, accepted in 1996. **195** *Reading abbey cartularies*, ed. Kemp, I, p. 395; II, p. 157. The Christian names are: 'Ricardus de Cimiterio', and 'John de Cimiterio'. **196** *Cal. Pap. Reg.*, XV, No. 920, Innocent VIII. Such opportunism did not end with the Middle Ages. 'Bully's Acre', the ancient graveyard in Kilmainham, had been considered common ground even after the establishment of the Royal Hospital in 1680 and was supposedly exempt from burial fees, making it an an especially popular place for the interment of Dublin's poor. However, Sir John Trail testified in 1795 that at that time people had for decades been paying burial fees – albeit reduced ones – for interment in Bully's Acre. Andrew Cullen, a farmer, dairyman and publican of Gallow's Hill, who farmed lands by lease from the Royal Hospital, charged from 1*d.* to 1*s.* for every funeral at Bully's Acre, according to the means of the mourners. See Murphy, *Bully's Acre*, p. 6; Kenny, *Kilmainham*, pp 49–50. 'Chyllmeorbych' may be Kilmore (Co. Galway, barony of Clare, parish of Tuam). See *Ind. Townlands*, p. 584. **197** Doherty, 'The monastic town', p. 51.

sources. In the vernacular 'Life of Brendan of Clonfert', for example, we hear of a jester whose body was thrown ashore and devoured by mice.[198] Stories collected by S.H. O'Grady and published in *Silva Gadelica* contain a number of references concerning wild animals and the dead. For example, St Ciarán of Saighir is exhorted by a company of men to 'go fetch the bodies of that company, so that the wild beasts should not devour them'.[199] In 'The Tribute' one of the benefits of burial in a particular cemetery is that any body buried in it will not be eaten by wolves.[200] In the 'Life of St Ruadán', Diarmait, son of Fergus Cerrbél, wishes that a wild boar will attack a tomb and root up the corpse in it'.[201] The medieval Irish attitude towards the contact of a corpse with an animal is well illustrated by the passage in 'Mac Carthaigh's book' which tells how the 'English' gave Diarmait MacMurchada (Dermott Mac Murrough) the opportunity to 'avenge the wicked slaying of his father by the people of Dublin … when a dead dog was buried with his body in the ground as a mark of hatred and contempt'.[202]

Numerous statutes of the English and Scottish churches are concerned with the proper enclosure of the cemetery for the purpose of keeping out animals. The Constitutions of David, bishop of St Andrews in Scotland, drafted in the thirteenth century, decree that 'in the first place it be seen to that churchyards be suitably enclosed all the way round, so that no access be open to unclean and brutish beasts … the custom prevails that the whole of the churchyard be enclosed by the parishioners'.[203] Statutes adopted in the mid-thirteenth century at Exeter, Wells, Winchester and Worcester also speak of the need to protect cemeteries from beasts.[204]

In the Middle Ages, any open space which could be used for grazing was valuable, and the enclosed space of the cemetery was perfect for confining animals. Adomnán described a laywoman taking refuge in the church of Derry, and driving her sheep over the grave of a holy man.[205] French historical sources indicate that grazing rights in the cemetery were often leased out.[206] In 1377, the bailiff of the abbot of St Thomas', Dublin, was fined 12s. when a pig exhumed a corpse, and the record carefully notes that the abbot had been fully aware that

---

198 *Lives*, II, p. 51. **199** 'St Kieran of Saighir', *SG*, I, p. 8; II, p. 8: '*ar nach ithedaois bethadaig allta iad*'. **200** 'Cipé bés for ghreis Cholaim . ní bia a cholainn fó chuana': i, p. 388; 'whosoever shall be under Columbkill's protection, his body shall not be a prey to wolves': *SG*, II, p. 423. **201** *Lives*, I, p. 388. **202** *MacCarthaig's book, s.a.* 1170. **203** *Stat. Scot.*, 'Constitutions of David, Bishop of St Andrews', p. 57. **204** *Councils and Synods*, ed. Powicke & Cheney, II, p. 1009, 'Statutes of Exeter II', §114, explicitly mentions pigs; ibid., p. 601, 'Statutes of Wells', §20; ibid., II, p. 708, 'Statutes of Winchester III', §35; ibid., p. 174, 'Statutes of Worcester II', §21, p. 174; ibid., I, p. 297, 'Statutes of Worcester III', §5. **205** So it came about that that one day a woman was observed driving her sheep over the grave of this man, soon after his burial …' *Adomnán*, eds Anderson & Anderson, pp 248–9, §26a: 'Hic homo … sed illo in loco sepelietur ubi oves femina trans sepulchrum ejus minabit.' **206** Ariès, *The hour*, p. 56.

the animals were being allowed to feed in the cemetery.[207] A papal letter of 1471 regarding the diocese of Lismore speaks of one

> William Oronayn [who] ... has not resided in person in the said church, nor appointed anyone to exercise the cure ... has caused and allowed horses and other animals to be fed and stabled in places of the said church consecrated to God ...[208]

The wording of this passage leaves some room to question whether the animals were in the actual church-building itself, or in the cemetery.

Grazing in cemeteries did not end with the dawn of the modern period. In the early sixteenth century, Archbishop Alen's register notes that the existence of unenclosed cemeteries was still a problem.[209] It has previously been mentioned that in the mid-eighteenth century, one Andrew Cullen had grazing rights in the 'Bully's Acre' cemetery in Kilmainham which was very heavily used as a burial ground at that time. Apparently, leases for grazing rights were not normally given for this cemetery; this particular lease was given for the purpose of discouraging the common people of the area from using as a common thoroughfare a track which had been made through the cemetery for the convenience of the earl of Galway, then lord justice.[210] However, the very fact that such an arrangement should have been made, and that the following public outcry was over the walling of the cemetery rather than the grazing of animals in it, suggests that the practice did not offend public sensibilities – perhaps because it was a common one. Indeed, in at least some parts of Ireland, the practice of turning a goat out in the cemetery to eat the weeds and grass continued well into the mid-twentieth century.[211]

Any list of animals that posed a danger to graves must also include humans. Sanctuary status was supposed to provide safety and protection from plunder and violence, yet ironically, cemeteries were often defiled as a direct result of this status. Presumably robbers and raiders often crossed through the cemetery in their forays, and people seeking protection inside the cemetery often imported their conflicts.

Thus, the 'Annals of Ulster' record that in 1121 'Gilla Escoip Eogain Ua Aindiaraidh, king of Cianacht, was killed by his kinsmen in the middle of the cemetery of Bennchor',[212] and the 'Annals of Inisfallen' tell that in 1180 Ardfert was plundered by the MacCarthys who 'put many good people to death inside its sanctuary and graveyard'. A case regarding homicide within a cemetery was

---

207 *Calendar of Archbishop Sweteman*, ed. Lawlor, p. 263. **208** *Cal. Pap. Reg. 1458–1471*: 7 Paul II, 1471, p. 811. **209** *Calendar of Archbp. Alen's reg.*, ed. MacNeill, p. 289, No. 11 (1529–34). **210** Kenney, *Kilmainham*, p. 48. **211** Dr Katharine Simms recalls that when she visited Youghal, Co. Cork, in the 1960s, it was common for goats to be placed in the cemetery for this purpose. **212** *AU* 1121.3. The Irish word used here is *relig*.

heard in the Crown court at Kildare in 1298,[213] and in 1307 a case concerning an axe-fight in a cemetery was brought before the justiciar in Cork.[214]

The so-called 'Venedotian Code' (*Llyfr Iorwerth*) of medieval Welsh law, which dates from the thirteenth century, states the fine to be paid for a wrong done in a church, and that a fine of half the amount was to be paid for wrong committed in the churchyard.[215]

Additional proof of the violation of cemeteries can be found in church documents which record ceremonies of reconciliation, that is, the reconsecration ceremony required before any burials could be made in a cemetery which had been defiled by the spilling of blood or semen[216] or the burial of excommunicates. William Reeves, who edited Primate Colton's Visitation, noted that part of the liturgy of *reconciliare uolens* (which he included in an appendix to his edition) dates from the twelfth century and once belonged to the diocese of Canterbury.[217] Some fifteenth-century papal letters specifically grant the right – and sometimes state the need – to reconcile cemeteries.[218] In locations where cemeteries were not physically connected with the local church, a cemetery could be defiled without violating the sanctity of the church itself, a possibility which is clearly stated in one of the decretals of Pope Boniface VIII.[219] Because of this, a separate ritual of reconciliation was created for cemeteries.

In his visitation of 1397, Primate Colton of Armagh had to reconcile the cemeteries of Ardstraw (near Derry), Dungiven, and the church of 'sancti Brackani' in Clone after each of them had been polluted by blood.[220] The rite was also employed on the Scottish border. In 1419, a letter from monastery of Kelso was sent to the pope explaining that

> on account of outbreaks of war between the two realms it often happens that some holy places of the said monastery and subject to it are polluted by the effusions of blood

---

213 *CDI*, 25–26 Edward I. Mem. 10, pp 202–3.   214 *CDI*, 35 Edward I, 29 May 1307; pp 397–8.
215 *The ancient laws and institutions of Wales*, ed. & trans. Owen, I, p. 37, §20.   216 'Furthermore, we decree that when a church or churchyard shall have been profaned by the shedding of blood or of sexual seed … he who profaned it … shall pay the dues in respect of the reconciliation': from the fourteenth-century 'Synodal Statutes of St Andrews, *Stat. Scot.*, pp 76–7.
217 *Acts of Archbishop. Colton*, ed. Reeves, pp 100–4 (Appendix B). Colton was archbishop of Armagh from 1328 to 1404.   218 See, for example, *Cal. Pap. Reg.*, p. 51 (17 Kal. Aug. 1405); p. 108 (2 Kal. Mai 1405); p. 228 (17 Kal. Jan. 1410); p. 245 (11 Kal. Mai 1412).   219 *Acts of Archbishop Colton*, ed. Reeves, p. 105: 'Si Ecclesiae pollui sanguinis aut seminis effusione contingat, ipsius Caemiterium, si contiguum sit eidem censetur esse pollutum; unde antequam reconciliatum fuerit, non debet in eo aliquis sepeliri. Secus si remotus fuerit ab eadem. Non sic quoque in casu converso sentimus; ut videlicet polluto Caemiterio, quamvis Ecclesiae contiguo, debeat Ecclesia reputari polluta, ne minus dignum majus, aut accessorium principale ad se trahere videretur.' Cited from Catalani, Rituale Romanum, ii, p. 126.   220 *Acts of Archbishop Colton*, pp 15–16, 31–2, 41–2.

and requesting that the pope

> grant a faculty to the said Abbot William and his successors to reconcile by
> themselves and the religious of the said monastery all and sundry the holy
> places, churches and cemeteries … which may be polluted, interdicted or
> suspended by bloodshed profanataion or the burial of excommunicates.[221]

The opening of graves

The few mentions of grave-robbing contained in written sources come almost
exclusively from tales about pre-Christian Irish warrior society, and generally con-
sist of an account of entering a burial mound for the purpose of stealing the
empowering weapons of a dead warrior – a theme which is well-known throughout Western mythology and folklore.[222] For example, in the 'The colloquy of the
ancients', the warrior Caeilte breaks into a burial cairn and brings up the head
buried within, along with valuable grave-goods, among which is a chain which
he gives to St Patrick.[223] Another segment of the same story tells how Caeilte
plundered a 'sod-covered grave' although he was 'loath to do it' and takes out
weapons which he gives to Oengus, the son of the king of Ulster, before 'the dead
were returned to their grave and their stone restored over their resting-place'.[224]

The commentary to 'The martyrology of Oengus', tells of the disinterment
of the corpse of Niall of the Nine Hostages by St Cainnech, who said a mass
over the corpse before re-burying it.[225] In 836, *Chronicum Scotorum* records that
when the Vikings plundered Brega 'they entered into many crypts, a thing not
often done before'. This entry is usually taken to mean that they plundered the
famous Boyne Valley group of tombs.[226] When the Scottish Bruce brothers and
their troops harried Ireland in 1316, they are reported to have 'plundered the
churches and opened the tombs' in Naas, although this would have been done
for the insult rather than to obtain valuables.[227]

In medieval Ireland, goods were not normally interred with the dead (with
some exceptions, notably in the case of high-ranking ecclesiastics). This, of course,
eliminated the most obvious reason for robbing graves. Yet the absence of grave-
goods does not mean that Christian graves did not contain anything of perceived
value; as we have seen, the remains of prominent religious or political figures
were highly prized for the miraculous powers they were believed to hold, and
were sometimes stolen.[228]

---

221 *Calendar of Scottish supplications*, ed. Lindsay and Cameron, 1419, 12 June, Florence, p. 73.
222 Geary, *Living with the dead*, pp 49–50, 61–7.   **223** 'The Colloquy,' *SG*, I, p. 140; II, p. 153.
224 Ibid., I, p. 165; II, p. 183.   **225** 'His body afterwards taken out of the ground by Cainech
… Now a mass was said by the clerics over Niall's body and at the (sprinkling of) holy water
the herbs part from him.' *Félire*, p. 245.   **226** *Chronicum Scotorum*, *s.a.* 836; Cuffe, 'History of
Duleek', p. 140. The famous tombs of the Boyne Valley include Newgrange, Knowth and
Dowth.   **227** 'Grace's Annals', *s.a.* 1316.   **228** See below, 'Chapter 3 : The stealing of corpses

Of course, grave-robbing was nothing new. Bart Jaski has pointed out that both the laws of the native Irish and the law-codes of the Roman emperor Justinian (promulgated in 553) list grave-robbing as acceptable grounds for a woman to divorce her husband.[229]

We also find passages which describe the disinterment of human remains and their re-interment in a newly consecrated cemetery. This was done for the purpose of 'Christianizing' the deceased, thereby creating a sense of cultural continuity in burial ritual. Religious texts from the early Middle Ages, including *Collectio Canonum Hibernensis* show that the violation of graves was a general problem at this time.[230] The penalty for violating graves varied, depending upon the status of the people buried within them, which may reflect the survival of the concept of 'body-price' which was a cornerstone of native Irish law.[231]

The Church alone had the right to disinter bodies. Specifically, it had the right to disinter from consecrated Christian cemeteries the corpses of unrepentant excommunicants and others who had not died in a state of grace. This right is referred to in a statute adopted by the Twelfth General Council summoned by Pope Innocent III in 1215, which prohibited members of the Knights Hospitallers and 'certain other religious orders' from giving burial to the bodies of 'persons excommunicated by name' or 'public robbers or violators of churches or other places' and ordered that any bodies 'so buried be removed from consecrated ground'.[232]

and relics'. **229** Jaski, 'Marriage laws', p. 32, citing Brundage, *Law, sex and Christian society in medieval Europe* (Chicago, 1987), pp 14–17. **230** Doherty, 'The monastic town', p. 51. **231** Ibid., p. 58. **232** *Stat. Scot.*, pp 73–4.

CHAPTER 3

Burial ritual in medieval Ireland

A series of ritualized activities was performed between an individual's death and interment. These included the formal period of waiting preparatory to the burial of the corpse – known as the 'wake' – during which time various activities, both of a religious and of a secular nature, might be performed. Religious activities might include the recitation of prayers and the singing of hymns; secular activities might include games, lamenting for the dead, funeral processions, and a funeral feast. Often, the body also needed to be transported to the place of burial, which could require a lengthy and arduous journey. Depending on the distance, some kind of embalming might have been done.

Here again, Irish medieval sources generally preserve information regarding the ritual used for members of the upper levels of society. They record information about those who were admired, and also concerning what befell the corpses of people who were held in contempt. This evidence is considered below, along with some observations about the language used to record 'honorable' burial. I have found almost no explicit information on burial ritual for people who were not of the élite classes, with the exception of men who had fallen in battle.

THE 'WAKE'

Judging from the written evidence, the time between the death and burial of the corpse varied from less than twenty-four hours to as long as twelve days in medieval Ireland. Finucane has stated that in the later Middle Ages, a period of three days between death and burial was normal, at least for élite members of society. Prior to that time, there seems to have been some variance.

The 'Dialogues' of Pope Gregory the Great show that in later sixth-century Italy it was the normal practice to bury non-clerics and the non-élite on the same day as death occurred, and that the washing of the corpse was an integral part of the burial ritual.[1] However, in the 'Life of St Columba' by Adomnán (697

---

1 *The dialogues of St Gregory*, p. 44, on Marcellus: '... because he was to be carried far off, he could not be buried that day. His sisters having now longer respite for his burial, with heavy

x 704) the great Gaelic saint prophesies that one full day is to pass between death
and burial: 'At the end of the week, on a Friday, your son will die, and on the
eighth day from now, that is on the Sabbath, will be brought here for burial;'[2]
yet Adomnán wrote that Columba's own wake lasted for three days.[3]

Regularis concordia, a monastic agreement drawn up by English nuns and
monks at the synod of Winchester *c*.970 also prescribes that a monk be buried
on the day of his death, 'provided that those things necessary for a burial can be
prepared'.[4] Otherwise, monks were to keep watch over the body through the
night in shifts, continuously chanting psalms until burial was given early the following morning.[5] The 'Monastic constitutions of Archbishop Lanfranc', which
postdate the arrival of the 'Anglo-Normans' in Ireland give similar instructions,
stipulating that a monk was to be buried within a very few hours of his death,
the exact time depending on the hour at which he had died.[6] In general, the
constitutions of Lanfranc are the same as those of Le Bec (Lanfranc's mother-
house), and closely resemble the constitutions drawn up at Cluny between 1030
and 1048.[7]

Monasteries employing Continental monastic rules began to be founded in
Ireland from 1127.[8] It is reasonable to expect that the burial procedures followed
by these communities would also have been followed in post-Reform medieval
Ireland, and we do indeed find this. For example, Cellach – the reforming 'suc-
cessor of Patrick', who had imposed new rules at Armagh in 1126 – appears to
have been buried 'in the burial ground of the bishops' within twenty-four hours
after his body was brought to the cathedral at Lismore, Co. Waterford.[9] However,

hearts ran weeping unto the bishop'; p. 136: '… a poor woman's husband died … (and she)
made him ready to be buried, yet it was so late, that it could not be done that day …' **2**
Adomnán's Life of Columba, ed. & trans. Anderson & Anderson, pp 24–5: 'Nonne sabbati dies
hodierna est. Filius tuus sexta feria in fine morietur septimanae; octavaque die, hoc est sab-
bato, huc sepelietur', p. 24. **3** Ibid.: 'And for three days and three nights the funeral ceremonies were duly carried out in a worthy and honourable manner'; 'Honestaeque ternís
diebus et titidem noctibus honorabiles rite explentur exequiae', §133a, pp 230–31. **4** *Regularis
Concordia*, ed. & trans. Symons and Cross, p. 65; *The Oxford dictionary of the Christian church*, ed.
Cross, p. 1147. **5** Ibid., p. 65: 'If the brother died before dawn, in the night or after the dark
house, in the early morning, let him be buried before the brethren have their meal, when the
Masses have been celebrated, provided that those things necessary for a burial can be prepared: otherwise let the brethren be appointed by turns to chant psalms unceasingly by the
body throughout that day and the following night until early morning when it shall be committed to the earth.' **6** *The monastic constitutions of Lanfranc*, ed. & trans. Knowles, pp 127–8.
My thanks to Prof. A.P. Smyth for bringing this to my attention. Jewish law requires that
burial be made before sundown of the day of death, which would have checked the spread
of disease, and would also have been an obvious reason for this rule. **7** Ibid., p. 59. **8** The
monastery of Ibracense, founded in Munster in 1127, seems to have been Augustinian; a
Savignac abbey was founded in Dublin in 1139, A. Gwynn & Hadcock, *Medieval religious*,
p. 3. **9** *AU*, 1129.3 records that Cellach died in 1129, on the Kalends (1st) of April on the
second feria, and that his body was brought to Lismore on the third of the Nones (3rd) of
April, and was buried on the second of the Nones (4th) of April, on the 5th feria.

the dates regarding the arrival of Cellach's body and his burial are recorded with such exactitude that they arouse suspicion that there may have been something unusual about the burial. It could be that Cellach's burial was effected with unusual speed; however it seems more likely that the annalist wished to prove that the burial of the great reformer himself was performed in full accordance with the monastic rule which he championed. The burial of Aedh O'Gibellan, a Premonstratensian canon at Trinity Island who died in 1236, also conforms exactly to Lanfranc's constitutions. Aedh 'was waked in the choir that night and until mass on the morrow, and was honourably interred afterwards'.[10]

The sources also contain a number of exceptions to 'next day' burial. A three-day wake is noted in the seventh-century 'Life of St Samson of Dol' (a sixth-century Welshman who travelled and lived in Ireland and Cornwall before settling in Brittany). It tells of the burial of a man possessed by demonic forces who was waked by the community 'for three whole days, as many nights, continuing steadfast at the accustomed prayers, remaining without food and without sleep'.[11] The wording in this passage seems to suggest that this wake may have been longer than usual – whether this was due to the generosity of the community on the afflicted soul's behalf, or to their wish to ensure that the demonic force has been fully exorcised, is not stated. What seems to be clear is that a longer delay before burial seems to have become unusual, at least for the socially élite,[12] that segment of society with which most of our sources are concerned. I have previously mentioned that in 597, the waking of St Columba, who was both prince and saint, is said to have lasted for three days.[13] Under the year 1230, *AFM* note that the corpse of the erenagh of Tibohine, 'Dermot Macgillacarry' (Gillacoimdedh O'Duilin) was held in the 'temple at Drum for two days and two nights' after his death while the monks of Saints' Island and Boyle fought over it. On the third day, the monks of Boyle Abbey, Co. Roscommon, where he had chosen to be buried, and the clerics of Moylurg, assembled and chose two men to oversee his burial.[14]

Other Irish sources also mention 'wakes' which continued for seven and eight days, with twelve-day wakes recorded for men of especially high status.[15] The vernacular life of St Ciarán of Saighir, reports that his body was waked for seven days and seven nights,[16] and the 'Book of Fenagh', the verse portions of which

---

10 *ALC*, I, s.a. 1236; *AB*, §298 (1236). 11 *Life of St Samson of Dol*, trans. Taylor, p. 70. 12 Finucane, 'Sacred corpse', p. 41. 13 *Adomnan's Life of Columba*, ed. Anderson & Anderson, see n. 3 above. 14 *AFM*, s.a. 1230; *ALC*, I, s.a. 1230. *AB* §390, p. 297 provide the following details: 'Clari Elfinensis archdiaconi ad Insolam Sanctae Trinitatis … Qui dixit quod apud monachos de Buellio sepiliri elegit … quod corpus in templo de Druim duabus diebus et duabus noctibus de consensu utrusque partis fuerat sequestratum. Porro die tertia omnibus monachis de Buellio et clericis de Mag Luirg in unum collectis compromisionem in duos uiros ydoneos fecerunt. Facta autum compromisione et lite contestata et alleg(atis) omnibus factis demum ipsum corpus Insole Sancte Trinitatis ad sepiliendum adiudicatum est'. 15 *Vitae sanctorum*, ed. & trans. Plummer, I, pp cxlix–cxlx. 16 Ibid., II, p. 119. For the dating of this life, see *Sources*, p. 316.

may have been composed in the thirteenth century, preserves a description of the 'men of Ireland' mourning the death of one 'Cobthach' for a period of seven days.[17] St Senán's hagiographer wrote that the saint was 'waked' for eight days,[18] while the 'wakes' of St Patrick, SS Ethnea and Fedelmia[19] and St Bairre continued for twelve days. The 'Book of Fenagh' also contains a passage in which St Caillin instructs Manchan of Mohill to disinter his body from Relig Mochaemhog after twelve years and translate his bones. These uses of the number 'twelve' may suggest that it had particular significance within the culture.[20]

The entry regarding the funeral ritual for St Bairre has close parallels with the entries for both Brian Bóruma and Domnall, coarb of Armagh. The Irish life of St Bairre records that 'the monks and disciples of the churches of Desmond came to wake and honour the body of their master, St Bairre, and bear it with them to the place of his resurrection' in Cork.[21] The author of the saint's life also wrote:

> The churches of Desmond were busied about the body of their master with hymns and psalms and masses and recitations of hours for twelve days, during which time the sun did not go beneath the earth …[22]

Similarly, after the death of Brian Bóruma in 1014, the 'archbishop' of Armagh and his senior cleric travelled south to Swords, collected his body and carried it to Armagh, and waked it for twelve days before its burial.[23] A third example exists: when Domnall, coarb of St Patrick, died at Duleek in 1105, the *AU* record that his body was also carried north to Armagh for burial.[24] Domnall's wake is

---

17 *Bk Fen.*, p. 262–3: 'Uair batas se rectmain ann / Ag golgairi na timchell'; 'For they were there during a week/ Engaged in loud wailing about him.'   **18** '*Vita S. Senani*', in *Acta Sanctorum Hiberniae*, ed. Colgan, p. 528. For the dating of this life, see Kenney, *The sources*, p. 365.   **19** Ibid., p. 254. These were the daughters of King Loeghaire who lived in the fifth century.   **20** *Bk Fen.* also records that Caillin came to Ireland 'twelve years' after Patrick's arrival. In the same source, on pp 110–11: 'Ó ló m'adluichti co becht / Bid da bliadain decc co cert / Tan dobera co maisi / D'fidnacha mo chaomhthaisi' ('from the day of my burial, exactly, 'Twill be just twelve years / 'Till thou shalt gloriously bear / My fair relics to Fidhnacha'. Another reference to twelves years in *Bk Fen.*, appears on p. 37. These are just two examples. The 'Life of St Brendan of Clonfert' states that 'the prayer of Brendan … should be recited twelve times in a day for the soul of every sinner and twelve genuflections after each recititation': *Lives*, II, p. 89. The number nine may also have been important; see *Bk Fen.*: pp 260–63: 'Nine kings fell', 'Nine days was Cobhthach under the lake…'; and pp 264–5: 'Nine paces on this side of the Corrginds/ Is Cobhthach'; p. 92: And when assuming arch-kingship / the power of nine in each man'.   **21** *Lives*, ii, p. 20, xxvi.   **22** '*Beatha Bharra*', ed. & trans. Ó Riain, pp xxvii, 89–91. This is recorded in the 'Early vernacular life', argued by Ó Riain to have been composed between 1196–1201, but does not occur in the later Latin life.   **23** *AFM, s.a.,* 1014; *AI, s.a.* 1013; *ALC, s.a.* 1014; *AU, s.a.,* 1014.2; *Leabhar Oiris*, ed. Best, §39.   **24** *AU, s.a.* 1105.3: 'ocus co tucadh a sin co Dam Liac co nderbailt ann 7 tucadh a chorp co hArd macha .i. I Prod. Id. August 7 i Sathurn 7 I feil Lasrein Innsi Muren 7 in *ocht*mad *fich*it ocus co tucadh

also said to have continued for the uncommonly long period of twelve days, as had King Brian's.[25]

The *ALC* alone records that Brian's wake lasted just two days; however, this may be a scribal error, since in other sources, twelve-day wakes seem to be connected with people of high status, and thus appear to have specific social connotations.[26]

Brian's unusual twelve-day wake puts him in the illustrious company of the two saints mentioned above who had wakes of the same length. This may be indicative of an Irish desire to attribute sanctity to its political rulers, a practice which reached its height on the Continent in the mid-twelfth century, when Barbarossa had Charlemagne canonized. Ó Corráin has noted this preoccupation among Uí Briain (the O'Briens) of twelfth-century Ireland.[27]

The speed with which the corpse was carried to the church also seems to have had some significance, probably as an indication of the status of the deceased and the esteem in which he was held. The stealing of satins' relics (or items that could be passed off as saints' relics) was a lucrative occupation in medieval Europe.[28] In Ireland, the written sources reveal that the relics of prominent churchmen and political rulers were also in demand, and a quick burial after death would have reduced the danger of having the corpse stolen. This may be another reason why we find so much detail about the timing of Cellach's wake and burial. The importance of quickly transporting the corpse to the place of burial is also indicated in the late twelfth-century obituary notice of Domnall, the son of Aed Mac Lochlainn (Hugh O'Loughlin), 'Lord of Ailech and presumptive heir to the throne of Ireland'. In recording his death and burial, *AFM* state that 'his body was carried to Armagh on the same day'.[30] The inclusion of this detail is unusual, and the annalist also tells that Domnall 'alone received a thrust from an English spear'. Thus, the speed with which the body was brought to Armagh may have been recorded to show that Domnall's comrades had 'done the right thing' by their fallen leader. It is also possible that such speedy transportation may have been deemed necessary in order to protect the body from retaliatory mutilation by the enemy. Because Donal's date of burial is not mentioned, we do not know the length of his wake.

While it is difficult to draw conclusions from this small amount of evidence, the indications are that monks were generally buried the following day, while members of the social élite (territorial kings, chieftains, warriors, etc.) were given

ann inda ghalur.' **25** *AU, s.a.* 1014.2: 'Dí aidci dhec immorro do samhadh Patraicc'. **27** 'Dí aidce, umorro, dósum ocus do ts(h)amad Padraig ag aire na gcorp …' *ALC s.a.* 1014. **27** See Ó Corráin, 'Foreign connections', p. 228. King Brian is mentioned by Colgan and in the English Martyrology; the Bollandists did not feel he merited inclusion as a saint ('Praetermissi, et i alios dies rejecti'). See *Acta Sanctorum*, ed. Bolland, 12 March (xii Martii), p. 102. **28** For general comments on medieval European relic thieves, see Geary, *Furta Sacra*, p. 44. **30** *AFM s.a.* 1188.

wakes of three days or longer. An entry regarding Diarmaid Mac Carthaigh (Demott MacCarthy), king of Desmumu, provides a noteworthy exception. Mac Carthaigh was slain at the monastery of Tralee, Co. Kerry, in 1320 but the annalist makes a point of mentioning that it was not until a fortnight later that he was buried at Inisfallen, some twenty miles away. The annalist surely had a reason for including this detail, but we can only guess at what it was. If the delay had been caused by an unusually long wake or because of a dispute over his corpse, we would expect this to have been mentioned. Since Mac Carthaigh had been slain, the answer may be that some time passed before his remains were recovered or released by the enemy (a humiliating detail which a friendly annalist would not have been eager to record), or inclement weather may have delayed transportation of the corpse back to the place of burial, as it often must have.[31] Records relating to Richard Burke, who died in 1326, indicate that an inordinately long amount of time may have passed between his death, which *AI* record as having occurred before the first of August, and his burial at Athassel, which the records of St Mary's Abbey, Dublin say took place shortly before the Feast of St John the Baptist, held on 29 August.[32]

An intriguing reference from an Irish annalist refers to the slaying of one Íomhair Ó hÁinle (Ivor O'Hanly) in 1408 on 'Lá-na-m-Bruach-n-Dubh'. O'Donovan stated that he had not been able to discover the meaning of this phrase, which he believed was 'some day of mourning', and which he translated as 'the day of the black borders'.[33] Whether this indicates a particualar type of mourning ceremony, some annual commemoration of the dead, a public confirmation of the territorial borders, or simply relates that the day on which Ó hÁinle died was a very 'black' day for his people, remains unknown.[34]

THE REQUIEM MASS, 'KEENING', AND THE ELEGY

Singing and chanting over the corpse during the liminal waking period, and even after burial, was an important part of the funeral ritual. In introducing his *Vitae Sanctorum Hiberniae*, Plummer notes references to the singing of a requiem after the burial of Christians,[35] and the Irish 'Life of St Brendan of Clonfert' contains the assurance that 'it does profit the dead for their surviving friends

---

31 *AI*, 1320.2. **32** *AI, s.a.* 1326, and *Chartularies of St Mary's*, ed. Gilbert, ii, p. 364. **33** *AFM*, IV, p. 796, n. 'v'. **34** It may be useful to note this passage included in an extract from 'the death of Dermot', in *SG*, II, p. 469: 'ocus nogniithí anaenach sin la gach ríg la cach nogebedh Eirinn ro táinic Pátraic. Ocus. Cccc. Oenach I Tailtin ó Pátraic co dubaenach nDonnchada meic Flainn m. Maeilshechlainn'; II, p. 514 (translation): 'and that meeting was made by every king that had Ireland until Patrick came, and in Taillte there were four-hundred such from Patrick to the "black gathering" of Donough, s. of Flann mac Melachlin'. The death of Flann Maelshechlainn is recorded in *AFM s.a.* 942. **35** The Irish word is 'ecndairc': Plummer *Vitae sanctorum*, I, p. cl.

to sing their requiem'.[36] The body of St Bairre of Cork was honored 'with psalms and hymns and spiritual songs'.[37] Brian Bóruma's twelve-day wake included the 'reading of psalms and prayers and chanting of hymns'. There is no mention in either of these excerpts of a Mass being said for the deceased, though records of later funerals tell of Masses. We have already seen that in 1129 Cellach of Armagh was 'honourably' buried with 'hymns, psalms and masses', as was Amlaíb Ó Donnchada (Aulay O'Donough), overking of Eóghanachta Locha Léin of west Co. Kerry), who died in 1158, and 'was honourably buried by them with hymns and psalms and Masses'.[38] Perhaps requiem-masses did not become part of the Irish funeral ritual until after the twelfth-century reforms. The 'Book of Fenagh' includes this passage:

> I shall be entreating the king of the stars
> And singing psalms over his grave
> Along with thirty men of grade
> For 'tis a joy to me how he believed.[39]

In the Middle Ages, the 'waking' of a corpse was accompanied by lamentations (also known as 'keening', from the Irish *caoine*, 'lament'), a custom which presumably dated from pre-Christian times. The Church sought to eliminate the practice and replace it with ecclesiastically more acceptable forms of mourning, presumably in an effort to have burial ritual standardized and controlled by the ecclesiastical élite.[40]

Two early Penitentials – the 'Bigotian penitential' and the 'Old Irish penitential' – express markedly different views regarding keening. The 'Bigotian penitential', written in the late seventh or early eighth century and possibly in Ireland,[41] takes an accommodating attitude, citing Biblical examples of public lamentation such as the weeping of the women for Christ, in an effort to show that keening should be tolerated. The Penitential concludes by stating that 'for whom no lament is made to him it is reckoned as bad merit'.[42] But in the 'Old Irish Penitential', written *c.*800, keening is sharply censured. Specific penances are prescribed for keening which vary according to the social status of the deceased: the lower the social status of the person being keened, the more severe the penance. These penances suggest that a concentrated effort was made to stamp out keening among the unfree classes.[43]

36 *Lives*, ed. Plummer, II, p. 89. **37** *Mon. Hib.*, I, note p. 112. **38** *Mac Carthaig's book, s.a.* 1158, no. 7. **39** *Bk Fen.*, p. 147. **40** For a discussion of the critical role women played in funeral ritual on the Continent, and how that role was usurped by the church in the he eleventh century for political and ideological reasons, see P.J. Geary, *Phantoms of remembrance*, pp 48–80. **41** See Kenney, *The sources*, No. 74. **42** *The Irish penitentials*, ed. & trans. Bieler & Binchy, p. 231. **43** Ibid., p. 163. The keening of a 'layman or laywoman' carried a punishment of '50 days on bread and water', while the keening of 'an anchorite or a bishop or a scribe or a great prince

A poem by the mid-eighth century writer Blathmac mac Con Brettan describes the death of Christ in terms of contemporary Irish burial ritual and contains numerous references to keening. One example tells that 'it is incumbent upon' anyone who 'has seen him (Christ) lying in his blood … to keen him perpetually'.[44] The Latin 'Life of St Ruadan', the recensions of which Sharpe has argued to be traceable back to an original dating from 750 x 900, notes that 'the people were in great lamentation and mourning' after his death.[45] The 'Book of Fenagh' tells that after the death of the semi-mythical Cobhthach 'the game of sorrowing' was celebrated by 'the kingly hosts of the Fir Fuinidh who

> … were there during a week,
> engaged in loud wailing about him.
> there came to us – 'twas a sad tale –
> The women of Ireland, a great band.
> To mourn Cobhthac, 'twas no deceit,
> The red-lipped female band did come.[46]

Caithréim Thoirdhealbhaig states that in 1310, after the body of Sheeda Mac Conmara was buried in 'St Bredan's churchyard' in Birr, 'his households mourning for him raised three loud cries of sorrow'.[47] Edmund Campion, writing *c.*1571, described the public grieving of the Irish, which had become proverbial. He noted that the corpse was carried

> To grave with howling and barbarous owt –
> Cries, pitifull in appearance, whereof grewe as
> I suppose the proverbe to weepe Irishe.[48]

The Latin Life of saints Ethnea et Fedelmia (written in the late twelfth or early thirteenth century) tells of the great lamentation and ululations made for dead friends which continued for three days before burial.[49] A poem in the fourteenth-century 'Book of Magauran' tells of women keening over 'Fearghal, Brian's son'.[50]

Hand-clapping also seems to have been a important element of this ritual, as shown by these excepts:

---

or a righteous king' was punishable by 15 days on bread and water. For dating, see *Sources*, No. 75. **44** *Poems of Blathmac son of Cú Brettan*, ed. & trans. Carney, p. 47, stz. 133. **45** Sharpe, *Medieval Irish saints' lives*, pp 329, 331–3, 397. **46** *Bk Fen.*, p. 262–63. **47** *Caithr. Th.*, I, p. 53; II, p. 51. **48** Campion, *Two bokes*, p. 19, lines 17–20. **49** *Acta sanctorum Hiberniae*, ed. Colgan (11 Jan), pp 54–5: 'postea sacramentum corporis, & sanguinis Christi de manu S. Patricii acceperunt; ac deinde in lecto uno posite, et vestimentis suis cooperte dormierunt in morte: quod videntes amici, et nutrices earum, planctum, et ululatum magnum fecerunt.' **50** 'Book of Magauran', ed. McKenna, pp 45–9, poem V, st. 14 & 29 (English trans. pp 306–8); pp 44, 48 (English trans. pp 306–8). For dating, see p. viii.

> Every splendid household beats hands over their lord[51]

and

> They would come to you and me to keen your royal son. So that with
> beating of hands without … with women, children and men, they might
> keen on every hill-top the king … [52]

The medieval Welsh romance 'The Lady of the Fountain' which may have been
composed as early as the second half of the twelfth century, contains this description of lamenting, which is similar to those found in Irish sources:

> And following that host he could see a yellow-haired lady with her hair
> over her shoulders, and many a gout of blood on her tresses, and a torn gar-
> ment of yellow brocaded silk about her, and two buskins of speckled cord-
> wain upon her feet. And it was a marvel that the ends of her fingers were
> not maimed, so hard did she beat her two hands together … And louder
> was her shrieking than what there was of man and horn in the host.[53]

As these examples indicate, keening appears to have been the responsibility of
women, or at least they played the most prominent role in this aspect of funeral ritual. The poem '*Sliab Betha*', suggests that the duties of a wife may once have
included digging her husband's grave.[55]

Men more particularly are recorded as eulogizing the deceased, often in the
form of a chant. The vernacular 'Life of St Cellach', which has been called 'a comparatively late literary romance',[56] tells that the saint's brother, Cucoingilt 'chant-
ed a short dirge over the grave of his brother'; presumably the dirge was short
because he was in a hurry to find his brother's murderers. In the 'Book of
Magauran' we hear of 'famous Teallach's host' chanting over the grave of
'Fearghal, Brian's son'. The poem goes on to recount that 'every man gave his
testimony' that the prince had been killed with a blow from the front, and that
more tributes were given after his funeral Mass.[57]

Elegiac verses were also written upon the death of a chief or king, and these
might be spoken over his grave after his burial. Irish poems and the Irish chronicles include numerous medieval examples of these verses, and this tradition was
a feature of native Irish funeral ritual well into the modern period.

A description of the twelfth-century funeral of King Toirrdelbach Ua Brian
(Turlough O'Brien), speaks of both lamenting and pipe-playing as part of the

---

51 Ibid., p. 43, st. 126. **52** Ibid., p. 51, st. 146–47. **53** *The Mabinogion*, ed. and trans. Jones, pp
ix, 166. **55** *Met. Dind.*, IV, p. 77. Gwynn equates the spot with *Slieve Beagh* in the parish of
Clones, Co. Fermanagh. **56** Kenney, *The sources*, p. 457. **57** 'Book of Magauran,' ed. McKenna,
pp 45–9, poem V, verses 14 & 29, (English trans., pp 306–308); pp 44 & 48 (English trans., pp
306–308). For dating, see p. viii.

funeral ritual for the over-kings of Ireland. The Latin 'Life of Mochulla' of Tulla, Co. Clare, which may have been written by the same author, contains similar information.[58] *Caithréim Thoirdhealbhaigh*, written in the fourteenth century, presents a vivid scene in 1311 at Donough O'Brien's grave:

> After this his violent death, all left the chief to lie there; but his poets and his clergy of the higher orders came to seek him, even as his poet tells us when he, standing over Donough and setting forth Ireland's grief, did enunciate this lay: 'Weary this night ...'[59]

FUNERAL 'GAMES'

As mentioned above, the 'Book of Fenagh' tells that the death of the semi-legendary Cobthach was celebrated with *cluiche caine* ('games'; lit. 'game of weeping'), and seven days of 'sorrowing and lamenting'.[60] This text source was composed *c.*1300, indicating that the knowledge of such practices was still alive in the high Middle Ages, and that such games may still have been performed at that time. This is hardly surprising, since funeral games are known to have been a feature at Irish wakes into the twentieth century.[61] The high merriment often associated with wakes is also recorded in medieval Scotland – and eastern Scotland at that. The statutes adopted by the Scottish church at Aberdeen in the thirteenth century 'forbid singing and dancing to take place' at the funerals and exequies of deceased lay persons 'since it does not become us to laugh at the weeping of others, but in a case of the kind rather to grieve as they do'.[62]

FUNERAL PROCESSIONS

The first funeral procession noted in Irish sources is that of King Brian Bóruma in 1014. To anyone surveying the sources for burial in Ireland, the enormous

---

58 From *Codex Salmanticensis* (Brussels, Bibliotheque Royale, MS 76762–4 fols. 168a–17d) §22, quoted by D. Ó Corráin, 'Foreign connections', p. 217: '… description of the funeral of King Tairdelbach with its stress on the *planctus* (Irish: *caíned*) and pipe-playing as a custom of the "kings of the west" (that is, Ireland) … "sequenti proinde die, cunctis aduenientibus sanctis peregrinis et domesticis fidei, legitimo more uniuerse carnis obsequiis rite peractis, cum planctu et clangore tubarum ac tibicinum iuxta morem regum Occidentis et exempla, predicatorem Christi fidelem sepulchro digno honore condiderunt"', (SP 22). Ó Corráin has noted that descriptions of the funeral of Tairdelbach and St Mochulla appear to have been written by the same man, whose knowledge of the local customs and politics appears to have been excellent. **59** *Caithr. Th.*, II, p. 46. **60** *Bk Fen.*, pp 262–3:'Do ferad a cluichi caini'. **61** See Ó Suilleabháin, *Irish wake amusements*. **62** 'General provincial statutes of the thirteenth century', *Stat. Scot.*, p. 42.

social, political and religious importance of this event is obvious: no historical account of an Irish medieval funeral compares with that of Brian's for the amount of information and detail provided. The writers included information on the transportation of Brian's corpse from the battle-site at Clontarf to its tomb at Armagh. They noted that the clerics who met the body at Swords stopped at Duleek on the way to Armagh, the preparation of the corpse for burial, particulars about the wake, the tomb provided, its position in the church, and the payment of Brian's bequests *post-mortem*. Even if we had no other record regarding Brian's life and exploits, the accounts of his burial alone are enough to clearly indicate his pre-eminent status and unique position in Irish history. In spite of all of this, the information available regarding Brian Bóruma's funeral is still extremely limited. Much valuable detail which we might hope to find – such as who accompanied the corpse in addition to the clerics who journeyed from Armagh, and information about any commemorations held *en route* to Armagh – is not provided.

John McManners has stated that across Europe, 'a great change in mental attitude' regarding death 'comes in the twelfth century, among the intellectual and spiritual élite'. Men begin to realize their individuality, to 'insist on their personal and lonely destiny', rather than one which accepted the anonymity and commonality of death. From the thirteenth to the fifteenth century, McManners and others have noted:

> the growing sense of individuality ... the relatives and friends of the dead man are affirming his individuality and, looking ahead to their own inevitable end, affirming their own.[63]

Irish historical sources mention few funeral processions; generally we are left with only the vague assurance that the deceased was 'buried with honour', or a note that the body was 'conveyed', 'brought', or 'carried' to its place of burial. Yet even these few glimpses of Irish medieval funeral processions indicate that the funeral was gaining importance in English and Irish society at the same time.

During the central and late Middle Ages, the English funeral developed into a grander, more splendid and formalized ritual. This was designed to reaffirm the strength of the existing social hierarchy, and impress upon the general populace the wealth, power and prestige of deceased nobles and more importantly, of their descendants. Providing food and clothing to members of the poor was not only a means of distributing charity in the hope of generating prayers for the soul of the deceased, it was also an easy way to ensure the presence of an impressively large number of mourners. By the later Middle Ages, the new merchant-class' adoption of these practices caused the noble classes to create even

63 McManners, 'Death and the French historians', pp 118–19.

more elaborate rituals to emphasize and maintain the exclusivity of their social station. Claire Gittings' research reveals the scale that (at least some) English funerals had achieved by the high and late Middle Ages:

> Poor people flocked in droves to attend the funerals of their social superiors; many wills record the distribution of doles to a hundred poor folk, and it is not uncommon to find mention of an even bigger crowd.[64]

At William Marshal's funeral in London in 1219, the crowd was so large that it could not be contained within the gates of the city, and the ceremony had to be moved to the open spaces of Westminster.[65] When Hugh, earl of Stafford, was borne to his grave in 1385, he was 'followed by a hundred poor men clothed in white ...'[66] Given the small populations which inhabited cities in the Middle Ages, these figures are impressive; indeed, by the mid-fourteenth century, the custom of soldiers accompanying the body of a warrior to his grave seems to have been well-established in England, as shown by the fact that in 1368, Sir Otho de Grandison wrote, 'I entreat that no armed horse or armed man be allowed to go before my body on my burial day.'[67] These instructions make it quite clear that a nobleman was expected to have horses and armed men at the head of his funeral procession, and that de Grandison's request was exceptional.

The first record of a funeral having been attended by heralds and other members of the English College of Arms was that of the earl of Salisbury at Bisham in 1463,[68] but others which were not recorded may have preceded it, and probably did. Wearing the arms of the deceased, the heralds accompanied the earl's corpse to the church, where they presented his coat of arms, sword, shield, helmet and crest at the altar. These were then handed to the bishop of Worcester, who transferred them to the earl's heir.

The descriptions of later medieval Irish funerals available in Irish sources are few, and thus the opportunities for comparing the development of Irish funerals with those of other countries are limited. We are also missing evidence for roughly one-half of Ireland's medieval population since no contemporary description of a woman's funeral has survived, if indeed, one ever existed.

ALC preserve a colorful and unique account of the 1307 funeral procession of 'Domhnall (son of Tadhg), son of Brian, son of Andrias, son of Brian Luighnech, son of Toirdhelbhach Mor O'Conchobhair, tanist [heir presumptive] of all Connacht ...' Domhnall was wounded in battle, but 'God was merciful to him', and he lived to receive communion and last rites. After his death[69]

64 Gittings, *Death, burial*, p. 27   **65** Duby, *William Marshal*, p. 23.   **66** Gittings, *Death, burial*, p. 27.   **67** Ibid., p. 30.   **68** Ibid., p. 28.   **69** *ALC, s.a.* 1307, pp 539–40. *Corr Sliabh* (*Corr sliabh na segsai, i cCorann*) are the Curlew Hills just north of Boyle, between counties Sligo &

his body was taken to *Corr-sliabh*, and there was not taken with a dead body in later times such a quantity of droves, and garments, and cattle, of cavalry, and of kerns, as were taken in this procession with him to his sepulchre; and his remains were nobly and honourably interred in the monastery of the Buill [Boyle, Co. Roscommon].

The words 'there was not taken with a dead body in later times …' reveals that this was an exceptionally grand funeral procession. Domhnall was evidently a very wealthy man, judging from the report that 'droves' (presumably sheep, since cattle are mentioned separately), clothing, cattle, soldiers mounted on horses, and foot-soldiers went with him to his grave; rather, the words indicate that there was nothing exceptional about animals, clothing and soldiers accompanying a chief to the grave; in this instance, it was the *quantity* which was remarkable. We are not told why animals were included in the funeral ritual; Plummer noted that in the Latin lives of the Irish saints, cattle seem to have been slaughtered as part of the funeral ritual.[70] The date of this entry and the location of the funeral are of particular interest because the thirteenth century saw a resurgence in strength among the native Irish population at the furthest reaches of the expanded Anglo-Irish frontier, and 'Corr-sliabh' is in an area which would have remained essentially Gaelic. However, it is difficult to say whether this passage describes the type of funeral procession which traditonally accompanied an Irish chief to his grave, or features which may have been observed in the funerals of Anglo-Irish lords.

Pembridge's annals preserve a unique entry *s.a.* 1329 regarding the burial of the Anglo-Irish lord Thomas Botiller (Butler) which seems to indicate that, as in England, funerals were not private affairs, but events in which the general populace participated. We are told that after Botiller was killed by M'Geoghagan, he 'was honourably interred in the church of Saint Saviour by the citizens of Dublin'.[71]

The popular aspect of noble funerals is also described by Friar John Clyn, the Anglo-Irish chronicler. Clyn, who lived in Kilkenny, was probably an eyewitness when Sir William le Ercedekne and his two sons, his uncle, and 'three more of the name', were carried to be buried in the Franciscan convent at Kilkenny in 1335 'on seven biers together, one following after the other, through the town of Kilkenny, with the wailing of many'.[72] It seems clear that this funeral was of a type reserved for members of a noble family, since Clyn also noted

Roscommon. 'Kern' refers to a 'light-armed Irish foot-soldier' (*Shorter Oxford English Dictionary*, p. 1081). **70** Plummer, *Vitae sanctorum*, i, p. cl. **71** '… corpus dicti Domini Thome [le Botiller] portatum fuit per civitatem cum magno honore et sepultum apud Fratres Predicatores', quoted from 'Annals of Ireland', *s.a.* 1329, *Ann. Mon. Beata*, ed. Gilbert, 1329, p. 379. **72** '… in septem feretris simul et continue per villam Kilkennie, cum multorum planctu …' Clyn & Dowling, *s.a.* 1335, p. 26 (English trans., p. xxvi).

that Thomas de Bathe and Gerald Bagot, and 'others to the number of fifty' were killed with the le Ercedeknes, yet no mention is made of their corpses being included in the procession, or of their places of interment. Clyn also failed to note how many people wailed in the streets of Kilkenny as the biers bearing the le Ercedeknes to their graves passed. The entry does suggest that it was the number of le Ercedeknes being buried, rather than the number of mourners, which was notable. Clyn also recorded the apparently lavish funeral of Lord Nicholas de Verdun, who in 1347 was buried in the convent of Dundalk, 'honourably with great pomp and a solemn funeral and a gathering of many nobles'.73

Perhaps the closest Irish parallels to an English heraldic funeral are those of Enri MacCapa (Henry McCabe) and Tadhg Ua Conchobhair (O'Connor). McCabe died of a 'sudden sickness' at Lissardowlin, Co. Longford, in 1460 and the *AConn* record that he was 'buried at Cavan and there were fourteen score axes or more at his funeral procession'.74 The 'fourteen score axes' mentioned refer to the number of gallowglasses (Irish *gallóglách*, or Scottish mercenary soldiers), armed with broadaxes who accompanied his body as a guard of honor. This entry states that at least 280 gallowglasses were present. When Tadhg O Conchobhair Ruadh died four years later, 'Mac Firbish's Annals' record that

> Thady O'Connor, halfe king of Connaght, died … & was buryed in Roscomon in an honorable manner, by Cathal Crovderg's sept, by West & East, & by the Tuathas, viz. the countryes, of Silmuredhy Mullehan, as never a king in his dayes was, haveing so many grosses of Horse and foote companyes of Galloglaghes & other souldiers about his body; and too [*recte* 'and also'] it was difficult to account how many oferings both cowes, horses, and monyes were bestowed to God's honor for his soule …75

Regarding the above descriptions, the caveat should be entered that these funeral rituals were performed in a distinctively Irish (as opposed to English) social context. While the same trends may be evident in both, other influential factors — standards of wealth, for example — were not necessarily equivalent, and my research has not unearthed any descriptions of an Irish medieval funeral which rivals the opulence of some which were recorded for this period in England. Having said this, I must note that the fact that no description has managed to survive does not conclusively prove that one was never written, or that such opulent funerals never occurred in medieval Ireland. It should also be noted that the very idea of opulence is highly subjective, and depends on an individual society's standards of wealth and luxury: what is judged to be shabby and poor in one cultural context may be perceived as rich and rare in another.

---

73 '… dominus Nicholaus de Verdona apud Droukeda cum magno apparatu et solempni funere et multorum procerum conventu honorifice sepelitur'. Ibid., p. 34.   74 *AConn, s.a.* 1460.3.   75 *AMacF, s.a.* 1464; also *AFM, s.a.* 1464 (p. 1028, note 'y').

FUNERAL FEASTING

Adomnán's 'Life of St Columba' of Iona in Scotland tells of substantial quantities of food being consumed at a funeral at that foundation

> After some time, the saint foreseeing in the spirit the thief's imminent death, sent to Baíthéne, then living as prior in the plain of Long, and bade him send to that thief a fat beast and six measures of grain, as last gifts. When Baíthéne had dispatched these as the saint had asked him to do, the pitiful thief was found overtaken by sudden death on that day; and the gifts that had been sent were used at his funeral.[76]

Conversely, the rule enforced at the monastery at Tallaght, Co. Dublin, at the time of Bishop Maelruain (d. 792) prohibited the eating of meals in a monastery when a dead body was present.[77] This may have an interesting parallel in a story preserved in the 'Yellow Book of Lecan' which reads:[78]

> Then his cry of lament was raised, his grave made, and his stone set up, and to the end of three days no calf was let to their cows by the men of Ulster, to commemorate him.

The tradition of the 'funeral feast' is an ancient one, traceable to pre-Christian Rome, and there are indications that food was also connected with medieval Irish burial ritual.

Native Irish legal glosses require that payment for the burial of a *manach* (serf) included 'seven loaves and a funeral feast'.[79] The payment of these loaves was due after a week, and the feast after a month. This 'funeral feast' may have been a part of the 'month's mind' commemoration of the burial, or it may be that the period of a month was needed to locate and assemble the food.

In 1488, the Anglo-Irish lord Thomas de Bermingham and his wife made arrangements to supply eighteen 'milch-cows' as a funeral offering, an unspecified quantity of wax, a 'pipe' of wine and other beverages, twenty crannocks of

---

76 *Adomnán's Life of Columba*, eds Anderson & Anderson, §42b, pp 74–7: 'Quibus a Baitheneo sicut sanctus commendaverat transmisís ea die inventus este morte subita praeventus furax misellus; et in exequiis ejus transmisa expensa sunt xenia.' **77** 'Now to eat a meal with a dead man (though saintly) in the house is forbidden; but instead there are to be prayers and psalm-singing on such occasions', Gwynn & Purton, 'The Monastery of Tallaght', p. 153, §65. See above, Chapter 2, n. 164. The eleventh-century monastic constitutions of Lanfranc of Canterbury, based on monastic rule in France, do not prohibit eating, but dictate that if brothers were in the refectory when the 'board was sounded' announcing the death of one of their brethren, they were to 'wash their hands and return thither to resume the unfinished meal'. *Monastic constitutions of Lanfranc*, p. 125. **78** 'Death of Conla', ed. & trans. Meyer, p. 13. **79** Etchingham, 'Aspects of early ecclesiastical organisation', p. 138.

wheat, as well as meats and other comestibles from their own stocks for the sustenance of the brothers and the poor for eight days after the burial of their son John de Bermingham.[80] The English custom of enticing the poor to mourn the deceased with gifts of clothes and food has been cited above.[81] Into the twentieth century, paid keeners received food and drink at Irish wakes and funerals where the corpse was present.[82]

FUNERAL OFFERINGS

The evidence regarding funeral offerings provides another way to assess the rising importance of, and the increasing expenditures on, Irish funerals. By 1267, these were perceived to be becoming so exorbitant that the mayor and citizens of Dublin attempted to limit the funeral offerings made to the Church. Fearing the loss of income these provided, Archbishop Fulk de Sandford waged a vigorous protest, and the suggested limits were not enacted.[83] The same objections were registered by English parishioners in both Grantham and Grimsby, around 1300.[84] That funeral offerings grew increasingly excessive in Ireland in subsequent years is verified by a report dated 1305 that Michael le Browne, knight and secretary to the king, was buried in the church of St Francis, Dublin 'with more solemnity and a greater number of wax lights than was ever before seen on like occasion in this kingdom',[85] and also by the will of John Hammond of Dublin, written in 1388, in which the enormous sum of £50 was left for candles.[86]

THE PHRASE 'HONOURABLE BURIAL'

The words 'honour' and 'veneration' are commonly used by the Irish annalists to describe burial ritual. They make their first appearance in the Irish annals in 758, and are next found in *AFM s.a.* 921 and 933. Each of these references describes the burial of a member of the native Irish privileged classes (royalty, high-ranking clerics), which is not surprising since the aristocracy and high-level ecclesiastics are virtually the only people whose burials are mentioned in

---

80 'Item praedicti (Thomas Bermingham ac Anabala Edmundi de Burgo ejus uxor) dederunt dicte Conventui post mortem Johannis Bremigham filii et haeredis ipsorum die sepulturae ipsius decemocto lactiferas oblationibus et cera non computatis et per octo dies continuos post ipsius sepulturaram in eodem conventu morantes unam pipam vini cum aliis poculentis et viginti cranocis frumentineis in sustentationem Fratrum et pauperum supergredientium omissis carnibus et aliis esculentis de propriis bonis distribuebant.' *Reg. Mon. Athenry*, p. 219. 81 See n. 56 above. 82 Ó Suilleabháin, *Irish wake amusements*, p. 149. 83 *Crede mihi*, ed. Gilbert, pp 103–4. 84 Murphy, 'The high cost of dying', p. 114. 85 *Mon. Hib.*, II, p. 75, c.f. Harris' *Collectanea*, II, p. 311. 86 *Calendar of the ancient records of Dublin*, i, p. 123.

the chronicles. However the second use of this phrase in 921 is notable because it occurs in conjunction with the burial of a woman: Lighach, daughter of Flann [king Flann Sinna], who was 'buried with great veneration at Cluain-mic-Noise' (*7 ro i hadhnacht co nairmitin móir hi cCluain mic Nóis*).[87] The similarity of this phrase to the one used to describe the wake of Brian Bóruma, the first king of all Ireland, prior to his burial at Armagh in 1014 is striking: 'Maelmuire and his clergy waked the bodies with great honour and veneration …' (*Maoilmaire co na ramhadh acc aire na ccorp co nonóir 7 co nairmittin mhóir* …).[88] The similarity of these entries does not suggest that noble women were regarded as 'inferior' to men a this time – at least not in death.

The first burial notice in the *ALC* is that of Brian Bóruma in 1014. The passage, written in Irish, changes to Latin to tell that the king was buried with 'honor proper to his position as king' (*propter honorem regis positi*). A similar phrase is employed by the author of the entry regarding Brian's death in the *AB*.[89] This feature is not uncommon in entries referring to burial.[90] *ALC* even employ both languages for the same word *s.a.* 1118, where we read that 'Diarmaid Ua Briain, king of Mumha … died (*dhéc*) at Cork', but that 'Maria … daughter of the king of Alba … *mortua est*'.

In *AFM*, a change in language occurs between the obituary of Ardghal MacLochalinn *s.a.* 1064, and that of Cellach, comarb of Patrick under 1129, when the Irish word for 'honor' changes from *onóir* to *honorach*. After this, the word *onóir* is never used again in connection with burial. Both *ALC* and *AU* employ the same Irish phrase (*adhnaiced go honórach*) in their entries regarding the burial of Cellach in 1129, while *AI* describe the burial using the Latin phrase *cum gloria*.

By 1188, *AFM* return to the Irish form used in 921 to record that Domhnall, the son of Aed Mac Lochlainn, Lord of Aileach was interred at Armagh 'with great honour and solemnity' ('*co nónoir, 7 co nairmhidhin móir*'); *ALC* and *AFM* also express this in Irish, but use the phrase *co honórach* ('honourably').[91] In 1385, another 'honourable' burial is noted in *AFM*, but the description of the burial as having been *co honórach* is applied not to a chieftain, king or cleric, but to 'Tany O'Mulconry' the chief poet (*ollav*) of Connacht. *AConn* also include O'Mulconry's burial notice, but does not express the sentiment under discussion here, nor is it found in his obituary in *AU*.

---

87 *AFM.* **88** *AFM, s.a.* 1014. **89** Freeman, 'The annals in Cotton MS. Titus A.XXV', XLI, (1924), p. 329: 'Brian mac Chennetig meic Lorcain … ro hadlaichit gu honorach iat 7 cu uasal ormitnech ard.' **90** *Occisi sunt, sepultus est* and *quievit* are found throughout. It is interesting to note that in the seventeenth-century transcription of the *AClon* (*s.a.* 1251) the obituary for Clarus of Elphin (*s.a.* 1251), is rendered completely in Latin, for which there is no comparison in the entire chronicle, excepting the entry in 1210 recording the death of Richard Tuite at Athlone castle. **91** There is a lacuna here in the *AI*; *AU* records that the burial was completed *co honorach*.

In 1249, *AFM*, *AConn*, and *ALC* note the burial of Mulkieran O'Lenaghan, a 'noble priest of Tuam-mna',[92] and for the first time, the word *uasal* appears in relation to burial. The passage in *AFM* reads *a adhlucad co husassal onorach*, while *AConn* offers *adnacal co huasal onórach*; the same phrase is also used in *ALC*.[93] It could be that this appearance of the word *uasal*, meaning 'noble' may indicate that the burial ritual was becoming longer and/or more complex, or being influenced by European concepts of nobility. The appearance of the word *uasal*, meaning 'high' (and also 'noble', for example, *duine uasal*, meaning 'gentleman') in a burial-related context is interesting. It was at this time that concepts of nobility were becoming more complex, and elaborate burial rituals were being developed to reflect this. The word also appears in the mid-thirteenth century – the same period to which the first Irish-carved effigies are dated, showing that 'Anglo-Norman' funerary art was also being adopted by the native Irish. Perhaps the appearance of the phrase '*co uasal*' in 1249 and other changes in the 'language of burial' also reflect the adoption of 'Anglo-Norman' social customs.

DISHONORABLE BURIAL

Not all bodies were buried 'with honour and veneration'. Some were disposed of in ways which were clearly intended to publicly dishonour the deceased and humiliate the affiliated kin-group. The written sources refer to a number of instances in which this was done, some of which may preserve vestiges of pre-Christian burial practice.

Separate burial of parts of the body
The Christian belief in the literal physical resurrection on the Day of Judgement made it very important that the body be whole at the time of burial or at least that all of the parts of the body be interred together. However, the historical record offers evidence that this was not always achieved, and that sometimes the separation of various parts of the body prior to burial was done intentionally. Paradoxically, while this was sometimes done to humiliate the deceased and the kin-group, it could also indicate that the person – and the remains – were held in high esteem.

The 'Life of St Ruadan', who in the sixth century established the religious foundation at Lorrha, Co. Tipperary, contains a prophecy made to King Diarmait which emphasizes the horror of not being buried 'intact':

---

92 'Tuam-mna' is near Carrick-on-Shannon, Co. Offaly. **93** This entry does not occur in the *AI*.

thy thigh, which was raised before me shall not be buried in the same place with thy body, but a man shall cast it in sheep's ordure.[94]

The text goes on to report that 'King Diarmait fell at Rath-Beag in Ulster. His head was cut off and sent to Clonmacnoise for interment, while his body as buried in Connor'.

In Celtic culture, the head was considered the most important part of the body. Pádraig Lionard has suggested that small recumbent slabs of the type found at Clonmacnoise and other early Christian sites may originally have been placed over the head of the deceased, often identifying him or her with the sign of the cross and a name.[95] The heads of chieftains and warriors were flaunted (it is supposed) in order to shame opponents, and the portability of a severed head made it especially suitable as a trophy of war.

Christianity enhanced the meaning of head-stealing because medieval Christians believed a corpse without a head would not be able to enjoy physical resurrection on the Day of Judgment. A variety of sources indicate that the Celtic cult of the head was still being practiced in Ireland in the Middle Ages and later, and some of the passages indicating this have already been noted in this chapter.

In 1185, Gilla-Crist Mac Cathmail 'head of counsel of the north of Ireland', was killed and his head was taken. The fact that it was obtained by his people a month later, may suggest that it had been held for ransom.[96] The Anglo-Irish chronicle, 'Grace's Annals' contains numerous mentions of heads being taken as trophies by Irishmen and Englishmen alike between 1315 and 1318. Under 1315, for example, it records that Edmund Butler retaliated against the O'More's depredations in Laois by killing 'a great number' and bringing back 'eight-hundred heads to Dublin'.[97] The year 1315 seems to have been a fine year for head-harvesting: William Comyn slew O'Byrne and twelve of his men and 'brought their heads to Dublin', the Irish of Uí Máil 'attacked Tullow, and lost 400 men, whose heads were brought to Dublin'; and

> John Hussee, butcher of Athenry, by the orders of his lord went from Athenry by night to look of O'Kelly among the dead … he slew his own servant, then O'Kelly and his servant; he brought back their three heads to his lord; for this deed he was knighted and gifted with great estates.[98]

The account of the battle of Magh Rath notes 'thereafter the heads were brought before Domnall son of Aed'[99] and goes on to record:

94 *Lives*, ed. & trans. Plummer, I, pp 316–29; II, pp 308–20.   **95** Lionard, 'Early Irish', p. 100.
96 *AU, s.a.* 1185.   **97** *Annales Hiberniae*, ed. & trans. Butler, *s.a.* 1315.   **98** Ibid., *s.a.* 1316.
99 Marstrander, 'A new version of the battle of Mag Rath', pp 242–3.

Then Comgal was brought into the abandoned fortress and they washed him and his head was placed upon the mound of the rath.[100]

In 1318, after Edward Bruce failed in his attempt to subjugate Ireland, his head, hands and heart were brought to Dublin, while his limbs were sent to different places.[101] In 1317, Sir John Athy took as prisoner the pirate Thomas Don, killed him along with some forty of his men, and brought their heads to Dublin.[102] The *Caithréim Thoirdhealbhaigh* contains numerous descriptions of heads being collected as trophies in the late thirteenth and early fourteenth centuries,[103] and other sources make it clear that the practice was not uncommon through the end of the fifteenth century.

The diversity of these sources, combined with the fact that these activities are noted throughout the six centuries which are the focus of this study, leaves little doubt that the practice was not a rare aberration.[104] It also leaves little doubt that archaeologists should expect to find decapitated heads and headless bodies, especially in administrative centres like Dublin and native Irish strongholds. The skull-burial surrounded by rib- and hip-bones excavated by Etienne Rynne at Ballinlough in 1962 and my suggestion that it could possibly be of a far later date than originally thought has been discussed above.[105] Excavations such as the one at Isolde's Tower on the south bank of the River Liffey in Dublin have uncovered the remains of bodies which had probably been hung from the city walls, and may have been decapitated.[106]

The written sources contain a few reports of the head and body of one person being buried separately. The earliest is a chronicle entry *s.a.* 900 that tells

---

100 Ibid., pp 244–5. **101** *Annales Hiberniae*, ed. & trans. Butler, *s.a.* 1318. **102** Ibid., *s.a.* 1317. **103** 'Bestir yourselves now like men and, these nobles being prize of war, strip them; their notables' heads take', *Caithr. Th.*, *s.a.* 1279, I, p. 15; II, pp 16–17; 'the heads and battle-spoils were brought to be exposed upon the green', ibid., *s.a.* 1304, I, p. 26; II, p. 28; 'the good chieftain was beheaded and, for fear lest his friends might recover him, he also was not left both head and body in one place'; ibid., *s.a.* 1312, I, p. 59; II, p. 56; 'they made incredible slaughter of the enemy … each one of them according as he felt death upon him would either hand carry to the Shannon's brink a head to hold up and show to his noble lords, then heave them from him to sink in the abyss', ibid., *s.a.* 1313, I, p. 75; II, p. 68; 'from among those heroes to seek out and to set aside your own dead friends; to count the spoils and heads', ibid., *s.a.*, 1317, I, p. 117; II, p. 104; a sudden and successful effort from which he brought back divers loads of heads to exhibit to his own side. This hardy exploit gained him worship in the sight of those battalions …', ibid., I, p. 92; II, p. 85. **104** See *AConn s.a.* 1462; *AFM, s.a.* 535, 1000, 1062, 1072, 1085, 1089, 1172, 1266, 1452, 1468; *AI s.a.* 1073; *Annals of Ireland* (Dowling), ed. & trans. Butler *s.a.* 1341; 'A new … battle of Magh Rath', ed. & trans. marstrander, pp 261, 275; *FAII*, p. 67, s.a 1457; *Calendar of Documents, Ireland*, ed. Sweetman & Hadcock, 29 Dec. 1250, no. 3090; *MacCarthaig's Book*, *s.a.* 1394; Molyneux, *Journey to Connaught*, p. 164; *Song of Dermot and the Earl*, ed. & trans. Orpen, p. 111; *Scottish verse*, ed. & trans. Watson, IX, st. 4; *Suibhne Geilt*, ed. & trans. J.G. O'Keeffe, p. 131; *AMacF* and *AFM s.a.* 1452; *AConn*, *s.a.* 1462. **105** See above, Chapter 2, n. 36. **106** Simpson, *The excavations*.

how the head of Cormac mac Cuileannáin, the king/bishop of Cashel, was delivered to Flann 'king of Ireland' so that he could follow custom and crush the foe's head with his thigh. The chronicler reported that Flann condemned this practice, took Cormac's head in his hands, and kissed it as a mark of honor. He then carried the 'consecrated head' around him three times, after which Cormac's head was taken to be reunited with the body, and buried in Dísert Diarmata (Castledermot, Co. Kildare).[107] It is obvious that this story is intended to prove that Flann was a good and Christian king, and the incident may be entirely fictitious. However, there would have been alternative ways of communicating this point; also, the statement that the skull of a vanquished opponent was ritualistically crushed, displayed as a trophy of war, or otherwise dishonoured is consonant with references regarding 'trophy' heads that date to as late as the fifteenth century, and of which there are doubtless later examples.[108]

There appear to have been three different and contradictory reasons why head and body might be buried separately. The first would be to show dishonor to the deceased and his kin. The head was regarded as a battle trophy, and stealing the head from the body was a customary way to emphasize dominance and sovereignty over a tribe defeated in battle, and to publicize its disgrace. However, the heads and bodies of mighty warriors and kings were sometimes buried separately because of a desire to possess their relics, believed to contain prophylactic powers.[109] Gaining the corpse of a powerful person was an important way for a religious foundation to ensure its future economic viability and survival, since the grave of an important person greatly enhanced a foundation's reputation for sanctity and power. Where progenitor was buried, progeny generally followed. A long series of family or kin-group interments, at least some of whom could be counted on to make substantial bequests both pre- and post-mortem, could guarantee the survival and continued prestige of a foundation.

Accounts of the separate burial of head and body occur in the annals as early as 558 when Diarmaid, the son of Fergus Cerrbél, who had been 'twenty years in sovreignty over Ireland' is reported to have been killed in Antrim by Aed Dubh, the Cruithin over-king of Dalriada. *AFM* state that his head was brought to Clonmacnoise for burial and his body interred at Connor, Co. Antrim.[110] This particular division of body and head could have been effected for the purpose

---

107 *FAII, s.a.* 900 (*recte* 908).   **108** See p. 98 above.   **109** Charles-Edwards, 'boundaries', p. 87.   **110** *AFM, s.a.* 558: 'After Diarmaid, the son of Fearghus Cerrbheoil, had been twenty years in sovereignty over Ireland he was slain by Aedh Dubh, son of Suibhne, King of Dal-Araidhe, at Rath-beag, in Magh-Line. His head was brought to Cluain-mic-Nois, and interred there, and his body interred at Connor'. St Ciarán was Diarmaid's friend, and Connor was near the place where he was killed. *SG*, II, p. 517: 'Thus perished the king (Dermot; and his body was consumed all but the head which with his relics was carried to Clonmacnoise and buried in (the slope called the "claen ferta", or otherwise the "céite", for there it was that he (what time he fasted in "eglais bheg", whereby he was healed of his headsickness after he had done

of increasing Diarmaid's chances of achieving heaven by being buried under the protection of two powerful saints (e.g. in two separate graveyards), and of increasing his kin-group's sphere of influence. *AClon* state that Diarmaid had requested that his head be interred at Clonmacnoise, the monastery of his friend, St Ciarán. Since Connor was near the place where Diarmait was killed, expediency may have helped determine where his body was buried.

The entry in *FAII* regarding the burial in 902 of Cormac mac Cuillennáin provides the first clear sign that the choice of burial place had become politicized. Cormac had requested that, if possible, his body should be brought to Cloyne, Co. Cork, for burial. His second choice was to be buried at Dísert Diarmata (Castledermot, Co. Kildare), 'where he had studied for a long time' because 'it was the burial place of Colmán MacLenine'. The entry gives no reason why Cormac was not buried at Cloyne; it says only that Móenach *preferred* to bury him at Dísert Diarmata. The reasons would seem to be political: Cormac was both king and bishop, and Dísert Diarmata was a church controlled by the *familia* of Comgall, to which Móenach belonged.[111] The collection of Irish canon law known as the *Collectio canonum Hibernensis* specifies that if an ecclesiastical subject departs from one abbot to another, the first abbot (if he has not tacitly approved the second vow) is to be left the subject's goods upon his death, and his body, clothing, horse and cow is to go to the second abbot.[112] This obligation may also have had some bearing on the decision to bury Cormac at Dísert Diarmata, since Cormac had studied there.

The three-fold advantages (spiritual, political and financial) of burying strong leaders in two places continued for many centuries. For example, *AFM* record that in 1068, after Murchadh Ua Briain, the grandson of King Brian Bóruma, was slain by the men of Tethba, his head was buried in Clonmacnoise and his body in the important Columban foundation of Derry.[113] The story of 'Mac Dá cherda and Cumainne Foda' tells that when Mac Ochtraig (MacGerrity) died

> the communities of Fid Dun and Lismore were contending for his corpse. They were a whole fortnight around the 'dun' and the community of Fid Dun stole it [the body] through the 'liss' at the back, put it in a vessel, and buried it at Fid Dun.[114]

his fasting against the saints of Ireland, his cure having previously been denied him) had elected to be laid'. In Irish, *SG*, i, p. 82: 'Marbtar ocus loiscter corp in rígh ann a négmais a chind. Dobretha iar sin a chend ocus a thaissi co cluain mac Nóis cor hadhnaicedh isin chlaoin ferta nó isin céiti. Ár is ann ro thogh féin a adnacal in tan do throiscc I neglais bicc dia ro híccadh do'n chenngalur iar fertain a throisci fri noemaib Erenn ocus iar néimded a ícca co riacht sin.' **111** *FAII, s.a.* 908 (*recte* 902). This is discussed in greater detail, in the 'Transportation' section of this chapter. See notes 163 & 164 below. **112** Etchingham, 'Aspects of early ecclesiastical organisation', p. 334; see also Ó Corráin, 'Early Irish Churches', pp 327–41. **113** *AFM, s.a.* 1068. **114** 'Mac Dá Cherda and Commaine Foda', ed. & trans. J.G. O'Keeffe, pp 39. *Fid Dun* is now Fiddown, Co. Kilkenny.

When the body of Hugh de Lacy, the conqueror of Meath, was recovered in 1198, two foundations vied for its possession, with the head receiving burial in the church of St Thomas, Dublin, and the body in Bective Abbey, Co. Meath.[115] The dispute went on for years, and was ultimately resolved when de Lacy's body was also interred at St Thomas'. Women's remains might also be considered valuable, as is shown by the dispute which arose in 1318 when the Friars Preachers of Mullingar refused to give up the body of Rosín de Verdun, who had left her body to be buried with the Friars Minors of Trim.[116]

In 1070, Connor Ua Maelshechlainn, king of Tara was slain by his brother's son. His head was stolen from its grave at Clonmacnoise by Toirrdelbach Ua Briain (Turlough O'Brien), who took it to his royal stronghold at Kincora on Good Friday. The prestigious trophy was retrieved by Easter, and the Uí Maelshechlainn also brought home two golden rings for their troubles.[117] The outrage caused by the theft of the head of a dead ruler is also preserved in a poem dating to the mid-thirteenth century, where we read of the distress caused by the transportation of the head of Brian O'Neill, king of Cenel-Eoghan, to London. It also specifically notes that the insult of having Brian's head buried separate from his body was exacerbated by the fact that it rested 'in a foreign church.'[118]

The burial of Melachlainn Macnamara's head and body at different spots is recorded in the *Caithréim Thoirdhealbhaigh* under the year 1312.[119] The author makes it clear that this was done 'for fear lest his friends recover him'. Again, this would have been done as an insult, since it prevented Macnamara's people from giving him a proper and honorable Christian burial. The same source also contains numerous examples of the beheading of enemy soldiers in the thirteenth and fourteenth centuries and clearly makes the point that heads were trophies of war.[120] The mid-fifteenth century case of Farrell Roe Oge Mageoghegan is unusual: Mageoghegan, a native Irish chieftain, was killed and beheaded in 1452 by the Anglo-Irish grandsons of Pierce Dalton. His head was carried to Trim and then to Dublin where it was exhibited. After an 'example' had been made of it, Macgeoghegan's head was 'brought back and buried along with the body' in Durrow, Co. Offaly.[121] This is the only record I have found for the burial of a head after public execution. By way of comparison, we may consider *Tobar na Ceann* 'the well of heads', near Inverary in Argyllshire, Scotland. It was at this site in 1663 – more than 200 years after Macgeoghegan's head was exhibited as a trophy – that Ian *Lom*, the poet of Clann MacDonnell, washed the severed heads of seven men who had murdered his chieftain, Alasdair MacDonnell,

115 *Chartularies of St Mary's Abbey, Dublin*, ii, pp 221, 276, 307. **116** *Cal. Pap. Reg.*, 2 John XXII, Kal. Jan. 1318, p. 171. **117** *CS, s.a.* 1070, also *AT, s.a.* 1073. **118** Mac Con Midhe, *The poems*, ed. J.G. O'Keeffe, poem XII, st. 4. 'To take Briain's head to London was as bad a hurt / as all that the Foreigner's did ...' **119** *Caithr. Th.*, I, p. 59; II, p. 56. **120** See p. 98 above. **121** *AFM, s.a.* 1452.

before presenting them to Glengarry. Today, a monument capped with a carving of the seven heads hanging from a dirk by their hair stands over the spring.[122]

Skulls were not the only parts of an enemy's corpse which were collected and displayed. Under 936, *AClon* record that the king of Ulster, 'Moraugh mcNeale' and his men, carried the bones of

> Kearvall mcMoregan 'king of Leinster' with them to the north, and there artificially caused to be made a payer [pair] of tables of the said kings [*sic*] bones, which for a very long time after was kept as a monument in the king of Ulsters [*sic*] house …

The story may be apocryphal, but this same treatment of bones is also mentioned by the thirteenth-century poet Giolla Brighde Mac Con Midhe as a mortal insult, eventually repaid in the battle of Down in 1260.[123]

Outright mutilation of corpses was also practiced. For example, 'Grace's annals' record that in 1318, Richard de Clare's body was 'cut into small pieces through hatred'. No mention is made of any type of burial, though the entry records that the rest of his men were buried in Limerick. The excavations at Hulton abbey in England, which was founded by Heny de Audley in 1219, provide a comparative example. Among the thirty-two burials excavated in the chancel, south transept and crossing, one skeleton, was found whose 'head had been cut off and the body split down the middle, his remains were buried in the chancel'.[124]

'Multiple' burial

The burial of different parts of the corpse in different locations came into fashion among Continental and English royalty and nobles in the twelfth century and generally seems to have been a means of improving their chances of attaining heaven, impressing their status and dominance upon a larger segment of the populace, and placating the ardent desires of religious foundations for relics of the rich and powerful.

Scotland provides two well-known examples of heart-burial. King Robert Bruce's deathbed request was honoured in 1330 when his heart was 'taken from his body, embalmed, and carried to the Holy Sepulchre [Jerusalem]', while his body was interred in the Scottish abbey of Dunfermline. His heart was eventually brought back to Scotland and buried in Melrose Abbey.[125] The powerful

---

122 Moncrieffe of that Ilk, *The Highland clans*, p. 128.   **123** Mac Con Mide, 'Poem on the battle of Dun', p. 162, lines 153–6: 'Chess of the shin-bones of Leinstermen / in our workshop was constructed / smooth chessmen were on the tables of our ancestors / of the bones of Leinstermen'.   **124** Klemperer, 'The study of burials at Hulton Abbey', p. 86. According to Kelmperer, the most likely identification is with William Audley, who had been killed in 1282 when his unit of the English army was massacred by the Welsh.   **125** G.W.S. Barrow, *Robert Bruce*, p. 323. Bruce had long had a desire to fight the 'saracens' in the Crusades. In

Douglas family (Sir James Douglas had been given the honour of bearing Robert Bruce's heart to Jerusalem) made separate heart burial something of a tradition, the most notable example of this being the burial of the heart of the notorious Archibald Douglas, the fifth Earl of Angus. His heart was interred at the family's parish church at Douglas in Renfrewshire, while his body was laid to rest in the monastery at Whithorn in Galloway.[126]

Separate burial of the heart was already an accepted custom in eleventh-century Germany and was known in Italy, but it was not adopted in northwestern Europe until about 1200. Richard I, King John, and King Philip IV of France are among the many documented examples of people whose hearts and bodies were buried separately.[127] Separate burial of entrails also began to be practiced in England at about this time. Probably the most notable example is the triple burial given to the English queen, Eleanor of Castile. After her death in Lincolnshire in 1299, Eleanor's body (which had been stuffed with barley) was entombed in Westminster, and her entrails were buried in Lincolnshire, in a tomb of Purbeck marble said to be more grandiose than the tomb encasing her heart, which was buried at Blackfriar's.[128]

Pope Boniface VIII was clearly concerned about the growth of these practices, and in 1299, he stigmatized the dismemberment of corpses on the grounds that it was against Canon law.[129] However, his pronouncements were soon relaxed by Benedict XI to appease Philip IV of France, no doubt in consideration of the financial advantages the church stood to gain by having more than one burial place for the wealthy and influential, and presumably the additional bequests and endowments which presumably accompanied them.

Given that a good deal of evidence exists for the separate burial of head and body in medieval Ireland, it is noteworthy that the Irish sources I have consulted do not contain any references to the separate burial of hearts or entrails. There is, however, some art-historical evidence for such burials: John Hunt has suggested that a miniature effigy of a man at Gowran, Co. Kilkenny, dated to the mid-thirteenth century, may commemorate a heart burial,[130] and the shrine containing the heart of St Laurence O'Toole is on view in Christchurch cathedral in Dublin, though he did not die in Ireland, but at Eu, in Normandy.

1330, Sir James Douglas began his journey to Jersualem with the king's heart. However, he was slain in battle and both his bones and Robert Bruce's heart were brought back to Scotland by Sir William Keith of Galston. Sir James was buried in the parish kirk of Douglas. Bruce's body 'was laid beneath the middle of the choir in the abbey church [at Dunfermline, which had by that time become the traditional burial-place of Scottish kings] and over [his body] was placed a "fair tomb" which the king had ordered to be made in Paris'. **126** Maxwell, *A history of the house of Douglas*, p. 22. Archibald Douglas' precise date of death is uncertain; he may have died in 1513, but 'in any event he was dead before 31 Jan [1514]'. **127** Hallam, 'The Eleanor crosses and royal burial customs', p. 16. **128** Ibid., pp 9–10; Daniell, *Death and burial*, p. 122. **129** Ibid., p. 16. **130** Hunt, *Irish medieval figure sculpture*, fig. 68, cat. no. 100.

'Defensive' burial

Charles Thomas-Edwards has noted that, in pagan Ireland (and possibly pagan Britain as well)

> The dead warded off the outsider from the land and thus protected the rights of their heirs; and this belief provided the basis for the part of the procedure for claims to land which showed the basis of any lawful claim; hereditary right.[131]

It seems that graves were often also used to guard the boundaries of the kindred's land,[132] and sources tell of burials made in ramparts, which also supports the idea that burials were thought to have defensive properties.

The 'Life of Maedoc of Ferns' tells how the 'race of Aed Finn' regarded the 'cemetery of the high kings' at Drumlane, Co. Cavan: 'to them it is a defence'.[133]

The poem 'Magh Dumach' tells of

> Mag Dumach of the bands that own it by right: after slaughter of armies, many are the stony grave-mounds therein, now turned to ramparts.[134]

The burial of warrior-kings in a defensive standing posture is also known. John O'Donovan noted that 'this custom of thus interring Irish kings and chieftains in a standing position is often referred to in Irish historical tales'.[135] Oengus mac Nad Froích, said to have given the Aran islands to St Éndae, was also believed to have been buried in a standing position facing north 'under the couch of the kings at Cashel' due to the enmity between Munster and Leth Cuinn.[136] Tírechán's 'Life of St Patrick', written in the late seventh century, tells that Loegaire, the king of Tara, refused to be baptized because his father Niall Noígiallach ('Niall of the Nine Hostages', who died *c.*450) had forbidden him to become Christian to prevent him from being interred in a Christian cemetery. Such an interment would have prevented him from fulfilling his duty to be buried standing and fully armed in the ramparts of Tara, facing Mullaghmast, home of Dúnlang of Leinster, who was the leader of the hereditary enemies of Loegaire's people.[137]

Similarly, Eogan Bél, a sixth-century king of Connaght is said to have

---

131 Charles-Edwards, 'Boundaries', p. 87. **132** Ibid., pp 83–7. **133** 'Life of Maedoc of Ferns (II)', *Lives*, I, p. 284: 'An chlannmaicne, doibh as díon / roimh adhlaicthe na naird-riogh'; II, p. 276. **134** 'Magh Dumach', *Met. Dind.*, IV, p. 263. **135** *Hy-Fiachrach*, p. 471. This practice is also known in the literature of Celtic Britain. In the 'Mabinogion' we read that the head of Bendigeid Vran, buried in the White Mount, protected Britain from attack: 'Branwen Daughter of Llyr', *Maginogion*, ed. & trans. Jones & Jones, pp 37–40. **136** Byrne, *Irish kings*, p. 194. **137** Bieler, *The Patrician Texts*, p. 133; Byrne, *Irish kings*, p. 65.

ordered himself to be interred in a standing position, with his red javelin in his hand, with his face turned towards Ulster, as if fighting with his enemies. This was done, and the talismanic result was, that as long as the body was left in that position the Connacians could not be defeated by the Ultonians, but whenever they came in collision the Ultonians were defeated by the Connacians. The Ultonians, on learning the cause of this, disinterred the body of Eoghan Beul, and carrying it north of the Co. Sligo, buried it with the face under, at the cemetery of Aonach Locha Gile near Lough Gill, in the present county of Sligo.[138]

An episode in the "Life of St Berach', records that after Cú-Allaid was killed in *Mag na Fert* ('plain of the graves'), he was carried up to a bluff in the mountains, because he had requested the opportunity to overlook the land of St Berach and curse it. The author tells that Cú-Allaid died there but not specifically that he was buried there and if so, whether he was buried standing or supine.[139] The reference to kerne (light-armed Irish foot-soldiers) being buried in earth 'heaped rampartwise', after the 'Battle of the Abbey' in Co. Clare in 1317, suggests that the custom of siting graves in ramparts was still being practiced at that time.[140]

P.W. Joyce notes a report that in 1848 a tumulus called Croghan Erin, located near Kilmessan in the parish of Kiltale, Co. Meath, was opened and a skeleton was found standing erect in a grave.[141] The latest mention of standing burial in Ireland is a non-contemporaneous account which refers to William Burke, one of the first wave of the 'Anglo-Norman invaders' (d. 1205/6), who was said to have been buried 'as he himself had prescribed ... in a standing posture for fear lest any man of the Maineachs [denizens of Uí Maine, or 'O'Kelly's country'] should trample him'.[142]

Women may also have been buried standing. Archdall reports that in the mid-nineteenth-century a body buried in a standing position at 'Temple Faratagh' in Armagh was discovered; it was believed to be that of St Patrick's sister, St Lupita.[143]

---

138 *The genealogies*, ed. O'Donovan, p. 471. **139** *Lives*, II, p. 37, §72. For dating, see Kenney, *Sources*, pp 402–3. **140** *Caithr. Th.*, I, p. 120; ii, p. 107. **141** Joyce, *A social history*, II, p. 552. **142** 'Genealolgy of the Burkes', *Caithr. Th.*, I, p. 153: '... do hádhlaiceadh Uilliam na seasadh fá mar do orrdaigh s'féin, d'eagla gu saltóradh énduine do mhaineachaibh air'; II, p. 163. Puckle noted that the poet Ben Jonson d. 1637) was buried standing in Westminster Abbey (presumably to economize on space), and the burial in Scotland of a 'Richard Hull' (no date given) who had been buried 'beneath the curious stone tower on Leith Hill, upside down on horseback so he would have advantages on Judgement Day when the world would be reversed'; see *Funeral customs*, pp 160–1. **143** A. Gwynn & Hadcock, *Irish medieval*, p. 313, cf. *Mon. Hib.*, I, p. 49. See Chapter 4, n. 128, of this book.

Burning of bodies

To date, Irish archaeological evidence has not been found for cremation after the fifth century AD.[144] However, hagiographical, poetic and historical sources indicate that corpses may sometimes have been cremated for the purpose of dishonoring their memory, and insulting their surviving kin.

The one extant hagiographical source we have for cremation appears in the second 'Life of Old St Ciarán of Saighir' (dated to the late sixteenth or seventeenth century, but based on earlier material), which records that Fergus Cindfaelad, chief of the king of Munster's household, strangled Ciarán's hospitaller. Ciarán retaliated by declaring that Fergus himself would be strangled as punishment, and that 'his body shall be burned in Rath Lochmaighe by the men of Eile'.[145] The literal medieval belief in the bodily resurrection of Christians necessarily precluded any hope that people who had been cremated could be resurrected on the Day of Judgment. Thus, by denying Fergus Christian burial and burning him like a pagan, Fergus was also pointedly denying Fergus the eternal life which Christian burial offered.

A poem included in the collection of the Dean of Lismore, which was written for the earl of Argyll exhorts the Earl to do the following to the *Sassenach* (English) invaders:

> Burn their women folk ungentle, burn their ungentle children; and burn their black houses, and rid us of the reproach of them … Send their ashes down the stream after burning of their bodies; show not pity for living Saxon …[146]

While caution must be used when interpreting hagiographical and poetical examples, these excerpts indicate that the medieval Irish regarded the burning of the body as the ultimate insult, and also suggest that it may have been done on occasion.

Historical sources provide an additional three examples of the burning of human remains. The first is an annalistic account that pre-dates this period so slightly that it seems to merit inclusion. It is the burning by the Fir Thulach in 891 of the writing and relics of St Finnian of Clonard, when the king of the Uí Failgi was killed in the church of Cluain Fota Fine Thulach.[147] Finnian was patron saint of the Uí Failgi, and in effect, their spiritual warlord. The burning of Finnian's relics would have been done to humiliate the Uí Failgi and deprive

---

144 E. O'Brien, 'Late prehistoric–early historic Ireland: the burial evidence reviewed', p. 54. 145 'The life of old St Ciarán of Saighir', *Lives*, II, p. 117. Plummer adds that '*Rath lochmaighe*' would seem to be at Eile, in the barony of Eliogarty, Co. Tipperary. 146 *Scottish verse*, ed. Watson, no. XX, '*Ar shlioct Gaodhal*', p. 163, st. 13 & 14. 147 *AU, s.a.* 890, *AFM, s.a.* 887, cited in P. Byrne, 'The community of Clonard', p. 541. The church of Cluain Fota Fine is Clonfad, Co. Westmeath (according to *AFM*, I, p. 541, note 'n').

them of their great cultural treasure as well as the supernatural power and protection the relics of St Finnian were believed to have provided.

Another example is found in *AFM* under 1500, where it is recorded that Barry Mór was killed by his own kinsman, David Barry, archdeacon of Cloyne and Cork. In retaliation, David himself was subsequently slain by Thomas Barry and the tribe (*muintir*) of O'Callaghan. Twenty days after David's murder, the earl of Desmond disinterred David's body, 'and afterwards burned it.'[148]

The *Caithréim Thoirdhealbhaigh* notes that in 1312, Lochlainn Mac Conmara was carried off by Hy-Blood 'for immolation', after first having been beheaded.[149] Under the year 1326 Thady Dowling records that Adam Niger (Adam Black or *Dubh*) O'Toole, who was believed to be possessed by Satan, was burned to death in Hogges Green (now 'College Green') in Dublin. No mention is made of what was done with his remains.[150]

Burial with an animal
Another way to dishonor a dead person (and thus grievously insult his kingroup) was to place the corpse in contact with an animal. Giraldus Cambrensis and the author of 'MacCarthaig's book' both recorded that Donnchad, father of Diarmait Mac Murchada, was buried under the Dublin assembly hall with a dead dog, 'as a mark of hatred and contempt'.[151] This type of insult was not unknown elsewhere in Europe, for example, Galbert of Bruges recorded that one of the murderers of Charles the Good, count of Flanders, was hanged without his breeches and a dog's intestines were then wrapped round his neck.[152]

SELECTION OF BURIAL PLACE,
TRANSPORTATION TO BURIAL, AND EMBALMING

Archaeologists Roberta Gilchrist and Richard Morris have argued that in Britain, conversion to Christianity must have been accomplished

---

148 *AFM, s.a.* 1500.   **149** *Caithr. Th.*, I, p. 59; II, p. 56.   **150** 'Adam Niger de familia de O Tooles in Lagenia spiritu satanicu obsessus negans incarnationem Christi … cremabatur in Hogges Greene juxta Dublin', *Clyn & Dowling, s.a.* 1326, p. 22.   **151** 'The English earl left the care of these, as well as of the town, in the hands of Diarmait MacMurchada to avenge the wicked slaying of his father by the people of Dublin … when a dead dog was buried with his body in the ground as a mark of hatred and contempt.' *MacCarthaig's book, s.a.* 1170. 'Diarmait … hated the citizens of Dublin … not without good reason. For in the middle of a large building, where it was their custom to sit as if before the *rostra* in the *forum*, they had buried his father, whom they had killed, along with a dog, thus adding insult to injury'. *Expugnatio Hibernica*, p. 67. (The reference in *MacCarthaig's book* is likely to have been derived from Cambrensis, see editor's note, p. x.)   **152** Galbert of Bruges, *The murder of Charles the Good*, pp 211-13.

Through existing frameworks of social behavior; that is through the customary formality of personal relationships. Any consciousness of the
Church as an institution must have been correspondingly slight ... to
what did the newly-baptized believe themselves to belong? A spiritual
family – a kin-group – headed by a heavenly lord fits the case.[153]

Historian Patrick Geary has noted that in the Middle Ages, when tradition was
passed on orally, the Church had enormous power to 'present and preserve the
structure of the family', creating:

> stability in the relationship between the living and dead, a stability that
> extends through the entire family structure, providing, before the reforms
> ... a core around which to organize continuity between past and future
> generations.[154]

Both of these views help explain why the church in which an individual was
buried held such enormous importance in medieval Irish culture, as well as how
much power the Church had as a result of its control of cemeteries and burial
ritual. The local church had the legal right to bury the corpse of anyone living
within its territory and to collect the related burial dues. The rules associated
with the ownership of the corpse and the burial fees are preserved in works
including the eighth-century collection of native Irish law known as the *Senchus
mór*, and the eighth-century *Collectio canonum Hibernensis*.[155] The *Senchus mór*
states that a 'will' originally meant that the deceased had 'left it on his tribe to
redeem him wherever he happens to be' and bring him back to his church for
burial, and that the body was literally said to 'belong' to that church.[156] Another
of its law tracts stipulates that if a person is wounded, and subsequently dies, the
'body-' or 'honour-price' of the person killed, are due to his original church
'because the body belongs to it'.[157]

A passage from the 'Brehon laws' indicates that there was some feeling that
churches were thought to be asking more than their fair share of the goods of
the deceased. It states that the territiorial church 'may not claim the property of
a dead man ... she is entitled to nothing but burial-clothes and seven cakes and
death feast ...'[158] The suggestion that the Church did not always fulfill its pastoral duties is also implied in this passage from the *Senchus mór*, which declare
that:

---

153 Gilchrist & Morris, 'Monasteries as settlements', p. 113.   **154** Geary, *Living with the dead*,
pp 91–91.   **155** For dating of the *Collectio Hibernensis*, see Kenney, *The sources*, pp 247–8.   **156**
Ancient laws of Ireland, ed. Atkinson, et al., I, pp 204–5.   **157** Ibid., III, pp 106–7: 'corab e in
tainmrainde sin ber don aithgin da eclais bunaid .i. uair is le in coland'.   **158** Ibid., V, p. 433:
'*Do fastad cirt ocus* dligid'. See section earlier in this chapter entitled 'Funeral Feasting'.

> ... the people have a right in the church ... the church is bound to give
> burial ... they demand their right from the church (regarding) baptism
> and communion and requiem of soul ...[159]

This statement is particularly interesting in light of a section of the seventh or
eighth century 'Rule of St Patrick' which, as previously noted, mentions no
obligation to bury the dead.[160]

People were supposed to be interred in their territorial churches. However,
as noted earlier, the choice of a particular burial place could be used to promote
the political aims of a powerful man or kin-group, and burial clearly seems to
have been exploited for these reasons from the very beginning of the period
presently under consideration. The first historical example of the selection of a
site other than the territorial church for a person's burial appears in connection
with Cormac mac Cuilennáin whose burial at Castledermot (*Dísert Diarmata*),
Co. Kildare, in 900 has been discussed earlier in this chapter.[161] Although Cormac
had preferred to be interred at Cloyne, Casterdermot was his second choice
because he had studied there. It may be that Cormac's reasoning reflected a custom
– or what later became a custom – that a monk should be buried where he had
been trained or ordained. Part of a monk's vows included the statement that he
was 'dead' to the world, a way of indicating that he had embarked on a new spiritual life.[162] Once spiritual vows had been taken, he was considered to have been
'reborn' and to have been provided by the Church with a new family. It is quite
possible that the religious foundation which had given him his new life was also
regarded as his new 'territorial' church. The case of Amhlaim Ua Muirethaigh,
bishop of Armagh, who died in 1185, makes it clear that his monastic family has
supplanted his biological one as far as burial ritual is concerned:

> He was carried honourably to Daire of Colum-cille and buried at the
> feet of his father, namely, the bishop Ua Cobhthaigh.[163]

This could also explain why two bishops of the isle of Man were buried at the
abbey of the Canons Regular at Bangor: Christian, who was interred at the
abbey *s.a.* 1179,[164] and Nicholas de Meaux, nephew of Olaf, king of Man, who
was buried there in 1215.[165] The chronicle states that both of these bishops were
natives of Argyllshire in western Scotland, so it is clear that Bangor was not their
territorial church. The great St Malachy had been abbot of the Augustinian

---

159 Ibid., III, p. 33, also *Corpus iuris Hibernici*, ed. D.A. Binchy, p. 529. For a more detailed consideration of the burial fees exacted by the church, see C. Etchingham, 'Aspects of early ecclesiastical organisation'. **160** 'The rule of Patrick', ed. & trans. O'Keeffe, §5–8, §12. **161** See
n. 110–11 above. **162** Finucane, 'Sacred corpse', p. 44. **163** *AU, s.a.* 1185. **164** A. Gwynn
& Hadcock, *Medieval religious*, p. 161. **165** *Chronica Regum Mannie et Insulae*, ed. Broderick, f.
50v & f. 51r. It is possible that the statement regarding Nicholas is wrong, since he appears to
have witnessed a deed in 1227. See A. Gywnn & Hadcock, *Medieval religious*, p. 161.

abbey at Bangor, and the fact that the abbot of Bangor enjoyed the townland of Clenanoy on the isle of Man shows a close connection between the two locations.[166] It may be that these bishops of Sodor were interred in the abbey at Bangor because they had been trained there.[167] There can be little doubt that this is how David Ua Bragar, bishop of Clogher, Co. Tyrone, came to be buried in the monastery of Mellifont, Co. Louth, in 1267. The annals record that this was done because 'he was a monk of its monks before that'.[168] Similarly, Dowling records *s.a.* 1414, that Thomas Fleming, the Augustinian bishop of Leighlin was buried at Kilkenny with the order to which he had been professed.[169]

King Brian Bóruma, provides another clear example of someone who used burial for political ends. Brian was of the Dál gCais kin-group whose territory was in Thomond in Munster, and whose family controlled the church of Killaloe, Co. Clare, where Brian's brother, Marcán, served as abbot.[170] Despite these strong connections, when Brian died in 1014, he was not buried at Killaloe – or even within in his own territory – but at Armagh, the great and powerful church of his subdued enemies, the northern Uí Néill. Brian had wooed Armagh in 1005 with a gift of twenty ounces of gold and supported its claims to the primacy of all Ireland.[171] Willing that his tomb be made at Armagh was Brian's final assertion of the supremacy of his line over the Uí Néill – and all of Ireland.

Written sources provide valuable insight into how the rules involving ownership of the corpse affected burial ritual. They reveal that Brian's body was not carried to Armagh by his own people, or even the clerics of Swords, Co. Dublin, where his body had been carried after his death. Instead, the archbishop and senior clerics of Armagh travelled south to Swords to take possession of Brian's corpse, which had become their legal property the moment he died.[172] The Armagh clerics' journey to Swords to collect Brian's corpse may have been an unusual act reserved only for extremely important people, and performed to ensure that the valuable royal remains were not stolen. Other sources may suggest that churchyards or cemeteries had a specific spot where the corpses of the deceased who 'belonged' to the churches in question were formally commended into their care.[173]

In or before 1133, Henry I of England made it clear to the bishop of London that chief barons and citizens of London could be buried in whichever church

---

166 *Mon. Hib.*, I, p 236; cf. King, p. 238. **167** *Calendar of papal letters to Scotland of Clement VII of Avignon*, ed. Burns (Scottish Historical Soc., Edinburgh, 1976) reveals another connection between Sodor and Ireland. In a letter dated 15 July 1387 Reg. Aven. 248, 153v.4: 'Michael, bishop of Sodor … removal of bishop John on account of his adherence to Bertolomeo Prignano [Urban VI]. Until now, Michael has been archbishop of Cashel in Ireland.' **168** *AU*, ed. Mac Carthy, II, *s.a.* 1267. **169** '… sepultus fuit in Kilkennia apud ordinem professionis sue'. **170** Ó Corráin, *Ireland before the Normans*, p. 127. **171** Ibid. **172** See the accounts of Brian's death and burial s.a. 1013 in *AI, AU, AFM, ALC*, & *Cogadh Gaedhel re Gallaibh* (*Wars of the Gaedhil with the Gaill*), ed. & trans. Todd, p. 211. **173** See section on 'pillarstones' in Chapter 4 below.

they wanted, provided that their own parish priest accompanied the corpse to burial.[174] In 1186 – more than 150 years after Brian's death – the *bulla* of Pope Urban III made it plain that corpses were regarded as the property of territorial churches, yet a provision was also made by which people could be buried at churches other than their 'own', just as Brian Bóruma had been. The *bulla* grants the people of Dublin 'freedom of sepulture, saving the mortuaries due to those churches from whence the bodies came'.[175] In other words, burial could be made at any church, as long as what amounted to a Christian version of the *eric* or traditional Irish 'bodyfine' was paid to the territorial church of the deceased. Presumably, however, only the élite could afford to be buried at a site other than their territorial church, since a burial fee was also due to the church where interment was made. The 'Registry of Clonmacnoise' sheds some light on how that great cemetery was partitioned over the centuries to accommodate the remains of members of important kin-groups who bought the right to be interred there. It shows that Clonmacnoise was a 'town of the dead', and reveals the complex commercial activity that helped to build and maintain it.[176]

The ownership of the remains of eminent people was sometimes disputed, as has already been shown regarding the case of Hugh de Lacy. Another example is that of Dermot MacGillacarry, erenagh of the old church of Tibohine, Co. Roscommon. After his death in 1230, MacGillacarry's body lay unburied for three days while a dispute over its ownership raged between the Cistercian monks of Boyle and the Premonstratensian canons of Holy Trinity in Lough Cé, who ultimately prevailed.[177] It seems odd that MacGillacarry, whose family had strong historical connections with Tibohine, was not buried there. Certainly the confusion about where he should be buried seems unusual, since Boyle and Trinity Island belonged to different orders. Both foundations are located near Tibohine, and both had strong MacDermott connections, with Boyle claiming precedence as the older establishment, having been founded in 1141 as opposed to *c.* 1215 for Trinity Island. Perhaps the cemetery at Tibohine had been profaned during its plundering in 1201 and had not been reconsecrated. If so, this would explain why MacGillacarry could not be interred there, and also account for the dispute over his corpse and the allied burial fees, etc. If this had been the case, however, one would expect that in the twenty-nine years between the plundering and MacGillacarry's burial, an alternate place of interment for the people of Tibohine would have been determined, and the dispute regarding MacGillacarry would not have been necessary. It seems that burial at Tibohine must have stopped for another reason, but we can only guess about what it may have been. Perhaps it was simply that Tibohine's status was eclipsed by the larger, more pow-

---

174 Harding, 'Burial choice', p. 120; cf. *Regesta*, ed. Davis et al., I, no. 1774. **175** Archdall, *Mon. Hib.*, I, p. 331, citing *Reg. of Christ Church*. **176** 'Registry of Clonmacnoise', ed. O'Donovan. **177** *AFM, s.a.* 1229; *AB* 1229.

erful monasteries of the Continental orders. The fact that MacGillacarry was ultimately buried at Trinity Island suggests that it was a more powerful house than Boyle at this time.[178]

Transportation of the dead to burial
In medieval Ireland, the body and the burial dues 'belonged' to the territorial church of the deceased. The return of the body to the appropriate church gained additional importance, because of both the associated burial fees which the territorial church stood to gain, and because it established a continuing burial tradition which usually led to additional burials, endowments and bequests from other members of the kin-group. The great efforts made during the period under study to transport corpses back to the appropriate territorial church testifies to the considerable importance of maintaining the relationship with the kin-group – even after death. Numerous such journeys are recorded in both native Irish and Anglo-Irish chronicles, and many of them involved significant distances. The limited number of roads in medieval Ireland, and the fact that much of the terrain was interrupted by rivers, streams, lakes and bogs, would have exacerbated the difficulty and danger of travelling overland with a corpse-laden wagon – especially during seasons of heavy rainfall and flooding while under danger of attack by enemies or relic-hunters. The transportation of a corpse by ship or boat could also easily be delayed by inclement weather.

The 'Book of Fenagh', which dates from *c.*1300, and relates lore from a much earlier period, contains a section highlighting the importance of returning a corpse to the proper church. In this case, the corpse is that of the local king, Aedh Find:

> This is the reason why to me was given
> The great tribute, for my use;
> And for bringing his body to my church,
> wheresoever in Ireland he might die.[179]

This suggests that corpses may commonly have been transported, and echoes the previously cited passage above which stated that the original purpose of a will was to assure the return of the corpse to the territorial church.[180] After Cormac died at the battle of Mag Ailbe,[181] his body was buried at Castledermot, Co. Kildare, a few miles to the north. His first preference was to be buried at Cloyne, Co. Cork, which would have required transporting his corpse (pre-

---

178 Loch Cé was captured by the 'Anglo-Normans' in 1235; during a later attack, the monks protected the 'Anglo-Normans', and in 1237 and 1239 the monastery's endowments were increased. The monastery was again plundered in 1249, but seems to have remained strong. Boyle was raided in 1243. 179 *Bk Fen.*, p. 83 (prose), p. 133 (verse). 180 See this chapter, n. 156. 181 This is Ballaghmoon, 2.5 miles north of Carlow, Co. Carlow.

sumably by wagon) a distance of some one hundred miles. Yet the chronicler gave no indication that such a long journey was deemed impossible or even that the proposition was unusual or remarkable. He recorded only that Móenach, 'preferred to bury him' at Castledermot. As we have seen, Moénach's decision may have been influenced by the prestige that would accrue to Castledermot once it became the site of Cormac's royal grave.

While transporting a corpse one hundred miles would certainly have been arduous, other entries do not suggest that such journeys were inconceivable. The royal remains of king Brian Bóruma (and those of other members of his family) were carried from Dublin to Armagh for burial,[182] a journey of some ninety miles. Written sources show that in the twelfth and thirteenth centuries, nobles were also transported long distances to their territorial churches for burial.

In 1181, Domnall and Maghnus O'Connor, and the sons of Aedh Ua Conchobair (O'Connor), Aed Ua Flathbertaig (O'Flaherty) and Donnchadh O'Fallamháin (O'Fallon), died in battle in the barony of Carbury in northwest Co. Sligo, and their bodies were transported to Clonmacnoise for burial.[183] Even on today's roads, this is a journey of about seventy-five miles through a very rough and watery landscape, and in the twelfth century it would clearly have been a far more challenging journey. We also find that in 1198, after Ruaidrí Ua Conchobair (Rory or Roderick O'Connor) died at Cong on the north shore of Lough Corrib in Mayo, his body was brought some sixty miles for burial at Clonmacnoise.[184]

To get a sense of the inconvenience that transporting corpses these kinds of distances would have caused, we need only remember the many petitions to the pope requesting consecration of new cemeteries at local chapels because it was so difficult during the wet seasons to transport corpses one or two miles to the parish church.[186] The early twelfth-century composition *Cocad Gaedel re Gallaib* (Wars of the Gaedhil & the Gaill) contains two references to the efforts made to transport members of the nobility to their territorial churches for burial. The quotation below refers to soldiers killed at the battle of Clontarf:

> On the next day they went to the field of the battle and buried every-
> one of their people that they were able to recognise, there ... and they

---

182 Killaloe was Brian's territorial church; but Armagh was the most powerful church in Ireland. For political reasons, Brian allied himself with Armagh, became its benefactor, and presumably arranged to be buried there. See above, notes 172 & 173. **183** *ALC*. **184** *AClon*, *AI*. I stress that these are approximate distances 'as the crow flies', and would not have been possible in the time under discussion. **186** It is also conceivable that the difficulty of transporting corpses was not the true reason for petitioning the pope for the right to buy in chapel cemeteries.

carried thirty of the nobles who were killed there to their territorial churches, wherever they were situated all over Erinn.[187]

The second passage recounts the attack of Donnchadh mac Gillapatrick on the soldiers of Dál Cais as they marched home from the battle of Clontarf in 1014:

> … thrice fifty of the wounded men died … and they were buried there, except such of their nobles as were brought to their native places and buried in their hereditary churches with honour, and they thus arrived at Cenn Coradh.[188]

As this source was written a long time after 1014, we cannot know if the corpses were really transported as reported. What these passages do show is that the twelfth-century writer thought that the proper and fitting treatment for warriors of the noble class honourably slain in battle was to carry them back to their territorial churches for burial.

In the fourteenth century, Diarmaid Mac Carthaigh, king of Munster, was slain at the monastery of Tralee, Co. Kerry, and the annals include the particular information that he was buried a fortnight later in Inisfallen, which is about twenty miles away.[189] In 1242, Meiler de Bermingham's body was carried from his place of death near Cashel, Co. Tipperary, to Athenry, Co. Galway – a distance of some sixty miles.[189a] Walter Burke's corpse was carried the even longer distance from Galway to Athassel, Co. Tipperary, for burial in 1271;[190] and in 1398, when Tadhg Mac Carthaigh of the royal line of Desmond died at 'Baile I Chairbre' near Cahirciveen in western Co. Kerry, his corpse was carried a similar distance back to Cork for burial. In 1468, Thomas, earl of Desmond, travelled to Drogheda, Co. Louth, on the east coast of Ireland to attend parliament, and was beheaded. His body was transported to the opposite side of the country for interment with his ancestors in Tralee, Co. Kerry.[191] The remains of the dead were also transported overseas for interment.[192]

The written record makes it clear that some Gaelic women of the élite classes were also transported for burial in their territorial cemeteries. Gormflaith was carried from Killaloe, Co. Clare, to Iniscealtra, Co. Clare, for her burial in 1076. In 1386, the body of Áine, daughter of Tadhg mac Donnchaid, was brought from Tuaim-senchaid at Garradice Lough near Drumlane in Co. Cavan, to Sligo for interment.[193] A poem concerning the wife of the Lord of the Uí Bhriain of Munster declares: 'Great had been our joy had she – or even her ashes – come back

187 *Cogadh Gaedhel re Gallaibh (Wars of Gaedhil & Gaill)*, p. 211.　**188** Ibid, pp 215–17.　**189** *AI, s.a.* 1320.　**189a** De Bermingham died near Cashel and was interred at Athenry: *Mon. Hib.*, II, p. 195.　**190** *AClon*, 1271; *AI*, 1272-4; *Reg. Mon. Athenry*, p. 213.　**191** *AFM*, iv, 1468.　**192** See section below: 'Methods of transporting corpses'.　**193** *AFM* & *AConn, s.a.* 1386.

from the harbour of the Bay of Duibhlinn …'[194] This record may suggest that it was not unknown for a woman's remains to have been transported home for burial, even if that involved a long distance; or it could be only poetic yearning. In light of the written evidence concerning the transportation of male corpses, the former interpretation seems more plausible.

The entries noted above – like almost all annalistic entries regarding burial – refer to the élite. What of the burial of non-nobles?

Two excerpts from the *Caithréim Thoidhealbhaigh* offer unique information regarding the burial of non-noble soldiers who were slain in battle in Co. Clare in 1317:

> Over their kerne (laid in one long trench) be the earth heaped rampart-wise; to their English allies be decent burial given.[195]

> … all that by you on this ground are fallen of Brian-of-the-Tribute's clans, to honour them with tomb and sepulture; from among those heroes to seek out and to set aside your own dead friends; to count the spoils and heads[196]

These passages seem to indicate that the non-élite were not transported to their territorial churches, but buried in mass graves dug on or near the site of battle. The same is indicated by a fifteenth-century reference in 'MacFirbis's annals', which tell of the fate of the men who fought for MacRichard in Waterford in 1443:

> after the account of them that knew it, there was the number of 410 of his men buried, besides all that was eaten by doggs and by foules of the aire …[197]

Presumably these 410 men were buried together, though this is not explicitly stated.

Methods of transporting corpses to burial

Corpses were usually transported from their place of death to the church for waking in a bier placed on a wagon. An account written perhaps *c.*1100 tells that when St Ruadhan (floruit sixth century) came:

---

194 *Aithdioghluim Dána*, ed. McKenna, II, p. 32, verse 17. The given translation of the word '*taise*' as 'ashes' is inaccurate. The word means 'remains' or 'relics' and does not have any connection with burning. See *RIA Dict*. **195** *Caithr. Th.*, II, p. 108: i, p. 1221: 'agus déntar clais múraig ar a gceithernaib agus réidadhlacad ar a rútadaib, adlacaidh festa na fednacha, ar in file; agus scaraid a néideda re a nuaislib.' **196** Ibid., II, p. 104; I, p. 118: 'ar tuit lib san láithirsi. do clandaib Briain boroma. onóir uagh is adlaicthi. do tabairt do'n triathfedhain. mórthinól bar marbcharad. ar leigh as an laochraidsi. faidb is cind do comáirem'. **197** *AMacF s.a.* 1462, p. 247.

Ruadan (of the blood of the kings of Munster) … went to the district of Cinel Cairpre Móir, to Snam Luthair. The king of this district died at this time, and was being carried to his burial as Ruadan arrived, and the people were in great lamentation and mourning …[198]

In the 'Life of St Brendan of Clonfert', the writer describes how once, when Brendan was 'traversing Magh Ai, they saw a bier, and a dead man on it, and his friends keening him'.[199] Later, the saint tells his companions that when he dies, his body is to be conveyed on a 'small chariot … lest if it were a large wagon with numerous attendance, the tribes should notice it and dispute for my body …'[200] This seems to indicate that a 'large wagon' would have been the vehicle normally used to transport the corpse of a man of his status. References to oxen drawing the burial wagon are common; for example, the remains of St Fanchea are reputed to have rested 'on a vehicle borne by two oxen.'[201] The anonymous Life of the Scottish St Serf (St Seruanus), which dates from the late twelfth century, tells that the saint was borne to his grave in a bier drawn by two bulls, an incident commemorated in a decorative boss in the ceiling of Glasgow cathedral.[202]

Corpses were also transported by ship, a fact attested to by the previously mentioned burials in Co. Down of two twelfth-century bishops of Sodor.[202a] Richard Burke's body was brought back from England for burial at Athassel, Co. Tipperary, in 1248,[203] and in 1321, the remains of Edmund fitzTheobald were also transported from England to Gowran in Kilkenny.[204] In 1420, 'Joanna de Wffler' had the bones of her husband, David Wedir, transferred from Bristol in England to Athenry, Co. Galway, to comply with his request to be buried there in the habit of a monk.[205] Such funereal traffic travelled across the Irish Sea in both directions: the corpse of Robert de Ufford, justiciar under Edward I, was shipped to England for interment in 1346, resting in a lead-lined coffin.[206] After Roger Mortimer, earl of March (the grandson of Lionel, who was the presumed heir to the English throne) was slain in 1397, Thady Dowling reported that his mother gave two chalices as ransom for his body, which was then sent to England for burial with his ancestors at the abbey at Wigmore.[207]

---

198 *Lives*, II, p. 309. **199** 'Life of St Brendan of Clonfert', *Lives*, II, p. 48. **200** Ibid., p. 91. **201** *O'Hanlon*, I, p. 10. **202** *Two Celtic saints*, p. 51. For dating, see *The Oxford dictionary of saints*, ed. Farmer, pp 249–50. **202a** See n. 167 above. **203** *AConn, AFM, ALC, Miscellaneous Irish Annals*, *s.a.* 1248, §9, p. 128. **204** 'Clyn's Annals'. **205** 'Item nobilis matrona Joanna de Wffler uxor dicti David Wedir … fecit transferri ossamenta mariti suit de conventu Bristol ad conventrum de Athnary …': *Reg. Mon. Athenry*, p. 207. **206** 'Grace's Annals'. **207** '… cujus mater ejus (?iis) dedit ij. calices, unum in Misheill, alterum in Garghill, ut haberet illum vel vivum vel mortuum, ad transmittendum illum in Angliam'. His death occurred near Kellistown, 'in O'Nowlan's country and its site is unknown', *Clyn & Dowling*, *s.a.* 1397, p. 25.

Obviously, transporting the dead across distances as great as one-hundred miles would have taken some time, and the accounts of the funeral rites of Brian Bóruma and his men provide an opportunity to make some estimations of how much time passed between his death and his burial.

I have already noted that after Brian was killed at Clontarf, Co. Dublin, in 1014, his remains were brought to Swords, about ten miles north of the battle site, and the archbishop of Armagh and his senior clerics are said to have immediately come down to Swords to collect the corpse.[208] However, it would have taken at least a day or two for word of Brian's death to reach the clerics, and at least the same amount of time for them to travel to Swords, by which time Brian would have been dead for at least three or four days.

The remains of Brian and his family would presumably have been borne to Armagh in some type of wagon, and therefore the funeral party would have had to travel slowly, up the *Slighe Midluachra*, one of the four great ancient roads of Ireland. Stops for the purpose of eating and sleeping would have been necessary, and we may reasonably speculate that at least two of these stops were made at the religious foundations of Duleek and Louth which were located along this route.[209]

Brian was a great king who had led the Irish to a decisive victory over the Vikings at Clontarf, but was killed during the battle. It is therefore reasonable to expect that some sort of mourning ritual occurred at each place his cortege stopped; the procession may have been slowed or stopped at other places not mentioned by the chroniclers. It seems likely that the trip from Swords to Armagh took another four or five days. If, as numerous chronicles report, Brian's body was then given a twelve-day wake at Armagh, Brian may have been dead for nearly three weeks before he was buried. The likelihood that a large amount of time transpired between death and burial – not only in this case, but in the others already noted – raises the obvious question of whether the written sources contain any evidence for embalming.

Embalming

Western European attempts to embalm corpses are well-documented for the early Middle Ages, although their levels of success seem to have varied significantly. For example, the first 'Life of St Samson of Dol' (who spent some of his life in Ireland), states that the saint 'left his wasted body to be embalmed and buried'.[210] The 'Dialogues' of Pope Gregory the Great tell of a search for a surgeon to disembowel a dead man 'and to embalm his body'.[211] The 'Annals of St

---

208 *AU, s.a.* 1013; *AFM, s.a.* 1013; 'Cottonian Annals,' A.M. Freeman, ed., LIII, (1916), p. 766; *ALC, s.a.* 1014; *Cogadh Gaill*, ed. Todd, p. 211. **209** The following may offer insight into why Brian's funeral cortège made three stops en route to Armagh: 'According to the thirteenth-century commentator, Guillaume Durand, the bier was carried by males of equal rank and three stops were to be made on the way to the grave', cf. R.E. Reynolds, 'Death and burial in Europe', *Dictionary of the Middle Ages*, IV, p. 120. **210** *Life of St Samson of Dol*, trans. Taylor, p. 70. **211** *Dialogues of Gregory the Great*, trans. E.G. Gardner, p. 224. **212** *The annals of St Bertin*, trans.

Bertin' record that, when Charles the Bald died at Tortona in 877, 'his attendants opened him up, took out his intestines, poured in such wine and aromatics as they had, put the body on a bier and set off to carry him to St Denis'. The annalist then proceeds to explain in extremely graphic detail just how futile these efforts were, with the result that the king's remains never reached St Denis.[212]

Written sources suggest that some kind of embalming was being practiced in Ireland by the twelfth century, and possibly many centuries earlier. The text in the *Yellow book of Lecan* quoted by Stokes in his edition of the *Martyrology of Oengus* (*Félire Oengusso*) refers to what would seem to be the embalming by the Irish pagan god *In Dagda* of his son by placing 'myrrh and frankincense and non-corrupting herbs round the corpse'.[213] The late Middle-Irish commentary in 'the martyrology of Oengus' tells that after the burial of the great fifth-century king Niall of the Nine Hostages 'his body [was] afterwards taken out of the ground by Cainnech, and thou wouldst think that there was no lack of shape or form upon him, for it is a tub with healing herbs that was around him in his grave'.[214] This passage echoes the earlier tale of the incorrupt body of St Cianán, found in the same source.[215] The fact that the comment regarding Niall is completely incidental to the point being made in the story suggests that some type of embalming procedure using herbs was practiced, as does the existence of a similar passage in the Early Modern Irish 'Life of St Ciarán of Saighir'. This hagiographical source is based on earlier materials, and describes how the monks waked the body of Ciarán 'singing hymns and canticles and other songs of praise, and with unguents such as spices and the like …'[216] The late 'life' of the seventh-century Irishman, St Fursa, a non-Irish composition of the twelfth or thirteenth century, specifically mentions embalming:

> Haymon hastened on horseback with all his household, to assist at the funeral obsequies … the clergy, monks and holy virgins were collected, with a crowd of villagers, singing requiem hymns to God, and preparing to embalm the body of His departed servant …[217]

That medieval embalming techniques in England were sometimes highly successful was shown when the coffin of Archbishop Godfrey de Ludham (d. 1265)

Nelson, pp 202–3. **213** 'So the Dagda put myrrh and frankincense and non-corrupting herbs round the corpse of his son Cernait Honeymouth', cf. *Félire*, ed. Stokes, p. 247, n. 2, cf. 'Yellow book of Lecan', 176a, 47. **214** Ibid., ed. Stokes, n. 2, §24; p. 176: 'Tucad immorro corp Neill a talmain iarsin la Cairnech 7 andar-lat isin uairsin atbath, conach bui esbaid crotha nó delba fair, uair is dabach co luibib ice bui ime ina folach'. Byrne has asserted that Niall of the Nine Hostage was indeed a historical figure, though much legend has attached itself to his name: *Irish kings*, p. 52. **215** 'Thus is Cianán's body, without corrupting, without dissolving in the tomb to the east of the *damliac* and the cause thereof is this'; *Félire*, p. 245, §24; ibid., p. 246: 'IS [*sic*] amlaid ata corp Cianain gan lobad gan leghad isin membrai frisin ndamliag anáir'. **216** *Lives*, II, p. 119. **217** Sharpe, *Medieval Irish saints*, p. 29. **218** Litten, *The English way*, pp 32–56. Regarding the

was opened in York minster in 1969.[218] If we may trust Archdall, an uncorrupted corpse of a prelate in his pontificals, supposed to have been Felix O'Ruadan, who had been buried at the foot of the altar in the monastery of the Blessed Virgin Mary in Dublin in 1238, was unearthed in 1787 and subsequently replaced.[219]

Julian Litten has stated that leaden coffins 'became fashionable in the fifteenth century' and seem to have been strongly associated with the burial vault, although he has remarked that leaden coffins 'very much like a mummy case' were used in the fourteenth century, with the leaden inner coffin usually placed in an outer wooden case. It is, therefore, quite interesting to find an entry dated 1346 in the annals of Friar John Clyn of Kilkenny which records that after Ralph de Ufford died in Ireland his corpse was conveyed in a style then being used in England: 'enclosed in lead, [his body] is carried by his wife to be buried in England'.[220] This account does not mention that de Ufford was embalmed, although we may be fairly certain that some embalming procedure was practiced. In fourteenth- and fifteenth-century England, embalming involved removing the soft organs, draining and cleaning the inner cavities 'with various aromatic and disinfecting fluids' which were sewn closed. The exterior of the body was then treated with preserving spices 'applied either as an ointment or a paste', after which the body was tightly wrapped in waxed linen ('cere cloth') with the seams sealed 'with beeswax so as to establish a near airtight condition'.[221] We may safely presume that this method was known and used in Ireland in the fourteenth century – although perhaps only for aristocratic 'Anglo-Normans' like Ufford, since the process was very labour-intensive and expensive.[222]

According to Litten, the preservation of the corpse was not always undertaken for reasons of vanity or as a way to hide the reality of death. The practice became something of a necessity:

> When a person of rank died far from home, and it was known that the funeral would therefore be delayed, embalming allowed the body to remain recognizable long enough for the relatives to make a positive identification on its arrival home ... not only to prove to all and sundry that the monarch was indeed dead but also to let the rightful heir be acclaimed and to deter any pretenders.[223]

case of Archbishop de Ludham, Litten has cited Ramm, et al.: 'The tombs of archbishops Walter de Gray (1216–55) and Godfrey de Ludham (1258–65) in York Minster, and their Contents', in *Archaeologia*, CIII, (1971), pp 101–48. **219** *Mon. Hib.*, I, p. 310, citing the 'Annals of Blessed Virgin Mary, Tristernagh' & Ware's *Antiquities* and *Bishops*, for the burial; no source is cited for the disinterment. **220** *Clyn & Dowling, s.a.* 1346, p. 141. **221** Litten, *The English way*, p. 37. **222** In 1471, one Hugh Brice was paid £15 3s. for the cerecloth (waxed linen) and spices used to embalm King Henry VI of England. See Litten, *The English way of death*, p. 38, quoting W.J. White, 'The death and burial of Henry VI', in *The Ricardian*, VI, 78, (September 1982), pp 70–80; and VI, 79 (December 1982), pp 106–17. **223** Litten, *The English way of death*, p. 37.

An interest in verifying that the person had not been murdered would have been another important reason for embalming, and this certainly would have been relevant in the case of Ralph de Ufford, who was so hated in England that even a cleric like Clyn felt compelled to record that his death was met with 'the greatest public joy and applause of all men'.

Other methods for preserving corpses were also used, including the grue-some – if exceedingly practical– *mos teutonicus*. This involved 'cutting the body into pieces and boiling it in wine and vinegar until fat and flesh separated … the skeleton was then shipped home for burial, and the remainder deposited at the place of death'.[224] Pope Boniface VIII tried to condemn the practice at the end of the thirteenth century, but his lack of success is shown by the fact that the procedure was employed on the corpse of the bishop of Hereford, who died in Italy in 1282, and also on King Henry V of England, who died in Normandy in 1422, and whose remains were shipped back to England for burial at Westminster some two months later. Clearly, a positive visual identification of the deceased must not have been required in these instances.

The number of references to the long-distance transportation of corpses and embalming contained in Irish sources composed in the Middle Ages, along with the fact that embalming was practiced (sometimes with excellent results) in England at this time, suggests that embalming was also practised in Ireland. However, what procedure might have been used, the circumstances that neces-sitated it, and how successful it might have been remain unclear, since written sources provide no detail. As with so many questions regarding the Middle Ages, we can hope that archaeology will provide additional information.

Disinterment and multiple burial of remains
Irish written sources testify to bodies being buried more than once However, a close analysis of these offer no indication that translations of burials were 'sec-ondary burials' of a type which might suggest that the Irish believed in any sort of a 'liminal' period between the actual moment of death and the time when the natural process of physical decay reduced the body to bones. Rather, record-ed instances of the disinterment of bodies (or parts of them), or the translation of bones clearly seem related to ideas of conquest and territoriality and the desire to possess the remains of people who were regarded as significant within the culture.

Place of burial was important to the Irish of the early Christian period, and bodies were sometimes disinterred in order to re-bury them at a place deemed more suitable – or where a particular group thought they could profit from them. The remains of powerful people were believed to retain their power after death, and it was thought wise to show them proper honor and keep them where

224 Ibid.

they could offer the greatest benefit to the kin-group. Conversely, bodies were sometimes disinterred and stolen in order to humiliate or intimidate opponents.

Eoghan Béul, the mid-sixth century king of Connacht, was buried in a standing position, facing north in the direction of his enemies, the Ulstermen, has previously been cited. When the Ulstermen learned of this, they disinterred his body, carried it north, and buried it face-down at the cemetery of Aonach Locha Gile, Co. Sligo.[225] Brian, who was killed by Crimthann at the second battle of Damchluain, was buried at 'tulcha Domhnaill', but we are told that 'after a long time', Beo-Aed 'came and carried away Brian's remains to Ros Caim where he laid him'.[226]

When St Cainnech disinterred the body of the Irish king Niall of the Nine Hostages it was said that the reason for exhuming it was to bless it by sprinkling holy water on it and re-inter it as 'Tuléin's first corpse'.[227] Clearly the story was intended to encourage the people of Tuléin to forsake pagan burial and seek Christian burial at the same place as this man who had held an elevated position in the history of his descendants. In 1207 the remains of Ruaidrí Ua Conchobair, king of Connaught, were disinterred and desposited in a stone shrine.[228]

In 1308, the bones of St Constans, who had been abbot and anchorite at *Inismhuighe-samh* (probably Lough Veagh) were translated into a shrine by Matthew, bishop of Clogher in Co. Tyrone.[229] Mervyn Archdall recorded that 'to the west of the cathedral of Kilmacduagh, in the church-yard, is a small cell, where, they say, the patron saint [Duach] was buried, and that the body was afterwards carried to Aughrim'.[230] Unfortunately, Archdall does not say when this was done, but Aughrim was the site of a great battle in 1691, raising the possibility that the relics may have been taken there in the belief that they could provide some protection against the enemy.

When Mór the granddaughter of Turlough O'Brien and wife of Cormac MacCarthy died in 1252, she was buried at Killone, a convent for Augustinian nuns founded by Donal Mór Mac Carthaigh, but 'her relics were brought to *Les na mBráthar*'.[231] 'Les na mBráthar' means 'enclosure of the brothers', and Killone was built on the lands of the Augustinian canons regular of Clare Abbey, also founded by Donal Mór. Possibly then, it was to Clare Abbey that her relics were brought. Her death is not noted in any other annals, and the translation of Mór's relics so soon after her death is unusual; while translations are certainly known, in the few Irish examples that we have, they were not effected until some years

---

225 See section above, 'Defensive burial'.   **226** 'Death of Crimthann', *SG*, II, p. 376; I, pp 333: 'ocus adnaicther Brian isin maigin sin. Tic iarum Beaed rois caim air céin móir iartain ocus beirid taise Briain co ros caim leis co ro adnocht iad I ros caim'. Brian was the king of Connacht, and son of Mongfhionn, daughter of Fidach. His brothers were Fiachra, Ailill and Fergus.   **227** *Félire*, ed. Stokes, p. 245.   **228** *AFM, s.a.* 1207.   **229** *Mon. Hib.*, I, p. 161, cf. Ware's *Bishops*, I, p. 183. See *Acta sanctorum Hiberniae*, ed. Colgan, p. 222.   **230** Ibid., p. 220, cf. *Acta sanctorum Hiberniae*, ed. Colgan, pp 219, 247.   **231** *AI*, 1252.4.

after burial. While one might suspect that Mór was a widow who had taken the habit of a nun at Killone prior to her death, the only person of the name 'Cormac Mac Carthaigh' whose death is noted in the chronicles for the thirteenth century died ten years after Mór. The annalist indicates the esteem in which Mór was held, recording that 'there was no woman in her time better than she', so her relics may have been removed to Clare abbey to rest with those of her husband's family. This may have been regarded as a more appropriate place, since there seems to have been a belief in the Middle Ages that the prayers of women (for example, nuns) were not as efficacious as those of men. A final example is that of Maurice FitzThomas, earl of Desmond, who was buried in 1355 at St Saviour, Dublin, and whose corpse was later disinterred and reburied in the Dominican friary of Tralee in Co. Kerry.[232]

The stealing of corpses and relics
The corpses of prominent people were valuable commodities in relic-worshipping medieval Europe, which gave rise to the stealing of corpses and relics, and we find clear examples of this in Ireland.[233]

The vernacular 'life' of Ciarán of Saighir tells of the death of St Columba of Iona, stating that Ciarán directed Odrán to carry Columba's body to burial 'concealed in wheat'.[234] The only similar reference I have seen is in Clare Gittings' study of burial in early modern England, where she cites a reference to the practice of filling the bottom of a coffin with bran 'that the body may lie the softer'.[235] This may have made sense in post-Reformation England, but doesn't seem applicable to medieval Ireland, where we have no evidence of any such squeamish sensitivities to the comfort of corpses.

Odrán's corpse was probably concealed in wheat to protect it from relichunters. Indeed, later in the same work, we find that in giving instructions regarding his burial, St Ciarán 'bade three worthy members of his congregation to guard his body'.[236] In the earliest life of Gildas, thought to date to 919, we find the fifth-century Briton requesting to be buried at sea to 'prevent any dispute regarding the immediate possession of his body'.[237]

Body-snatchers were also in the thoughts of St Brendan of Clonfert – or at least in those of the compiler of his Irish life – as shown in the instructions the saint is said to have given for his burial

> Make a small chariot, and let a single one of you go with it to convey my body, lest, if it were a large wagon with a numerous attendance, the tribes should notice it, and dispute for my body …[238]

232 *Mon. Hib.*, II, p. 71.   **233** For an excellent study of the significance and use of relics in medieval society, see Geary, *Furta Sacra*.   **234** 'Life of St Ciarán of Saighir', *Lives*, II, p. 117.   **235** Gittings, *The English way*, p. 115.   **236** 'Life of St Ciarán of Saighir', *Lives*, II, p. 120.   **237** O'Hanlon, *Lives*, I, p. 492.   **238** 'Life of Brendan of Clonfert', *Lives*, II, p. 92; also n. 200 above.

Corpse-pilfering was common enough that the 'Senchas Mór' contains detailed laws dealing with digging in a churchyard, breaking bones, and the theft of corpses.[239] Annalistic entries show that the squabbling over the remains of important and powerful people was so intense that outright body-stealing was not uncommon. These thefts may also have been linked with the desire of churches other than the territorial church to appropriate burial-fees or even the corpses of prominent people in order to elevate their status.

After Conchobar Húa Maelsechlainn (Connor O'Melaghlin), king of Tara, died in 1073, his head was taken 'by force' out of his grave by Toirdelbach Húa Briáin (Turlough O'Brien) and carried to Kincora – on Good Friday, no less.[240] The dispute over the body of Hugh de Lacy has already been mentioned, as well as the fact that the monastery of Bective in Co. Meath refused for ten years to relinquish his body so that it could be buried with his head at St Thomas', Dublin.[241] The case of Dermot Mac Gilacarry, erenagh of Tibohine, whose body was fought over by both the monks of Boyle and Loch Cé has previously been noted.[242] The fact that the annalist felt it necessary to include the defensive note that MacGilacarry's corpse had been 'lawfully obtained' by the monks of Loch Cé may or may not be special pleading, but it certainly points to the fact that there were instances where corpses were not. One of these occurred in 1300 – some seventy years later – when Roger, the prior of Colpe, Co. Meath, was fined 20s. for stopping some Dominican friars in Drogheda and robbing them of the body of Roger Wetherall – along with its bier and pall.[243]

239 *Ancient laws*, ed. Atkinson et al., I, 'Senchas Mor', pp 203–5. **240** *AT* (also, *AU*: 1073, *AI*: 1056, *CS*: 1070, *ALC*: 1073, *AFM*: 1073). **241** *Chart. St Mary's*, Gilbert, ed., II, pp 221, 276, 305 and 307; *Mon. Hib.*, II, p. 39; Lewis, *Topographical dictionary*, I, p. 190. **242** See this chapter, n. 14. **243** Lewis, *Topographical dictionary*, I, p. 389.

CHAPTER 4

Burial artifacts

The sources for medieval Ireland mention a number of burial-related artifacts, including shrouds, coffins, tombs, and various types of grave-markers. However, here again, the amount of evidence has proved to be meager. References may be found in a variety of sources, but the majority occur in the placename lore and heroic tales collected in the modern compilations *Duanaire Finn*, *The Metrical Dindsenchas*, and *Silva Gadelica* and relate – in fairly formulaic language – to the graves of warriors and kings and the monuments commemorating them. As a whole, the references provide some clues and suggestions as to what archaeologists might expect to find, add a bit of contextual information, and corroborate some currently held views, such as the rarity of coffins in medieval Ireland.

SHROUDS

Ludwig Bieler has noted that the custom in medieval Ireland was to wrap the corpse in a shroud and place it directly in the grave.[1] The Irish historical record contains evidence that shrouds were used as early as 668, under which year the *AU* record that Mael Fothartaig, son of Suibhne, king of Ua Thuirtri, 'was taken in his shroud to Daire (Derry)'. In a passage in Bede's life of the Northumbrian St Cuthbert (d. 687), Cuthbert directs that a certain piece of cloth which had been woven for him and given to him as a gift by a certain nun be used for his shroud.[2] This passage provides an interesting opportunity for comparison, since the word it uses for Mael Fothartaig's 'shroud' is *geimnen*. This word is related to *gemen*, meaning 'hide'.[3] However, it should not be presumed to mean that the shroud was necessarily made of leather or animal skin rather than cloth, as the word may possibly have originated at a period when shrouds were made of animal skin, but came, over time, to refer to a shroud in general.

    Other sources for the central Middle Ages, though not all Irish, indicate that shrouds were made of cloth, and probably linen, at least for those in religious

1 Bieler, *The Patrician texts*, p. 59. 2 Bede, 'Life of Cuthbert', *The Age of Bede* trans, J.F. Webb, p. 89. 3 *RIA Dictionary* under 'gemen'. Thanks are due to Dr Katharine Simms for pointing this out.

orders. The 'Life of Colmán Ela', thought to date to before 800, describes a death to come with the words 'when thou art in they single shirt of linen'.[4] The 'Life of St Ciarán of Saighir', which may date to the eleventh century,[5] vividly describes how after his wake, the saint was 'swathed in great quantities of white linen clothes, and was buried in them'.[6] The tenth-century *Regularis concordia* which prescribed the rule for English monks and nuns, required the corpse of every monk to be washed and clothed in clean 'shirt, cowl, stockings and shoes, no matter what his rank'. A stole might be added over the cowl of a priest.[7] Similarly, the eleventh-century French-based *Constitutions of Lanfranc* require washing the corpse and give very specific instructions regarding the burial-clothes:

> the chamberlain be present with grave-clothes of the right kind and thread and a needle for sewing ... When washed it (the corpse) shall be clad in a new shirt, or one newly washed, and a cowl; a head-cloth of linsey-wolsey belonging to the cowl shall be brought over this and attached in three places with thread. Gaiters of the same material reaching to the knees shall be put on the legs and night shoes on the feet. The hands shall be sewn together from arm to arm, and round the legs likewise. The night shoes also shall be joined together with thread. So dressed, the corpse shall be set in the hearse and covered with a pall.[8]

Regarding the burial-clothes of Irish laypersons, the written record is silent. Even the unusually detailed accounts concerning the eleventh-century burial of the great King Brian Bóruma offer no information on this subject. The *AFM* relate that the bishop of Armagh 'and his clergy washed the bodies (of Brian and his son Murchadh)' but there is no mention of shroud or burial-clothes. However, their existence can hardly be doubted, and it may be that shroud and burial-clothes at this time were so highly standardized that even the high king of Ireland would not have been buried in clothing that was different or remarkable in any way. What this standard might have been eludes us; but one would expect that a monk's funeral clothes would have differed in some way from those of a layperson – and certainly a king.

Corpses were also wrapped in branches, a practice which may possibly be recorded in the poem 'Cell Chorbbáin', which states that 'Corbbán, surpassing in poetry, rests under branches in the church'.[9] The term for this branchy cov-

4 'Life of Colman Ela', *Lives*, II, p. 165, §13. Richard Sharpe believes this source was written before 800. See Sharpe, 'Medieval Irish saints' lives', p. 334. 5 See Kenney, *Sources*, p. 316, in which he suggests that this 'is a work of considerable antiquity ... it was evidently composed at Saighir by a monk of Ciarán's community...'. 6 'Life of Old Ciarán of Saighir', *Lives*, II, p.119. 7 *Regularis concordia*, ed. & trans. Symons, p. 65. 8 *The monastic constitutions of Lanfranc*, ed. & trans. Knowles, p. 123. 9 *Met. Dind.*, IV, 'Cell Chorbbáin', p. 341.

ering is *strophaiss* (or *ses strophaiss* or *ses sofais*), and was commonly made of fresh
green branches, usually of birch. Its use is recorded in a marginal note in the
'Book of Leinster' which refers to the 'broom- or branch-covering that is round
the body' when it is being transported to the graveyard. The Royal Irish
Academy's *Dictionary of the Irish language* defines '*strophais*' as 'a covering of straw
or litter used as a shroud or winding sheet', and notes that it also occurs in
'Cormac's glossary' where it was called '*ses rapus*' or '*ses rophuis*', defined as '*scuab
adnacailu*' or 'broom of sepulture.'[10] A similar practice of wrapping a corpse in
rushes is also known to have occurred in medieval England. For example, excavations in the chancel at Hulton abbey uncovered a body which had been
'wrapped in organic rushes', and rush pollen appeared in other graves, suggesting that rushes may have been used for the burial rite and/or some sort of adorn-
ment in the church.[11] This may bring us full-circle, back to the quotation included above about Corbbán resting 'under branches in the church' and suggest that
the wrapping of the corpse in broom, which P.W. Joyce described as a pagan
Irish practice, actually continued well into the medieval period, and possibly
right up to recent times.

There is some evidence that fern fronds may also have accompanied some
Irish interments. James O'Laverty noted[12] that in an ancient Christian cemetery in the townland of Lisban, which seems to have been the site of the chapel
of 'Moyndele', there were found the remains of ferns, on which the heads of the
dead were cushioned.

The folklorist Anatole Le Braz tells that in France, before the Revolution, it
was customary for the parents of a dead child to make a receptacle for the body
by stripping the bark from a chestnut tree which they bound round the infant
with broom. This practice was outlawed in 1724 because of the extensive damage
it caused to the trees.[13]

COFFINS

This is a study of written sources, not artifacts, however it may be useful at this
point to provide some archaeological background. As Áine Brosnan has noted,
the opinion was long held among archaeologists that coffins were a late addi-

10 *RIA Dict.*; P.W. Joyce, *A social history*, II, p. 543. **11** Klemperer, 'Study of burials at Hulton
Abbey', p. 88. A mid-nineteenth century report tells that up to 1818, interments in the graveyard of the Augustinian Abbey of St John in Enniscorthy, Co. Wexford, were placed coffinless
in a grave that had been neatly lined with seasonal moss, dry grass and flowers, with a pillow
made of the same material supporting the head of the corpse. See 'Burial without coffins', *Jnl
Waterford & southeast archaeological society*, xv (1912), pp 197–8. **12** O'Laverty, 'Notes on pagan
monuments', p. 105. **13** Le Braz, *La légende de la mort*, I, p. 252.

tion to Irish burial ritual, though physical evidence of their use has occasionally been found. Views about the use of coffins have undergone revision, though it is still thought that they were not a general feature of Irish burial until the early modern period.[14] Excavations conducted in the 1950s at Dalkey Island, Co. Dublin, uncovered eleven burials, but no trace of coffins;[15] the medieval burials at St Mary's cathedral in Tuam, Co. Galway, were all found coffinless in shallow, unmarked pits.[16]

The medieval Irish situation seems consonant with that in England, about which Julian Litten has written 'no fifteenth-century peasant or artisan expected to be buried in a coffin; by contrast no noble would have been subjected to shroud burial in the churchyard'.[17] While coffins were almost unknown, stone sarcophagi were used in Ireland. John Bradley found thirty known 'Anglo-Norman' examples, but this small number indicates that they were uncommon even in their day. Sacrophagi seem mainly to have been used by the 'Anglo-Normans', and Irish examples are concentrated in the southeast of the country, in 'areas most prone to the adoption of English fashions', and 'appear to date to the thirteenth, fourteenth and perhaps the early fifteenth century, in what were probably the burial places of abbots and local dignitaries'.[18]

Excavations have uncovered coffin-shaped stone sarcophagi 'fitted together with joggled joints and shaped to the head and shoulders of the corpse' often without a lid, but covered with rough-hewn stone slabs, which Liam de Paor stated to have been 'a common type of medieval sarcophagus.'[19] Though rare, native Irish stone sarcophagi are known. As Bradley has noted, the one at Cormac's chapel on the hill of Cashel in Co. Tipperary, shows that the practice of burial in sarcophagi was present in Ireland before the coming of the Normans.[20] A hogback stone coffin, a type of sarcophagus dating from the Viking Age of the tenth and eleventh centuries, was found at Castledermot, Co. Kildare, in 1967, indicating another source of influence on Irish burial practice that predates the 'Anglo-Norman' incursions. Conleth Manning noted that this coffin most closely resembled English examples found in North Yorkshire and the coastal area of Cumberland, as well as one found in Dumfriesshire, Scotland, and pointed out that hogback coffins are not generally associated with Christian burial.[21]

In the excavation of the cemetery located on a sand dune on Omey Island, Co. Galway, where more than 250 individuals had been buried, evidence for only

14 Brosnan, *Mortuary practice*, pp 38–9. Also Candy & Hill, 'In the shadow of St Ninian', p. 95. **15** Liversage, 'Excavations at Dalkey Island', p. 128. **16** Clyne, 'Excavations at St Mary's cathedral', p. 94. **17** Litten, *The English way*, p. 86. **18** Bradley, 'Anglo-Norman sarcophagi from Ireland', pp 74–9. Anglo-Norman sarcophagi differ from the Irish versions because they were made from a single carefully hollowed block of stone, rather than a number of stones mortared together. **19** de Paor, 'Excavations at Mellifont abbey', p. 126. **20** See note 18 above. **21** Lang, 'The Castledermot Hogback', pp 154–8.

one coffin was discovered. This was the dark, purplish stain left from the coffin's disintegrated wood; the coffin itself had held the body of an adult and child, buried with their heads at opposite ends of the coffin.[22] The recent excavation of a small section of the disused Franciscan cemetery in Francis Street, Dublin, uncovered more than eighty interments datable to the thirteenth century, as well as the rare remains of two oaken coffins.[23] Other archaeological/artifactual evidence for coffins has been found, yet it is limited; the same may be said of written evidence for their use. None of the annalistic entries for the six-hundred years considered in this study mention a coffin. The limited physical evidence for medieval Irish coffins and the small number of written references suggest that, though coffins were used in Ireland from a fairly early date, their use was uncommon and they were probably reserved for élite burials.

The prologue to the *Cáin Adomnáin* written in the late tenth or early eleventh century, offers evidence that stone coffins were in use at that time: Adomnán's mother induced him to promulgate his law protecting women and children by burying him 'in a stone chest at Raphoe in Tirconnell'.[24] Excavations at the cathedral of the Holy Trinity in Downpatrick uncovered 'well-built coffins of mortared stone; the sides were roughly squared stones between 10 and 20 cm. thick … floored and roofed with thin slabs of shale'. These were dated to not later than the second quarter of the thirteenth century.[25] The 'Black book of Christ Church' records that Archbishops John Comyn and Luke were buried there in a 'stone tomb' in the southern part of the church.[26]

A medieval poem describes Holycross abbey as 'The true church of the Lord's Cross, with its stone monuments and coffins'.[27] The poem 'The battle of the sheaves', the written text of which has been dated to *c.*1200, contains the exhortation to 'Rise up, my friend, without fault, fix the coffin without stain, straighten its front to the wall …'[28] The Irish word for 'coffin' used in both of these poems is *comraid* or *comrar*, which means 'box, chest, basket or shrine for safekeeping', but in contexts relating to death, it has the explicit meaning of 'coffin'. Its other meanings of 'box or basket' which are items made of wood, willow or reed, may suggest that such coffins were made of these materials rather than stone.[29] At Whithorn, in Galloway, Scotland, three burials datable to the eighth

22 O'Keeffe, 'Omey and the sands of time'. **23** Information from Dr Declan Murtough, October 1995. **24** *Cáin Adomnáin*, ed. & trans. Meyer, p. 9, §14: 'a adnacul hi comrair clocha hi Raith-Both Thire Conaill'. **25** Delany, 'Monastic burials', pp 57–9. **26** '… Johannes comyng et lucas archiepiscopi sepelliunter in quadam tumba lapidea in australi latere ecclesie … Johannes de sancto paulo Archiepiscopus … corpus suum sub lapide marmoreo cum ymagine enea in secundo gradu ante predictum altare … ' Gwynn, 'Some unpublished texts', p. 310. **27** '… *na b(h)fert gloic(h)e is na gcom(h)raid.'* *Aithdioghluim dána*, ed. McKenna, poem LXXXVIII, st. 23. **28** 'Eirgid a cáirde gan cair. coirgid in ccomraid gan ail dírgid a hadort go fraig leabad ar ccarat claoidter'. 'The battle of the sheaves', *Duanaire Finn*, ed. Murphy, III, p. cxvi (dating) & pp 47–8. **29** *RIA Dict.*

and ninth centuries were found buried in what seem clearly to be household chests, complete with hinged lids and locks.[30]

Explicit written references to wooden coffins also exist. In the poem 'Cend Finnichair', we read of 'two hundred warriors ... laid ... under oaken bonds of death in a dwelling unloved'.[31] The 'Brehon law tracts' mention that the 'coffin of a patron saint', may be used to make judgements, and makes it clear that such a coffin would have to be wooden.[32] The 'Black book of Christ Church' records the burial of the archbishop of Dublin, Henry of London (d. 1228), in a 'wooden tomb'.[33] There is also the suggestion that bodies may have been interred in wicker coffins. An entry from the *AConn* dated 1424 tells that

> Ruaidri (Rory), son of Toirrdelbach Donn O'Conchobair (Turlough O'Connor), eligible prince of Connacht ... was buried in Roscommon in an ark made for him by his mother Graine, daughter of O Cellaig, wife of Tadc O Briain, king of Thomond[34]

In the accompanying footnote, A. Martin Freeman suggested that this 'ark' probably refers to a hollowed-out tree-trunk, but that if Ruaidhri's mother had actually made the 'ark' it could have been of wickerwork. It may be the case that this same practice survived long enough to be recorded in interviews made in the early 1960s with residents of Co. Westmeath. Interviewees described a funeral practice which had been common in their grandfather's (and sometimes their fathers') lifetimes, of placing a corpse in a 'wicker frame' and waking it for three days. These coffins were described has having been 'shaped like a wooden coffin with shoulders, the lid fastened on like a hamper' and 'sometimes made from sallies [willows] with green rushes interwoven'. Some interviewees reported that these wicker coffins were placed inside a wooden coffin for burial; others remembered only the wicker coffin being buried, so that the community's one wooden coffin could be re-used over a period of years.[35]

TOMBS

The laws of the native Irish required that a chief be buried and stipulated a penalty of 'distress of five days' for not 'erecting the tomb for thy chief ... '[36] Prior

---

30 Cardy & Hill, 'In the shadow of St Ninian', p. 95. **31** *Met. Dind.*, IV, 'Cend Finnichair', p. 325. **32** *Ancient laws*, ed. Atkinson et al., V, p. 473. **33** '... Henricus vero archiepiscopus sepellitur ex altera parte canselli mere ex opposito sub tumba lignea', A. Gwynn, 'Some unpublished texts', p. 310. **34** *'Adnacal a leburnai doroine a mathair'*. The *RIA Dict.* defines *'liberne'* as a 'galley or ship, a vessel'. **35** Fitzsimons, 'Miscellanea: wicker coffins', *Ríocht na Midhe*, III (1963), pp 67–8. **36** *Ancient laws*, eds Atkinson, et al., I, p. 185. The word translated here as 'tomb' is *fertad*.

to the arrival of Christianity, and perhaps for a 'cross-over' period of indetermi-
nate length afterwards, stone cairns were created above the graves of those the
local populace wished to commemorate. Adomnán told of a man who died 'as
the saint had prophesied, and his companions buried him there, constructing a
cairn of stones'.[37] Charles Plummer noted that the Latin *vitae* of the Irish saints
contain references to cairns;[38] and the poem 'Carn Furbaide', a place-lore poem
thought to have been composed before 1024, tells how a cairn was constructed
by every man putting a stone upon it.[39]

At least some tombs were above ground and could be entered. The eleventh-
century commentary on the *Martyrology of Oengus* (written in the eleventh century), tells that 'Adomnán went into the tomb to behold and touch the body.
Forthwith his eye is struck out ... Thenceforward no one dares to enter the
tomb.[40] The word translated here as 'tomb' is *membra,* which means a monument
over the dead, and also may have the sense of a shrine for relics.[41] Another passage in the same source tells that 'Cianan's hand (thrust) in through the southern side of the tomb even to the half', but here the word used is *slesa,*[42] meaning 'sides' or 'walls'.[43] Since Adamnán is said to have actually entered the tomb,
the *membra* seems to have been bigger than the stone slab-shrines known as *leachta*, unless it was only his hand or body which entered the structure. Perhaps the
slesa was something akin to one of the 'mortuary houses' mentioned in the previous chapter, which are believed to have been constructed for the purpose of
holding a single corpse.[44] If Cianán's arm was able to reach halfway across it, the
slesa would not seem to have been very large, and perhaps it was literally 'a shrine
with walls', and something akin to a *leacht*. It might be added that both *slesa* and
membra are words which are rarely used.

What, exactly, a *leacht* was has been pondered by many scholars, including
Charles Thomas, who wondered whether they served as a special type of altar,
actually contained or covered graves, or had uses which paralleled those for
Mediterranean altar-graves.[45] The excavations at Omey Island uncovered a hith-
erto unknown early monastic site and extensive cemetery which is not men-

---

37 *Adomnán's life of Columba*, eds Anderson & Anderson, pp 62–3, §35a.   **38** *Vita sanctorum
hiberniae*, ed. & trans. Plummer, p. cix, p. cxlix.   **39** 'A stone for every man that the axe clove
– so was the carn built,' 'Carn Furbaide,' *Met. Dind.*, IV, p. 35.   **40** *Félire*, pp 244–5, §24: 'Teit
dano Adamnan isin membra do deiscin 7 do lamachtad in chuirp. Benar a rosc fair focetoir
... Ni laim nech dono dul isin membra osin ille.'   **41** *RIA Dict.*   **42** '... & lam Cianain immech
col-leith in tslesa ...' The word used here for 'tomb' (*slesa*) seems to be problematical, as the
RIA Dict. precedes it with a question mark. The word closest to it in spelling is *slessach,* which
means 'having seats'. *Dineen's dictionary* contains no such entry.   **43** *RIA Dict.*, under 'slesa'.
44 Waterman, 'Banagher church, Co. Derry', pp 25–39, and 'An early Christian mortuary
house', (same author), pp 82–8. If the entombed body described in the passage from *Félire*
was buried in typical east/west Christian orientation, then Adamnán would have reached
across the tomb, not into it lengthwise.   **45** C. Thomas *The early Christian*, pp 169 & 175.

tioned in any of the historical sources, along with what appeared to be a 'two-story' *leacht* (that is, a second crude rectangular stone structure which had been built on top of the original), which was found to contain a group of disarticulated bones. No artifacts or evidence of a coffin were found in association with the structure.[46]

The 'Book of Fenagh', compiled no later than 1300 but containing traditional material referring to a far earlier date, tells 'I interred Conall truly, in my own penitentiary (*doirttaigh, durtech*)'.[47] This building would seem to be far bigger than the *slesa*, since *durtech* (or *dairthech*) is defined as an oak house or oratory, generally fifteen feet long and ten broad.[48] The 'Book of Leinster', written by different poets, uses the word *lecht* for 'grave'.[49]

Cuimin, the semi-historical progenitor of the O'Cuimins, was said to have been buried in the large *uluidh* at the feet of O'Suanaigh (O'Sweeney); John O'Donovan translated this word to mean 'altar-tomb'.[50] This word is also used in a description of the burial site of the great hero, Fergus, and legend says that the Irish word for the province of Ulster is derived from it.[51] In 1014, the same word is used for the tomb of king Brian Bóruma, rather than the more common *fert* (grave).[52] The English translators called the king's place of burial a 'new tomb', but the word *uluidh* or *alaid* more specifically means a stone tomb, sepulchre or cairn.[53] *Leabhar oiris* reports that the body of Brian's son Murchadh, as well as the heads of the fallen warriors Conaing and Mothla, were buried separately in another 'tomb'.[54] However, the words used for the receptacles of these heads is *cómraidh*, which has the more specific meaning of 'coffin' or 'casket', as has already been noted above.

The use of the word *uluidh* for the tomb of Brian Bóruma suggests that, as we might expect, his sepulchre was something extraordinary, and it would appear that the chronicler realized that his burial marked a huge break in tradition. There is certainly reason to think that other stone tombs already existed at Armagh before Brian's burial. We know that at least one great prince was interred at Armagh prior to Brian: Conor, the O'Donnell heir apparent to the great fortress at Ailach, was buried there 'with great honour' in 933.[55] In 1022, eight years after Brian's interment, Malachy, monarch of Ireland, was also buried at Armagh 'with great funeral honour'.[56] Despite these prominent burials, it is

---

46 T. O'Keeffe, 'Omey and the sands of time'. **47** *Bk Fen.*, p. 97. **48** *RIA Dict.* **49** '*Cúiced Lagen na lecht ríg*', pp 135–44 & '*Lecht Cormaic meic Culennáin*', i, pp 206–12, *Book of Leinster*. **50** *The geneaologies*, ed. & trans. O'Donovan, pp 44–5. **51** See 'Death of Fergus', *SG*, I, p. 256; ii, p. 285. **52** *AU*, 1014: '… coro adnacht i nArd Macha i n-ailaidh nui'. **53** *RIA Dict.* **54** '… do'n taoibh thiar-thuaidh do theampoll Ardmacha, i gcómhraidh ar leith, & Murchadh 7 ceann Conaing 7 Mhothla i gcómhraidh eile ar leith', *Leabhar Oiris*, ed. Best, pp 90–1. **55** *AFM; Mon. Hib.*, i, p. 37. **56** Ibid., I, p. 37. Though the obituary notices of Conor and Malachy contain no mention of tombs, the 'tomb of the kings' spoken of at Armagh in 1064 is called '*ttumba*'. See *AFM*.

not until fifty years after Brian Bóruma's burial that the sources first refer to Armagh as the 'tomb of the kings'.[57] This perhaps indicates that in the poet's time, it was not only well-known that king Brian had been interred at Armagh, but also that Malachy and others were believed to have been laid to rest there – although the annals are quite clear that Brian's tomb was new, and he was not buried with anyone else. Thus it is possible that 'tomb of the kings' means 'burial place of the kings', rather than indicating the existence of a single tomb in which royal remains were deposited.

When Brian died in 1014, it was the territory to which the deceased's kin-group belonged which determined place of burial. Brian's kindred were from Munster, not Ulster, and none of his line had previously been buried at Armagh. There were no cultural or historical reasons for Brian to be buried at Armagh – only political ones. A new grave had to be made for him, because no burial place for his family existed at Armagh. The statement that Brian was buried in a *uluid*, what is presumably at stone coffin, is notable since, like the reference from the *Cáin Adomnáin* (and the hogback tomb found in Ulster), it pre-dates the 'Anglo-Norman' invasion.

Later, the extremely eloquent obituary of Maol Sheachlainn Ó Ceallaigh (Melaghlin O'Kelly) records that he was buried at Knockmoy in 1402 'in his own stone tomb'.[58] Though written some 400 years later, this is the only annalistic entry comparable with the mention of Brian Bóruma's burial in a 'stone coffin' in 1014, and both of these references concern men who were held in very high esteem. O'Kelly is said to have been buried in *leabhaidh cloithi*, literally, a 'stone bed', rather than an *uluid* or 'tomb', but it is difficult to know exactly what the distinction between the two may have been. Unlike Brian Bóruma, Maol Sechlainn O'Kelly was not the first of his family to be buried at Knockmoy. In spite of this, it seems quite possible that there may not have been any O'Kelly family tomb at the abbey. Donnell Ó Ceallaigh (O'Kelly) 'Lord of Hy-Many', had been buried in the Cistercian abbey of Knockmoy in 1295, however, he was buried in the habit of a monk.[59] This is a telling detail, since Cistercian custom prescribed that monks be interred coffin-less in unmarked graves.[60] In other words, it seems that no O'Kelly family tomb existed at Knockmoy when Maol Sheachlainn died.

The *leabhaidh cloithi* in which O'Kelly was buried may refer to a slab-lined grave, the bottom (and possibly the sides) of which were lined with stones. 'The battle of Dun', a poem composed in the fourteenth century, tells that

---

57 ' ... et sepultus est in Ard-Macha, in mausoleo regum', *ALC* I, *s.a.* 1064.   **58** *MacCarthaig's Book*', ed. Ó hInnse, , Frag. II, 1402, §10, pp 166–7.   **59** *AFM, AU* ed. MacCarthy, I, p. 385.   **60** Brosnan, *Mortuary practices*.

> in Ard-Macha are the interments
> of the Ulaidh with their lime-stone graves[61]

Unfortunately, it is not clear whether this passage is speaking of slab-lined graves, or gravestones.

The case of Donnell O'Kelly bears comparison with the burial of another famous king, Cathal Crobhdearg O'Connor who, in 1224, was also interred in the habit of a Cistercian monk at Knockmoy, and whose obituary also makes no reference to his grave or tomb.[62]

As has become evident, medieval literary sources contain a number of different words which have been translated as 'tomb'. The poem *Suibhne Geilt*, a work which may have been composed as early as the twelfth century or as late as the close of the sixteenth, tells of the battle of Mag Rath in AD 637.[63] In it, the author tells of Suibhne's cairn being built by each man depositing his stone on it, and the word used for tomb is *leachtán*.[64] The fourteenth-century *Caithréim Thoirdhealbhaigh* dictates that after the end of a battle in 1317, Donough O'Brien, the chief, was to be interred in 'a permanent and worthy tomb' (*buanchóirigter innas nó fert cuibde do Donnchad*), while 'a cold lair' was to receive the bodies of the O'Hogans (*fuarálach d'úib Ogáin*), and 'habitations' were to be prepared for the O'Ahiarn dead (*adbada d'úib Eightigern*).[65] Despite the information included here, the lack of precise detail is frustrating.

The 'Book of Fenagh', sections of which date from the early fourteenth century, contains numerous mentions of burial, with *fert* being the favored word for grave.[66] We also find the words *lecht* and *uaig*, as well as *tiuglechtt*.[67] This last word is used in reference to the resting-place of the nineteen kings of Magh Rein (*ar Magh-Rein ta a tiuglechtt*).[68] Another poem of the same period contains a line which has been translated as 'raise ye a tomb to the band of women', the word

---

61 Mac Conmidhe, 'Poem on the battle of Dun', p. 149, lines 17–18. In Irish: 'Ulltaibh ar a n-Aelchlacha … a measg chloch are g-clann Néill-ne och nach ann a eiséirghe!' **62** It was long thought that the frescoes on the north wall at Knockmoy marked the tomb of Cathal Crobhdearg O'Connor, however it is now thought that these are datable to *c.*1400. Neither Cathal Crobhdearg's obituary notices in *AFM* or *ALC* contain any mention of a tomb, and it is difficult to believe that had such a fine memorial been created at the time of his burial, it would not have been noted by chroniclers. **63** O'Keeffe, in his introduction to his edition, remarked that on linguistic grounds the text might have been composed any time between 1200 and 1500. O'Donovan says its author must have lived before 1197. **64** *Suibhne Geilt*, ed. & trans. J.G. O'Keeffe, p. 157. 'The tomb of Suibhne here … from the grave and from the tomb!' (*os a lighe is ar a leachtán*). *Lighe* is associated with the word *lia* or monument stone; *leachtain* describes something akin to a small burial-mound. **65** *Caithr. Th.* re: the 'Battle of the Abbey' in Co. Clare in 1317, p. 107. The word *buanchóirighter* also suggests the tomb (or its stone) was 'dressed' or carefully prepared. **66** See *Bk Fen.*, eds Hennessy & Kelly, pp 260–1, 262–3, 264–5. 'Fertuib' is a compound meaning 'grave of the descendants of'. **67** *RIA Dict.* gives gives the meaning as 'grave, tomb', the first half of the compound ('*tiug*')meaning 'last' or 'final'. **68** *Bk Fen.*, eds Hennessy & Kelly, pp 260–1, 262–2, 264–5.

feart has been translated as 'tomb', while the grave of John, the local chieftain, is described as *uaigh Eoin*.[69]

In a four-line verse also written in the thirteenth-century, the poet Giolla Brighde mac Con Midhe describes the burial place of the king of Oileach as *uaigh*, and describes the graves of the Ulaid at Armagh as being 'in the midst of stones'.[70] For 'stones' the poet has chosen the word *chloch*, rather than *lia* or *coirthi*. The meaning of this phrase is open to interpretation. It could simply mean that the ground in the area was stony. It may refer to graveslabs marking graves there, or even that many tombstones were buried under the earth: the numerous small slabs found at Clonmacnoise are believed to have been enclosed in the graves, a practice that existed in Gaul and possibly in Northumberland as well.[71] Alternatively, this passage could refer to some sort of territorial stones – such a pillarstones, that were used to denote the area of the cemetery, like the pillar-stone at Clonshanville.[72] One is also reminded of interments found resting on crushed stone in graves formed by the careful placement of slabs set on their edges, and covered with flagstones, such as the ones discovered at Dundalk, Co. Louth, in 1881,[73] or those uncovered at Rossmakay, Co. Louth, in 1957.[74] Perhaps these are similar to the *leabhaidh cloithi* or 'stone beds' mentioned above.[75]

FUNERARY MONUMENTS

Excellent work has been done on recording and analyzing the inscribed and decorated funerary stones and monuments found in Ireland;[76] however, the limits of time and space demand that the focus here remain on the references found in the written sources.

Pillarstones

Charles Thomas stated that, although few *ogam* stones have been 'reliably record-ed … in direct association with graves,' no one 'seriously doubts that ogam stones

---

69 'The author of this is Eóghan MacEoin Mheic Eichthighearna', *Scottish verse*, ed. & trans. Watson, poem XIV, pp 170–1. The word 'uaigh' also means 'cave'. 70 Mac Con Midhe, 'Poem on the battle of Dun', p. 149, lines 17–18: 'Ulltaibh ar a n-Aelchlacha … a measg chloch ar g-clann Néill-ne'. 71 Lionard, 'The early', p. 100. 72 See below, n. 85. 73 Tempest, 'Graves discovered at Dundalk', p. 4. The account of these 'fifty or sixty graves' notes that although no traces of coffins existed, these burials might originally have been placed in coffins, since the stone-lined graves were 'built in the regular shape of coffins … the stonework of the graves on the inside representing an even and regular surface, as though the stones had been built against a shape'. The writer notes that 'graves of the same construction have turned up in open ground in the neighbourhood of Ardee where no evidence or tradition of burial grounds survives …' 74 Prendergast, 'Burial at Rossmakay', pp 38–9. 75 See above, n. 36. 76 Introduction to this volume. Also bibliography in *New history of Ireland*, II, pp 928–32.

ARE tombstones; no other explanation really fits'.[77] Ann Hamlin has agreed with Thomas, as has J.P. Mallory, who added that he was:

> unaware of a single example where an ogam stone in Ireland had been found directly associated with actual burial remains ... [However] it seems a fair presumption that some may have actually marked graves as opposed to commemorating the dead irrespective of place of burial.[78]

Pillarstones may also have been associated with territorial boundaries, a function which could have been linked to their connection with burial, since burials seem often to have been made at borders, as they were believed to have defensive or prophylactic properties. The great cemetery at Clonmacnoise is just one of many which were located at territorial boundaries.[79] Pillarstones may have served a function which was later taken over by stone crosses ('*termon* crosses') which were set up to denote the boundaries of the sanctuary lands of the church, and were thus also associated with the burials inside the consecrated land, if only because of physical proximity.[80]

Aside from medieval texts dealing with pre-Christian legend and mythology, we find few mentions of pillarstones. The Middle Irish commentary on the 'Martyrology of Oengus' contains the line: 'And get thee O Satan, into the pillarstone (*coirthi*) to the south of the cell, and thou shouldst cause no hurt there save to one who resist the Church'.[81] This would seem to indicate banishment to a pillarstone at the boundaries of a territory – and also suggest that pillarstones were regarded as non-Christian and perhaps even evil.

In 999, *AU* records that the *Lia Ailbe,* which was the chief monument in the territory of Mag Breg, fell and 'four mill-stones were afterwards made of it by Mael Sechnaill'. No additional information as to what function the *Lia Ailbe* served, or what its meaning might have been within this culture, is provided. F.J. Byrne states that the stone stood in the townland of Clonalvy, near Fourknocks, Co. Meath, and was purposely destroyed by the king.[82] The legendary origins of this pillarstone are preserved in the poem 'The colloquy of the ancients' (*Acallam na senórach*) which tells how three girls – Etaein, Aeife and Ailbhe – were beheaded by the Fianna warriors in an act of retribution, and then buried under 'three monoliths' (*trí cairtheda* and *trí cairthibsea*).[83] If the *Lia Ailbe* was

---

77 Thomas, *The early Christian*, p. 98.   **78** Mallory, 'The world of Cú Chulainn', p. 130.   **79** For a discussion of the possible connections between territorial boundaries and burials, see Ó Riain, 'Boundary associations' and 'Pagan example', p. 150. Ó Riain has noted that the tendency to locate churches on boundaries appears to be modelled completely on pagan custom, and to have existed only in the Celtic areas of Christendom.   **80** For one example, see Waterman, 'Banagher church', p. 37.   **81** 'Bid si immorro, for Mochuta, & eirgsi, a Satain, isin coirthi fil fri cill andes, & ni dernai irchoid ann acht dontí ticfa frisin eclais', *Félire*, p. 95.   **82** Byrne, *Irish kings,* p. 60.   **83** 'The Colloquy', *SG*, I, p. 225; II, p. 255.

destroyed on purpose, it must have been because it was offensive to the king in some way, and the recording of its destruction by the annalists shows that this event was significant and noteworthy. Presumably, by the end of the tenth century, the importance of the *Lia Ailbe* was associated with its symbolic representation of the former inhabitants of the territory, a symbolism which it initially acquired because it was believed to have been erected as Ailbe's gravestone. The fact that it was destroyed rather than appropriated is interesting as well: perhaps *Lia Ailbe* had lost its traditional importance, or its power was not believed to be transferable to a new kin-group. It is worth noting that trees which symbolized tribal kingship were also destroyed during this period.[84]

Samuel Lewis, writing in the mid-nineteenth century, may have noted a hold-over of the pillarstone's function as boundary and funeral marker when he observed that the cemetery at Clonshanville Abbey in Co. Roscommon which was 'still much used' at that time:

> one of the most remarkable relics is a cross of sandstone flag, rising eleven feet from the ground, said by tradition to mark the spot beyond which a corpse might not be carried by the relative and friends, but delivered up to the monk.[85]

Thus, the pillarstone at Clonshanville retained a link with the earlier tradition of using stones to describe the limits of a territory – the church's territory, in this case. This practice of 'handing over' the corpse to the church at the pillarstone has close similarities with the English custom of setting the corpse down at the covered 'lich-gate' at the entrance of the cemetery prior to burial.[86] At Lucan, Co. Dublin, Lewis recorded the survival of 'a very ancient and splendid cross' and noted that in the mid-nineteenth century it was 'still the custom at Roman Catholic funerals to bear the corpse (to the spot) previous to interment'.[87]

Archdall provided the curious information that John le Decer the mayor of Dublin, set up a 'large pillar stone in the church' of St Saviour's, Dublin in 1308.[88] The use of the term 'pillarstone' is odd. Perhaps this stone had previously been located outside, and had been brought into the church in an attempt to save it from theft, mutilation or destruction – or even in an attempt to 'Christianize' what may have been regarded as a pagan symbol.

84 See Byrne, *Irish kings*, 60n, p. 27.   **85** Lewis, *Topographical dictionary*, I, p. 63.   **86** 'At the entrance to most churchyards will be found a roofed timber erection known as a lich-gate. The term is derived from the German *leiche*, 'a corpse', for here it was that the corpse rested whilst the first part of the burial service was read in the days when it was not thought to be a fitting thing for the church to be used for the purpose.' Puckle, *Funeral customs*, p. 144.   **87** Lewis, *Topographical dictionary*, II, p. 321.   **88** *Mon. Hib.*, II, p. 70.

Gravestones

While some ogam-inscribed stones are pre-Christian, most are datable to the fifth or sixth centuries, although it has been argued that they continued to be erected into a later period. Upright stones with simple crosses incised on them are believed to have been the normal form of grave marker until the seventh century, after which time recumbent slabs became common.[89]

The terms used to describe monumental stones include: *ail, choirthe chrúaid, cloich, gloich,*[90] *lia, licc-bás, lid, láech-lía* (and its variant, *láochlíag*), *lechtaib, lecht leacca, marb-lia* and *uladh*.

Sources which record legendary stories speak of the graves of pre-Christian warriors being marked with stones which are generally described as having been 'raised' indicating that these were standing stones, rather than graveslabs. These references to the 'raising' of stones above graves indicate that they were monoliths of an impressive size. The large size of the stones is explicit in the following lines, as is the duty of making the grave:

> And he shall be under the shameful burden of the dead man, without mercy, till he find a stone that shall be a trophy of Aed's grave.' He marks a stone above Loch Goyle (it was a soldier's task), and raised it up with a champion's strength.[91]

The great height and weight of the stone enhanced the prestige of the deceased by proving that his companions were champions possessing the great physical strength needed to erect it. 'The colloquy of the ancients' also speaks of 'rearing' the stone over the place of rest,[92] and of the 'monumental stones of the Fianna' (*i lechtaib fiann*).[93]

References to inscribed monumental stones also occur. The tale of the burial of the great Celtic hero Fergus – with its mention of the soul and ogam stones – seems to combine Christian and pre-Christian elements:

> So Fergus's soul parted from his body: his grave was dug, his name written in the Ogham, his lamentation-ceremony all performed; and from the monumental stones (*uladh*) piled by Ulster this name of Uladh (Ulster) had its origin.[94]

89 Mytum, *The origins of early Christian Ireland*, p. 96. **90** '*Cloich*' and '*gloich*' are variations of the same word. **91** 'Ailech II', *Met. Dind.*, I, p. 103, lines 27–8: 'raib fo méla fon marbsin, cen nach cáemna/ co fagba lícc bas bert búada for lecht nAed'; Ibid, lines 29–30: 'Airgis líc ós loch F(h)ebail, ba feidm fénned, / co tórgab súas co crúas chórad, úais int én-f(h)er'. **92** 'The colloquy of the ancients', *SG*, I, pp 181–2: 'ocus do cuiredh fó fhochladaib talmen ann so í ar Cáilte. ocus ro tócbadh a lia ós a lige'. **93** 'The colloquy', *SG*, II, p. 181 (English), I, p. 163 (Irish). **94** 'Death of Fergus', *SG*, I, p. 285. *Uladh* = *ailad, aulad, ilad, elath* and is defined in the *RIA Dict.* as 'a tomb, sepulchre, burial cairn; *elath*: 'a calvary or charnel house'.

A passage from 'The colloquy of the ancients' indicates that stones may have been inscribed with a variety of information:

> ... a good story it is that thou hast told us; and be it by you others written on the tabular staves of poets and on monumental stones of Fianna.[95]

Numerous mentions of gravestones having been 'raised' for women also occur; the example of the 'Lia Ailbe' has already been noted.[96] The terms used for these stones are the same for both sexes, and interestingly, some of the funerary monuments erected for women are also called 'warrior'-stones, and said to carry ogam inscriptions. For example, regarding the grave of Medb (Queen Maeve), a poem records, 'tall is her gravestone'.[97] 'The colloquy of the ancients' tells of a women whose 'stone was reared over her resting-place, her funeral ceremony was performed, and her ogham-name inscribed'.[98] Tuadh, daughter of Aonghus, is said to have had a bare gravestone 'planted' over her, a stone which is later described as a 'warrior stone',[99] while in the poem 'Lia Nothain' a woman tells of her 'warrior-stone'.[100]

The main sources of information on monumental funerary stones are the legendary tales regarding the *fianna* warrior bands, and stories and poems which record placename lore. These tales present substantial difficulties regarding dating and content, and determining their value as historical sources is not easy. Obviously, they need to be used with great care. However, these tales comprise a major body of traditional lore committed to writing in the medieval period, and it would be irresponsible to ignore them altogether, since the references they contain contribute to a general understanding of burial in Ireland in the Middle Ages. Some of what they describe may be accurate descriptions of burial in prehistory. Other details may describe burial customs which were in use in the twelfth century, when these tales were committed to writing, and were interpolated into the earlier material. Yet even without close dating these references are instructive, for they indicate how a medieval audience would have wanted to believe the great legendary Irish kings, queens and warriors of a 'golden age' had been buried, and what would have been considered appropriate markers for their graves. They also provide valuable comparative information. For example, the fact that these tales tell that graves of high-ranking

Regarding the use of this word in the epitaph of Brian Bóruma, see the section of this work on 'tombs'. **95** 'ocus scribar líb in scél út i támlorgaib filid ocus i lechtaib fiann'; 'The colloquy', *SG*, I, p. 163; II, p. 181. **96** See n. 83 above. **97** '*is fata a ail*', 'Fert Medba', *Met. Dind.*, IV, pp 366–7. **98** ' ... lia ós a lige ocus ro feradh a cluiche cáintech. ocus do scríbadh a hainm ogaim': 'The colloquy', *SG*, I, p. 163: II, p. 181. **99** 'ro saith in gcloich os a cionn/ os feart Túaidhe atta oissi ann sin'; *Duanaire Finn*, II, poem XLII, verses 46–8, pp 79. The word *láochlíag* is later used to describe this stone. **100** '*mo láech-lía*', 'Lia Nothain', *Met. Dind.*, IV, p. 27 (English, p. 28).

women were marked with gravestones which were similar (if not identical) to those used to mark the graves of warriors indicates that this was a traditional practice. Although medieval sources which are generally accepted as being more historically accurate contain no explicit written references proving that this tradition continued into the high Middle Ages, given the conservative nature of burial, it is unlikely that it would suddenly have disappeared from Irish culture.

Charles Thomas and Pádraig Lionard have both noted that hardly any recumbent slabs were used in north Britain before the eighth century,[101] and Ann Hamlin has noted that the change from tall monolithic gravestones to recumbent slabs was a major one. The poem on the graves of the kings at Clonmacnoise, the earliest extant version of which is preserved in a fifteenth-century manuscript, contains many references to flagstones and states that numerous members of the same kin-group were buried under them. A few examples include:

> It is thirty kings in all of the folk of royal rank, of the kings of Cruachan who believe, that are under the flagstone of the kings in thy cemetery.[102]

> O great flagstone of the descendant of Maelrunach, to behold thee is not an order(?) of pride: twenty kings, and their heads 'neath thy cross, are under the mould which thou hast closed![103]

> O flagstone of Cuanu … eighteen men of excellence, from Cellach the Great to Murchad![104]

Datable inscriptions found on gravestones recovered from Clonmacnoise span a period from the eighth to the twelfth centuries but some of these would have been upright stones. Recumbent slabs may not have been used in Ireland at all before the seventh century, after which the recumbent slabs became more prevalent.[105] As has been noted above,[106] written sources referring to legendary or mythological events often describe 'tall stones' being 'raised' over graves. However, in passages describing contemporary events tombstones are generally called *lecca*. *AU* record that after the battle of Imlech Pich in AD 668, the poet

---

101 Thomas, *The early Christian archaeology*, p. 128. 102 R.I. Best, 'The graves of the kings at Clonmacnoise', lines 40–44; p. 167; Irish, p. 166: 'Is deich rígh fichet uili/do lucht réime rígraidhi,/do ríghaibh Crúachan do chreit, fo leic na rígh na reileic!' 103 Ibid., lines 53–56, p. 167; Irish, p. 166: 'A lec mór hui Maelruanaigh/do dechain ní hord uabhair,/ fiche ri[g] 'sa cenn fat crois,/atá fón úir do dúnois!' 104 Ibid., lines 57–60, p. 167; Irish: 'A lec Chuana ui Cellaig,/mairgh ard in c[h]ruaidh rodcennaigh,/ocht fir déc do glíri glan,/ó Chellach Mór co Murchad!' 105 Lionard, 'The early', p. 156; Brosnan, 'Mortuary practices', p. 33. 106 See above, n. 89–100.

recited these words: '... sorrowful are (your) glances at (their) grave-stones (*lecht leacca*),' and in 878, the same source records tells of 'cold flags over the temples (of the buried)' (*lecca huaire iar n-aire*).

Unfortunately, the annalists did not reveal whether the memorials were upright or recumbent, but other medieval Irish sources which are datable with greater certainty indicate that stones may have been recumbent by the eleventh century. The poem 'Ailech I' relates the place-lore of the Uí Néill stronghold of Ailech: 'A goodly shining grave was built in town wherein it is seen of all ... and a gravestone laid on the tomb'.[107] Since this poem is attributed to the poet Flann Mainistrech (d. 1056), and Edward Gwynn felt that it could not be dated earlier than the eleventh century, this detail probably reflects eleventh-century burial practice, rather than that from the pre- or 'early-Christian' period. A passage from the eleventh-century commentary on the 'Martyrology of Oengus' tells of Constantine's conversation with Mochutu in which he says 'I think I should like the flagstone [*lec*] on which thou repeatest thy paternoster to be over my face [when I am buried]', a request to which Mochutu assents.[108] This may suggest another reason – aside from the desire to protect the corpse from being disturbed or uprooted[109] – why stones came to be laid over the body, rather than placed upright at the head; it could also be that the author noted the request because such placement for the stone was unusual.

Samuel Lewis recorded the levelling of a bank of sand near the sea at Bray Head, Co. Wicklow, in 1835, at which time several human skeletons were discovered 'lying regularly east to west, with a stone at the head and another at the feet of each but which crumbled into dust on exposure to the air'.[110] These stones seems to have been below ground, buried with the corpse. One is reminded of the crosses buried at Armagh with the corpse thought to be St Lupita – perhaps these crosses were actually cross-inscribed stones.[111] Charles Thomas noted a burial from the Garvelloch islands in western Scotland which was characterized by 'two slabs at the (western) head end, and two marking the feet, one of which bore an incised cross of the seventh century type'.[112]

The fourteenth-century work *Caithréim Thoirdhealbhaigh* contains instructions for the types of tombs to be built for the noble dead and also details how the tombs of warriors slain in 1317 were to be marked after their death:

> For the Kennedys, have a litter strewn ... narrow flags laid over clan-Gillamochanna; a limestone flag, true to rule, over O'Flaherty. Have

---

107 'Dia do glan-f(h)ert glan rogníth fich inid faderc do chach ... cen marbh-lia mairt forsin fert', 'Ailech I,' *Met. Dind.*, p. 95.   **108** ' ... acht imraidim nama comad maith lim in lec forsa ngeibisi do pater cumad si no beith dar m'aigid.' *Félire*, p. 95.   **109** Lionard, 'Early Irish', p. 99.   **110** Lewis, *Topographical dictionary*, i, p. 223.   **111** Regarding St Lupita, see Chapter 3, n. 142, and below, n. 143.   **112** Thomas, *The early Christian*, p. 63.

O'Donnagan put down in a good place and, as by you heretofore these members of (your) highborn kindreds have been extinguished in the mighty battle, even so make you now ready and adorn their beds.[113]

The O'Kennedys are to have their 'litter strewn' (*Cóirigter cosair d'úib Chinneidid*)[114] and the order is given to 'adorn' the graves ('bed' means 'grave' here) of 'highborn kindreds', but information regarding what the litter was to be strewn with, or how the graves were to be 'adorned' is lacking. That considerable effort was to be expended is further indicated by the instruction to mark the O'Shanachan graves with 'dressed and polished stones', and the 'limestone flag, true to rule' (*aolchloch leicriaglach d'Ó Flaithbertaig*) which would mark O'Flaherty's grave. That bright or shining stones were to be 'planted over' the O'Shanahans (*snaidter solasleca tar úib Sencháin*) suggests that the stones were upright, though this is not clearly stated. The medieval poem cited above[115] describing Holy Cross Abbey, Co. Tipperary, as 'The true church of the Lord's Cross, with its stone monuments and coffins and hosts of angels in reference, is a fort, a sanctuary for souls', suggests that for a church to have a large cemetery was seen as a positive reflection of the church's worthiness and sanctity.[116] The 'Black book of Christ Church' records the burial of John of St Paul (d. 1362) under a marble stone at the second step of the altar of Christ church.[117]

The register of the monastery of Athenry contains what may be the only written record – although surely not the only occurrence – of the importation of an English tombstone into Ireland. It was brought to Athenry at a cost of 20 marks by Joanna de Wffler, for the purpose of marking the grave of her husband, David Wedir, who died in 1343.[118]

Crosses

Charles Plummer, in his *Lives of the Irish saints*, stated that 'for Christians, a cross was erected over the grave'.[119] It is all but certain that small wooden crosses were

113 ' … cuirter i ndeginad O Donnagáin; agus mar do marbad lib na degchineda sin go trásda sin trénchath degchóirigid anois a niamleptacha … ', *Caithr. Th.* re the 'Battle of the abbey' in Co. Clare in 1317, II, p. 107; I, p. 121. **114** The *RIA Dict.* translated *cos(s)ar* as the act of strewing lawyers, heap (esp. of dead bodies); Dr Katharine Simms has suggested 'Arrange a bed (or couch) for the O Kennedys' as an alternate translation. **115** See n. 27 above. Dr Katharine Simms has pointed out that the *RIA Dict.* translates *snaidid* as 'carved', rather than 'planted' which appears in O'Grady's translation. **116** *Aithdioghluim dána*, poem 88, st. 23. The author of this poem is unknown, and Lambert suggests no date for it (see p. xx). Dr Katharine Simms has suggested that it may have been connected with the major restoration work undertaken at Holy Cross in the fifteenth century. **117** ' … corpus suum sub lapide marmoreo cum ymagine enea in secundo gradu ante predictum altare … ', A. Gwynn, 'Some unpublished texts', p. 310. **118** '… nobilis matrona Joanne de Wffler uxor dicti David Wedir … transferri ossamenta mariti sui de conventu Bristol ad conventum de Athnary … Item fecit transportare unum lapidem in quo est sculptura de partibus transmarinis pro quo solvit quoad emptionem et quoad navem et quoad omnia alia xx marcas et hic lapis est super sepulturam ipsius et sui mariti … ' *Reg. Mon. Athenry*, p. 207. **119** Thomas, *The early Christian*, p. 92; H.C. Mytum, *The origins*, p.

used in Britain before the Norman Conquest of England and Charles Edwards has argued that such crosses 'were placed on or at graves from the early seventh century', but that these crosses have not survived.[120] The work of R.A.S. Macalister and others have detailed the large number of Irish cross-inscribed graveslabs which survive from the early Christian period.[121]

Written sources, however, contain almost no mention of crosses as grave-markers. The Irish annals contain only two mentions of crosses. The first occurs in 871, slightly before the period of this survey, and tells of hazel crosses used to mark a soldier's grave in Drumcliff, Co. Sligo.[122] The second entry tells of the burial in 1244 of Magnus son of Muirchertach Muimnech; the *AConn* relates that he

> was buried outside the doorway of the church of Fenagh … A beautiful monument of stone with an excellently wrought stone cross was afterwards made (and set up) over him, but after awhile the Uí Ruairc in their enmity demolished it.[123]

ALC also describe it as 'a splendid monument of hewn stones, surmounted by a beautiful stone cross', indicating that it had a substantial base.[124]

Literary references to crosses are also rare: the poem on the graves of the kings at Clonmacnoise tells of the 'great flagstone of the descendant of Maelruanach – 20 kings and their heads 'neath thy cross'.[125] In the tale *Buile Shuibhne* composed sometime between the early twelfth and the fourteenth century, the author asked

> What plain is a match for Magh Line, unless it be the plain that is in Meath, or Magh Femin of many crosses …[126]

An early Irish lyric refers to a warrior buried with a cross 'above his head',[127] but whether this refers to a cross-marked stone, a stone carved into the shape of a cross, or a wooden cross is unknowable.

In his entry regarding the disinterment at Armagh early in the eighteenth century of a body buried in a standing posture, and believed to be that of St Lupita, Archdall noted that 'crosses were also discovered closely guarding the body before and behind'.[128] Unfortunately, no further description of the cross-

---

97; *Lives*, p. xclix, citing pp 294, 325–6. **120** Plummer, *Vitae sanctorum Hiberniae*, I, p. xclix, citing I, pp 294, 325–6. **121** Macalister, *Clonmacnoise* and *Inscriptionum*. **122** *AFM s.a.* 871. **123** *AConn*, 1244.5. **124** *AConn*, *ALC s.a.* 1244, No. 5. **125** Best, "The graves of the kings at Clonmacnoise", p. 167, st. 14. **126** *Suibhne Geilt*, ed. O'Keeffe, p. 107. 'Magh Femin' is in Co. Tipperary, south of Cashel, on the border of Desmond, at the boundary between the baronies of Offa and Iffa. **127** 'Grievous to me has been the death of the warrior who used to lie with me – that the son of the woman from Daire Dá Dos should have a cross above his head.' 'Créide's Lament for Cáel,' *Early Irish lyrics*, ed. & trans. Murphy, v, pp 148–9, No. 48. **128** *Mon. Hib.*, I, p. 49.

es was given. If the body did date from Patrician times, as Archdall wrote, the crosses must have been of stone, since it is unlikely that wooden crosses would have survived for so long.

Writing in the sixteenth century of the great battle of Clontarf where Brian Bóruma was slain, Edmund Campion stated that by his own time there was

> … Only a memory left of theyer felde in Clontarf,
> where dyvers noble yryshmen were slayne,
> that lye buryed before the crosse of Kylmaynam.[129]

Whether Campion meant that he believed the slain had been buried before a cross erected specifically as a monument to the dead, or simply that the dead were buried in close proximity to an existing *termon*-cross marking the boundaries of the sanctuary lands of Kilmainham, is not clear. European medieval cemeteries commonly erected a cross at each of the four points of the compass as well as in the centre,[130] and it is likely that a cemetery had existed at Kilmainham for many centuries prior to the battle of Clontarf. A belief that the slain from this battle were buried at Kilmainham has persisted well into the present century, and modern writers also sometimes state that the present grounds of the Royal Hospital at Kilmainham were used as a staging-ground by the Irish prior to the battle of Clontarf in 1014.[131] Presumably, this idea originated in a passage from the *Leabhar Oiris*.[132]

Inscribed epitaphs

Ogam-engraved pillar-stones have already been discussed[133], and are concentrated in the west of Ireland. Many ogham inscriptions commemorate the dead, and as I have noted,[134] Irish heroic and legendary tales also record the practice of commemorating the dead on vertical stones. Written sources describe the practice in highly formulaic language that is usually almost identical with the following passage regarding the burial of Fionn's princely opponents:'Over the grave of the fallen the monumental stone was raised, their names written in ogam above them all …'[135]

---

129 Campion,'Two bokes of Ireland,' p. 61, line 23. **130** Gyug,'Consecration of cemeteries', p. 541. **131** Stanihurst's influence is also strong and enduring: see, for example,'Ancient monuments in the hospital fields, Dublin,' *Dublin Penny Journal*, i, 1832–3, pp 68–9; S. Murphy, *Bully's Acre*, p. 5; Kenny, *Kilmainham*, p. 26. **132** *Leabhar Oiris*, ed. Best, p. 90, §39:'…7 do bhá dar ameasg a gcarad, ag iarraidh a gcorp; 7 as e comha[i]rle do rinne Cian mac Maoilmhuaidh 7 Tadgh mac Briain, dul go Cill Mhaighneann an oidche sin …' I am indebted to Dr Tina Hellmuth for the folllowing translation: '… and they were amongst their friends asking for their corpses; and Cian mac Maoilmhuaidh and Tadhg mac Briain suggested to go to Kilmainham that night …' **133** See section on 'Pillarstones' in this chapter. **134** See section on 'Gravestones' in this chapter. **135** 'do tócbad a lia ós a lecht ocus do críbad a nanmanna I nogaim ós cionn cach énfir díob', 'The gilla decair', *SG*, I, p. 307; II, p. 272.

Inscriptions on Irish funeral sculpture of the medieval period are rare, and it is important to remember that the population of Ireland during the Middle Ages was small and social organization centered around the kin-group. R.A.S. Macalister noted the difficulty of positively associating historical people with the inscriptions he recorded and in reminding his readers that doing so was not his goal, he noted that[136]

> the inscriptions were addressed primarily to contemporaries, presumed to know already everything necessary to know about the owners of the monuments; not to us, a vaguely-realized posterity.[136]

Despite these disclaimers, Macalister was able to associate three inscribed graves-labs to the third quarter of the ninth century, and two each to the tenth, eleventh, and twelfth centuries – including the gravestone of the twelfth-century king Toirrdelbach ua Conchoboir (Turlough O'Connor) which he thought matches an illustration in the manuscript of the 'Annals of Tigernach'. Of the stones which carry more than a name, and on which the beginnings of the inscriptions are still legible, all use the '*oroit do*' ('pray for') convention.

The earliest inscribed 'Anglo-Norman' funeral monument in Ireland would seem to be a damaged graveslab bearing a floriated cross and a woman's head. It was found in St Mary's church in New Ross, Co. Wexford, and is inscribed 'ISABEL: LAEGN …' This was once believed to commemorate the burial place of Isabel, the daughter of Strongbow; however H.G. Leask convincingly argued that the 'Isabel' commemorated by this stone could not have been Isabel de Clare, who died in 1220 and was buried at Tintern in Monmouthshire, Wales. In his judgment, the stone is a centotaph and based on the relative simplicity of its Lombardic lettering, dates from 'soon after 1220'.[137]

The earliest inscribed stone listed in John Hunt's masterly work, *Irish medieval figure sculpture*, was dated by the author to the late thirteenth century. It comes from Bannow, Co. Wexford, the area where the first 'Anglo-Norman' soldiers landed in Ireland, and commemorates '*Ioanes Colfer*' (John Colfer).[138] The second is from St Mary's parish church in Kilkenny. Dated to the late thirteenth or early fourteenth century, it commemorates Helen, the wife of William of Armayl.[139] The earliest inscription commemorating a native Irishman remarkably commemorates neither king nor cleric, but a civilian named 'Thomas S', whose dress reveals him to be of the middle classes. It was found at Jerpoint, Co. Kilkenny, and bears an inscription which dates it to the fourteenth century; art historians

---

136 Macalister, *Corpus inscriptionum*, ii, introduction (not paginated).   **137** Leask, 'A cenotaph of "Strongbow's Daughter"', pp 65–7.   **138** This stone was recorded in the last century by Du Noyer, but no longer exists. See Hunt, *Irish Medieval*, pl. 98, cat. no. 260.   **139** Ibid., pl. 25, cat. no. 160.

have assigned it to the first half of that century.[140] However, the fact that the name 'Thomas' inscribed on the stone is not an Irish name (nor the Irish spelling of the name) raises the question of how much certainty there can be about this man's origins.[141] If he was a native Irishman, then he is one who had anglicized his name (or whose family thought it expedient to bury him under the anglicized version of his name). Alternatively, he could be a *gall* ('foreigner'), who had adopted the native Irish style of clothing.

The first written reference to epitaphs or inscriptions in Ireland occurs in 1220 in regard to Meiler FitzHenry (whose father was natural son to King Henry I). Meiler was interred in the chapter house of the priory at Great Connell, Co. Kildare, and his grave is said to have been marked with the words:

> Conduntur tumulo Meyleri nobilis ossa
> Indomitus domitor totius gentis Hiberniae.[142]

The next mention of an inscription is preserved among the 'Charter of the Cistercian abbey of Duiske'. The editor records that Ralph, the rector or parson at Gowran, died in 1253, and that his monument was 'a huge slab with the recumbent effigy of an ecclesiastic in vestments … with the following inscription in hexameters':

> Dum uixit sanus, Radoulfus erat Julianus,
> Dum uixit sospes, Ruptis fuerat pius ospes,
> anno domini MCLIII XIII Kal. April[143]

John Hunt has verified both the existence of this slab and that its inscribed date is indeed 1253.

The register of Archbishop Swayne contains a reference to the curious and lengthy epitaph, datable to 1348, of 'John Raby'(?), son of Andrew', which reads:

> Hic Jacet Andreae notissimus orbe Johannes
> Primo qui Sexti Clementis, atque Novellas
> Jeronimi laudes speculique jura peregit,
> Raby Doctorum Lux Censor Normaque Morum
> Occubit fato praebere pestis in anno.[144]

---

140 Ibid., pl. 52, cat. no. 119. 141 I wish to thank Dr Katharine Simms for pointing out this inconsistency. 142 *Annales Monasterii*, ed. Gilbert, ii, p. 314; Archdall printed what he called a 'very inelegant translation': 'Intombed [*sic*] are the bones of him they noble Meyler call, Who was the tameless tamer of the Irish nation all': *Mon. Hib.*, II, p. 261. 143 *Charters of the Cistercian*, eds Butler & Bernard, pp 11–12. 144 *The register of John Swayne*, eds Butler & Bernard, pp 11–12.

No other information is provided, and neither John nor Andrew Raby is mentioned elsewhere in the register (nor is anyone of the same name indexed in Sweteman's or Fleming's register). The wording 'here lies' certainly suggests that this refers to an inscribed epitaph, rather than to words from a funeral eulogy.

Mervyn Archdall, quoting Meredith Hanmer, recorded an inscribed monument dated 1402 at Abbeyknockmoy, Co. Galway, commemorating 'muileachaind O Ceallaid' (Melaghlin O'Kelly) chief of Uí Maine. Macalister recorded the stone as lying in the ruins of the Cistercian abbey-church at Knockmoy, and recorded the inscription as being 'four lines of medieval 'Gothic' lettering executed *in cavo relievo* as follows:

DO MULEACHLAIND O KEALLAID DO RI O MANI
AGUS D'INDBUALAIND INGE(N) I CHONCHUR
DORINE MATHA O COGLI IN LEABAIG SEA

Macalister translated this as 'For Mael-Sechlaind Ó Ceallaigh king of Uí Maine, and for Fionnguala, daughter of Ó Conchobair, Matha Ó Cogli made this bed'. Both died in 1402 and Macalister does not indicate that he believes the stone to have been carved later than O'Kelly's stated date of death in 1402.[145] The wording of the inscription is quite different from the '*oroit do*' formula formerly employed in inscriptions on memorials of the native Irish. The O'Kelly monument is the only inscription found which honours a fifteenth-century Irish chieftain. While it may not have been unique, one must surmise that it was highly unusual.

Effigies
Unfortunately, the primary Irish written sources which have been consulted for this study contain no mention of effigies, but a brief overview of Irish effigial tombstones may be of use.

Since the 'Anglo-Normans' did not arrive in Ireland until the fourth quarter of the twelfth century, it comes as little surprise that the earliest Norman-style funerary monuments are scarcely earlier than the thirteenth century,[146] and that the earliest effigies of abbots and knights – an art form imported from Norman culture – appear in the late thirteenth century. Examples from this early period still exist in western Ireland at the sites of Ardfert, Co. Kerry, and Hospital, Co. Limerick, where they were erected to commemorate Anglo-Irish graves. In the century between the burial of Donnell O'Kelly in 1295 and Maol Sechlainn O Kelly in 1402, the Anglo-Irish funerary art used to mark the graves of nobility and high ecclesiastics would have become familiar to the native Irish élite. Hunt states that[147]

145 Macalister, *Corpus inscriptionum*, II, pp 8–9.   **146** Hunt, *Irish medieval*, pp 6–7.   **147** Ibid., the influence of the Norman invasion is interestingly mirrored in the effigies traditionally said to be those of Felim O'Connor of Roscommon and Conor na Siudaine O'Brien of Corcomroe, Co. Clare. These effigies were made in imitation of the effigies of English kings, but were executed in a flat, distinctively Irish style of carving. They date to no earlier than *c.*1300, and a date of *c.*1330 is possible for that of Conor na Siudaine – meaning that it could have been carved some thirty years after his death.

Hunt suggests that the effigy may possibly commemorate a later monarch.

It might be useful to compare the situation in Ireland regarding effigies with that in northern Wales, the area from which so many of the 'Anglo-Normans' came.[148] Interestingly, the earliest known surviving northern Welsh effigial monument stone depicts a woman. It is the coffin-lid bearing the semi-effigy of Princess Joan, found in Anglesey, and dated to 1237 – a few decades earlier than the earliest surviving Irish effigy. The earliest extant inscribed slab is the floriated cross-slab of Johannes, son of Nicholas, which comes from Chirk Castle in Denbighshire, and is dated to the late thirteenth century. Its main inscription, executed in sunken Lombardic capitals, is quite poetic, and conforms to a type which was common in England during this period.

Of the ten inscribed northern Welsh slabs which date from *c.*1300 or earlier, the sex of the person commemorated is known for eight. Interestingly enough, seven of the ten extant slabs commemorate women, and six of these seven appear to be native Welsh women.[149] Presumably the high percentage of inscriptions commemorating women is due simply to an accident of survival, but it testifies to the attention and money that were lavished on the burial of high-status women in twelfth-century Wales.

A double-effigy of two children in swaddling clothes or 'chrisoms', carved in high relief, have been found at St John's church in Tralee, Co. Kerry. Tradition claims that the children commemorated are Geraldine twins. The only comparable Irish effigy is known as the 'Bambino' stone, and is located in St Mary's, New Ross, Co. Wexford. It has been dated to some time in the late thirteenth or early fourteenth century.

Monumental brasses

Referring to England, Clare Gittings says that the erection of monuments to the deceased

---

pl. 43, cat. no. 3; & pl. 42, cat. no. 212, pp 6–7. **148** This includes the counties of Anglesey, Caernarvonshire, Cheshire, Denbighshire, Flintshire, Merioneth, Montgomeryshire & Shropshire. **149** Gresham, *Medieval stone carving.* I refer here to slabs nos. 22, 23, 27, 29, 30, 31, 35, 36, 37 & 38. My observation about the women's being 'native Welsh' is based solely on the names as they appear on these monuments.

became common from the fourteenth century ... as is reflected in the spread of monumental brasses. Unlike earlier tombs which were often anonymous, the name of the person commemorated was now displayed on the monument. Both developments are symptomatic of a growing emphasis on the individual ...[150]

Due to the great popularity of memorial brasses in England, it is reasonable to expect that this trend found its way to Ireland – particularly as a method of commemorating the merchant classes – just as it might be expected that the grander and far more expensive effigial monuments which became so popular among the English nobility would also have become popular with Anglo-Irish lords. However, no mention of monumental brasses in Ireland has been found in either the written or art historical sources surveyed for this period.[151]

150 Gittings, *Death, burial*, p. 33. **151** See H.A. King 'Irish memorial brasses to 1700', *PRIA*, XCIV (1994), pp 111–40.

CHAPTER 5

Evidence of social stratification in burial

Medieval Irish sources contain a good deal of information regarding the placement of burials both inside churches and out. The placement of burials in relation to the church, and the positions of the graves and the corpses in relation to each other, provide insights into how Irish society was stratified during the period under study, and also suggest the social status of the deceased during life. As R.C. Finucane has stated:

> In the Middle Ages as in other epochs, death ritual was not so much a question of dealing with a corpse as of reaffirming the secular and spiritual order by means of a corpse.[1]

Written sources indicate that the Irish thought it appropriate for members of the same kin-group to be buried together (especially if they had died together), and we find examples of this regarding kings, bishops, warriors, soldier-boys and royal women. It was common for more than one interment to be made in a grave; for example, recent excavations in the city of Waterford found as many as thirteen individuals in a single stone-lined grave, though these burials were probably not deposited at the same time, but over a number of years.[2] Three of these groups are mentioned in one section of the prose text 'The colloquy of the ancients' (*Acallam na senórach*), written *c.*1200, in which Conall tells of three earthen burial mounds or *tulaig*:

> *tulach na laechraidhe* or 'grave of the laechs' one is called; *tulach an bhanchuire* or 'tulach of the woman-bevy' another; and *leacht na macraidhe* or 'grave of the boys' is the third tulach's name ...[3]

Centuries later, the 'Register of the monastery of Athenry' preserves a variation on this theme, recording that David Wedir and Robertus Gardiner, the two husbands of one Joanna de Wffler, were buried under the same tombstone in 1440.[4]

---

1 Finucane, 'Sacred corpse', p. 41. 2 Power, 'Human skeletal remains', p. 763. 3 'The colloquy,' *SG*, I, p. 155; II, p. 172. A 'laech' is a 'boy-warrior'. 4 '... et hic lapis est super sepultur-

149

BURIAL OF WARRIORS AND SOLDIERS

The medieval sources referring to the warrior-society of pre-Christian Ireland
often speak of warriors being buried together. The poem *Tulach Eogain* tells:

> Here rest a brave quartet in one place, in one abode … Four there were,
> as is well known, that did red deeds of valour … Those are the ten sons
> of stern Cathair, and his six grandsons, in one tomb: a band of lions
> undaunted were they, here round Eogan …[5]

Another poem, '*Lumman Tige Srafáin*' states: 'together likewise do we lie in
the grave, we four stout fighters',[6] and in a poem from *Duanaire Finn* we read
that 'Caoil met his death beside Patrick himself … and he was buried in *Crosa
Caoil* with the son of Lughaidh beside him'.[7] A mid-thirteenth-century poem
on the battle of Ballyshannon tells of 'three noble heroes, who do not seek praise-
poetry, are in one pale, tapering limestone grave, a trio of warriors side by side
…'[8]

The fourteenth-century composition *Caithréim Thoirdhealbhaigh* directs how
in 1317, after the 'Battle of the Abbey' at Corcomroe, Co. Clare, the slain noble
warriors were to be interred side by side with due consideration given to their
relative 'ranks':[9]

> … for Donough the chief be there made a permanent and worthy tomb
> … At the prince's side have Brian of Berra laid … Murtough's grand bulk
> beside the stripling; by him again, Teigue of Limerick; next in order be
> Turlough mac Teigue also set.[9]

The 'Annals of St Mary's, Dublin' record that the Scottish lord Fergus
Ardrossan, along with Lord Walter of Moray and all who died with them, were
buried in the convent at Athy, Co. Kildare, in 1315; however, we do not know if
they were interred in one grave, or if the nobles were given separate burial. It is
worth noting that their bodies were not sent back to Scotland for interment.[10]

---

am ipsius et sui mariti videlicet Daird (*sic*) ut dictum est et sub eodem lapide jacet unus nobilis
armiger nomine Robertus Gardiner … secundus maritus praenominatae matronae …': *Reg.
Mon. Athenry*, p. 207. **5** '*sind oen-uaig*', '*Tulach Eogain*', *Met. Dind.*, iv, pp 284–5. **6** '*Lumman
Tige Srafáin*', *Met. Dind.*, iv, p. 333. **7** *Duanaire Finn*, ii, poem XXXCIII, st. XXXIX, p. 31. **8** Mac
Con Midhe, *The poems*, ed. Williams, No. iv; st. XXXI, p. 49. This poem dates to the mid-thir-
teenth century. **9** *Caithr. Th.*, ii, p. 107; i, pp, 120–121: 'buanchóirigter innas nó fert cuibde
do Donnchad in degháirdríg ar órdugad bus oirderca ná a uasalbráithrecha .i. Brian agus
Muirchertach agus mór Thadg. cóirígter Brian berrai go buanáithesach re táib in áirdríg
Donnchaid, agus cuirter Tadg luimnigh le a remhartáib sin. cuirter Toirdelbach rígchoscrach
mac Taidg re táib na cosrach sin mar in gcédna'. **10** 'Occiduntur ex parte Scotorum Dominius
Fergus Andressan, Dominus Walterus de Morrey, et multi alii interficiuntur, quorum corpo-

Writing of pre-Christian Irish heroic society, the author of 'The colloquy of the ancients' reports that, like warriors, members of the non-élite who died together were also often interred together, indicating that tribal affinity was the tie which bound:

> The Fianna came and in excavations of the earth buried those four hundred of Finn's people, the manner in which each one of these was found being with a man of the sons of Morna dead under him.[11]

In this case, the burial duties were performed by the élite warriors of the Fianna. Other passages indicate the type of burial given to common, non-élite soldiers. In 980 we read of the 'measuring rod' employed to reckon the number of men felled in battle at Tara, Co. Meath.[12] A cross-base in the graveyard of Inis Cealtra was described by Macalister as bearing the inscription 'ILAD Í DECHENBOIR', meaning 'the grave of the ten men',[13] while *Caithréim Thoirdhealbhaigh* provides the following description of the burial of footsoldiers in Co. Clare in the early fourteenth-century: 'Over their kerne [laid in one long trench] be the earth heaped rampartwise.'[14] This allusion to burial in 'ramparts' must refer to the fact that the earth was built up over the burial trench, but it echoes earlier references to pre-Christian warriors being buried in ramparts, a practice which I discuss below in the section entitled 'location and position of graves and tombs'.

Written evidence records that members of the Anglo-Irish warrior-élite were also buried together. The 'Register of Athenry' records that in 1415 'Lord Thomas de Burgh' the son of the count of Ulster was buried in the habit of a brother next to William Prendergast and Maurice Prendergast, 'captain' of the 'nation' of Clanmorris.[15] This entry is particularly notable because, although de Burgh had died as a friar, he was not buried with the friars but according to the social position which he had held in his earlier, secular life.

For obvious reasons, the burial of soldiers was not always accomplished immediately, and the grim consequences could be equally obvious: an entry in 'MacFirbish's annals' describes a battle between the earls of Ormond and Desmond in 1462, when 'after the account of them that knew it, there was the number of 410 of his men buried, beside all that was eaten by doggs and foules of the aire …'[16]

---

ra sepulta sunt apud Athy, in conventu Fratrum Predicatorum': *Ann. Mon. Beatae*, ed. Gilbert, p. 347. **11** 'The colloquy', *SG*, I, 157, ii, p. 174. **12** 'A great battle between Mael Sechnaill and the son of Amláib … at Temuir, a measuring rod being required everywhere.' *AFM*, s.a. 980. This suggests that the bodies had been gathered into one area, and perhaps stacked. **13** Maclister, 'The history and antiquities of Inis Cealtra', p. 146. The author did not suggest a date for the inscription. **14** 'agus déntar clais múraig ar a gceithernaib …' *Caithr. Th.*, I, p. 120, II, p. 107. **15** ' … juxta quem jacent diversi nobiles Willelmus Pindigast et Mauricius Pindigast capitani nationis de Clanmuiris.' 1415, *Reg. Mon. Athenry,* pp 211–12. **16** *AMacF, s.a.* 1462.

BURIAL OF KINGS

That kings were buried together is recorded in numerous sources. The 'Book of Fenagh', whose verse sections date from before 1300, tells that a total of nineteen kings were buried at Magh Réin (the plain on which Fenagh is located), many of them in one grave (*i n-aen uaigh*).[17] Chronicles refer to the 'tomb of the kings' at Armagh,[18] while other sources tell of royal cemeteries at Drumlane[19] and Cell Corbbáin.[20] The 'cemetery of the kings' at Clonmacnoise is well known, and the poem on the graves of the kings buried there indicates that two kings were buried under the altar, with Toirrdelbach buried on the altar's southern side and Ruaidrí interred on the 'other lofty side'. Additionally, thirty kings are said to have been buried under the same gravestone, while a different stone, the 'great flagstone of the descendents of Maelruanach' is reported to have twenty kings buried beneath it.[21]

There seems to be as little reason to believe that any of the locations referred to in written sources as a 'cemetery of the kings' should be regarded as one in which *only* kings were buried, any more than the statement that Luke, archbishop of Dublin, was interred in 1255 in 'the same tomb' with his predecessor, John Comyn[22] means that burial in Christchurch cathedral was reserved exclusively for the archbishops of Dublin.[23]

The poem *Cell Chorbbáin* clearly illustrates this point. It presents an inventory of the cemetery at Cell Náis (Naas, Co. Kildare), in which were buried 'nine kings, a martial line, shining in splendour', before stating that this 'royal cemetery' contained not only the graves of kings, but also those of women, clerics and other members of the community:

> there are nine women … yonder beside the Cross rest their remains …
> Aillend and Áine in one tomb … Nine kings, nine queens brought long
> renown to their meeting-place, with nine saints … Many are the kings
> and the queens and hawklike favourite squires, the clerics and musicians
> in array, beside those three bold nines.[24]

17 *Bk Fen.*, ed. & trans. Hennessy, p. 265.   **18** 'Conchobur m. Domnaill, ridomna Ailigh, mortuus est et sepultus est in cimiterio regum i nArd Macha', *AU*, 935; '… ri Ailigh do ec i Telach Og ocus sepultus est in nArd Macha in mausolio regum', *AU, s.a.* 1064; '… co nairmidin i ttumba n riograide', *AFM, s.a.* 1064.   **19** 'Life of Maedoc of Ferns (II)', ed. & trans. Plummer, i, p. 284, § 271: '*ar uaigh an rígh go Ferna*', ii, p. 276, §271.   **20** *FAII, s.a.* 909: 'Cerball, son of Muirecán, king of Laigin died … and was buried among his forefathers at the graveyard of *Cell Corbbáin*'. (*Cell Chorbbáin* was at Naas, Co. Kildare.)   **21** *Ibid.*, lines 41–44. of the poem states: 'It is 30 kings in all of the folk of royal rank of the kings of Cruachan who believe, that are under the flagstone of the kings in the cemetery (*fo leic na rígh at reileic*)'.   **22** *Mon. Hib.*, II, p. 4; date cited from *Handbook of British. chronology*, edd. Fryde et al., p. 350.   **23** For example, the 'Black book of Christ Church' records that Richard de Clare ('Strongbow') was buried there in 1176.   **24** '*Cell Chorbbáin*', *Met. Dind.*, IV, p. 341.

Annalistic entries and studies of gravestones offer additional evidence that the cemetery at Clonmacnoise also received the bodies of bishops, abbots, women[25] and poets.[26] The 'Life of St Colman Ela' tells that the saint

> gave them in return [that is, the Uí Duibhginn, in exchange for 200 milch cows] a place in the choir of my church, / a little way from the bed (grave) of the kings, / without disturbance assuredly.[27]

Thus, the renowned 'cemetery of the kings' may have been a particular area of the graveyard, or the information may only mean that it was traditional for the kings of Connaught to be buried at Clonmacnoise. The same probably holds true for the royal graveyards said to have been at Armagh, Glendalough, Naas, and Lismore. A close reading reveals that the sources do not say that other people and social groups were excluded from burial at these sites, although, when they refer to the 'tomb' of kings or bishops, we may presume that these burials were concentrated in one area of the cemetery.

BURIAL WITH ANCESTORS

Thomas Charles-Edwards has pointed out that the wooden church-buildings during the early medieval or early Christian period were hardly permanent, which gave added importance to the continuity of place provided by generations of burials in one cemetery:

> … allegiance descended in the kindred and was expressed in burial. A man was normally buried where his father was buried, so that the solidarity of kindred might be expressed by burial in the same cemetery. As a result, the church would serve a set of lay kindreds, its fortunes and its continuity depended upon their fortunes and their continuity as they were, by the very nature of Irish kinship, accustomed to per-

---

25 See, for example, Macalister, *Corpus inscriptionum*, II, XXXVII, p. 46, commemorates ADMOER INGEN DUNA ('Admoer, daughter of Dúna'), ibid., CXXXIX, p. 57, probably commemorates Conn na mBocht, bishop and anchorite, who died in 1059 or 1060; ibid., CLXXXIII, p. 62, commemorating a prince of Tethba who died *c*.950. Another stone at Clonmacnoise dating to 932–34 commemorates 'Uallaig', which is a woman's name. See Lionard, 'Early Irish', p. 264. **26** 'Poem on the graves of the kings at Clonmacnoise', ed. & trans. Best, st. 18: 'Beneath thy chaste mould, O church, are two ollaves of Erin: Mac Coisse, sway over whom I have not heard of, and Cuchuann of Connacht!' **27** 'Life of Colman Ela II', *Lives*, I, p. 175 § 25; II, p. 168, §25. Richard Sharpe has argued that the original text was written before 800: A. Gwynn & Hadcock, *Medieval religious*, p. 334.

ceive contemporary reality and its validity as a bequest from dead ancestors ...[28]

The written evidence shows that burial with previously deceased members
of the family was normal. When Cerball son of Muirecán, over-king of Leinster,
died in 909 he 'was buried among his forefathers at the graveyard of *Cell Chorbbáin*
which was in Naas, Co. Kildare.[29] Although Naas is not mentioned in the chronicles after the year 1000 in relation to burial, it had been renowned as the burial
place of the Uí Fhaeláin kings of Leinster and may have served this function from
738.[30] The role of Clonmacnoise as a royal cemetery has been noted above.[31] The
lines below, taken from the poem 'The graves of the kings at Clonmacnoise' show
the importance of burying members of the same kindred together:

> O great flagstone of the descendants of Maelruanaid ... twenty kings,
> and their heads 'neath thy cross, are under the mould which thou hast
> closed.
>   O flagstone of the descendants of Tadg of the Household, noble this
> folk to follow them: eighteen men of pure excellence ...
>   O stone of the descendants of Concenainn, thou hast concealed men
> of estate: seventeen men of shining valour 'neath thy comely angelic
> cemetery!
>   O chaste temple of the children of Niall, in the time of Diarmait of
> the smooth face, fifty kings, 'tis no small portion, have come to thee, O
> cemetery![32]

The 'Registry of Clonmacnoise' provides much additional detail about which
kindreds were buried there, how they acquired their 'part' of the cemetery, and
how much was paid for it, for example:

> Mac Dermoda ... purchased for hymself the proportion for three church-
> es of that cemeterie, for wch he gaue in Cnocauicarie 48 daies, Kill-
> eathraght 48 daies, Rath Salainn 48 daies, and this hath he giuen to Cluain
> for hym and his heires ...[33]

Caithréim Thoirdhealbhaigh notes the continuity of burials among Maic
Conmara (MacNamara), as expressed in this reflection on the death in 1317 of
Hugh mac Donough Mac Namara: 'How happy we must deem one that met

---

28 Charles-Edwards, 'The pastoral role', p. 76. For continuity of burial, see Wasserschleben *Die
Irische Kanonensammlung*, Liber XVIII, cap. 2, 4–5. **29** *FAII, s.a.* 909. **30** Fáelán, the progenitor
of this line of kings, died in 738 (*AU* 738.1). The annals do not record his burial; so we do not
know if he was interred at Naas, which would seem to have been established in early Christian
times. **31** See n. 26 in this chapter. **32** 'The graves of the kings at Clonmacnoise', ed. & trans.
Best, st. 14, 15, 17 & 19. **33** 'The Registry', ed. O'Donovan, pp 452–3.

with such an end, in that he came decked with honour to his grandfather's [Cumea More's] place of sepulture, to Ennis!'[34]

A belief in the importance of burial with one's ancestors was not restricted to the native Irish. In 1317 the pope was required to settle the matter of the burial of the knight Thomas de Mandeville, who was killed at 'a distance' from his parish church of Carrickfergus and could not be buried there 'by reason of the power of his enemies'. The pope decreed that de Mandeville should be interred in Drogheda, but noted that it was 'contrary to the will of the said knight, none of his ancestors having been buried there'.[35] The register of the monastery of Athenry contains detailed records of the burials of the 'Anglo-Norman' family of de Bermingham with their ancestors, such as[36]

> Raymond the son of Thomas fitz Walter near the son of Richard, son of the aforesaid John ... near which lies William MacUllis Remundus his son ... in the presbytery lies William Canus de Burgo and Walter his son and [blank] and Richard the young burgher near whom lies Raymond de Burgo with his sons and daughter who lie with his son William Brudi and others who *lie a muro usque ad murum et diversi quorum nomina sunt in libro vitae.*

By the end of the fourteenth century the amount of attention which chron-iclers give to recording generational continuity in burial increases significantly. Under the year 1398, the *AFM* record that Morrough Bane O'Farrell, 'a worthy heir to the lordship of Annaly', was interred in Lara 'in the tomb of his father and grandfather'.[37] In 1403 Tadhg, the son of Cathal óg Ó Conchobair (O'Connor) was 'buried in the tomb of his grandfather Cathal son of Domnall',[38] and in 1405 Tadhg Mac Diarmada (MacDermott, king of Moylurg), 'was brought to be interred in the tomb of his ancestors'.[39] Soon afterwards, Teige MacBranan, the grandson of the chief of Corco Achlann, was interred at Roscommon 'in the tomb of his father and grandfather'.[40]

---

34 *Caithr. Th.,* I, p. 130; II, p. 114.   **35** *Cal. Pap. Reg.*, ed. Bliss, II (1305–42), Ka. Nov., p. 171.
36 A few examples: 'Ricardus de Brimigham ... sepultus est cum parentibus suis AD MCC-CXXII. (1322), *Reg. Mon. Athenry*, p. 205; ...'dominus Petrus qui sepultus est cum patre suo a dextris', ibid., p. 205; 'Idem Ricardus fuit austerus bellicosus nobilis et prudens ... sepultus cum patre suo videlicet dicto Petro in conventu Fratrum Ordinis Praedicatorum de Athinary anno D. MCCCXXII, ibid., p. 205; ' ... Et huic domino Ricardo successit dominus Thomas ut supradictum est et huic domino Thomae successit dominus Walterus de Brimigham ... et sepultus est cum antecessoribus suis apud predictum conventum in sepultura propria anno D. Millesimo CCCC. vicessimo octavo', ibid., p. 206.   **37** *AFM, s.a.* 1398 '... ocus a adhnacul i mainistir leathratha i ttomba a athar ...'   **38** *ALC, s.a.* 1403: 'Tadc mac Cathail óicc .h. Conchubhair for machaire na noi-leach, in hoc anno, fo feil Brighidi, et sepultus est illebaidh Cathail mic Domhnall a shenathar; also *AConn, s.a.* 1403.   **39** *ALC*: 'ocus tucadh Tadcc da adnacal a nothar lige a shensir ...' also *AConn, s.a.* 1405.   **40** *ALC*: ' ... et sepultus est hi man-

By the early fifteenth century, burial entries begin including much more detail, probably in response to the growing importance of funeral processions and tombs. A comparison of the spare thirteenth-century entries regarding burial offer a sharp contrast with the lengthy, descriptive fifteenth-century entries in 'MacFirbish's annals'.

In general, the entries which tell of the founding of abbeys at this time – especially Franciscan foundations – make a point of noting that the abbey was founded so that a 'tomb' or 'place of burial' could be established in it for the founder and his descendants. In the Middle Ages, confession was only made once, usually as close to the time of death as possible. The Franciscans took a particular interest in hearing confessions, and many of the laity sought burial at their foundations. The Franciscans are also known to have employed the Irish language, a fact which must have contributed to their popularity among the native Irish, although it caused trouble for them among the Anglo-Irish.[41]

Thus, in 1420, *AFM* record that the earl of Desmond founded the monastery at Askeaton, Co. Limerick, and 'erected a tomb in it for himself and his descendants'. MacCarthy More laid the foundations for the abbey of Muckross, Co. Kerry, in 1430 where he 'erected a tomb for himself and his posterity'.[42] In 1447 O'More erected the monastery of Stradbally, Co. Laois, and 'selected a burial place for himself and his descendants in it',[43] and in 1464 Thomas, earl of Kildare, and his wife (Joan, daughter of the earl of Desmond) founded the monastery at Adare, Co. Limerick, and 'erected a tomb for themselves in it'. Before O'Connor Kerry died in the monastery of Lis Laichtnín, Co. Kerry, in 1470, he 'selected a burial place for himself' in it,[44] and in 1495, when the MacCarthys established Kilcrea in Co. Cork, 'they erected an honourable tomb in it for the interment of the gentlemen and chieftains'.[45]

The rising status of the merchant classes in Ireland is indicated by the fact that Edmund Lynch, a 'burgher' of Galway and a benefactor of the monastery of Athenry, is said in the monastery's register to have been buried in a tomb which he had had made in the chapel of the Blessed Virgin in his parish church in Galway in 1462.[46] With the exception of this 'lady chapel', all these examples relate to Franciscan foundations, and the careful notation of them in the *AFM*, a chronicle compiled by Franciscans, may reflect this link.

istir Rosa Cummana notharligi a senathar ocus a athar'; *AConn, s.a.* 1410.14.   **41** Williams, 'The Latin Franciscan', pp 28, 52–3, 65.   **42** *Mon. Hib.* II, p. 240, n. 7, 'according to the Franciscan records'.   **43** *AFM; 'Mainistir Laoighisi i Laighnibh'*, should not be confused with Abbeyleix, the Cistercian house founded in 1183 by Connor O'More, as was done by John O'Donovan in his edition of *AFM*. My thanks are due to Prof. G. Mac Niocaill for pointing this out.   **44** *AFM.*   **45** *AFM.*   **46** '... in tumba sua quam sibi et suis fabricari fecit in capella Beatae Virginis Ecclesia parrochiali ipsus villae de Galway anno Domini 1462': *Reg. Mon. Athenry*, p. 211.

The native Irish had strong cultural and social connections with their cemeteries.[47] The importance of being buried in the cemetery of the local saint not only offered great benefits to the individual seeking the shortest route to heaven, but also helped ensure the prosperity of the kin-group in general. Because the medieval Irish believed that they would literally experience physical resurrection after death, to be buried in a place other than one's territorial cemetery was tantamount of abandoning one's kin-group for all eternity.

The taboos against burial in a cemetery that had no connections with the kin-group tended to be both ancient and strong. Territorial cemeteries were often believed to have been established by a local saint during the early Christian period, and hagiography preserves dramatic examples of the powerful curses and misfortunes which threatened anyone who dared to be buried in a cemetery other than that of their local patron saint.[48] Therefore, the conscious decisions to build these foundations as new places of burial and the abandonment of traditional burial sites suggest changes in traditional Irish culture. This is hardly surprising given the series of events that occurred in Ireland during this period which would have affected burial practices, including the Gregorian monastic reforms, the adoption of the highly regulated monastic system and the arrival or new monastic orders, and the 'Anglo-Norman invasion'.

Thomas Charles-Edwards has pointed out that heirs to land could use gravestones inscribed in *ogam* writing to confirm their hereditary claims to territory, and that 'the inscriptions over the graves have the same role in showing title to land as charters or other deeds in a more literate age'; he added that unmarked graves had the same ability to decide disputes over land.[49] The period here under study was, indeed, a 'more literate age' than the seventh century of which Charles-Edwards writes; this does not mean, however, that literacy was general, even among the élite Irish, or that graves were not a way of stating land ownership in the central Middle Ages.

In the fourteenth century, English burial practice was quickly evolving away from the earlier communal and largely undifferentiated style of burial towards practices which were increasingly – and increasingly visibly – concerned with commemorating the individual's status, power and wealth. The native Irish, strug-

---

47 Writing in the 1830s of Kinvara, Co. Galway, Samuel Lewis offered an indication of how strong they could be when he wrote: 'there are some remains of the old ch., which was for ages the burial-place of the O'Haynes and Magraths, no others being allowed to be interred within its walls': Lewis, *Topographical Dictionary*, ii, p. 234. **48** See, for example, *Bk Fen.*, p. 198: 'Heaven they should have if they chose [to be buried] in Fidnacha by Ailliín; or else every plague and pestilence, every war and vengeance, of the foregoing to come upon them; they should have a short life in evil plight here, and hell at last while Caillin might be in Heaven, if they chose [to be buried] in any other church, however exalted'. See also the 'Life of St Maedóc (II)', *Lives* I, p. 284; II, p. 277. **49** Charles-Edwards, 'Boundaries in Irish law', pp 84–5.

gling to defend their status and lands in the face of Anglo-Irish encroachments, may have seen the adoption of funerary monuments in the native Irish style as a way to show that they were equal in status with the Anglo-Irish nobles and kings, and they may have used burial to help them do this. Even as the native Irish adopted ideas imported from England with their emphasis on ceremonial splendor and creating 'a tomb of one's own', it appears that burial retained aspects of its traditional meaning and power within the culture.

Christopher Daniell has shown that such prominent people as the duke of Norfolk and members of the Clare family changed their traditional places of burial to strengthen their claims in territories which had not previously been theirs.[50]

BURIAL IN RELIGIOUS HABIT

In the Middle Ages, burial *ad sanctos* (that is, near saints' relics) was highly desirable, since it was believed that saints' bones contained stored-up power which would help anyone buried near them gain entry to heaven. Saints' relics were kept in the church, usually at the altar; therefore, people desired to be buried as close to the altar as possible.

Limitations of space obviously made it impossible to offer burial *ad sanctos* to everyone who wanted it. While historical and archaeological evidence clearly shows that burials were made inside churches from an early period, the Church for centuries put up at least a pretense of prohibiting burial in churches, and succeeded for some time in more or less restricting it to the élite – both laics and clerics. In 1070, the Legatine Council which met at Winchester in England in 1070 it decreed that there was to be no burial in churches,[51] but numerous documents show that the decree was not heeded. In 1180, for example, one Alexander of Chester, a commoner, was buried in the priory of the Holy Trinity (Christchurch) in Dublin.[52] In 1152 the Cistercian general chapter ruled to restrict burial in their churches to persons of royal descent, bishops and archbishops, indicating that before that time Cistercian houses had been giving church-burial to a wider cross-section of society.[53] In England, the restrictions on burials were also weakening: the statutes of Chichester in 1292 allowed burials to include lords of the village, patrons of the church and their wives.[54]

In light of the discussion above regarding 'cemeteries of the kings' it is interesting to note that when Cellach, the coarb of St Patrick died at Ardpatrick, Co. Limerick in 1129, his body was taken to burial at Lismore, Co. Waterford, where both *AU* and *ALC* note that he was buried in the 'cemetery of the bishops':

---

50 Daniell, *Death & burial*, pp 92–3. **51** *Councils & synods*, edd. Brett, et al., II, p. 576. **52** *Mon. Hib.*, I, p. 327. **53** Stalley, 'Mellifont Abbey', p. 269. **54** Daniell, *Death and burial*, p. 186.

Monks were allowed to be buried within the church, and many of the recorded instances of laypersons endowing religious foundations and/or retiring to monasteries were probably motivated by a desire to receive a monk's burial.[55]

The Irish chronicles mention a number of people – including two women – who are said to have retired to religious foundations or to have been buried in monastic habit. I have assumed that all of these people were accorded the burial of a person in religious orders, even though some of the obituaries do not specifically mention burial. With three exceptions, all of the people mentioned were native Irish.[56] The two women are 'Gormlaith, daughter of Dauid Ó Duibgennáin [O'Duignan], wife of Brian mac Aedacáin', an anchorite who died in 1437,[57] and 'Finduala' (Fionnuala) O'Connor, who retired to the Augustinian convent at Killeigh in Co. Offaly in 1447.[58]

The earliest description of burial in monastic habit for the period of this study relates to Rory or Roderick O'Connor (Ruaidrí Ua Conchobhair), king of Connacht, who died at Clonmacnoise in 1118.[59] Seven O'Connors appear to have been buried in monastic habit – a greater number than any other family-group. While it is true that the chronicles in which these entries are found have a particular interest in the O'Connors, when the relatively small amount of specific burial information included in the chronicles is taken into consideration, it still appears that burial in monastic habit had become something of tradition among the O'Connor kings. Rory's death in monk's habit was followed by that of another Rory, the son of Toirrdhealbhach (Turlough) and powerful king of Connaught, who died in 1198.[60] Although the entry does not specifically say that he was buried in the habit of an Augustinian monk, the fact that he was a great benefactor to Cong would make this highly likely.[61] In addition to the burial of the two aforementioned O'Connors of the twelfth century, Cathal Crobhdearg O'Connor (d. 1224), Tadhg, great-grandson of Turlough Mór O'Connor (d. 1313), Murrough O'Connor (d. 1421), Fionnuala O'Connor (d. 1447), and Felim O'Connor (d. 1467) were also buried in religious habit.[62]

---

55 *AU, s.a.,* 1129; *ALC* says it was 'tomb of the bishops'. 56 The exceptions are: David Wydyr, *Reg. Mon. Athenry*, p. 207 (from a fifteenth century document – exact date unknown); 'Oliverus de Fraxineto (*Annals of Nenagh, s.a.* 1347); Adam de Feipo (*Chart. St Mary's*, I, p. 93, No. 69). My thanks are due to Dr Katharine Simms for also pointing out that *Leabhar Chlainne Suibhne*, ed. P. Breatnach (Dublin, 1920) tells of Máire, daughter of Ó Máille, wife of the early sixteenth-century chieftain Ruaidrhri mac Suibhne, died in the habit of the 'friars of Mary' [Carmelites] in the monastery which she had founded. 57 *AConn, s.a.* 1437. 58 *AMacF* do not actually note her burial in habit; only that she retired to Killeigh. 59 *ALC, s.a.* 1118. He had been overking of Connaught from 1067 x 1076 until his blinding by an opponent in 1092 (*AFM; AU* 1092.3). 60 *AFM, s.a.* 1198. 61 A. Gwynn & Hadcock, *Medieval religious*, p. 166. 62 *AFM, s.a.* 1224; *ALC, s.a.* 1313; *AFM, s.a.* 1421; *AMacF, s.a.* 1447; *AMacF,* 1467.

The choice of houses to which the O'Connors retired prior to death corresponds with the historical pattern of monastic development in Ireland: the first retired to Clonmacnoise, founded in the sixth century by St Ciarán, while Rory O'Connor retired to Cong, an early foundation which had been refounded by his father as an Augustianian abbey, and where he had built a new monastery.[63] In 1180, Cathal Crobhderg O'Connor colonized the Cistercian abbey of Knockmoy, Co. Galway, from Boyle,[64] and retired there prior to his death in 1224; and in 1313, Tadgh O'Connor chose to retire to Boyle. But the newer Franciscan foundation of Killeigh in Co. Offaly, which had been founded by O'Connor Faly in 1293(?) was the place of retirement for Murrough O'Connor in 1421, and in 1447 Fionnula O'Connor retired to the convent of Augustinian nuns located there.[65] In 1265, Felim O'Connor died in the habit of a friar at the Cistercian abbey of Kilcooley which had been rebuilt a few years earlier, but was buried at Tulsk, Co. Roscommon, in the Dominican priory which he himself had endowed shortly before his death.[66]

Three O'Donnell (Ua Domhnaill) kings or chieftains of Tirconnell were buried in Cistercian habit at Assaroe over a 180-year period. In 1241, Domhnall Mór O'Donnell, who had ruled as king of Tirconnell for fourteen years, died at Assaroe, Co. Donegal, in the habit of a Cistercian monk; he was followed in 1333 by Hugh, the son of Donnell Oge O'Donnell, and later by Turlough O'Donnell, who is said to have retired to Assaroe *s.a.* 1422 where he died 'in the habit of a monk' a year later.[67] It is likely that three O'Briens also assumed the habit before their deaths: Turlough at Ennis, Co. Clare, in 1306;[68] Dermot at the friary at Corcomroe, Co. Clare, in 1313;[69] and Murtough O'Brien, buried at Ennis in 1343.[70] Two MacDermotts elected to die in Cistercian habit at Boyle, Co. Roscommon: Maelruanaidh in 1331, and Diarmaid Ruaidh (Dermot Roe) in 1341.[71]

Two MacCarthys also adopted religious habit: Diarmaid MacCarthy at the Cistercian foundation of Abbeymahon, Co. Cork, and Domhnall MacCarthy at the Augustinian abbey in Cork.[72] Domnall O'Kelly (Ua Cellaigh) died in Cistercian habit at Knockmoy, Co. Galway, in 1295, and Melachlin (Maol

63 A. Gwynn & Hadcock, *Medieval religious*, p. 166. The Augustinian canons regular seem to have een introduced into Ireland before 1137, possibly as early as 1127. Mellifont, the first Cistercian abbey, was founded in 1142, and the Franciscans may have been in Cork as early as 1214, although 1224 x 1226 may be more plausible. See ibid., p. 123 and pp 146–7. **64** Ibid., p. 124. **65** Fionnuala O'Conor lived in the Augustinain convent that neighbored the Franciscan friary. See A. Gwynn & Hadcock, *Medieval religious*, pp 253 & 321. **66** *AFM, AClon.*, An early foundation in Co. Roscommon also had the name of 'Kilcooley', however it seems doubtful that it was still occupied in the fifteenth century. See A. Gywnn & Hadcock, *Medieval religious*, p. 389. **67** *ALC, s.a.* 1241; *AFM, s.a.* 1333; *AFM, s.a.* 1422 and 1423. **68** *MacCarthaigh's Book, s.a.* 1306. **69** *Mon. Hib.*, I, p. 75. **70** *Annals of Nenagh, s.a.*, 1343. **71** Maelruanaidh, *s.a.* 1328 (*AU*) and 1331 (*ALC*); and Dermot Roe, *s.a.* 1341 (*AFM*). **72** *AI, s.a.* 1278, 1302.

Sheachlainn) O'Kelly, who *AFM* say was also brought there before his death in 1402, may have done the same.[73] John O'Dugan (Seán Ua Dubhagáin), 'arch-historian of Ireland', who died at the monastery of the Fratres Cruciferi at Rindown, Co. Roscommon, in 1372, provides us with the only undisputed example of a person of the traditional Irish learned classes being buried in monastic habit.[74] Gormlaith O Duignan (Ua Duibgennain), 'ultimately an anchorite', was buried at Loch Cé in 1437, which would suggest that she was accorded the burial of a person in religious orders.[75]

In addition to the family groups noted above, the chronicles also record the burial in habit of an O'Donoghue (Ua Donnchadha, d. 1231) Magrath (d. 1243), MacCarthy (d. 1302), Mac Conmara (d. 1349), MacClancy (d. 1418) , and MacBranan (d. 1448).[76]

Most of those mentioned as having died or been buried in monastic habit were kings or chieftains – or their children. It is worth bearing in mind that these were men of conflict and war, a fact which may have made burial in church especially important to them. *AFM* tell us, for example, that Maelruanaid Dermott (Mac Diarmada), king of Magh-Luirg', committed 'a great depredation … in the territory of Carbury' in 1310. The same source reports that he 'slew many of the people of Muintir-Eolais and Muintir-Cearbhallain' in 1315,[77] before 'resigning his kingdom and sovereignty' to retire to Boyle in 1325.[78] Similarly, when Murrough O'Connor, Lord of Offaly, who is reported to have killed over three-hundred people in 1406, was 'attacked by a dangerous disease' in 1421, he retired to the monastery of Killeigh and took the habit of a friar.[79] The obituary of Hugh O'Donnell under 1333 makes his fierceness plain: he was 'dreaded by his enemies … had slain the largest number both of the English and Irish who were opposed to him'.[80] Murder, raiding and pillaging were endemic in medieval Gaelic Ireland and, even allowing for exaggeration, these chieftains would still seem to have had good reason to seek all the assistance available to avoid eternal damnation.

Five men not of native Irish stock are also recorded as having been buried in the habit of a monk, two of whom were Anglo-Irish aristocrats. Meredith Hanmer related that Maurice fitzGerald retired to the Dominican monastery at Youghal, Co. Cork, after having served as lord justice of Ireland, where he was interred 'in the habit of his order' in 1257.[81] Thomas de Burgo, son of the Lord of Ulster, was buried in Dominican habit at Athenry, Co. Galway, in 1316.[82] Adam de Feipo (whose family had been barons of Skreen, Co. Meath, until the four-

---

73 *AFM, AU s.a.* 1295; *MacCarthaigh's Book, s.a,* 1467.   **74** *AU, s.a.* 1372.   **75** *AConn, s.a.* 1437.
76 *Mac Carthaig's Book, s.a.* 1231; *AFM, ALC, s.a.* 1243; *AI, s.a.* 1302; *Annals of Nenagh, s.a.*. 1349; AFM *s.a.* 1418; and *AFM s.a.* 1448 (MacBranan).   **77** *AFM, s.aa.* 1308, 1315.   **78** *AU, s.a.* 1328. It seems that his wife, Gormlaith, had died the previous year, which may have put him in mind of his own mortality. Her obit appears in *AFM, s.a.* 1327.   **79** *AFM, s.a.* 1406. **80** AFM, *s.a.* 1333.   **81** *Mon. Hib.,* I, p. 159.   **82** Ibid., II, p. 196.

teenth century)[83] willed his body to St Mary's abbey in Dublin in 1495, where it is said that his brother, Thomas, had assumed the religious habit.[84] Oliver de Freyne was buried in Kilkenny in 1347 after assuming the Franciscan habit,[85] and in 1343 David Wydyr, *uenerabilis burgensis quondam de Athenry* who died at Bristol, chose to be buried at Athenry in the habit of the brothers there.[86]

Two of the men who are said to have taken the habit prior to death provide what may be evidence of the changes taking place in burial. They are Oliver de Freyne, who was buried in Kilkenny in 1347,[87] and Seán O'Dugan (Ua Dubhagáin), 'the arch-historian of Ireland' mentioned above, who was buried at Rindown in monk's habit in 1372. De Freyne was part of a leading 'Anglo-Norman' administrative family. His father was Fulk de la Freyne, who had served as both a sheriff and a seneschal.[88] O'Dugan was a member of the learned-class of secular professionals trained in native genealogy, history and poetry.[89]

Widowed women sometimes became nuns and presumably these women would have been buried in nun's habit, as were the men who adopted monastic habit late in life. The cartulary of St Mary, Clerkenwell, in London, contains two documents dated 1175 in which 'Roger son of Remfrid' states that, after their death, his wife 'may become a nun if she desires and that her corpse is to be borne to the church at Clerkenwell and buried there in the habit of a nun'. The second document gives the same permission to his mother.[90] The only example of this in Irish sources is that of Gormlaith, daughter of Dauid Ó Duibgennáin'. *AConn* record that she was the wife of Brian Mac Aedacáin (MacEgan) and 'ultimately an anchorite', which indicates that she was a widow when she entered religious life at Loch Cé, Co. Roscommon, where she died in 1437. How soon before her death she adopted the habit is not known. The *AFM* and *AMacF* record the retirement of Fionnghuala, daughter of Calvagh

---

83 Orpen, *Ireland under the Normans*, II, p. 85.   **84** ' … frater Thomas, germanus meus, habitum religionis assumpserat': *Chart. St Mary's*, I, p. 93, No. 69.   **85** *Annals of Nenagh*, 1347. **86** 'Joanna de Wffler uxor dicti David Wedir de consilio fratrum fecit transferri ossamenta mariti sui de conventu Bristol ad conventum de Athnary …' *Reg. Mon. Athenry*, p. 207. I have not yet been able to identify 'David Wydyr,' perhaps because this is an unusual – or unique – variation of a surname. Professor David Dumville has suggested that this may be the same as the Welsh name 'Gwydir'.   **87** *Annals of Nenagh*, 1347.   **88** St John Brooks, *Knights' fees*, p. 185; *Reports of the Deputy Keeper of the public records*, XXIX, p. 47. I am indebted to Gerard McGrath for making me aware of this connection with Fulk de la Freyne.   **89** Consider the parallels in function between the medieval administrative class and these (below) noted by F.J. Byrne for the Irish *áes dána*, bearing in mind that he was writing of this learned class at the height of its pre-Conquest vigour: '… the áes dána formed a distinct social class, equal in status to the nobility … It was this mandarin class of poets and pedants who were largely responsible for the cultural unity of the country They alone, together with the Christian clergy who were accorded their privileges, enjoyed legal status outside the confines of their own tuath … in an aristocratic society they were aristocratic to a degree … ' Byrne, *Irish kings*, pp 13–16.   **90** '… vbi ipsa dedit corpus suum sepeliendum in quocumque habitu obierit et facient seruicium pro illa sicut pro sua moniali': *Cartulary of St Mary Clerkenwell*, pp 67–8

O'Connor Faly and Margaret O'Carroll, to the monastery of Killeigh in 1447, in order to 'prepare for life eternal' where, according to *AConn*, she lived until 1493 when the *AFM* records that she was 'a woman who had preserved her widowhood for the period of forty-nine years'.

LOCATION AND POSITION OF GRAVES AND TOMBS

There is some reason to think that, for interments made outdoors in the cemetery, the center or middle of the cemetery was the position of highest honor, which may relate to what is known of the typical development pattern for early cemeteries, where burials were grouped around a 'founding' or 'focal' burial. The 'Book of Fenagh,' contains the following lines, which are notable because they indicate that when burying a king, the yew tree, flagstone, and position in the center of the cemetery were regarded as important:

> At the yew of the kings afterwards,
> Aedh was certainly buried;
> under the flag of the Angels, truly
> in the middle of the Relig of Dun-baile.[91]

Regarding the placement of burials in terms of direction, it appears that Ireland may have had somewhat different customs than those which prevailed in England, where the north side of the church was unpopular for burial and usually reserved for the interment of 'unfortunates' such as murderers, suicides or unbaptized children.[92] This custom seems to have arisen because the north was the side of the altar from which the Gospel was delivered, while the Epistle was read from the South. It was thought appropriate to bury those who had died outside the grace of God on the north side, where they might benefit from 'hearing' the word of God in the form of the Gospel.[93]

In Irish custom however, the north of the house 'was always the side of honour', as F.J. Byrne has pointed out, and this may explain why, in Ireland, burial on the north side does not seem to have had the negative meaning which it carried in England. In fact, both written and archaeological evidence suggests that for interments in Ireland, the north was regarded as a position of honor – particularly if the interments were made inside the church. However, the sources contain evidence for burial on both northern and southern sides.

'The Battle of the Sheaves', a poem found in *Duanaire Finn,* mentions burial on both sides of the church:

& 70–1. Nos. 101 & 105. **91** *Bk Fen.*, p. 133. In Irish: 'Ac ibar na rig arsin / Ro hadhnacht Aed go deimhin / Fa leic na naingel gan gai / ar lar relgi Duin Bhaili.' **92** Brosnan, 'Mortuary practices', p. 351. **93** Puckle, *Funeral customs*, p. 150.

Lay Oscar on this southern side – it is a bitterness to my heart and body – MacLugach without quarrel or hatred, lay him quickly on the northern side.[94]

A preliminary analysis of the hundreds of burials excavated from Ardfert Cathedral in Co. Galway showed that the north side of the churchyard was used for burial to an extent which would indicate that it had not been reserved merely for the burial of 'unfortunates', and Áine Brosnan has suggested that reserving the northern section for 'unfortunates' may have developed later in the Middle Ages.[95] The 'Poem on the battle of Dún', written in the thirteenth century, contains the following lines:

> The tomb of the king of Oileach of thick hair …
> I would point out to you the grave
> on the north side of the church.[96]

These lines do not explicitly say whether the grave was inside the church. If it was outside, the grave may have been placed on the northern side of the church because death occurred in battle – and therefore without Last Rites.[97]

John Gwynn, who edited the texts of the 'Book of Armagh', noted that the first part of Tírechán's memoirs preserves a conversation between St Patrick and an angel which

> relates how … It was ordered that certain classes of these 'virgins, Pentitents, and Married Servants of the Church', should worship in 'the Chuch of the North quarter' but the rest, with the Bishops, Presbyters, and Anchorites, in 'the Southern Basilica'.[98]

The first abbey to be established in Ireland by a Continental order was Mellifont, Co. Louth. Donough O'Carroll, the king of Oriel who gave Mellifont its initial endowment of lands, is thought to have been buried there in a tomb in the arched recess at the north side of the altar. This came to be the standard position for the burial of founding patrons in the Cistercian abbeys of Ireland.[99] The written record shows that this position was also popular for burial among other orders, and for bishops as well as founders.

The cartulary of Llantony Secunda in Gloucestershire, England, contains the information that St Cianán was buried in the north part of his church at Duleek,

---

94 'Battle of the sheaves', *Duanaire Finn*, I, p. 164. In Irish: 'Cuir osgar don taob ro tes – is goirt lem croide is lem cnes / Mac Lugdac gan fioc gan fuath. cur don taob thuaid go lan-luat.'   **95** Brosnan, 'Mortuary practices', pp 75–7, 116.   **96** 'Poem on the battle of Dún', ed. & trans. O'Donovan, st. 54.   **97** Note 'f' marking this passage notes that slain people were buried to the north, and this is still called *taebh na bh-fear n-gonta* (side of the slain men). See section below entitled 'Burial of excommunicants', n. 201.   **98** *Liber Ardmachanus*, ed. J. Gwynn, Book I.26 to end and b. II. I, 2.   **99** Stalley, 'Mellifont abbey', p. 269. See below, under section entitled

in the chancel.[100] Blessed Felix O'Dullanus, bishop of Ossory, was buried at St Mary's abbey in Jerpoint, Co. Kilkenny, on the north side of the high altar after his death in 1202.[101] In 1261, John fitzThomas fitzMaurice fitzGerald, founder of the monastery of Tralee, Co. Clare, was buried on the north side of that abbey,[102] as was Thomas fitzMaurice fitzRaymond, founder of the Franciscan friary at Ardfert, Co. Kerry, in 1280. His descendants were probably also interred near his tomb.[103] Thomas O'Kelly, bishop of Clonfert, Co. Galway (d. 1263), had a vault for human bones built 'near the north side of the high altar'.[104] As noted above,[105] in 1452, Lord Thomas de Burgh was buried in the monastery of Athenry in a monk's habit *'in parte boriali prope murum.'*[106]

Despite this evidence, it is far from clear that one side was generally preferred over another. The poem 'Cell Chorbbáin' tells that at that site, 'the space on the south side of the great church' became the cemetery. The 'Poem on the graves of the kings at Clonmacnoise' tells of King Toirrdelbach being buried on the southern side of the altar, suggesting that it was the favored position, although it goes on to state that Ruaidrí was interred 'on the other lofty side' of the same altar.[107] The *Martyrology of Oengus* specifically records that the 'union of Colum cille and Cianán' was accomplished by 'Colum Cille putting his hand in through the south side of the tomb and Cianan's hand (thrust) out even to the half'.[108]

Christian burial practices supported ideas of social stratification. As Peter Brown has written:

> The practice of *depositio ad sanctos*, for instance, threatened to make only too plain the play of family influence around holy graves … Once obtained, it mapped out in a peculiarly blatant manner, in terms of proximity to the saint, the balance of social power within the Christian community.[109]

While this observation was not made regarding medieval Ireland in particular, the 'mapping out of the balance of social power' he speaks of was certainly a concern in medieval Ireland and sources indicate that this was probably a tradition with a long history. For example, old-Irish texts preserve information about the seating arrangements at royal social occasions, and the amount of detail they contain reveals the importance of such etiquette. It may be that this traditional social ordering is echoed in burial. Irish texts sometimes use the word 'house' (*tech*) to mean 'a grave', which may suggest a connection between the customs

'Burial in the church'.   **100** Cf. Hughes 'The offices of S Finnian of Clonard & S Cíanán of Duleek', p. 355.   **101** *Mon. Hib.*, II, p. 321.   **102** *Caithr. Th.*, I, p. 168; II, p. 178.   **103** *Irish Memorials of the dead*, II, p. 137; A. Gwynn and Hadcock, *Irish medieval*, p. 242.   **104** *Mon. Hib.*, II, p. 195, cf. 'Burke', p. 226.   **105** See Chapter 2, 'Charnels, ossuaries and mortuary houses', above.   **106** *Reg. Mon. Athenry*, pp 211–12.   **107** 'Graves of the kings at Clonmacnoise', ed. & trans. Best, p. 164 & 165, lines 9–10.   **108** *Félire*, ed. Stokes, §24, pp 244–5.   **109** P. Brown *Cult of the saints*, p. 34.

pertaining to the social order in life and in death.[110] For example, in 'The colloquy of the ancients' we read that 'one shall pay him an ounce of gold to have his house (*tech*) within his [Moling's] cemetery'.[111] The Irish life of St Berach, which Kenney described as 'a late composition', says that the saint's body was 'buried in the dark house with honor'.[112] A lament written for King Maelsechlainn II, which was probably composed in the early eleventh century, describes the burial ground as follows:

> The house in which the kings lie is closed …
> there are twelve score in their house (*tech*) yonder,
> two hundred there against each fair wall.[113]

The eighth-century law-tract *Críth Gablach* makes it quite clear that the north is the side of honor.[114] 'The long rectangular building faces east, and the king sits near the far end on the north side'.[115] The order, as stated in *Críth Gablach*, is as follows:

> The king's mercenaries on the south … a man whom he saves from violent death; a man whom he saves from capture; a man whom he saves from captivity; a man whom he saves from servitude, from serfdom, from unfree tenantry. He does not have a man whom he saves from the field of battle, lest he betray him or slay him on account of private grievances or family loyalties … a front guardsman, a rear guardsman, and two flankers … it is they that are proper to be in the south of a king's house to accompany him going out … The personal surety for base clients to the west of these. Envoys to the west of him (the personal surety). Guest companies after them. Poets after them. Harpers after them. Pipers, horn-players, jugglers to the south-east. In the other half, on the north, a warrior, a champion guarding the door … the king's noble clients west of these

---

110 Prof. David Dumville has reminded me of the existence of Irish house-shaped reliquaries.   **111** '… uinge d'or (dherg) ó (gach) nech. ar a thech na chill bennán Moling luachair.' 'The colloquy of the ancients' (Acallamh na Senorach), *SG*, I, p. 153; II, p. 170.   **112** 'an chorp annsa tigh dorcha co onóir', 'Life of St Berach', *Lives*, I, p. 43, §90; II, p. 42.   **113** 'Dúnta in tech i-táit na ríg … dá fichet déc 'na taig tall, 's dá chét ann fri cach fraig finn', 'A Lament for Maelshechlainn II', st. 1& 2, the *Ó Cianáin Miscellany*, pp 143, 145. As its editor, James Carney pointed out: 'the tech is the graveyard which, according to the poet's estimate … contained over 1,000 bodies: twelve score and two hundred along each of the four walls', p. 147, n. 3d. The large number of kings in one tomb, as well as the indication that numerous graves were 'against the wall' may suggest that the walls of the cemetery were viewed in something of the same way as the boundaries of the territory, along which burials were often made in pre-Christian times. I am indebted to Dr Katharine Simms for her assistance with the dating of this lament.   **114** Byrne, *Irish kings*, p. 38. 'Lánellach tigi rích 7 ruirech' gives position but unfortunately, not direction.   **115** Byrne, *Irish kings*, p. 38.

– they are the company who are in attendance on the king. Hostages after them. A judge after them. The king's wife west of him, and then the king. Forfeited hostages in chains in the north-west.[116]

Judging from the amount of detail provided in this passage, the established etiquette regarding seating would seem to have been of enormous importance, a view bolstered by the first recension of the account of the battle of Mag Rath. The battle was fought in 637 and this version of the poem may date from the beginning of the tenth century. The battle itself was said to have been necessitated by a breach in the usual – and expected – seating order of the nobles.[117]

If the individual's social status was a determining factor in deciding the location of a native Irish person's grave in relation to the graves of relatives and associates, then a comparison of descriptions of native Irish burials with the 'seating plan' laid out in *Críth Gablach* may prove instructive.

None of the main chronicles tell where the tomb of Brian Bóruma was located, though the *Leabhar Oiris* states that his tomb was on the northwest side of the church at Armagh.[118] A fourteenth-century poem by Giolla Brighde Mac Con Midhe, records that:

> Brian Bóraimhe is in the church in the north, Brian Ó Néill of Aileach of red weapons, the descendant of Conn of Cabha, is well to the west and his feet face Brian Bóraimhe.[119]

This could literally be true, since according to *Críth Gablach* this is the position in which the king would have been seated in his hall. If the author had no real knowledge of where the tomb was, it could well be that, at a time when information about social status was often transmitted through symbols, he might have chosen to locate King Brian's tomb in the north, to communicate his high rank.

The same source also tells us that Brian's son Murchad, and the head of Conaing, were buried in another coffin on the south side of the church. Here again, the author may have specified this location to communicate to his audience what relationship these men had with the king. The south side is the position which the king's son would have occupied in relation to his father when

---

116 Ibid., p. 33, cf. *Críth Gablach*, ed. Binchy. For Welsh seating arrangements, see 'Of appropriate places' in the 'Venedotian Code', *Ancient laws and institutions of Wales*, ed. Aneurin, I, p. 5. 117 Dillon, *The cycles*, pp 65–6; *The battle of Magh Rath*, ed & trans. O'Donovan, p. 29. 118 'Ríghe hÉireann do'n taoibh thiar-thuaidh do theampoll Árdmacha, i gcómhraidh ar leith, & Murchadh & ceann Conaing & Mhothla i gcomhraidh eile ar leith.' *Leabhar oiris*, ed. & trans. Best, p. 90. See Best's introduction for dating information.   119 Mac Con Midhe, *The poems*, 'Poem XIII', pp 152–3.

he was seated in the great hall, and it may therefore also have been considered the appropriate position for his grave. A poem on the graves of the kings at Clonmacnoise tells that Toirrdelbach is buried 'on the southern side' of the altar, with Ruadhri's grave 'on the other lofty side',[120] while Ruaidrí's own son was buried to the west of the chancel. 'The colloquy of the ancients' (*Acallam na senórach*) also refers to this southern position as a king's burial place:

> Patrick enquired: 'and who, Caeilte, is in this the tulach's southern end?' 'Salbhuide, son of Feidhlecar, king of Munster' …[121]

According to *Críth Gablach*, the south was the position appropriate for mercenaries or the 'personal surety for base clients',[122] but it contains no reference to sons or daughters; only the queen is mentioned. Her place is to his west – at the king's 'right hand'. If the father was interred in traditional Christian burial position, with his head to the west and his feet to the east and his son was buried to the south, then the son was necessarily buried 'at the right hand of the father'. This is a well-known reference to the position of Jesus Christ in relation to God the Father, as stated in the Nicene Creed in the Mass. It may be that it was followed literally in medieval Irish burial practice, since the medieval Irish believed that the bodies of the dead would literally come to life on the Day of Resurrection. For example, when Richard fitzThomas, son of the 2nd earl of Kildare, was interred in the Franciscan foundation of Kildare in 1329, he was buried at 'the right hand of his father' who had been buried there the previous year.[123] When Peter de Bermingham was buried in Athenry in 1322, he may also have been buried in this position, although the reference to the position of his grave is unclear and may mean that he was buried at the right side of the church.[124]

The written record also includes references to sons being buried at their fathers' feet. This may be an indication of a 'string-grave' pattern of burial, where the feet of the previous interment respected the head of the most recent – a method practiced in early Anglo-Saxon England. It may be worth noting that, for medieval Ireland, the references we have to this burial placement are mentioned in connection with the native Irish, not the Anglo-Irish. Both the Irish hagiographical tale, 'The expulsion of St Mochuda from Rahen', and *Genealogies of Uí Fhiachrach* contain the information that 'Cuimín son of Dioma' was buried in the 'great monument' or 'the large *uluidh* or altar-tomb' at the feet of the mid-eighth century grandsons of Suanach (Sweeney) of Rahan.'[125] And in 1186,

---

120 'Graves of the kings at Clonmacnoise', ed. & trans. Best, pp 164–5, lines 9–10.   **121** *Sálbhuide mac Feidhlecar mac ríg Muman*, 'The colloquy of the ancients', *SG*, I, p. 188; II, p. 128.   **122** See above, n. 116.   **123** Gwynn & Hadcock, *Medieval Religious*, p. 252.   **124** 'Item successit ei filius et haeres praedicti Mylseri qui multum dilexit ordinem et concessit fratribus redecimationes omnium terrarum suarum et fecit dicto conventui plur abona cujus nomen fuit dominus Petrus qui sepultus est cum patre suo a dextris.' *Reg. Mon. Athenry*, p. 205.   **125** 'The Expulsion of

Amlaíbh Ua Muiredaig, the bishop of Armagh and Cenél Feradaig, died in Dún Cruithne, an early Christian foundation near Macosquin, Co. Londonderry, and was interred in 'the side' of the church at Derry, 'at his father's feet'.[126] This positioning is also given in a poem by Giolla Brighdhe Mac Con Midhe mentioned above, which refers to Brian Ó Néill's burial at Armagh cathedral 'well to the west, and his feet face Brian Boru'.[127]

Burial in the church

Burial at the altar, especially burial at the right side of the altar, is often referred to as the burial place of honor for bishops. In 1010, *AFM* record that Muireadhach mac Crícháin, coarb of Columba and lector of Armagh, was buried before the altar there,[128] and in 1074 Dúnán, archbishop of Dublin, was buried at the right side of the altar of the church of the Trinity.[129] In 1156 Toirrdelbach Ua Conchobair, overking of Connaght, died and was buried 'beside St Ciarán's altar' at Clonmacnoise.[130] In 1185, Felix O'Dullany, bishop of Ossory, was interred on the north side of the high altar,[131] and in 1235 Felix O'Ruadan, the archbishop of Tuam, Co. Galway, was buried in the abbey of the Blessed Virgin Mary in Dublin, at the foot of the altar, at the left hand side.[132] Ruaidrí Ua Conchobair was buried at the north side of the altar in 1198.[133] Thomas fitzJohn, the second earl of Kildare, was interred in the Franciscan 'Grey Abbey' in Kildare, before the great altar,[134] while it is recorded that Richard, the third earl, was buried in 'our Lady's chapel, before the great altar' in 1329.[135] In 1361 Richard Ledred, bishop of Ossory, was buried at the north side of the altar of Kilkenny cathedral,[136] and in 1400 'those of the nation of Lynch' were buried around the altar at Athenry.[137] Odo O'Molloy, son of Nellan O'Molloy, founder of the Carmelite monastery of Kilcormac, Co. Offaly, was buried there in 1454 before the high altar.[138]

The choir is also frequently noted as a favored place for burial of the élite, founders, or great benefactors of religious houses – both native Irish and Anglo-

Mochuda from Rahen,' *Lives*, I, p. 312, 'Cuimin mac Dima, meic Diarmata, I cCill Cuimin I tir Ó nEachdach .i. isin Ulaigh moir fo chosaibh hUa Shuanaigh .i. I rRathain ro hadhnacht Cuimin'; II, p. 303. See also 'Pedigree of O'Mochain,' *The genealogies, tribes*, ed. J. O'Donovan, p. 45. Fidmuine Ua Suanaig, anchorite, and Fidairle Ua Suanaig, abbot, both lived in the mid-eighth century, according to *AU*. Kenney, offers no date for the text of 'The Expulsion' (see Kenney, *The sources*, p. 452). **126** *ALC*, pp 174–5: 'Ca adnacul a taob an teampuil fo corraib a athar'. **127** See above, n. 119. **128** *AFM*, 1010. **129** *Annales Hiberniae*, ed. & trans. Butler, p. 6, and note 'm', p. 7. 'Mr. Petrie informs me that this body was found in the situation described, on the repairing of the choir a few years since, with his mitre, which was an exquisite work of art.' **130** *AFM, s.a.* 1156; *AT*, p. 182. **131** *Mon. Hib.*, I, p. 310. **132** *Chart. St Mary's*, II, ed. Ware (1658), p. 229 No. 4: 'Felix O-Ruadan, Archipiscopus Tuamensis, in qua ipse sepultus est anno 1238, ad gradum altaris, in sinistra parte'. Ibid. In 1718, a body was found in this position, buried in pontificals. The coffin seems to have been replaced. **133** *AFM, s.a.* 1198. **134** *Mon. Hib.*, II, p. 278. **135** *Mon. Hib.*, I, p. 23. **136** Galloway, *Cathedrals of Ireland*, p. 129. **137** *Reg. Mon. Athenry*, p. 210. **138** Lewis, *Topographical dictionary*, I, p. 635.

Irish. For example, in 1218 Hugh, bishop of Ossory was interred 'under a high monument in the middle of the choir'.[139] MacCarthy Reagh, who founded the Franciscan monastery of Timoleague, Co. Cork, was buried in the choir in 1240.[140] In 1296, the Anglo-Irish lord of Desmond, Thomas fitzMaurice fitzJohn fitzThomas, was buried in the middle of the choir in the Franciscan abbey of Tralee, Co. Kerry,[141] while in 1298 Ragnailt, 'daughter of Brian's son', was buried in the choir of the Discalced Friars in Cork.[142] In 1443, John Prene, archbishop of Armagh, was buried in the choir of the parish-church of Termonfeckin in Co. Louth.[143]

Two mid-fourteenth-century burials at the Dominican priory of St Saviour in Dublin may offer a glimpse of social status reflected in burial. In 1351, Kenelbreck Sherman, 'who had been mayor of Dublin, and was a generous benefactor who had glazed the great east window, roofed the church and performed many other works, died and was interred in the friary under the belfry which he had built'; yet ten years later, 'Moris Doncref, citizen of Dublin' – who had given the huge sum of £40 sterling to the friars for the purpose of glazing their church – was buried in the churchyard.[144]

An intriguing but partly illegible entry in the register of the Dominican monastery of Athenry seems to indicate that the 'family [*muinter*] of Bruader' was buried in the choir in Clonfert in 1462.[145] The wording of this is reminiscent of the notice of the burial of 'those of the nation of Lynch', previously noted.[146]

Burial at entryways and boundaries

Élite native Irish burials are also noted as having occurred in outdoor locations, and references indicate that burial at an entryway, threshold or boundary may signify high status. The poem on the royal burials at Clonmacnoise records that three kings 'Murgal and Tomaltach the mighty, and Muirgius are under thy wall'.[147] The 'Life of St Senán' of Scattery Island (Inis Chathaig) tells of two boys whose

> bodies were buried in the cemetery, near the monastery. They were the first deposed within the graveyard, and they were interred in a conspicuous place before the entrance.[148]

---

139 *Mon. Hib.*, II, p. 321. In England, the nave seems sometimes to also have been called the 'choir': see Daniell, *Death and burial*, p. 97.   **140** 'tighearna cairpreach 7 a tumba fein do denomh hi ccoraidh na mbrathar', *AFM, s.a.* 1240.   **141** *Caithr. Th.*, I, p. 168; II, p. 178.   **142** *AI, s.a.* 1298, No 1: Ragnailt, daughter of Brian's son [probably Ó Briain) died, and was buried in the choir of the Discalced Friars in Corcach on the first of July.   **143** *Reg. John Mey*, No. 284, pp 21–2.   **144** *Mon. Hib.*, II, p. 71.   **145** 'Item in choro ante sedem subprioris jacent muintir bruader omnino (blank) …': *Reg. Mon. Athenry*, p. 213. There are two townlands in the barony of Loughrea, Co. Galway, by this name: *Index to the townlands*, p. 64.   **146** See n. 137 in this chapter.   **147** 'The graves of the kings at Clonmacnoise', ed. & trans. Best, p. 165, st. 2 & 7.   **148** *Lives*, I, pp 242–4. O'Hanlon, *Lives*, VII (1892). Kenney (no. 157)

A similar reference from *ALC* tells that Magnus, son of King Muircheartach 'Muimhneach' O'Connor, was buried in 1244 'outside the doorway of the church of Fenagh'.[149]

These stories may indicate that there was special meaning associated with interments made 'in a conspicuous place before the entrance' to the church. The tale of the boys buried at Inis Chathaig found in the 'Life of St Senán' is reminiscent of other hagiographical tales of 'first interments' in new cemeteries[150] – but this could hardly have been the case regarding Maghnus, since Fenagh was an ancient cemetery, not a new one. The church of Fenagh was not a suitable place of burial in 1244, since it had lost its roof and been desecrated in a raid. But the fact that the annalist carefully recorded the boy's burial 'outside the doorway of the church' suggests that the position of the grave was meaningful.[151] Maghnus' death came during a raid on the church of Fenagh, an event which put an additional strain on the already tense relations between the O'Connors and O'Rourkes. This is reflected in Maghnus' burial notice, which tells of the huge offering which was given to the church as an oblation in reparation for the damage caused to the church by his men, which included the death of this child. His obituary is unique in the native Irish chronicles because it contains the sole mention of a stone cross. The *ALC* describes it as a 'beautiful monument of stone' which had been set up over his grave and was destroyed a short time later by the O'Rourkes. It could be that Magnus' grave – and the others mentioned above – were sited at church entrances and boundaries because of a belief that they might ward off enemies or offer some other kind of protection. Christopher Daniell has noted that in England, thresholds and rood-screens also seem to have been 'liminal areas', perhaps suggesting the boundary between earthly life and the afterlife.[152]

Burial of native Irish women

Legendary tales contain references to women of the same kindred being buried in the same grave, as we have seen was the case with men. The passage quoted above from 'The colloquy of the ancients' regarding the *tulach* of the 'woman-bevy' is one;[153] we find another in the same text, where Caeilte tells of 'ten score

---

who says Life of St Senán is not later than tenth century, while Version 2 of the Life 'dates in all probability from the eleventh century, author was an Irishman, Conchubranus. **149** *AConn*, 1244.5; *ALC, s.a.* 1244. **150** The account of Odhrán's burial in Adomnán's 'Life of Columba', for example. See above, Chapter 2, n. 155. **151** Could this have been a 'defensive' burial? See also Astill and Wright, 'Perceiving patronage', p. 135, where they note that the earliest burials made (after 1471) in the south transept of Fountains Abbey, Yorkshire, were placed before the entrances to the transept chapels. **152** Daniell, *Death and burial*, pp 100–1. **153** See above, n. 3.

men, and women as many' buried in a *tulach* known as 'the hill of slaughter' (*cnoc an áir*).[154] The 'girls' graves' (*ferta na n-ingen*), said to have been near Tara, are also mentioned.[155] Among the poems dating from the early fourteenth to early sixteenth centuries which were collected by the dean of Lismore in the fifteenth and early sixteenth centuries, we find an exhortation to 'raise ye a tomb to the band of women as broad as the grave-slabs of the spouses of Cruacha'.[156]

In the five hundred years between 1000 and 1500, the native Irish chronicles record the burial of just nineteen women. All were of high status – territorial queens or princesses – and all but four were native Irish women. The first exception is the daughter of the earl of Ulster, wife of Miles MacCostello. Her burial in the monastery of Boyle is recorded *s.a.* 1253 in both *AFM* and *AConn*, and she presents an interesting case, as she was an 'Anglo-Norman' woman, born and raised in Ireland, and married into the 'Anglo-Norman' family of Angulo or Nangle, which was the first such family to adopt an Irish surname (Mac Coisdealbha/Costello). The other three Anglo-Irish women were Desideria fitzMorris (*s.a.* 1345), Joanna de Burgo (*s.a.* 1359), and Sebhán, daughter of Garret the Earl (*s.a.* 1428).

The burial notices for women found in the Irish chronicles between the years 1000 and 1500 are listed in the table opposite.

Unfortunately, these notices from the Irish chronicles do not provide any information regarding funerary ritual for women, the position in which they were buried in the church (with one exception), or even whether each was interred in her own separate grave or buried in a grave containing other members of the kin-group. The sole reference to the position or location of a woman's grave occurs in the obit of Ragnailt, 'daughter of Brian's son'. Her burial in the choir, which was a location reserved for élite-burials, is recorded in *AI s.a.* 1298.

From their places of interment we can see that native Gaelic women of the élite-classes were not obligated to be buried in the territorial churches of their husbands, but could be interred in their native church, among their own kindred. Burial notices of men from this period sometimes say that the deceased had been buried 'according to his wish'; but no such statement occurs regarding the burial of a woman. However, *Cáin Adomnán*, a set of laws adopted at the council of Birr, Co. Offaly, in 697, states that 'every woman who would choose (for herself) his burial place would be taken to Heaven without judgment …';[157] and women were also able to make bequests to churches of their choice, independently of their husbands.[158]

---

154 'The colloquy of the ancients', *SG*, I, p. 126; II, p. 137. 155 '… Brí therefore with her bevy of women went to ferta na ningen by Tara …': 'Translation of extracts', *SG*, II, p. 476 (Irish text); II, p. 522. 156 'Tógbaidh feart don bhéinne bhan leithead leacht gcéile gCruachan': 'The Author of this is Eóghan MacEoin Mheic Eichthighearna', *Scottish verse*, ed. & trans. Watson, p. 171, st. 14. 157 *Cain Adomnáin*, ed. & trans. Meyer, §25, pp 14–15. 158 Bitel, 'Women's Donations, p. 13.

Burial date	Source	Person	Burial site
1076	AI	Gormfhlaith, dau of Ua Fócarta, Q. of of Mumu, wife of Toirrdelbach Ua Briain	Inis Chealtra, Co. Clare
1226	AFM ALC	Nuala, dau. of Roderic O'Conor, Q. of Ulidia	Cong, Co. Mayo
1252	AI	Mór, daugher of Conchobar, son of Tairdelbach Ó Briain and wife of Cormac MacCarthaig	Killone (Cell Lonáin), Co. Clare; relics transferred to 'Les na mBrathar'
1253	AConn	?, dau. of earl of Ulster (Hugh de Lacy), wife of Miles MacCostello	Boyle, Co. Roscommon
1298	AI	Ragnailt, 'dau. of Brian's son'	Cork, Co. Cork
1340	AU AFM	Dervorgilla (Dearbhaill) dau. of, O'Donnell, repudiated wife of O'Connor	Boyle, Co. Roscommon
1345	ANen	Desideria FitzMorris, daughter of Gerald	Ardfert, Co. Kerry
1353	ANen	Gormlaith O'Donnell, wife of Donald O'Neill	Armagh, Co. Armagh
1359	ANen	Joanna de Burgo, countess of Kildare	Nenagh, Co. Tipperary
1373	AU	Mór, dau. of Ua Fergail, wife of Diarmait Mag Raghnaill	Cloone, Co. Leitrim
1386	AFM AConn	Áine, dau. of Tadhg mac Donnchaidh, wife of Tiernan Ó Ruairc	Sligo, Co. Sligo
1395	AFM	Cobhlaigh Mór, dau. of Cathal, king of Connaught, wife of (1) O'Donnell, (2) Hugh O'Rourke, (3) Cathal, son of Hugh Bréifneach O'Conor	Boyle, Co. Roscommon
1428	AI	Sebhán, dau. of Garret the earl, wife of Tadhg Mac Carthaig★★	Tralee, Co. Kerry
1417	AConn	Ragnailt, dau. of Donnchad Ó Birn, wife of (1) Diarmait Mac Diarmata (2) William Burke, (3) Cumscrach Mac Ragnaill	Roscommon, Co. Rosc.
1417	AConn	Catirfina, dau. of Cathal Ó Ruairc, ?, wife of Toirrdelbach Mac Domnaill Gallóclach	Roscommon, Co. Rosc.
1437	AConn	Gormlaigh, dau. of Dauid Ó Duibgennáin, wife of Brian Mac Aedacáin, ultimately an anchorite	Loch Cé, Co. Rosc.
1446	AMacF	Sara (Sadhbh) 'daughter of William fitz Conner mac Branan Maelyn O-maelconary … Banollamh of Silmuiredhy fitz ffeargus and a nurse to all guests and strangers, and of all the learned men in Irland'	Elphin, Co. Roscommon
1474	AU	Margaret Mag Mathgamna, wife of Donnchadh Mag Uidhir	Clonmacnoise, Co. Offaly
1498	AU	Margaret Mag Uidhir, dau. of Domnall, wife of Ua Flannagán	Donegal, Co. Donegal

★   Dates are given exactly as found in the published sources.
★★ See *AI*, n. 3, p. 437.

Thus we find some native Irish women buried with their own kindred, while others were buried with their husbands' families. Gormlaith Ní Fhócarta (Fogarty) was buried in 1076 at Inis Chealtra, Co. Clare, in her father's territory. The body of Mór MacCarthy was interred in 1252 at the nunnery of Killone, Co. Clare, which had been founded by her ancestor Donal Mór O'Brien before 1189; later her remains were removed to Clare Abbey itself. In 1226, Nuala O'Connor was interred not in the territory of her husband, MacDonslevy, king of Uladh,[159] but at Cong in Co. Mayo, deep in the heart of her father's territory. When Mór, the daughter of Ua Fhearghail died *s.a.* 1373 (*recte* 1378), she was not buried with her husband's people, but at Cloone, Co. Leitrim, safely within her native territory.

Áine, daughter of MacDonough and wife of Tiernan O'Rourke, was not buried in the O'Rourke territory of Bréifne in 1386, but at Sligo. Cobhlaigh Mhór, daughter of Donnell O'Connor, king of Connaught, was married first to Niall O'Donnell, lord of Tirconnell, then to Hugh O'Rourke, lord of Bréifne, and finally to Cathal, son of Hugh Bréifneach O'Connor. She seems to have been buried in her own territory.

The traditional burial place of the O'Donnells was the abbey of Assaroe in Donegal; however, Derbail (Dervorgilla) O'Donnell was buried at Boyle, Co. Roscommon, in 1340. This is probably due to the fact that 'the illness of her death seized her' while she was at Inis Dhoighri (Inisterry) visiting Connor MacDermot (Conchobhur Mac Diarmada). The MacDermot burial place was at Boyle, and it was also the traditional place of burial for the O'Connors, of which MacDermots were essentially a branch. Derbail had been married to O'Connor but, since she had been repudiated, it seems likely that Connor MacDermot had Gormlaith interred at Boyle abbey because it was the burial place of his own people. Ragnailt, daughter of Donnchadh O'Byrne (Ó Birn), was first married to Dermot then to William, the grandson of Sir David Burke and, lastly, to Cumscrach Mac Raghnaill. Her interment at Roscommon in 1417 continued a burial tradition that is documented in the chronicles from 1133 – and may have predated these records.[160] Sebhán, daughter of Garrett the earl, died in 1428, and was buried in Tralee, Co. Kerry, the Dominican priory founded in 1243 by John fitz Thomas (Fitzgerald, called John of Callan).

This same situation existed in medieval England, where high-status women were not uniformly buried either with their own or their husbands' families. Jennifer Ward has considered medieval Englishwomen's instructions regarding their place of burial and concluded that:

> it is unknown how much independence they had in deciding these matters … there does appear to be an element of individual choice … it was

159 *AFM.*   160 *AT* & *AFM, s.a.* 1133; *ALC, s.a.* 1133; *CS, s.a.* 1129.

often heiresses, 'the last of their own line', who sought to be buried in locations that emphasized their own lineage.[161]

In Ireland, we find no record of women being buried in their husbands' territory until the fifteenth century, which may indicate a shift in custom among the female Gaelic élite. Raghnailt, the 'daughter of Brian [O'Brien]'s son', was buried in her husband's territory in Cork in 1417. Catirfina, daughter of Cathal O'Rourke, was the wife of Turlough Mac Donnell (Toirrdelbhach Mac Domhnaill 'Gallóglach') who was slain in 1419 while leading a battalion of Mac Donnell gallowglasses against the Burkes. Catirfina's death preceded her husband's, and Sligo and Drumlane, Co. Cavan, were the traditional burial places of her own family, the O'Rourkes. However, Catirfina was buried at Roscommon which had strong ties with the O'Connors, and her burial there was probably linked to her husband's service as a 'gallowglass' or mercenary soldier to the O'Connors. A convent of nuns – perhaps a double monastery – had been established at Roscommon *c*.1223, and we know that a convent was there in 1400, but no mention is made of Catirfina's having become a nun prior to her death, or that she died in a convent.[162]

The written record also makes it clear that the remains of élite Gaelic women were sometimes transported great distances for burial in their territorial cemeteries, as were the bodies of men. I have previously noted that Gormlaith Ní Foíarta was carried from Killaloe to Inis Chealtra (both in Co. Clare) for her burial in 1076; and that in 1386, the body of Áine, daughter of Tadhg mac Donnchaid (Mac Donough), was brought from Tuaim-senchaid at Garradice Lough (near Drumlane, Co. Cavan), to Sligo for interment.[163]

As discussed in Chapter 4, the Irish tradition of honorably burying women and marking their tombs is well-documented in semi-historical writings such as the *dindsenchas* poems of the Fionn cycle, and hagiographical sources. The literature also gives examples of the graves of high-status women being marked with cairns, pillar-stones or other memorials, and recounts numerous sites which are said to be called after the women who are buried there.[164] While most of the inscribed stones which have been found commemorate men, stones commemorating women are not unknown.[165] In her study of the distribution of male and female burials both inside the church and in the cemetery surrounding the church at Ardfert, Co. Kerry, Áine Brosnan concluded that 'gender was not necessarily related to status'.[166]

Some women were accorded the honor of burial in an abbey. The non-Irish 'Chronicle of Kings of Man and the Isles' (*Cronica regum Mannie & Insularum*)

---

161 Ward, 'The English noblewoman', p. 133.   **162** A. Gwynn & Hadcock, *Medieval religious*, p. 323.   **163** See Chapter 3, n. 193.   **164** See Chapter 4: 'Artifacts', notes 83, 96–100.   **165** For example, a stone at Knockmoy, commemorating Melachlin O'Kelly (d. 1401), and his wife, Fionnuala, daughter of Turlough O'Connor. Macalister, *Corpus*, II, No. 541, p. 8.   **166** Brosnan, *Mortuary practices*, p. 84.

notes that Affreca de Courcy, who had founded Grey abbey in Co. Down in 1193, was 'even buried there'.[167] The phrase seems to indicate that this was exceptional in some way. Affreca was the daughter of the king of Man and the wife of the 'Anglo-Norman' baron John de Courcy. The phrase may indicate that the burial of a woman in an abbey was considered to be unusual at the time; alternatively, it could mean that it was considered unusual that she was buried in her husband's territory, rather than her father's.[168] In 1357, Joan de Burgh, the wife of Thomas, the earl of Kildare, was interred in Kildare, at the side of her husband.[169] We also find women mentioned in a charter of 1290, in which Walter de Lacy grants a number of chapels and churches (including Dunshaughlin, Co. Meath) in *Frankalmoign* to the church and canons of St Thomas the Martyr, Dublin, 'for the salvation of his soul and the souls of his father and mother whose body reposes there'.[170] Finally, *ANen* record that Desideria, the daugher of Gerald fitzMorris and a great benefactor to the Franciscans, was buried in 1345 with the brothers of Ardfert, Co. Kerry, and that Gormlaith O'Donnell, wife of Donald O'Neill, was buried with the brothers of Armagh in 1353.[171]

SEPARATE BURIAL OF WOMEN AND MEN

Hamlin and Foley have argued that evidence from the fifth century to the twelfth indicates that men and women were separated for burial.[172] It seems clear from placename and other evidence that separately cemeteries for women did exist in Ireland, yet a number of sources tell of men and women being buried together. The written sources surveyed for this work have not yielded any statements to corroborate the view that separate burial of the sexes was the standard practice during the Middle Ages.[173]

If separate interment of Irish men and women in prehistoric times was standard, medieval manuscripts written on legendary themes in widely disparate areas do not prove this; rather, they provide examples of men and women having been interred together. For example, in a passage in 'The colloquy of the ancients' Caeilte tells St Patrick that the king of Leinster and Fithir, the daughter of Tuathal

---

167 *Cronica regum Mannie & Insularum*, ed. & trans. Broderick, f. 41r.   **168** John de Courcy's role in the history of this period cannot be overstated; yet no record of his place of death or burial is known.   **169** *Ann. Mon. Beata*, ed. Gilbert, *s.a.* 1357, p. 393.   **170** *Calendar of documents, Ireland*, ed. & trans. Sweetman & Hadcock, p. 381, No. 839 (6), The wording suggests that only his mother is buried there.   **171** ' … sepulta que est cum eisdem fratribus in Ardart', and 'et sepulta cum fratribus de Ardmacha', 'Annals of Nenagh'.   **172** Hamlin & Foley, 'A women's graveyard'; Edwards, *The archaeology*, pp 129–30.   **173** The case of Finlaggan on the island of Islay, Scotland, is noteworthy, although it is not named in any of the written Irish sources for this period. Finlaggan was built before 1380 by John, Lord of the Isles, and was the burial place for 'the wives and children of the island lords … while these latter were buried at Iona': O'Hanlon, *Lives*, I, p. 56, also noted by Hamlin & Foley, 'A woman's graveyard'.

Techtmar, were 'in this sodded grave … laid together'.[174] In the poem 'Cerna' we read of the

> yellow-haired host that lie beneath Cerna, sloping home of hundreds …
> his wife lies under the cloak of each man of the host I have enumerated
> thus far.[175]

The author of 'Créide's lament for Cáel', thought to date from *c.*1175, tells how the daughter of the king of Ciarraige Luachra, in what is now northeast Co. Kerry, 'laid down by Cáel's side and died for grief of him; and they were both buried there in a single tomb'.[176]

'The Book of Fenagh', whose verse portions were composed before 1300, tells that Cobhthach, a prehistoric king of Brega, was buried with his nurse, Rian, near his side.[177] That St Brigit and St Patrick were believed to share the same grave is related in a poem composed in the mid fourteenth century.[178] These examples show that medieval writers were familiar with the practice of burying men and women together and saw it as an honorable custom, though it is worth considering the possibility that these interments were recorded because they were considered unusual.

The 'Dialogues' of Gregory the Great refer to the burial of a nun and a monk in the same grave and do not censure or condemn the action.[179] However, with the coming of Christianity to Ireland, the propriety of burying men and women together was questioned. The so-called second synod of St Patrick, possibly dating from the seventh century, decreed that 'Each one shall consider in his conscience whether the love and desire of sin have ceased, since a dead body does not harm another's dead body. If this is not the case they shall be separated.'[180] The written evidence does not indicate that any procedures for separation were ever adopted.

As I noted earlier, written Irish sources contain references to the 'cemetery of the kings', 'tomb of the kings' and 'tomb of the bishops'.[181] In the light of these notices, if women were buried separately from men, we might reasonably expect to find similar references to separate burial places for women, such as a

---

174 'The colloquy of the ancients', *SG*, I, 183; II, p. 206.   **175** 'Cerna', *Met. Dind.*, II, p. 209.
176 *Early Irish lyrics*, ed & trans. Murphy, p. 151. For dating, see ibid., pp 229–230 of the same source.   **177** *Bk. Fen.*, pp 252–3 (prose); pp 260–1 (verse). 'On this side of brave Cobhthach's grave / is her grave and resting place.'   **178** Ó Dubhagain and Gilla na naomh Ó Huidrín, *The topographical poems*, ed. & trans. O'Donovan, p. 39.   **179** '… he [Benedict] sent presently to bring her corpse to his Abbey, to have it buried in that grave which he had provided for himself: by means whereof it fell out that, as their souls were always one in God while they lived, so their bodies continued together after death': *Dialogues of Gregory the Great*, ed. Gardiner, p. 96.   **180** *The Irish penitentials*, p. 129, §11. For dating, see Kenney, *The sources*, p. 245.   **181** See section above entitled 'Burial of kings'.

'cemetery of the queens'. Yet, with two exceptions, none of the diverse sources which I have surveyed has produced any reference to a Christian 'women's cemetery' or even the 'women's section' of a cemetery. 'The Book of Fenagh', mentions 'the hill of the women' (*Cnoc-in-Banntrochta*) located on the south of the plain, named for the fifteen queens who died on the plain which it overlooks but, because it is being pointed out by Finntan to St Patrick, this is clearly a reference to a pre-Christian site. This passage is interesting, however, because it indicates that the graves of queens – not only those of kings – may have been thought to offer protection to their people.[182] The second mention is found in *AFM* under the year 1082, in an entry which records the burning of 'the cemetery of the nuns at Cluain-mic-Nois'; this would have been the cemetery that was attached to the nunnery, the existence of which is first noted in 1026.

Two high-status women were buried at Clonmacnoise: the mother of Flann Sinna, king of Mide, was buried there in 886, and her granddaughter Ligach (Flann Sinna's daughter), was buried there in 921. Yet neither of these obituary notices mention a separate women's cemetery, nor do they give any indication of where their graves were located.[183] It could be that a separate women's cemetery did exist at Clonmacnoise in the ninth and tenth centuries, and that its existence was so well known that it was taken for granted. However, the annalists and poets did not take the 'cemetery of the kings' for granted; they wrote a great deal about it, and it was definitely well known. If such cemeteries for women existed, it seems odd that they were not noted, especially if, like the 'cemeteries of the kings', they were the final resting place of members of the élite classes.

Medieval monks generally had their own graveyard or section of the graveyard, separate from that in which the laity was interred; therefore, the existence of a separate cemetery for nuns does not necessarily indicate that the general lay population was separated at burial according to sex.[184]

We do, however, find references to women and men having been buried together in the Middle Ages. The 'Register of the monastery of Athenry' records that in 1363 William Wallace, a 'noble burgher' of Dublin, was buried 'in his stone tomb with his wife and children'.[185] In 1413 'Thomas Brayneoc' was buried with his children as well as 'Catylyne', a relative of Thomas, who was the wife of John Reed.[186] In 1415, Thomas Bovanter, a burgher, chose to be buried in the monastery of Athenry with his wife, Christina Lynch, and his children who had pre-deceased him in 1413.[187] The last will and testament of John Lytill, whose

---

182 *Bk Fen.*, p. 253. **183** *AFM* places Flann's death *s.a.* 886; the death of Ligach is noted in *AFM, s.a.* 921 and *AClon, s.a.* 919. For the dating of the nunnery at Clonmacnoise, see A. Gywnn & Hadcock, *Medieval religious*, p. 315. **184** *AFM, s.a.* 1082. **185** '… cum sepelitur sua uxor cum suis filiis.' *Reg. Mon. Athenry*, i, pp 206–7. **186** 'Thomas Brayneoc fuit amicus fratrum et benefactor et in eadem cappella est sepultus cum ipsius progenie et Catylyne Brayneoc germana praedicti Thomae quae fuit uxor Johannis Reed', ibid., p. 209. **187** 'Item praedictus venerabili burgensis elegit sepeliri sub altari beati Petri Martyris, et ibi sepultus est

probate was granted in St Patrick's cathedral in Dublin in 1434, contains the request that he be buried 'near the body of Alianora Comyn, his former wife.'[188]

The argument that these examples refer to the 'Anglo-Norman' population, and should therefore not be taken as an exemplars for the social practices of the native Irish is a reasonable one. However, archaeological excavations conducted at early Christian and later medieval cemeteries in such disparate areas of the country as Millockstown[189] and Mellifont, both in Co. Louth;[190] Ardfert[191], Co. Kerry; Omey Island, Co. Galway;[192] Kilshane, Co. Dublin;[193] Church Island, Co. Kerry;[194] Knocklea, Co. Limerick;[195] and Waterford city[196] have found men, women and children buried together in the same sections of the cemetery. An inscribed stone found at Knockmoy commemorating the graves of the native Irishman Melachlin Ua Cheallaig (O'Kelly, d. 1401) and his wife, Fionnuala, daughter of Turlough O'Connor, certainly seems to suggest that the two were interred together.[197] An elegy written *c*.1444 by Tadhg Óg Ó hUiginn (O'Higgin) tells that Gráinne Ní Chellaig (O'Kelly) and her husband, Tadhg Ó Briain (O'Brien) were buried together at Ennis, Co. Clare, but suggests that it was considered unusual that she was not buried by 'her own people':

> No shame for the swan of Áth Truim not to be buried by us; Sláine's son insisted that he and she share one grave.[198]

Excavation of sixteenth-century interments at Tintern abbey, Co. Wexford, revealed five women and one man buried together in what seems to be one tomb located in the wall of the north chancel. The only 'high-status' burial among the eighty-eight excavated was a female buried in a stone-lined grave, and the exca-

cum uxore et prole …': *Reg. Mon. Athenry*, p. 208. **188** Robinson, 'Ancient deeds of the parish of St John', p. 198. **189** Manning, 'Archaeological excavation of a succession of enclosures', pp 135–81, esp. pp 164–5. **190** de Paor, 'Excavations at Mellifont Abbey'. **191** Brosnan, 'Mortuary practices', pp 88–9. **192** Excavated in 1992–3 by a team led by Dr Tadhg O'Keeffe, of which the author was a member. See O'Keeffe, 'Omey and the sands of time'. The Ordnance Survey map also records the presence of a cemetery of women on Omey, but this could date from a much later period or have been an unconsecrated cemetery – see the section below entitled 'Burial of the unfortunate'. **193** Brosnan, 'Mortuary practices', p. 36. Excavation revealed the extremely dense burial of 123 skeletons, including children and adolescents. **194** See M.J. O'Kelly, 'Church Island'. **195** M.J. Kelly 'Knocklea'. This excavation produced sixty-six burials, thought to represent a single extended family over a period of 200 years. **196** Power, 'Human skeletal remains', p. 762. **197** The inscription reads DO MULEACHAIND O LEALLAID DO RI O MANI AGAS D'INDBUAILAIND INGE(N) I CHONCHUIR DOIRE MATHA O COGLI IN LEABAIG SEA, as recorded by Macalister, *Corpus*, ii, p. 8, No. 541. It bears noting that this stone is from the early fifteenth century, by which time traditional native Irish burial practices had been eroded to a degree which must have varied considerably, depending on the strength of the Anglo-Irish presence in the area. **198** 'Ní gut d'ealaid Áta truim / gan a hadlacad aguinn; / mac Sláine 's sé nar ceaduig / gan Gráinne 's é i n-éinleabaid': 'An elegy on Tadhg O'Briain', *Aithdioghluim Dána*, poem XIV, st. 18, p. 32.

vators felt that there was no reason to think that monks from the abbey had not also been buried in the same church, although this could not be conclusively proven.[199]

The written evidence shows that women were accorded élite burial inside Irish religious foundations from at least the late twelfth century, and no written evidence indicates that interments were made in areas separate from the men's graves. It is not possible, however, to prove from Irish written sources that women's and men's graves were intermingled, since the specific locations of the women's graves are not given. Affreca de Courcy's burial at Grey abbey in 1193 has already been noted, along with the thirteenth-century burial of Walter de Lacy's mother in St Thomas the Martyr, Dublin.[200] *ANen* record that Desideria, the daughter of Gerald fitzMorris, and a great benefactor to the Franciscans, was buried with the brothers in Ardfert in 1345, and Gormlaith O'Donnell, wife of Donald O'Neill, was buried with the brothers of Armagh in 1353,[201] though this may not necessarily indicate physical placement of the corpse in the midst of the monks' graves.

While the sources provide no evidence that separate burial of the sexes or children was normal in Ireland from 900 to 1500, there is a good deal of evidence to show that there were cemeteries in Ireland devoted exclusively to the burial of men or women or children.[202] We do not know, however, whether these customs existed – or even if the graveyards existed – during the Middle Ages, since most of the evidence for these cemeteries comes from placenames. Many of the graveyards which are known to have been used for the burial of unbaptized children (called *ceallúnaigh*) were once consecrated cemeteries which had been abandoned at earlier times due to population-shifts, and were not turned to this use until well into the modern period.[203] I have also not found any indication that these cemeteries were used for burial of the general population; rather, they seem to have been used expressly for the interment of people who died in circumstances which were thought to make their burial in consecrated ground ill-advised.

BURIAL OF 'THE UNFORTUNATE'[204]

The canon law adopted for cemeteries (1205–14) stated that Christians were not required to be buried in a consecrated cemetery, though Canon law stipu-

---

199 J.F. O'Donovan, 'A study of the human remains', pp 49–52, 198.   **200** See above, notes 167–71.   **201** '… *sepulta que est cum eisdem fratribus in Ardart*', and '*et sepulta cum fratribus de Ardmacha*', 'Annals of Nenagh'.   **202** Notably by W.F. Wakeman, Foley, and Hamlin; see Edwards, *The archaeology*, pp 129–30.   **203** Aldridge, 'Notes on children's burial grounds in Mayo'.   **204** I have borrowed this term from Claire Gittings' *Death, burial*, where she has used it as a title for one of her chapters. It seems both a humanitarian and efficient way to

lated that each grave must be blessed at burial, and that those who could not receive Christian burial were to be laid in a place set apart.[205] However, because burial near saints' relics (*ad sanctos*) was believed to have a very beneficial effect, Christians had a fervent desire to be buried in the same cemetery (or in the same church) where a saint's relics rested.

A non-Christian could not be buried in ground consecrated for Christian burial. Christians who died by suicide, or while excommunicate or unrepentant, were also denied burial in the consecrated ground of the churchyard. Canon law stated that those who were not allowed to receive Christian burial were to be laid in a place set apart. The Church also had the right to disinter the bodies of those who had not died in a state of grace and remove them from the consecrated cemetery, as stated in a statute adopted by the Twelfth General Council convened by Pope Innocent III in 1215. Additionally, members of the Knights Hospitallers and 'certain other religious orders' were prevented from giving burial to the bodies of those 'excommunicated by name or public robbers or violators of churches or other places' and instructed that any bodies 'so buried be removed from consecrated ground.'[206]

The constitutions of the Irish diocese of Ossory, approved by Bishop Richard de Ledred in 1317, state that any priest who had 'in ignorance' given ecclesiastical burial to any person excommunicated for having done harm to the clergy or their property':

> when he learns the truth, he shall cause the body to be exhumed, and to be removed from sanctuary and cast upon a dunghill. Otherwise the church and cemetery are placed under interdict till the body is removed.[207]

The burial of the English religious dissenter John Wyclif, who died in 1384, provides an example of such a disinterment. Wyclif was buried in his parish church at Lutterworth, Lincolnshire, but his works were later judged to be heretical, and in 1428 remains thought to be Wyclif's were disinterred, burned, and tossed into a stream.[208]

Papal letters to Englishmen and Scotsmen show how critical burial in consecrated ground was for members of the Christian community in medieval society: The letters threaten the men with life-long excommunication if a particular mission is not properly completed, but if enforced, the excommunication was to remain in effect only until 'the hour of death'.[209]

Separate, unconsecrated cemeteries for 'the unfortunate'
Groups for which separate, unconsecrated cemeteries are thought to have existed include men who had died in battle, and thus had not received last rites (or

---

refer to a very diverse group of people.   **205** Podradsky; *New dictionary*, p. 52.   **206** *Stat. Scot.*, pp 73–4.   **207** Lawlor, 'Calendar of the Liber Ruber', p. 168.   **208** *Heresy trials,* ed. Tanner, p. 7.   **209** *Papal reg.*, IV, 5 Greg. XI, 8 Id. Sept. 1375; *Papal reg.*, 6 Bon. IX, Id. July 1395.

possibly made their last confessions); children who had died before receiving baptism; and women who had died in or shortly after childbirth, and thus before receiving the ritual cleansing in church which was standard post-partem custom in medieval Ireland.[210] Documentary evidence exists to show that in England, some churches also denied burial in consecrated ground to women who had died giving birth.[211]

Strangers might also have been buried separately.[212] Both Irish and Welsh law contain highly detailed prescriptions for what must be done regarding the burial of a stranger. John O'Hanlon wrote of a town called Ballyfoile, where it is marked on the Ordnance Townland survey 'a burial place for children'. In the neighborhood, this ancient cemetery is said to be used for unbaptized children and strangers'.[213]

Burial is one of the most conservative of social practices, and Irish medieval society was localized, homogeneous, superstitious, and fearful of people and situations which were outside the narrow range of known 'normal' experience. Excommunication was a severe and commonly used punishment, and giving burial in consecrated ground to a person whose status in relation to the Church, and whose 'state of grace' were unknown could mean incurring the wrath of the Church. Further, since the members of a local kindred had often been promised special blessings by their patron-saint if they were buried in his cemetery, it is possible that the kindred might not have been eager to share either its cemetery or its blessings with an outsider.[214]

The sources surveyed contain no references to women who died either in childbirth or before they were 'churched', and stories referring to pre-Christian Irish society suggest that a woman who had died in childbirth did not carry any stigma of uncleanliness. On the contrary, mythological tales speak of extreme honor being given to women who had died in such circumstances. Áine, the wife of Finn, who died in childbirth, is described as having been buried in a respectful and honorable manner:

> laid in excavations of the earth … her stone was reared over her resting-place, her funeral ceremony was performed and her ogham-stone inscribed.[215]

The rituals described are the same as those enacted for the burial of the most respected male members of the society. The legendary Tlachtga had the *roth*

---

210 Hamlin & Foley, 'A women's graveyard'; also Bitel, 'Women's donations'. Finucane notes that there was also the fear that blood falling from the woman's body would pollute the church. See Finucane, 'Death in the later Middle Ages', p. 55.   **211** Daniell, *Death and burial*, p. 103.   **212** Plummer, *Vitae sanctorum*, p. cx.   **213** 'St Breacc Fele', O'Hanlon, *Lives*, I, p. 220.   **214** For a good example of the kinds of blessings promised – and the curses for those of the kin not buried in the cemetery, see *Bk Fen.*, p. 81; also, 'Life of Maedoc of Ferns (II)', *Lives*, II, p. 277.   **215** 'The colloquy of the ancients', *SG*, I, 163; II, p. 181.

ramhach (the Flagstone in the Forcharth) set up over her after she died in child-birth, 'and over her the *dún* was erected'.[216] This is not to suggest that pre-Christian myth and medieval reality are the same but only to point out that the written record contains no evidence that pre-Christian Irish society had a tradition of marginalizing women who had died in childbirth. Further, if medieval Irish society did marginalize them, these sources show that medieval writers did not feel compelled to revise these early tales to make them conform to contemporary social practices.

Archaeological excavations of late-Viking age and medieval Irish cemeteries have found three full-term foetuses, all buried with a female (*in* or *ex-utero*). It was thought that the absence of infants aged less than one year might indicate that they had been interred elsewhere.[217].

It may be that the use of 'separate' burial grounds was a regional custom, rather than a pan-Irish one. Surviving medieval Irish records offer commentary on only a small section of the country, and it is quite possible that contemporary customs in areas remote from where the extant sources were produced would not have been noted or even known. It is also possible that the practice of separating these marginalized groups at burial developed after the period under study. Clearly, more research on this subject is needed before conclusions can be drawn.

Burial of excommunicants, unbaptized children and those who died by suicide
In surveying the sources used in this study, no information regarding the burial of unbaptized children, of persons who had taken their own lives or of those who had died while excommunicate has been found.

However, information about the burials of these 'unfortunates' in England and Scotland may be of value for purposes of comparison.

Clare Gittings, writing of the early modern period in England, notes 'the vital distinction' between children who had been baptized and those who had not, and that the usual fate for these latter unfortunate children was to be laid by the midwife in some 'secret place' or even thrown on the rubbish tip. She continues by pointing out that such treatment indicates that early modern English society did not regard these children as being as fully human as adults or older children.[219]

In England, suicide was regarded as having committed a three-fold crime – 'an offence against nature, against God, and against the king'. Evidence from the mid-sixteenth century shows that in England, those who committed suicide were buried in or near to the highways (preferably at a crossroads) with a wooden

---

216 'Translation of extracts', *SG*, II, p. 466 (Irish text); II, p. 511 (English trans.).　**217** Power, 'Human skeletal remains', p. 769.　**219** Gittings, *Death, burial*, pp 83–5.

stake thrust through their bodies. Crossroads were chosen in order to diffuse the evil influence of the body by sending it in several different directions, thus rendering it less harmful; the stake was to prevent the ghost from walking.[220] This was more than superstitious tradition: it was the law in England, and remained so until 1821,[221] and it is probably safe to assume that the practice was an old one. Christopher Daniell has pointed out that this law was only rigorously enforced from the late fifteenth century onwards,[222] and individual priests may have chosen to disregard the rules – at least on occasion – and provide cemetery burial to those who had died by suicide. A letter to Archbishop Wishart of Glasgow dated 1446 is notable not only because it accuses a local vicar of having

> buried within the sanctuary of the cemetery of the said church the body of William Ade, a parisioner of his who had hanged himself with a rope in his own barn[223]

but more interestingly, because it notes that he did so 'without consulting his diocese'. The inclusion of this phrase suggests that such burials may have been permitted if some sort of permission could be obtained. By the late Middle Ages in Europe in general, people who were deemed to have taken their lives by reason of insanity were generally allowed burial in the churchyard.[224] Daniell has noted that in England 'the church was curiously silent about suicides', and that cases in which a suicide was judged to have been wilfull and fully conscious and therefore barred from burial in consecrated ground, seem to have been rare.

Burial of criminals

In England the bodies of executed criminals usually received Christian burial – at least by the end of the Middle Ages – unless the crime was high treason, in which case burial was sometimes denied entirely.[225] The treatment of the body of the condemned person, both before and after execution, could be exceedingly gruesome, although there was a certain logic behind it. For example, when the Welsh prince Dafydd ap Gruffudd was executed by Edward I, he was dragged

---

220 Ibid., pp 72–3.   **221** Ibid., pp 72–3. A similar practice is also recorded in Book XIX of the Decretum of Burchard of Worms (Germany). Burchard noted the practice – unsanctioned by the Church – of piercing with a stake the corpse of a child who had died before being baptized and burying the body in a secret place. According to Burchard, it was believed that this would prevent the child from returning and causing harm. Puckle wrote that the practice was abolished in 1823, when it was 'decreed that they [people who had died by suicide] should be buried in unconsecrated ground between nine and midnight'. See Puckle, *Funeral customs*, p. 152.   **222** Ibid., pp 72–3. Daniell, *Death and burial*, p. 106.   **223** *Cal. Pap. Reg.* 1 Nicholas V, 14 Kal. April 1446 (–7), p. 320.   **224** Finucane, 'Death in the later middle ages', p. 56.   **225** Gittings, *Death, burial*, p. 70.

to the scaffold by horses (because he was a traitor); hanged alive (for the crime of homicide); after which he was disembowelled and his bowels burned (for committing offenses during the holy season of Easter). Finally, his body was drawn and quartered (for plotting against the king).

Yet, after all of this, Dafydd's remains were not buried, perhaps to deny him any chance of resurrection. 'The Hagnaby Chronicle' reports that:

> There then followed some unseemly squabbling over the distribution of the pieces of the body: The Londoners carried off the head in triumph, but the citizens of York and Winchester disputed possession of the right shoulder. The men of Lincoln refused to accept any part, and as a result incurred royal displeasure, only remitted once a substantial fine had been paid.[226]

A passage in the 'Brehon law tracts' specifically limits the amount of damages the living may seek from the kin of the dead:

> Stock does not increase on a tomb; his crime dies with the criminal, if he has been lawfully buried after death under the sod of any lawful tomb.[226a]

The Irish sources also contain many examples of men who were executed, such as Muirchertach Ua Braen, a Leinster chief who had betrayed Diarmait Mac Murchada (Dermot MacMurrough), and whose beheaded body was brought to Strongbow, who had it thrown to the hounds, which 'wholly devoured him'.[227] In 1197, Mac Gilla-Eidich was hanged after robbing the church of Derry.[228] After his capture in 1172, Tigernán Ua Ruairc (Tiernan O'Rourke) was pierced with spears and decapitated before his body was hung upside down at the north side of *Cell na Truan* (near Dublin).[229] In 1295, Thomas O'Brochan was sentenced to hang for the death of Ralph de Cantelup in Kerry and have his limbs cut off, and in 1432, Maghnus MacMahon placed the heads of Englishmen on the stakes of his stronghold at Lurgan, Co. Monaghan.[230] Yet none of these grisly descriptions mention that the remains were buried.[231]

Philippe Ariès, writing of medieval France, has observed that executed criminals' bodies were generally not taken down, but remained exposed to the elements – sometimes for years – as an example to the public.[232] Clare Gittings'

---

226 Prestwich, *Edward I*, pp 202–3. **226a** *Ancient laws*, eds Atkinson et al., 'Brehon law tracts', p. 449. **227** *The song of Dermot and the Earl*, ed. & trans. Orpen, p. 159. **228** *AU*. **229** *AT*, *s.a.* 1172 (*AU*); 1171 (*ALC*); 1171 (*AFM*). **230** *AU*, *AFM*, *s.a.* 1432. **231** CJI, 23 Edw. I, Memb. 6d, p. 25. **232** Ariès, *The hour*, pp 44–45.

research revealed that in early modern England those executed were generally given Christian burial, except traitors, whose bodies were laid to rest 'near or under the gallows', although this was usually not done until some time after the execution.[233] Christpher Daniell has noted that excavations in England have revealed that bodies of people who had been hanged were sometimes buried 'backwards' – that is, with their heads to the east, instead of the west, as was normally done – buried with hands tied behind their backs or thrown face-first into the grave. Some had also been buried fully clothed.[234] In the light of the examples above, we may deduce that the same practices may have prevailed in Ireland.

Technically, the bodies of executed criminals could be buried in holy ground, on the grounds that a man paid for his crime by his execution, and God would not punish a man twice for the same transgression.[235] This is illustrated by the case of Lord William de Bermingham, a friend and supporter of the earl of Desmond. De Bermingham was arrested in Clonmel, Co. Tipperary, then hanged in Dublin in 1332 by order of Anthony de Lucy, the lord justice. Despite being in disfavor with the government, de Bermingham was given burial in the Dominican friary in Dublin. The sources record that numerous people were sentenced to hanging for robbery and other crimes,[236] but remain silent about the ultimate fate which befell their bodies. I have found one exception: *AFM* records *s.a.* 1452 that Farrel Roe Oge Mageghegan was beheaded at *Cruach-abhall* by the son of the baron of Delvin, who carried his head back to Trim, Co. Meath, and later Dublin 'for exhibition'; but it was afterwards buried, along with his body at Derry.

There is evidence that burial was sometimes refused for reasons beyond the well-known ones of non-baptism, excommunication and suicide. An incident regarding St Cellach shows that in reality burial might have been refused for far less lofty reasons. In the 'Life of St Cellach', he is said to have been murdered by four of his students, who were in the employ of Guaire Aidne, king of Connaught. The saint's body was found by his brother in the hollow trunk of an oak-tree, torn by ravens, scald-crows and wolves. He carried the mangled body to the church of Turloch for interment, but the clergy there would not give it burial because they feared King Guaire's wrath. The brother then carried the remains to the church of *Lis Calláin*, where it was also refused burial. In the end it was carried to the church of *Eiscreacha*, where it was interred with due honors.[237] While this tale may be fabulous, it supports the theory that political considerations could interfere with burial, and affect the choice of burial place.

233 Gittings, *Death, burial*, pp 68–70.   **234** Daniell, *Death and burial*, p. 149.   **235** Ariès, *The hour*, p. 44.   **236** See, for example, *Calendar of Justiciary Rolls, Ireland*, 33 Edw. I, 1305, memb. 58d, p. 86; 25–26 Edw. I, Memb. 9d, 1297, p. 176; Ibid., 23 Edw. I, Memb. 9, 1295, p. 44.   **237** 'Genealogy of the Hy-Fiachrach' (notes on St Cellach), *The geneaologies*, ed. O'Donovan, p. 415; *Caithréim Cellaig*, ed. Mulchrone, p. 17.

Another early example of refusal to bury a Christian in consecrated ground occurs in the first life of St Samson of Dol of Brittany. In this instance, a man is denied burial because he is believed to be possessed of the devil. After the man's death, St Samson ordered his monks 'to carry that poor body outside the gate of the monastery to be buried'. After it was interred in unconsecrated ground, the saint and his monks beseeched God for three days and three nights to accept the man's soul, as recorded above.[238]

It seems that both discomfort about devilish connections and fear of reprisal were the reasons why the body of Lord Arnold Poer, seneschal of Kilkenny, 'lay a long time unburied' in the friary of St Saviour's in Dublin in 1328: Richard de Ledred, bishop of Ossory, had accused Arnold Poer of the crime of heresy and tried to connect him with Lady Alice Kettler who had been accused of witchcraft.[239] In 1349, ecclesiastical politics also led to a refusal to bury the body of Alexander de Bicknor, archbishop of Dublin, who had been involved in a heated dispute over whether the archbishop of Dublin had precedence over the archbishop of Armagh. His body lay unburied until he was given special *post-mortem* absolution by the primate.[240]

238 *Life of St Samson of Dol*, pp 68–70. See Chapter 3 above, n. 11.   **239** *Annales Hiberniae*, ed. & trans. Butler, p. 111.   **240** Lewis, *Topographical Dictionary*, II, p. 70.

CHAPTER 6

What the dead have to tell us

Western Europeans in the Middle Ages believed that the dead were a part of their community long after their demise. Paradoxically, the influence of the dead was long-lived, and continued to affect the living – often for many generations. Research on burial involving numerous disciplines continues to prove that the dead do, indeed, have a great deal to tell us.

The historical evidence for burial presented here does not support a view of Ireland as a country that was markedly different from her Western European neighbors during the Middles Ages, a view which has been based on the fact that Ireland was never invaded by the Romans, and has therefore often been presumed not to have been shaped by the same cultural influences as those which transformed her neighbors to the west. Giraldus Cambrensis may, indeed, have found Irish customs strange but in his time, what the Irish were doing regarding burial was probably similar to, if not exactly the same as, what was being done in parts of his own native Wales. This is hardly surprising given the close geographical proximity of the countries and their common experience as Gaelic societies recently subjugated by 'Anglo-Normans'.

Although the historical information available to us regarding burial in medieval Ireland is quite limited it strongly suggests that Irish medieval burial practices did not differ significantly from those in the neighboring countries. I base this statement on the fact that rituals and practices comparable with those in Ireland can also be documented for the present-day countries of England, Scotland and France.

What follows is a distillation of the findings discussed in greater detail in the previous pages.

IRISH CEMETERIES

Burial in unconsecrated ground is known to have persisted in other parts of Western Europe until at least the ninth century, and a letter to the pope concerning Co. Londonderry shows that burial in unconsecrated ground that was not associated with a church continued in Ireland until at least the early fifteenth century. English evidence from the same period parallels this, telling of burials in ordinary fields and proving that this practice was not restricted to Ireland.

Late medieval sources from both England and Ireland tell of interments which were not made in any known cemetery or proximate to any church or chapel, and which presumably conformed to the customary pattern for Christian burial, that is, the east-west orientation of the corpse, which was interred without grave-goods. In the absence of laboratory tests which would date the remains with precision, there is a high probability that archaeologists would probably date such burials to the time when Christianity was just supplanting the earlier, non-Christian religion in Ireland. Yet the historical evidence shows that interments with these characteristics could have been made as late as the fifteenth century – some 800 to 900 years later. This shows the need to exercise caution in dating such burials, and suggests that reconsidering the dates assigned to previously excavated burials may also be valuable.

The social uses of Irish medieval cemeteries

Philippe Ariès has shown that medieval French cemeteries hosted a wide range of activities, and Irish sources either suggest or explicitly record that these also occurred in Irish cemeteries.

Written evidence testifies that the open, public sanctuary space of Irish medieval cemeteries was used to perform penitential rituals, store foodstuffs, and even provide living space. Fairs, games, contests, and meetings about contractual and legal matters are also known to have been associated with medieval Irish cemeteries.

While the written evidence does not prove conclusively that all of these activities continued through the end of Middle Ages, it is clear that in Ireland during the medieval period cemeteries were used as public spaces and hosted a wide variety of activities, both spiritual and secular in nature. Certainly no evidence has been found to suggest that the activities carried out in medieval Irish cemeteries differed in any significant way from those documented for the same period in France, Scotland and England.

Care of cemeteries and respect for the dead

The practice of disinterring bare skulls and bones from graves (presumably in order to accommodate a new corpse) and depositing them in charnel-houses is well known in France and other parts of continental Europe, where it survived into the twentieth century. Written evidence testifies to the existence of medieval charnel houses in each region of Ireland, and eyewitness testimony records that the practice of displaying the bones and skulls of the dead continued into the late nineteenth century. Small buildings known as 'mortuary houses' are also known to have existed in Ireland, although their exact function and period of use is not clear.

The sources show that cemeteries were supposed to have 'keepers', although what their responsibilities and functions were is not known. Before 1222, the

Dublin merchant-guild rolls contain the names of four men who are described as 'de Ciminteria' perhaps indicating that the family were 'keepers' of one cemetery (perhaps more) or had some other special relationship with it. Thirteenth-century English records also record the similar surname 'de Cimiterio', which could have been the same family or (more probably) indicates that its members performed a similar function.

The Irish sources show that the possibility of corpses being uprooting by animals was very real and greatly feared. Sources attest to the fact that animals were allowed to graze in the cemeteries, and documents also exist which forbid this practice. It may be that a distinction was drawn between grazing animals and animals that root and dig.

BURIAL RITUAL

The written sources record that formal mourning periods between death and interment (the wake) ranged from less than a day to as long as twelve days. However, most of the wakes are said to have lasted two or three days. This is consonant with prescriptions found in Continental monastic rules, and is not surprising since the majority of wakes reported are those of saints, monks and clerics. Twelve-day wakes appear to have been reserved for men of particularly high status. It may be that high-status women were also accorded such lengthy wakes, but the sources make no note of it.

The medieval Irish funeral ceremony seems to have included hymns, psalms and Masses, although Masses may have been a somewhat later addition. Keening (the traditional Irish lamentation for the dead) seems to have been ubiquitous, and a cause of great irritation to the Church which attempted to stamp it out.

Hand-clapping and the recitation of elegiac poetry were an integral part of the lamentation-ritual, at least among the noble classes, and a twelfth-century account of a royal wake in Co. Clare records the playing of pipes, indicating that music may also have been a feature. The 'funeral games' (*cluiche caínte*) mentioned in Irish literature are not referred to in the sources surveyed. However, they are mentioned in medieval Scottish sources and are also known to have been held in Ireland until quite recent times, which suggests that they were probably part of medieval Irish burial ritual.

The sources contain little information regarding the funeral procession. Even the (comparatively) rich description of King Brian Bóruma's (Brian Boru's) burial offers no detail about his funeral procession or commemorations. The sources do, however, contain information indicating that an Irishman's status would have been reflected in the number of cattle, sheep, cavalry and foot-soldiers which were part of the funeral procession. Whether these would also have been included in a woman's funeral is unknown. Descriptions of Anglo-Irish funerals from around the same time do not mention animals, and even the report of a funeral for a number of men slain in the same battle (the funeral of le Ercedekne family-members) does not specifically note the presence of soldiers. There is some indication that Irish funeral processions became more important and more elaborate as the Middle Ages progressed. For example, the funeral of Nicholas de Verdun in 1347 is described as an occasion of great pomp and solemnity, possibly reflecting the importation of English funeral ritual into Ireland.

The language of burial

The burial of a member of the élite-class is sometimes described in native Irish chronicles as having been carried out with 'with honour and veneration'. The phrase first appearing in the early tenth century. These chronicles uniquely describe the burial of King Brian Bóruma as having been completed 'with honour proper to his position'; the *AI* describe the burial of Cellach of Armagh in 1129 as having been conducted *cum gloria*, which is the only such annalistic use of this phrase in connection with burial.

'Dishonourable' burial

It seems that the ultimate insult was to bury a corpse with an animal, and an enemy's head and body were sometimes buried separately as a way of preventing recovery of the remains – an act which was also thought to preclude participation in the Resurrection. However, this is problematic since there are also instances in which the head and body of celebrated people were buried separately. Presumably the soul of the deceased was thought to benefit by having the prayers of two congregations, not just one. The desire to satisfy the greed of medieval churchmen for the relics of powerful people – laity or ecclesiastics – provided another strong motivation for dismemberment after death, since prestigious burials enhanced a foundation's appeal as a burial site, which in turn generated additional monies in fees for burial and memorial Masses.

Irish sources contain no mention of the separate burial of the heart and/or entrails which became fashionable among the royalty and aristocracy in England and northwestern Continental Europe in the thirteenth century. There is also no indication that cremation was part of burial practice in medieval Ireland during this period, though there are some isolated references to the burning of bodies.

The sources consulted make quite clear the importance of interring the corpse in the territorial church to which it belonged. Cemeteries had territorial and dynastic associations, and there are numerous examples in which corpses – both male and female – were transported over distances as great as one hundred miles for burial in the church of their family group. Corpses of members of the Anglo-Irish élite were sometimes shipped between England and Ireland for burial. Members of the native Gaelic élite who died in battle were generally brought to their territorial churches for burial; non-élite soldiers seem to have been given burial in mass graves on the battlefield. The church in which a cleric took his orders appears to have gained the right both to his body and to burial fees.

Given the long distances over which some corpses are said to have been transported for burial, embalming certainly would have been desirable, or even necessary. The written sources indicate that some type of embalming was known, and perhaps occasionally practiced in Ireland before the tenth century, when this study begins. This is not surprising, since embalming is also recorded in Continental sources of the same period. However, it is impossible to tell from the written sources what the procedure was or how prevalent – or successful – embalming might have been.

References to the disinterment of bodies occur in Irish sources. This is sometimes said to have been done so that the relics could be returned to the territorial church for burial. In other instances, a particular church or foundation wanted to possess the remains of an important person. Examples also exist from the twelfth and thirteenth centuries of disputes between monasteries for possession of corpses, as well as of the outright stealing of corpses.

BURIAL ARTIFACTS

Irish sources for the period under study contain no information about shrouds or burial clothing. The only mention found comes from the seventh century, and the Irish word used in that instance seems to suggest that the shroud was made of cow's hide. Reformed monastic rules – such as the 'Constitutions of Lanfranc' – give highly detailed instructions about burial clothing, and Irish monks in Continental orders were presumably buried in the same type of clothing as their non-Irish brethren. I have found no information about the burial clothes of the general lay population.

References to coffins are almost non-existent in Irish sources. This is consonant with the extremely small amount of physical evidence for the use of coffins, and seems to support the current view that coffins were rarely used. The warriors' heads which were carried with the body of Brian Bóruma to Armagh for burial in 1014 seem to have been interred in wooden caskets. Stone coffins are sometimes mentioned, and I have found an unclear reference to a coffin which seems to have been made either from a hollowed-out log, or from wickerwork. Irish literature referring to an earlier period tells of the wrapping of corpses in branches – especially broom – which invites comparison with the known medieval English practice of wrapping corpses in rushes for burial.

Words used for tombs and graves
Irish medieval sources contain many references to tombs and graves. These contain a number of different words, some of which have not been clearly defined.

It appears that tombs of different sizes and types existed. These might range from the cave-like *uaigh* to the Irish stone 'slab-shrines' or *leachta*. Burial is also recorded in a 'penitentiary' (*durthech*). The *uluidh* (which has been translated as 'altar-tomb') seems to have had special social significance and may therefore have had features deemed appropriate for high-status burials, although no mention of any such features occurs.

The sources contain the words *lecht* and *fert*, both of which have been translated in the sources as 'grave'. The words *tuiglecht* (meaning 'final bed') and *leabaidh cloithi* (literally 'stone bed') are also used; although it is difficult to say whether the latter form refers to a stone sarcophagus or a grave with bottom and sides made from slabs of stone.

Funeral memorials
By the tenth century, tall pillar-stones no longer seem to have been used as funeral monuments, having been replaced by smaller stone memorials, and a commentary written in the eleventh or twelfth century appears to suggest that pillar-stones had come to be regarded as un-Christian by that time. Pillar-stones may have retained some symbolic importance as boundary markers, and some may have signified the place where the corpse was relinquished by the deceased's relatives and given into the care of the Church.

Written sources – particularly literary sources – contain numerous mentions of gravestones, most of which occur in legendary tales set in the pre-Christian period. Some of these tell of women's graves marked in a way identical to that of the graves of male heroes and warriors – such a tombstone is even given the same name: 'warrior-stone' (*láech-lía*). The sources show the great concern given to the burial of fallen warriors of the élite-class, and to the marking of their graves; common, non-noble soldiers were interred in mass graves where they fell. A monastic record from 1343 provides singular testimony that tombstones were being imported from England to Ireland – in this case from Bristol to Athenry.

It would seem that graves were commonly marked with a cross, although references to crosses are rare. I know of only one reference to a carved stone cross erected over a grave, and this is a thirteenth-century reference regarding Fenagh, Co. Leitrim. The other mentions of crosses give no detail regarding their size or the material from which they were made.

Native Irish written sources include statements and bits of verse which appear to have been proclaimed over the grave of the deceased, but the first written reference to an inscribed epitaph is that of the 'Anglo-Norman' lord, Meiler FitzHenry, in 1208. The epitaph of 1348 for another Anglo-Irishman, 'John Raby', is both lengthy and flowery in its wording. As might be expected, both of these epitaphs are in Latin.

While fragments of inscribed funerary memorials exist from pre-colonial Ireland, the earliest complete epitaph written in Irish which has been recorded is that of Melaghlin O'Kelly, chief of Uí Maine, and his wife, both of whom died in 1402 and were interred at Knockmoy, Co. Galway.

Art historians have argued that effigies were introduced to Ireland by the 'Anglo-Normans,' and first appeared there in the early thirteenth century. The earliest surviving effigies of native Irishmen are distinctively Irish attempts to imitate English royal effigies and have been dated to the first third of the fourteenth century. The written sources consulted for this study contain no mention of effigies or of the monumental memorial brasses which were becoming so popular in England during the fifteenth century, some examples of which can be seen in St Patrick's cathedral in Dublin.

EVIDENCE OF SOCIAL STRATIFICATION IN BURIAL

The tendency was strong in medieval Ireland to bury 'like with like', and the sources tell that members of the same kin-group were buried together. Among the groups mentioned as having been interred together are kings, bishops, and 'boy-warriors'. This may indicate that profession and social status were seen as forming a kind of kinship, but it is important to consider that, because medieval Irish society had a strongly local character, there is a good chance that those interred together were – at least distantly – related. It is clear that the 'Anglo-Normans' and the Anglo-Irish of a later period continued to bury their aristocratic warriors together.

It appears that prestigious and powerful families whose members included kings were often buried for many years in a particular section of a cemetery. However, while references to 'cemeteries of the kings' are well known, a close examination of the written sources shows that a far wider cross-section of the population was also buried in these cemeteries. Therefore, uses of the term 'cemetery of the kings' should not be taken to mean that the specified cemeteries were reserved for the exclusive burial of royalty. Additionally, no written evidence has been found indicating whether, or how, the graves of kings were separated from the rest of the burials, or if they were marked in a particular way.

Burial with one's ancestors was important to the Irish, but towards the end of the fourteenth century, both the Irish and non-Irish chroniclers show a new preoccupation with explicitly stating that multiple generations of a family had been buried in one and the same place. These statements may have been an attempt by the native Irish who had been displaced from the lands they traditionally held to establish 'roots' in new homelands. Similar passages in the Anglo-Irish annals may suggest that they also used continuity of burial to help justify their familial claims in new territories. The chronicles also suggest a new preoccupation at this time with the erection of family tombs and burial places. This is particularly true in entries relating to the establishment and endowment of

Franciscan abbeys, and probably reflects the order's success in convincing the population that burial with them offered advantages over burial in other orders' foundations

Burial in monastic habit assured interment inside the church. There is a long history both in Ireland and in continental Europe of members of the élite classes 'retiring' to a monastery late in life, or when an illness set in. For the period under study here, the first example recorded in the chronicles of an Irishman 'retiring' to take monastic habit is that of Ruadhrí Ua Conchobar (Rory O'Connor) who died at Clonmacnoise in 1118. Judging from the entries in the Irish chronicles, it seems that retirement to a monastery became something of a tradition among the Ua Conchobair kings, and prominent Anglo-Irishmen also availed themselves of this option. By the end of the fourteenth century, monastic retirement prior to death, which seems once to have been reserved for the aristocracy, was being undertaken by members of the Anglo-Irish administrative and merchant classes. The retirement of widowed women to convents was a popular practice elsewhere in medieval Europe, and the sources indicate that it also occurred in Ireland, though how often is impossible to ascertain.

It appears that in the Middle Ages, graves continued to be thought to have defensive properties, a belief which dates from prehistoric times. We may read of the siting of graves on ramparts, and even the Anglo-Norman lord of Connaught, William Burke, is reported to have been buried standing. While this story may well be apocryphal, it shows a knowledge of tales such as those concerning the burials of Laeghaire and Eogan Bél, both great semi-legendary Irish kings, and indicates that this type of burial was still had symbolic meaning to the medieval Irish.

Burial on the north side of the church may not have carried the stigma which it bore in England, and the written sources record that inside the church, members of the élite were often buried on the north side. This may have some connection with the fact that in Irish custom, the north was the side of honour in the king's house or hall and the place where the king himself sat. A preliminary analysis suggests that there may be some connection between the placing of graves and the relationship between different members of Irish society as specified in the 'seating order' used in the king's hall, although more research and analysis are needed before we can presume that this was the case.

The written sources suggest that it may have been customary among the élite classes to bury sons either 'at the feet' of their fathers or at their right-hand sides. Burial 'at the foot' of the father may be the earlier – and perhaps native Irish – tradition. Other frequently noted places for the burial of the élite were before the high altar, on the steps of the altar, and in the choir. Burial at walls, the entry to the cemetery, and before the door of the church are also noted. This may suggest either the continuing belief that burials offered some sort of protection from unwelcome intruders, or it could simply be a burial ritual which was continued after its meaning had been forgotten.

Separation at burial according to gender or circumstance of death
It is clear from native Irish chronicles that high-status native Irishwomen were given burial in religious foundations. The evidence shows that élite native Irishwomen were customarily buried with their own kin-groups, rather than with their husbands'. The first clearly recorded examples of native Irishwomen being buried in their husbands' churches appear in the fifteenth century.

I found no written evidence for the separation of the sexes at burial. Passages in medieval Irish literature which describe events in the pre-Christian period contain references to men and women being buried together and, despite the fact that the propriety of burying the sexes together in Christian cemeteries was questioned in the seventh century, there is no indication in the written record of any such segregation being practised between 900 and 1500. On the contrary, the sources contain examples from the fourteenth and fifteenth centuries of men and women – both native Irish and Anglo-Irish – being buried together.

The written sources contain no mention of cemeteries devoted exclusively to the burial of women, warriors or unbaptized children, nor does existing archaeological evidence indicate that such separation at burial was commonly practiced in medieval Ireland. Placename evidence for the existence in Ireland of such exclusive cemeteries is plentiful, and has been discussed by Ann Hamlin, Claire Foley, and others. However, since this placename evidence for separate cemeteries has not been dated, it is not known whether 'separate' burial was being practiced in the period under study, or was adopted at a later time.

It is important to note that each of the groups for whom separate cemeteries have been identified could have been thought to have died in specific circumstances which would have made the community loath to bury their bodies in consecrated ground. Therefore, even if it can be proved that such separate Irish cemeteries existed during the Middle Ages, this will not necessarily demonstrate that it was normal practice to separate the *general* population at burial by sex, age or social status. Additional evidence suggests that if such segregation of 'the unfortunate' was made at burial, strangers from outside the local kin-group's territory may also have been denied Christian burial, since their personal history, such as their status *vis-à-vis* the Church would have been unknown.

The Irish sources consulted contain no references to suicide. Irish annalistic and administrative sources contain numerous examples of executions, but I have found no record of how – or even whether – those executed were buried. Political expediency could also sometimes prevent Christian burial; the sources note two examples where burial was delayed for political reasons.

SUMMARY

I undertook this study of burial in medieval Ireland to see what information was contained in the Irish medieval sources. I wondered what they might reveal about native Irish culture during the period which saw the introduction of both Scandinavian and 'Anglo-Norman' culture. The historical sources have yielded some hard factual information and tantalizing hints on a wide range of subjects. The material also presents many questions for historians and those working in other disciplines to consider, and hopefully, to answer.

The burial practices of the native Irish population do indeed seem to have changed between 900 and 1500. The power of the old territorial churches and their insistence on the burial of the bodies of the local populace in their local, traditional cemeteries eroded in the face of the enormous changes that occurred between 900 and 1500. However, the upheaval and displacement caused by the coming of the 'Anglo-Normans' was just one of a number of factors which caused these changes, factors which include the twelfth-century Church reforms and the arrival of Continental monastic orders (especially the Franciscans in the thirteenth century). The marked growth of the merchant-class during the later Middle Ages and the effect which it had on social structure, commerce and the dissemination of ideas should also be taken into account.

Burial studies is a mirror which captures the image of many aspects of medieval society. When considered as a whole, the information available about burial using the various disciplines of anthropology, archaeology, and history, makes it possible to catch the reflection of such diverse aspects of society as religious beliefs, ritual, social organization, diet and diseases. This survey of the historical sources for information on burial in medieval Ireland indicates that medieval Ireland, despite its non-Roman history, was not markedly different from other western European societies; it is the similarities between England, Scotland, France and Ireland – rather than the differences – which are notable.

Bibliography

PRIMARY SOURCES

Account roll of the priory of the Holy Trinity, Dublin: 1337–1346, ed. James Mills (Dublin, 1891; reprint ed and annotated, Dublin, 1996).

Acta sanctorum, see 'Bollandus, Johannes'.

Acta sanctorum Hiberniae, ed. John Colgan (Louvain 1645 & 1647; facsimile reprint; Dublin, 1948).

Acts of Archbishop Colton in his metropolitan visitation of the diocese of Derry, AD MCCCXCVII, with a rental of the see estates at that time, ed. William Reeves (Ir. Arch Soc., Dublin, 1850).

'A description of Clogher cathedral in the early sixteenth century', ed. M.J. Haren, *Clogher Record*, VII (1985), pp 48–54.

Adomnán's Life of Columba, ed. & trans. Alan Orr Anderson & Marjorie Ogilvie Anderson (2nd edition, Oxford, 1990).

Adomnán of Iona/Life of St Columba, ed. & trans. Richard Sharpe (London, 1995).

Ailred of Rievaulx, 'Life of St Ninian', *Two Celtic saints: the lives of Ninian and Kentigern*, ed. & trans. A.P. Forbes (Edinburgh 1874; reprint, 1989).

Aislinge meic con Glinne, ed. K.H. Jackson (Dublin, 1990).

Aislinge Oengusso, ed. Francis Shaw (Dublin, 1976).

Aithdioghluim dána: a miscellany of Irish bardic poetry, ed. Lambert McKenna (2 vols, Irish Texts Society XXXVII and XL, Dublin, 1939–40).

The Amra of Colum Cille of Dallan Forgaill, ed. J. O'B. Crowe (Dublin, 1871).

'Ancient deeds of the parish of St John, Dublin', ed. J.L. Robinson, *PRIA*, XXXIII (1916), pp 175–224.

Ancient laws and institutions of Ireland, ed. & trans. R. Atkinson, W.N. Hancock, W.M. Hennessy, T. O'Mahoney & A.G. Richey (6 vols, London, 1865–1901).

Ancient laws and institutions of Wales comprising laws opposed to be enacted by Howel the Good, ed. Owen Aneurin (2 vols, London, 1841).

'*Annala as Breifne*', ed. & trans. Éamonn de hÓir, *Breifne*, IV (1970–5) pp 59–86

Annala Connacht: the annals of Connacht, ad 1224–1544, ed. A. Martin Freeman (Dublin, 1944; reprint 1970).

Annála ríoghachta Éireann: Annals of the kingdom of Ireland by the Four Masters from the earliest period to the year 1616, ed & trans. J. O'Donovan (7 vols, Dublin, 1848–51; reprint Dublin, 1990).

Annála Uladh: Annals of Ulster; otherwise Annála Senait, annals of Senat: a chronicle of Irish affairs 431–1131, 1155–1541, eds W.M. Hennessy & B. MacCarthy (4 vols, Dublin, 1887–1901).

Annála Uladh: The Annals of Ulster (to AD 1131), eds Seán Mac Airt and Gearóid Mac Niocaill. Pt I: text and translation (Dublin Institute for Advanced Studies, Dublin, 1983).

Annales de Monte Fernandi (Annals of Multifernan), ed. Aquilla Smith (Irish Archaeological Society, Dublin, 1842) (In *Tracts relating to Ireland*, II).

Annales Hiberniae ('Grace's Annals'), ed. & trans. R. Butler (Irish Archaeological Society, Dublin, 1842).

'Annales monasterii Beata Marie Virginis, juxta Dublin', ed J.T. Gilbert, *Chartululary of St Mary's abbey, Dublin*, II (1886), pp 241–92.

'The annals in Cotton MS Titus A. XXV', ed. A.M. Freeman, *Revue Celtique*, XLI (1924), pp 301–30; XLII (1925), pp 283–305; XLIII (1926), pp 358–84; XLIV (1927), pp 336–61.

The annals of Boyle, see 'The annals in Cotton MS Titus'.

Annals of Christchurch, see 'Some unpublished texts from the Black book of Christ Church'.

Annals of Clonmacnoise, being annals of Ireland from the earliest period to AD 1408, translated into English, ad 1627, by Connell Mgeoghagan, ed. Denis Murphy (RSAI, Dublin, 1896; facsimile reprint 1993).

Annals of Connacht, see Annála Connacht.

The annals of Inisfallen (MS Rawlinson B 503), ed. and trans. S. MacAirt (Dublin, 1951).

The annals of Ireland by Friar John Clyn and Thady Dowling, together with the annals of Ross, ed. Richard Butler (Irish Archeological Society, Dublin, 1849).

Annals of Ireland: fragment: AD 1308–1310 and 1316–1317, ed. J.T. Gilbert, *Chartulary of St Mary's abbey, Dublin*, II (1886, reprint 1965), pp 293–302

'The annals of Ireland, from the year 1443 to 1468 ... translated by ... Dudley MacFirbisse', ed. John O'Donovan, *Miscellany of the Irish Archaeological Society*, I (Dublin, 1846), pp 198–302.

Annals of Loch Cé, a chronicle of Irish affairs, 1014–1590, ed. W.M. Hennessy (2 vols, Rolls Series, LIV; reprint Irish Manuscripts Commission, London, 1871; Dublin, 1939; Vaduz, 1965).

'Annals of Multifernan', *see Annales de Monte Fernandi.*

'The annals of Nenagh', ed. D.F. Gleeson, *Analecta Hibernica*, no. 12 (1943), pp 155–64.

'Annals of Ross' (*see* Clyn's Annals), ed. R. Butler, *Miscellany of the Irish Archaeological Society* (Dublin, 1849).

'Annals of Roscrea', D. Gleeson & S. MacAirt, eds, *Proceedings of the Royal Irish Academia*, LIX(C), (1958), pp 138–80.

Annals of St Bertin, ed. & trans. Janet L. Nelson (Manchester, 1991).

'Annals of St Mary's Abbey, Dublin' *see* 'Annales monasterii Beata Marie Virginis, juxta Dublin'.

Annals of the Four Masters, *see 'Annals of the kingdom of Ireland by the Four Masters'.*

'The annals of Tigernach', ed. & trans. Whitley Stokes, *Revue Celtique*, XVI (1895), pp 374–419; XVII (1896), pp 6–33; 119–263; 337–40; XVIII (1897), pp 9–59; 150–97, 267–303; repr. in 2 vols, Felinfach, 1993).

Annals of Ulster (to AD 1131), ed. S. MacAirt & G. MacNiocaill (Dublin, 1984).

'Annals of Ulster' *see Annála Uladh.*

'Archbishop Cromer's Register', eds L.P. Murray & A. Gwynn, *Louth Archaeological Society Jnl*, VII (1929–32), pp 516–24; VIII (1933–6), pp 38–49, 169–88, 257–74, 322–51; IX (1937–40), pp 36–41, 124–30; X (1941–4), pp 116–27, 165–79.

'*Ban Senchus*', ed. M.E. Dobbs, *Revue Celtique*, XLVII (1930), pp 282–339; XLVIII (1931), pp 163–234; XLIX (1932), pp 437–89.

Battle of Mag Rath, ed. J. O'Donovan (Dublin 1842).

'A New Version of the Battle of Mag Rath', ed. C. Marstrander, *Ériu*, VI (1911), pp 226–47.

Beatha Bharra, ed. P. Ó Riain, Irish Texts Society, LVII (London, 1994).

'*Beatha Lasrach* (Life of St Lasair)', ed. & trans. Lucius Gwynn., *Ériu*, V (1911), pp 73–109.

Bede, 'Life of Cuthbert', *The age of Bede*, ed. & trans. J.F. Webb (London, 1983).

Bethada Náem nÉrenn, see Lives of Irish saints.

'*Bethu Brigte: Vitae S. Brigitae*: the oldest texts', ed. Richard Sharpe, *Peritia*, I (1982), pp 81–106.

Bethu Phátraic, 'The tripartite life of Patrick', ed. & trans. Kathleen Mulchrone (Dublin & London, 1939).

'The birth of Aedán Mac Gabrán and Brandub Mac Echach', ed. & trans. M.A. O'Brien, *Ériu*, XVI (1952), pp 157–70.

'Black book of Christ Church', *see* 'A Calendar of the *Liber niger* and *Liber albus* of Christ Church Dublin'.

The black book of Limerick, ed. J. MacCaffrey (Dublin, 1907).

The book of Armagh, ed. A. Gwynn (Dublin, 1913).

The book of Fenagh, ed. & trans. W.H. Hennessy & D.H. Kelly (Dublin, 1875).

The book of Lecan; *Leabhar Mór Mhic Fhir Bhisigh Lecain*, (facs., Ir. Manuscripts Comm., Dublin, 1937).

The book of Leinster, eds R.I. Best, M.A. O'Brien & A. O'Sullivan (6 vols, Dublin, 1954–1983).
The book of Llan Dav (The Book of Landaff), eds J.G. Evans & John Rhys (Cardiff, 1843).
The book of Magauran (Leabhar Méig Shamhradháin), ed. Lambert McKenna (Dublin, 1947).
The book of obits and martyrology of the cathedral Church of the Holy Trinity, commonly called Christ Church, ed. J.C. Crosthwaite (Dublin, 1844); reprint in *The Register of Christ Church Cathedral, Dublin*, eds Raymond Refaussé & Colm Lennon (Dublin 1998).
'A breviary from St Mary's Abbey, Trim', ed. Aubrey Gwynn, *Ríocht na Midhe*, III (1964), pp 290–98.
Buile Shuibhne, ed. J.G. O'Keeffe (London, 1931).
'The Burning of Finn's House', ed. E.J. Gwynn, *Ériu*, I (1904), pp 13–37.
'*Cáin Adamnáin*: an old-Irish teatise on the law of Adamnán, ed. & trans. Kuno Meyer (Oxford, 1905).
'Cáin Domnaig: the epistle concerning Sunday', ed. J.G. O'Keeffe, *Ériu*, II (1905), pp 189–214.
Caithréim Cellaig, ed. Kathleen Muchrone (Dublin, 1971).
Caithréim Thoirdhealbhaig, *see* 'O'Grady, Seán mac Ruaidhrí'.
Calendar of Archbishop Alen's register, c.1172–1534; prepared and edited from the original in the registry of the united diocese of Dublin and Glendalough and Kildare, ed. & trans. Charles MacNeill; index by Liam Price (Dublin, 1950).
Calendar of documents relating to Ireland, 1171–[1307], eds H.S. Sweetman & G.F. Handcock (5 vols, London, 1875–86; reprint Nedeln, 1974).
Calendar of documents relating to Scotland ... 1108–[1509], ed. Joseph Bain (4 vols, Edinburgh, 1881–8).
Calendar of entries in the papal registers relating to Great Britain and Ireland: papal letters, eds W.H. Bliss et al. (I–XIV, Public Records Office, London 1893; XV–XVIII, Ir. Manuscripts Comm., Dublin, 1978–89).
Calendar of Scottish supplications to Rome, eds E.R. Lindsay & A.I. Cameron (Scottish History Society, 3rd series, 23, Edinburgh, 1934).
Calendar of the ancient records of Dublin in the possession of the municipal corporation, eds J.T. Gilbert & Rosa Mulholland Gilbert (19 vols, Dublin, 1889–19).
Calendar of the Gormanston register, eds James Mills and M.J. McEnery (Dublin, 1916).
Calendar of the justiciary rolls or proceedings in the court of the justiciar of Ireland ... Edward I [1295–1307], ed. James Mills (2 vols, Dublin, 1905–14).
Calendar of the justiciary rolls ... of Ireland: I to VII years of Edward II (1308–14), eds Herbert Wood & A.E. Langman; revised by M.C. Griffith (Dublin, 1956).
'A Calendar of the *Liber Niger* and *Liber Albus* of Christ Church Dublin', ed. H.J. Lawlor, *RIA Proc.*, XXVII C (1908–09), no. 1, pp 1–93.
'Calendar of the *Liber Niger Alani*', ed. G.T. Stokes, *JRSAI*, XXVII (1897), pp 164–76.
'Calendar of the *Liber Ruber* of the diocese of Ossory', ed. H.J. Lawlor, *RIA Proc.*, XXVII (C) (1908), pp 159–208.
Calendar of Ormond deeds, 1172–1603, ed. E. Curtis (6 vols, Dublin, 1932–43).
'A calendar of the register of Archbishop Fleming', ed. H.J. Lawlor., *PRIA*, XXX (C) (1912–13), pp 94–190.
'A calendar of the register of Archbishop Sweteman', ed. H.J. Lawlor, *PRIA*, XXIX (C) (1911–12), pp 213–310.
Campion, Edmunde, *Two bokes of the histories of Ireland*, ed. A.F. Vossen (Assen, Netherlands, 1963).
Cartulary of St Mary, Clerkenwell, ed. W.O. Hassall (Camden 3rd Ser., LXXI, London, 1949).
Cath Ruis na Ríg for Bóinn (The Battle of Rosnaree), ed.. E. Hogan (Dublin, 1892).
'Charters of the Cistercian abbey of Duiske in the County of Kilkenny', eds C.M. Butler & J.H. Bernard, *RIA Proc.*, XXXV (C) (1918–20), no. 1, pp 1–188.
Chartularies of St Mary's Abbey, Dublin; with the register of its house at Dumbrody, and annals of Ireland, 1162–1370, ed. & trans. .J.T. Gilbert (2 vols, Rolls series LXXX, London, 1884–6; reprint Nedeln, 1965).
Christchurch, Dublin, *see* 'Some unpublished texts from the Black book of Christ Church'.
Chronicle of the abbey of Bury St Edmunds, *see* 'Jocelin of Brakelond'.
Chronicle of Melrose, ed. & trans. J. Stephenson (Felinfach, 1988).

Chronicum Scotorum: a chronicle of Irish affairs...to 1135, with a supplement ... 1141–1150, ed. W.M. Hennessy (Rolls Series XLVLI, London, 1866; reprint Vaduz, 1964).

'Clyn's annals', *see Annals of Ireland by Friar John Clyn and Thady Dowling.*

Cogadh Gaedhel re Gallaibh: the war of the Gaedhil with the Gaill, or the invasion of Ireland by the Danes and other Norse men, ed. J.H. Todd (London, 1867).

'Colman Mac Duach and Guaire', ed. J.G. O'Keeffe, *Ériu*, I (1904), pp 43–47.

Colton's visitation, ad 1397, see Acts of Colton.

Conchubranus, 'Life of St Monenna by Conchubranus', ed. Ulster Society for Medieval Latin Studies, *Senchus Ardmacha*, IX (1979), pp 250–73; X (1980–1), pp 117–41.

Cormacan Eigeas, 'The circuit of Ireland by Muirchertach MacNeill', ed. & trans. J. O'Donovan, *Tracts related to Ireland*, II (Dublin, 1841).

Corpus Iuris Hibernici, ed. D.A. Binchy (6 vols, Dublin, 1978).

The coucher book of Furness abbey, ed. & trans. J.C. Atkinson & J. Brownbill (2 vols, Chatham Soc., Manchester, 1886–1919).

Crede Mihi: the most ancient register book of the bishops of Dublin before the reformation, ed. John T. Gilbert (Dublin, 1897).

Cronica regum Mannie & Insularum, ed. George Broderick (Belfast, 1979).

'*Dán do Chormac Mág Shamhradháin, easpag Ardachaidh', 1444–?1476*, ed. G. Mac Niocaill, *Seanchas Ardmhacha*, IV (1960–1), pp 141–6.

Dánta Grádha: an anthology of Irish love poetry, ad 1350–1750, I: text, ed. T.F. O'Rahilly (Dublin, 1916; 2nd edition, Cork, 1926.)

'Death of Conla', ed. & trans. K. Meyer, *Ériu*, I (1904), pp 113–21.

De Praesulibus Hiberniae, ed. J. Lynch (2 vols, Dublin, 1944).

'De Síl Chonairi Mór', ed. Lucius Gwynn, *Ériu*, V (1911), pp 30–143.

The dialogues of St Gregory, surnamed the Great, Pope of Rome ... translated into our English tongue by P.W. and printed at Paris in MDCVIII. Re-edited with an Introduction and Notes by Edmund G. Gardner (London, 1911).

Die Irische kanonensammlung, ed. Hermann Wasserschleben (Leipzig, 1995; reprint, 1966).

The 'Dignitas Decani' of St Patrick's cathedral, Dublin, ed. N.B. White (Dublin, 1957).

'Documents relating to the medieval diocese of Armagh', ed. A. Gwynn, *Archivum Hibernicum*, XXIII (1947), pp 1–26.

Dowling's Annals, *see Annals of Ireland by Friar John Clyn and Thady Dowling.*

Duanaire Finn, I, ed. & trans. Eoin MacNeill (Dublin, 1908); II, ed. & trans. Gerard Murphy (Dublin, 1933); III, ed. & trans. Gerard Murphy (Dublin, 1953).

The Dublin Guild Merchant Roll c.1190–1265 (supplement to the *Calendar of the Ancient Records of Dublin*), eds P. Connolly & G. Martin (Dublin, 1992).

Early Irish lyrics, ed. & trans. G. Murphy (Oxford 1956; reprint Dublin 1998).

Early statutes of Ireland: the statutes of Kilkenny, ed. H.F. Berry.

Early sources of Scottish history, I, ed. A.O. Anderson (Stamford, 1990).

The English martyrology, ed. John Wilson (London, 1975).

Extracts from the account rolls of the abbey of Durham, ed. Joseph T. Fowler (Surtees Society, XCIX, C, CIII, Durham 1898, 1899, 1901).

Félire Oengussa Céli Dé (The Martyrology of Oengus the Culdee), ed. Whitley Stokes (Henry Bradshaw Society, XXIX, London 1905).

'A fragment of Irish annals', ed. B. Ó Cuív, *Celtica*, XIV (1981), pp 83–104.

'A fragment of Old Irish', ed. O.J. Bergin, *Ériu*, II, 1905, pp 221–25.

'Fragmentary annals from the west of Ireland', ed. E.J. Gwynn, *PRIA*, XXXVII (C) (1925–7), pp 149–57.

Fragmentary annals of Ireland, ed. & trans. J.N. Radner (Dublin, 1978).

Galbert of Bruges, *The murder of Charles the Good, Count of Flanders*, ed. J. Ross (New York, 1967).

The geneaologies, tribes and customs of Hy Fiachrach, commonly called O'Dowda's country, ed. & trans. J. O'Donovan (Dublin, 1844).

Gerald of Wales, *see* Giraldus Cambrensis.

Giraldus Cambrensis, *Expugnatio Hibernica: the conquest of Ireland*, eds A.B. Scott and F.X. Martin (Dublin, 1978; Penguin, London, 1982).

—, *The history and topography of Ireland* (Topographia Hiberniae), ed. J.J. O'Meara (Mountrath & London, 1982).

—, *The journey through Wales / The description of Wales*, ed & trans. Lewis Thorpe (London, 1986).

Gormanston register, see Calendar of the Gormonston Register.

'Grace's Annals', *see Annales Hiberniae.*

'The graves of the kings at Clonmacnoise', ed. R.I. Best, *Ériu*, II (1905), pp 163–71.

'The guarantor list of the Cáin Adamnáin', ed. Máirín Ní Dhonnchadha, *Peritia*, I (1982), pp 178–215.

Heresy trials in the diocese of Norwich, 1428–31, ed. & trans. N.P. Tanner (Camden 4th Series, XX, London, 1977).

Historic and municipal documents of Ireland, 1172–1320, ed. J.T. Gilbert (Rolls Series LIII, London, 1870; reprint [Nendeln?], 1964).

Historical documents Scotland 1286–1306, I, ed. J. Stevenson (Edinburgh, 1870).

'Hy Fiachrach', *see The genealogies, tribes and customs of Hy Fiacrach.*

'Incipit vita S. Laurencii archiepiscopi Dublinensis', ed. Charles Plummer, *Analecta Bollandiana*, *xxxiii* (1914), pp 121–86.

The instructions of King Cormac mac Airt, ed. Kuno Meyer (Dublin, 1909).

Instructio pie vivendi et superna meditandi, ed. & trans. J. McKechnie (2 vols, London, 1933–46).

The Irish cartularies of Llanthony Prima and Secunda, ed. E. St. John Brooks (Dublin, 1953)

Irish historical documents 1172–1922, eds E. Curtis & R.B. McDowell (London, 1943).

'An Irish litany of pilgrim saints, composed *c.*800', ed. K. Hughes, *Analecta Bollandiana*, LXXVII (1959), pp 305–32.

Irish monastic and episcopal deeds, A.D. 1200–1600, transcribed from the originals preserved at Kilkenny castle ... ed. N.B. White (Dublin, 1936).

The Irish penitentials, ed. Ludwig Bieler (Dublin, 1963).

Jocelin, 'Life of St Kentigern', *Two Celtic saints: the lives of Ninian and Kentigern*, ed. & trans. A.P. Forbes (Lampeter, 1989).

Jocelin of Brakelond, *Chronicle of the abbey of Bury St Edmunds*, eds D. Greenway & J. Sayers (Oxford, 1989).

King, William, *The state of the Protestants in Ireland under the late King James* (Dublin & London, 1886).

'*Lánnellach Tigi Ríchh & Ruirech*', ed. & trans. Máirín O Daly, *Ériu*, XIX (1962), pp 81–6.

'Lament of Crede, daughter of Guaire', ed. & trans., Ruth P.M. Lehmann, *Études Celtiques*, XV (1978), pp 549–52.

'Late medieval Irish annals: two fragments', ed. K.W. Nicholls, *Peritia*, II (1983), pp 87–102.

Latin lives of Irish saints, see Vita sanctorum Hiberniae.

Leabhar Branach (The Book of the O'Byrnes), ed. S. MacAirt (Dublin, 1944).

'*Leabhar Oiris*', ed. R.I. Best, *Ériu*, I (1904), pp 74–112.

Leabhar na g-Ceart, ed. John O'Donovan (Dublin, 1847).

Lebor na Cert: The book of rights, ed. Myles Dillon (Dublin, 1962).

Lex Salica ('Laws of the Salian Franks'), I, ed. & trans. K.F. Drews (Philadelphia, 1991).

Liber Ardmachanus, ed. J. Gwynn (Dublin, 1913).

Liber primus Kilkenniensis: the earliest of the books of the corporation of Kilkenny now extant, ed. C. McNeill (Dublin, 1931).

—, *Liber primus Kilkenniensis*, ed. & trans. A.J. Otway-Ruthven (Kilkenny, 1961).

Life of St Samson of Dol, ed. T. Taylor (London, New York & Toronto, 1925).

Lives of Irish saints (Bethada Náem nÉrenn), ed. Charles Plummer (2 vols, Oxford, 1922).

The Mabinogion, eds & trans. G. Jones & T. Jones (London, 1949, reprint, 1966).

'MacCarthaig's Book' (MacCarthy's book), *see Miscellaneous Irish Annals.*

Mac Con Midhe, Giolla Brighde, *The poems of Giolla Brighde Mac Con Midhe*, ed. N J.A. Williams (Irish Texts Society LI, London, 1980).

—, 'Poem on the Battle of Dun [1260]', ed. John O'Donovan., *Misc. of the Celtic Society* (Dublin, 1849), pp 145–83.

MacCraith, Seán Mac Ruaidhrí, *Caithréim Toirdhealbhaigh*, ed. & trans. S.H. O'Grady (Irish Texts Society, 2 vols, London, 1929; reprint Dublin, 1988).

'Mac Dá Cherda and Cummaine Foda', trans. J.G. O'Keeffe, *Ériu*, V (1911), pp 18–44.

'MacFirbish's Annals', *see* 'The annals of Ireland, from the year 1443 to 1468 ... translated by ... Dudley MacFirbisse'.

Martyrology of Donegal, eds J. O'Donovan, J.H. Todd, & W. Reeves (Dublin, 1864).

The Martyrology of Oengus the Culdee, see Félire Oengussa Céli Dé.

Medieval Irish lyrics, ed. J. Carney (Dublin, 1967; reprint Dublin, 1985).

Metrical Dindsenchas, ed. E. Gwynn (5 vols, Dublin, 1903–35).

'A middle Irish poem on the Christian kings of Leinster', ed. & trans. M.A. O'Brien, *Ériu*, XVII (1955), pp 35–51.

Miscellaneous Irish annals (AD 1114–1437) ('MacCarthaig's Book'), ed. & trans. Seámus Ó hInnse (Dublin, 1947).

The monastic constitutions of Lanfranc, ed. D. Knowles (London, 1951).

Molyneux, Samuel, *Journey to Connaught*, ed. A. Smith, *Miscellany of the Irish Archaeological Society*, I (Dublin, 1846), pp 161–78.

Moryson, Fynes, *An Itinerary continaing his ten yeers travell through the twelve dominions of Germany, Bohmerland, Sweitzerland, Netherland, Denmarke, Poland. Italy, Turkey, France, England, Scotland and Ireland*, II, ed. C. Hughes (2 vols, Glasgow, 1907).

Muirchú, 'Life of St Patrick', *St Patrick: His writings & Muirchú's Life*, ed. & trans. A.B.E. Hood (London, 1978).

Obits of Kilcormmick, ed. J.H. Todd, *Miscellany of the Irish Archaeological Society*, I (Dublin, 1846), pp 99–105.

The Ó Cianáin Miscellany, ed. James Carney, *Ériu*, XXI (1969), pp 122–47.

Ó Dálaigh, çongus Rúadh, 'O'Conor's house at Cloonfree', ed & trans. E. C. Quiggin., *Essays and studies presented to W. Ridgeway* (Cambridge, 1913), pp 333–52.

Ó Dálaigh, Gofraidh Fionn, 'A poem', ed. & trans. O. Bergin, *Essays and studies presented to W. Ridgeway*, ed. E.C. Quiggin (Cambridge, 1913), pp 323–32

—, 'Filidh Éireann go haointeach: William Ó Ceallaigh's Christmas feast to the poets of Ireland, AD 1351', ed. & trans. Eleanor Knott, *Ériu*, V (1911), pp 50–69.

—, 'Historical poems', ed. & trans. L. McKenna, *Irish Monthly*, XLVII (1919), pp 1–5, 102–7, 166–70, 224–8, 283–6, 341–4, 397–403, 455–9, 509–14, 563–9, 622–6.

Ó Dálaigh, Mathghamhain, 'A poem for Fínghin Mac Carthaigh Riabhach', ed. & trans. Brian Ó Cuív, *Celtica*, XV (1983), pp 96–110.

Ó Dálaigh, Muiredhach, 'A religious poem ascribed to Muiredhach Ó Dálaigh', ed. trans. W. Gillies, *Studia Celtica*, XIV & XV (1979–80), pp 818–86.

Ó Dubhagain and Gilla na naomh Ó Huidrín, *The topographical poems by Seán Mór Ó Dubhagain and Gilla na naomh Ó Huidrín*, ed. & trans. John O'Donovan (Dublin, 1862).

O'Grady, Sean mac Ruaidhrí, *Caithréim Thoirdhealbhaigh*, ed. S.H. O'Grady (2 vols, Cambridge, 1929; reprint, 1988).

Oidheadh chloinne hUisneach (The violent death of the children of Uisneach), ed. & trans., C. Mac Giolla Léith (Irish texts society, London, 1993).

'Old Irish table of penitential commutations', ed. & trans. D.A. Binchy, *Ériu*, XIX (1962), pp 59–72.

'On the graves of Leinster men', ed. & trans. M.E. Dobbs, *Zeitschrift für Celtische philogie*, 24 (1954), pp 139–53.

Patrick, St, 'St Patrick's Confession', 'Letter to Coroticus', *St Patrick: his writings and Muirchú's Life*, ed. A.B.E. Hood (London, 1978).

'A poem ascribed to Flann MacLonáin, an elegy on Echnechán, son of Dálach, king of Tír Conaill', ed. & trans. M.E. Dobbs, *Ériu*, XVII (1955), pp 16–37.

'A poem composed for Cathal Croibdhearg Ó Conchubhair', ed & trans. B. Ó Cuív, *Ériu*, XXXIV (1983), pp 157–74.

Poems of Blathmac, son of Cú Brettan, together with the Irish Gospel of Thomas and a poem on the Virgin Mary, ed. & trans. James Carney (London, 1964).

Poems of the marcher lords, ed. & trans. Anne O'Sullivan & Pádraig Ó Riain (Irish Texts Society, London, 1987).

'Poems on the cemetery of Clonmacnoise', ed. & trans. R.I. Best, *Ériu*, II (1905), pp 163–71.

Reading abbey cartularies, ed. B.R. Kemp (Camden Society, 4th ser. XXXII & XXXIII, London, 1987).

'Records of the Dublin gild merchants, known a the gild of the Holy Trinity, 1438–1671', ed. H.F. Berry, *JRSAI*, XXX (1900), pp 44–68.

The red book of the earls of Kildare, ed. Gearóid Mac Niocaill (Dublin, 1964).

'*Regestum monasterii fratrum praedicatorum de Athenry*', ed. Ambrose Coleman, *Archivum Hibernicum*, I (1912), pp 201–21.

'The register and records of Holm Cultram (*c*.1236)', eds Francis Grainger and W.G. Collingwood, *Cumberland & Westmoreland Antiquarian Society Record* (Kendal, 1929).

'Register of All Hallow's, Dublin', *see Registrum prioratus omnium sanctorum juxta Dublin*.

'Register of Archbishop Alen', *see* 'Calendar of the *Liber Niger Alani*'.

'The register of Clogher', ed. K.W. Nicholls, *Clogher Record*, VII (1971–2), pp 361–431.

'The Register of John Mey', *see Registrum Johannis Mey*.

Register of John Swayne, Archbishop of Armagh and primate of Ireland, 1418–1439, ed & trans. D.A. Chart (Belfast, 1935).

'The register of Kells', ed. N.B. White, *Irish monastic deeds: 1200–1600* (1936), pp 300–13.

'Register of St John the Baptist, Dublin', *see* 'An unpublished fragment of the register of the hospital of St John the Baptist, Dublin'.

'Register of St Saviour's Chantry, Waterford', *see Registrum cantariae S. Salvatoris Waterfordensis*.

Register of the Priory of the Blessed Virgin Mary at Tristernagh, ed. M.V. Clarke (Dublin, 1941).

Register of wills and inventories of the diocese of Dublin ... 1457–1483, ed. H.F. Berry (Dublin, 1898).

Registrum cantariae S. Salvatoris Waterfordensis: B.M. Harl. 3765), ed. Gearóid Mac Niocaill, *Analecta hibernica*, no. 23 (1966), pp 135–222.

Registrum cartarum monasterii B. V. Mariae de Tristernagh ... register of the priory of ... Tristernagh, ed. M.V. Clarke (Dublin, 1941)

Registrum chartarum hospitalis Sancti Johannis Bapistae extra novam portam civitatis Dublin: register of the hospital of S. John the Baptist without the New Gate, Dublin, ed. E. St. John Brooks (Dublin 1936).

Registrum de Kilmainham: register of chapter acts of the hospital of St John of Jerusalem in Ireland, 1326–1339 ..., ed. Charles McNeill (Dublin, 1932).

Registrum Iohannis Mey: the register of John Mey, archbishop of Armagh, 1443–1456, eds W.G.H. Quigley & E.F.D. Roberts (Belfast, 1972).

'*Registum monasterii fratrum praedicatorum de Athenry*', ed. Ambrose Coleman, *Archivum Hibernicum*, I (1912), pp 201–21.

Registrum prioratus omnium sanctorum juxta Dublin, ed. Richard Butler (Dublin, 1845).

'Registry of Clonmacnoise', ed. J. O'Donovan, *Kilkenny & South-East of Ireland Archaeological Society*, II, new series (1856–57), pp 444–60.

'The Rights of MacDiarmada', ed. & trans. Nessa Ní Shéaghadha, *Celtica*, VI (1963), pp 156–72.

Regularis concordia: the monastic agreement of the monks and nuns of the English nation, eds T. Symon & F.L. Cross (London, 1953).

Reports of the Deputy Keeper of the Public Records in Ireland (Dublin, 1859–?).

'The rule of Ailbe of Emly', ed. & trans. J. O'Neill, *Ériu*, III (1907).

'The rule of Patrick', ed. & trans. J.G. O'Keeffe, *Ériu*, I (1904), pp 16–224.

Scottish verse from the book of the Dean of Lismore, ed. & trans. W.J. Watson (Edinburgh, 1837).

Select documents of the English lands of the abbey of Bec, ed. M. Chibnall (Camden 3rd Ser., LXXIII, London, 1951).

'Senchas fer n-Alban', ed. J. Bannerman, *Celtica*, VII (1966), pp 142–62; VIII (1968), pp 90–111; IX (1971), pp 217–65.

Silva Gadelica, ed. & trans. S.H. O'Grady (2 vols, London, 1892).

'Some ancient deeds of the parishes of St Catherine and St James, Dublin: 1296–1743', ed. & trans. Henry F. Twiss [Berry], *RIA Proc.*, XXXV (C) (1918–20), no. 7, pp 265–81.

'Some ancient deeds of the parish of St Werburgh, Dublin, 1243–1676', ed. & trans. H.F. Twiss [Berry] *PRIA*, XXXV (C) (1918–20), pp 282–315.

'Some unpublished texts from the Black Book of Christ Church, Dublin,' ed. & trans. Aubrey Gwynn, *Analecta Hibernica*, 16 (1946), pp 281–337.

The song of Dermot and the earl, ed. & trans. G.H. Orpen (Oxford, 1892).

Statutes of the Scottish Church: 1225–1559 (Scottish History Society, LIV, Edinburgh, 1907).

Statute rolls of the Parliament of Ireland ..., 3 vols, ed. H.F. Berry (Dublin, 1907).

Suibhne Geilt, ed. & trans. J.G. O'Keeffe (London, 1913).

Tain bó Cúailnge, ed. Cecille Ó Rahilly (Dublin, 1984).

'A thirteenth–century poem on Armagh cathedral', eds S. MacAirt & T. Ó Fiaich, *Seanchas Ardmhacha*, II (1956-7), pp 145–62.

'Three Old Irish accentual poems', ed. & trans. J. Carney, *Ériu*, XXII (1971), pp 23–80.

Topographia Hiberniae, *see* 'Giraldus Cambrensis, History and Topograhy of Ireland', *Topographical poems*, ed & trans. James Carney (Dublin, 1943).

'The Tragic Death of Cúroí Mac Dáiri', ed. & trans. R.I. Best, *Ériu*, II (1905), pp 18–29.

'The tribes and customs of Hy Many, commonly called O'Kelly's country', ed. John O'Donovan (Irish Archaeological Society, Dublin, 1843).

Tripartite life of Patrick, ed. & trans. Whitley Stokes, I (London, 1887).

'Two old Drogheda chronicles', ed. & trans. D. Mac Iomhair, *Jnl Louth Archaeological Society*, XV (1961–4), pp 88–95.

Vie et miracles de S. Laurent, archévêque de Dublin, see *Incipit vita S. Laurencii*.

'*Vita Sancti Flannani*', ed. P. Grosjean, *Analecta Bollandiana*, XLVI (1928), pp 124–41.

Vita Sanctorum Hiberniae, ed. & trans. Charles Plummer (2 vols, Oxford, 1910).

War of the Gaedhil and the Gaill, *see Cogadh Gaedhel re Gaillaibh*.

SECONDARY WORKS

Aalen, F.H.A. & Whelan, Kevin, *Dublin: from prehistory to present* (Dublin, 1992).

Alcock, E., 'Burials and cemeteries in Scotland', *The early Church in Wales and the West*, ed. N. Edwards & A. Lane (Oxford, 1992), pp 90–103.

Aldridge, R.B., 'Notes on children's burial grounds in Mayo', *JRSAI*, XCIX (1969), pp83–7.

Amt, E., *Women's lives in medieval Europe: a sourcebook* (New York and London, 1993).

Archdall, Mervyn, *Monasticon Hibernicum* (3 vols, Dublin and London, 1786).

Ariès, Philippe, *The hour of our death*, trans. H. Weaver (London, 1981); originally published as *L'homme devant la mort* (Paris 1977).

Armstrong, E.C.R., 'An account of some early Christian monuments discovered at Gallen priory', *Royal Society of Antiquaries, Ireland*, XXXVIII (1908), pp 61–6.

—, 'An incised cross-slab from Gallen Priory, Ferbane, King's Co.', *JRSAI*, XVIII (1908), pp 173–4.

Barrow, G. Lennox, 'Knights Hospitallers of St John of Jerusalem at Kilmainham', *Dublin Historical Record* (1973–5), pp 108–12.

Barrow, G.W.S., *Robert Bruce and the Community and the Realm of Scotland* (Edinburgh, 1988).

Barrow, Julia, 'Urban cemetery locations in the high Middle Ages', *Death in towns*, ed. Steven Bassett (Leicester, 1992), pp 79–100.

Barry, T.B., *The archaeology of medieval Ireland* (London, 1987).

Becker, Patricia, 'An analysis of the Dublin Guild merchant roll *c.*1190–1265', unpublished MPhil thesis, University of Dublin (Trinity College), 1995.

Bennan, P., 'Incised effigial slab at Athassel Priory', *Jnl Tipperary Hist. Soc.* (1990), pp 193–6.

Bennett, D., *Encyclopedia of Dublin* (Dublin, 1991).

Berry, H.F., 'The records of the Dublin guild of merchants,' *JRSAI*, VI (1900), pp 44–68.

Bethell, Denis, 'English monks and Irish reform in the eleventh and twelfth centuries', *Historical Studies*, VIII (1971), pp 111–35.

Bieler, Ludwig, *The Patrician texts in the Book of Armagh* (Dublin, 1979).

Bigger, F.J., 'Inis Chlothrann (Inis Cleraun), Lough Ree: its history and antiquities', *JRSAI*, VI (1900), pp 69–90.

—, 'The Franciscan friary of Kilconnell', *Jnl of the Galway Archaeological and Historical Society*, I (1900–1), pp 145–67; II (1902), pp 3–20.

Binchy, D.A., 'The fair of Tailtiu & the feast of Tara', *Ériu*, XXVIII (1958), pp 111–38.

—, 'Irish law tracts re-edited', *Coibnes Uisi Thairidne*', *Ériu*, XVII (1955), pp 52–85.

—, *'Lawyers and chroniclers', Seven centuries of Irish learning*, ed. B. Ó Cuív (Dublin, 1961; reprint Cork, 1971), pp 58–71.

—, *The linguistic and historical value of the Irish law tracts* (London, 1943).

—, 'Old Irish table of penitential commutations', *Ériu*, XIX (1962), pp 59–72.

Bitel, Lisa, *Isle of the saints* (Cornell, 1990).

—, 'Women's donations to the churches in early Ireland', *JRSAI*, CXIV (1984), pp 5–23.

Blair, John, 'Purbeck marble' in *English medieval industries*, eds J. Blair & N. Ramsay (London, 1991), pp 41–56.

Boase, T.S.R., *Boniface VIII* (London, 1933).

—, *Death in the Middle Ages* (London, 1972).

Boddington, Andy, 'Pagans, Christians and agnostics: patterns in Anglo-Saxon burial practice', *Medieval Europe: death & burial*: pre-printed papers, IV (York, 1992), pp 99–104.

Bollandus, Joannes, *Acta Sanctorum* (Paris, 1865).

Boyle, Alexander, 'St Ninian & the Life of St Monenna', *Analecta Bollandiana*, XCI (1973), pp 21–30.

Bradley, John, 'Anglo-Norman sarcophagi from Ireland', *Keimelia*, eds Gearóid Mac Niocaill & P.F. Wallace (Galway, 1988), pp 74–94.

—, 'A medieval figure at Calliaghstown, Co. Meath', *JRSAI*, X (1980), pp 149–52.

— and Manning, Conleth, 'Excavation at Duiske abbey, Graiguenamanagh, Co. Kilkenny', *PRIA*, LVI (C) (1981), pp 397–426.

Bradley, Richard, 'Anglo-Saxon cemeteries: some suggestions for research', *Anglo-Saxon cemeteries 1979*, eds P. Rahtz, T. Dickinson, & L. Watts, BAR British Ser. 82 (Oxford, 1980), pp 171–8.

Bradshaw, Brendan, *The dissolution of the religious orders in Ireland under Henry III* (Cambridge, 1974).

Brannon, N.F., 'Five excavations in Ulster 1978–1984', *UJA*, XLIX (1986), pp 89–98.

Brindley, Anna L., *Archaeological inventory of County Monaghan* (Dublin, 1986).

Brooke, Christopher, *Medieval Church and society* (New York, 1982).

Brosnan, Áine, 'Mortuary practices in the cathedral cemetery, Ardfert, Co. Kerry: a preliminary assessment', unpublished MA thesis, Univ. College Cork, Dept. of Archaeology, 1993.

Brown, Cynthia Gaskell & A. E. J. Harper, 'Excavations on Cathedral Hill, Armagh 1968', *UJA*, XLVII (1984), pp 109–61.

Brown, Peter, *Cult of the saints* (Chicago, 1981).

Buckley, Victor M., *Archaeological inventory of County Louth* (Dublin, 1986).

Butler, L., 'The churchyard in Eastern England, AD 900–1100: some lines of development', *Anglo-Saxon cemetery studies 1979*, eds P. Rahtz, T. Dickinson, & L. Watts, BAR British Ser. 82 (Oxford, 1980), pp 383–90.

—, 'Two twelfth-century lists of saints' resting places', *Analecta Bollandiana*, CV (1987), pp 87–103.

Byrne, Francis J., *Irish kings and high-kings* (London, 1973, reprint, 1983).

—, 'Senchas: the nature of Gaelic historical tradition', *Historical Studies*, IX (1974), pp 137–59.

Byrne, Paul, 'The community of Clonard, 6th–12th centuries', *Peritia*, IV (1985), pp 157–73.

Cardy, A.H. & Hill, P.H., 'In the shadow of St Ninian', *Medieval Europe: death and burial*: pre-printed papers, IV (Oxford, 1992), pp 93–8.

Carney, James. 'Literature in Irish, 1169–1534', *New history of Ireland*, A. Cosgrove, ed. (Oxford, 1993), pp 688–706.

Carver, Martin, ed., *In search of cult: archaeological investigations in honour of Philip Rahtz* (Woodbridge [England] & Rochester, New York, 1993).

Charles-Edwards, Thomas, 'Boundaries in Irish law' in *Medieval settlement*, ed. P.H. Sawyer (1976), pp 83–7.

—, 'The pastoral role of the church in the early Irish Law', in *Pastoral care before the parish*, eds J. Blair & R. Sharpe (Leicester, 1992), pp 63–77.

Childers, E.S.E. & Robert Stewart, *The story of the Royal Hospital, Kilmainham* (London, 1921).

Clyne, Miriam, 'Excavations at St Mary's Cathedral, Tuam, Co. Galway', *Jnl Galway Archaeological & Historical Society*, XLI (1987–8), pp 90–103.

Constable, Giles, 'The Liber Memoralis of Remiremont', *Religious life and thought* (London, 1979), pp 258–79.

Cooney, Gabriel. 'Irish prehistoric mortuary practice: Baurnadomeeny reconsidered', *Jnl Tipperary Hist. Society* (1991), pp 223–9.

Cosgrove, Art, *Late medieval Ireland, 1370–1541* (Dublin, 1981).

—, '*Hiberniores ipsis Hibernis': Studies in Irish history presented to R. Dudley Edwards*, eds A. Cosgrove & D. Macartney (Dublin, 1979), pp 1–14.

Crawford, Henry S., 'The early slabs at Lemanaghan, King's Co.', *JRSAI*, XLI (1911), pp 151–6.

—, 'The mural paintings and inscriptions at Knockmoy abbey', *JRSAI*, XLI (1919), pp 25–34.

Cuffe, P.. 'History of Duleek', *Riocht na Midhe*, III (1964), pp 140–54.

Curtis, Edmund, *A history of medieval Ireland from 1110 to 1513* (London, 1938).

—, 'The wars of Turlough: an historical document', *Irish Review*, II (1912–13), pp 577–86, 644–7, II (1913–14), pp 34–41.

Daniell, Christopher, *Death and burial in medieval England: 1066–1550* (London, 1977).

Davies, J.G., *A dictionary of liturgy and worship* (London, 1972).

Davies, R.R., *Conquest, coexistence and change: Wales 1063–1415* (Oxford, 1987).

—, *Domination and conquest: the experience of Ireland, Scotland and Wales, 1100–1300* (Cambridge, 1990).

—, 'Lordship or colony?', *the English in medieval Ireland*, ed. J.F. Lydon (Dublin, 1984), pp 142–60.

de Paor, Liam, 'Excavations at Mellifont abbey, Co. Louth', *PRIA*, XLVIII (C) (1969), pp 109–64.

Deiss, Lucien, *Early sources of the Liturgy* (London, 1967).

Delaney, T.G., 'Monastic burials and a gilt bronze book-cover fragment from the cathedral of the Holy Trinity, Downpatrick', *UJA*, XXXVIII, pp 57–61.

Dickinson, Tania, 'The present state of Anglo-Saxon cemetery studies', *Anglo-Saxon cemetery studies 1979*, eds P. Rahtz, T. Dickinson, & L. Watts, BAR British Ser. 82 (Oxford, 1980), pp 11–34.

Dillon, Myles, *The Cycles of the Kings* (London, 1946; reprint Dublin, 1994).

—, *Early Irish literature* (Chicago, 1948; reprint Dublin, 1994).

Dobson, Barrie, 'Citizens and chantries in late medieval York' in *Church and city: 1000–1500*, eds D. Abulafia, M. Rubin, M.J. Franklin & C. Brooke (Cambridge, 1992), pp 279–310.

Doherty, Charles, 'The basilica in early Ireland', *Peritia*, III (1984), pp 303–15.

—, 'The monastic town in early medieval Ireland', *Comparative history of urban origins in non-Roman Europe*, eds H.B. Clarke & A. Simms, BAR International Series CCLV (2 vols, Oxford, 1985), pp 45–76.

—, 'Saint Máedóc and Saint Molaisse', *Breifne*, VI (1982–86), pp 363–74.

Dolley, Michael, *Anglo-Norman Ireland* (Dublin, 1972).

Duby, Georges, *William Marshal*, trans. Richard Howard (New York, 1985).

Duffy, Seán, 'The Bruce brothers and the Irish Sea world, 1306–29', *Cambridge Medieval Celtic Studies*, XXI (1991), pp 55–86.

Duncan, A.A.M., 'The Scots' invasion of Ireland, 1315', *The British Isles, 1100–1500*, R.R. Davies (Edinburgh 1988), pp 100–17.

Edwards, Nancy & Lane, Robert, 'The archaeology of the early Church in Wales: an introduction' in *The early Church in the Wales and the West*, eds N. Edwards & A. Lane, Oxbow Monograph XVI (Oxford, 1992), pp 1–11.

—, *The archaeology of early medieval Ireland* (London, 1990).

Edwards, R.D., 'An agenda for Irish history', *Interpreting Irish history: the debate on historical revisionism, 1938–1994*, ed. Ciaran Brady (Dublin, 1994).

Empey, C.A., 'County Waterford: 1200–1300', *Waterford: history & society*, eds W. Nolan & T.P. Power (Dublin, 1992), pp 131–46.

Ennen, Edith, 'The early history of the European town: a retrospective view', *Comparative history of the urban origins of Non-Roman Europe*, eds H.B. Clarke & A. Simms, BAR International Series, CCLV (2 vols, Oxford, 1985), pp 3–14.

Etchingham, Colmán, 'Aspects of early ecclesiastical organisation', unpublished PhD thesis, Univ. of Dublin (Trinity College), 1993.

Etheridge, D.J., 'Some aspects of early medieval burial practice in southern Scotland, AD 400–1100', unpublished M.Phil thesis, Glasgow University, 1993.

Evans, E.E., *Irish folk ways* (London 1957; sixth edition, London, 1988).

Fanning, Thomas, 'Excavations at Kells priory, Co. Kilkenny', *Old Kilkenny Review*, XXV (1973), pp 61–4.

—, 'An Irish medieval tile pavement: recent excavations at Swords castle, Co. Dublin', *JRSAI*, CV (1975), pp 47–82.

—, 'Excavations at Clontuskert Priory, Co. Galway', *PRIA*, LXXVI (C) (1977), pp 97–162.

—, 'Excavation of an early Christian cemetery and settlement, Co. Kerry', LXXXI (C) (1981), pp 3–172.

Finucane, R.C., *Miracles and pilgrims: popular beliefs in medieval England* (Totowa, 1977).

—, 'Sacred corpse, profane carrion: social ideals and death rituals in the later Middle Ages', *Mirrors of mortality: studies in the social history of death*, ed. J. Whaley (London, 1981), pp 40–60.

Fitzgerald, Walter, *The historical geography of early Ireland* (London, 1925).

Fitzpatrick, William J., *The history of the Dublin Catholic cemeteries* (Dublin, 1900).

Fitzsimons, H., 'Miscellanea: Wicker Coffins', *Ríocht na Midhe*, III (1963), pp 67–8.

Fleming, Andrew & Woolfe, Alex, '*Cille Donnáin*: a late Norse church in South Uist', *Proceedings Society of Antiquaries, Scotland*, CXIII (1992), pp 329–350.

Fleming, Robert, 'Christchurch's sisters and brothers: an edition and discussion of Canterbury obituary lists', *The culture of Christendom*, ed. M.A. Bleyer (London, 1993).

Frame, Robin, *Colonial Ireland, 1169–1369* (Dublin, 1981).

Galloway, Peter, *Cathedrals of Ireland* (Belfast, 1992).

Gaskell-Brown, Cynthia, 'Excavations at Greencastle, Co. Down 1966–1970', *UJA*, XLII (1979), pp 51–65.

Geary, Patrick, *Furta Sacra: thefts of relics in the Middle Ages* (Princeton, 1990).

—, *Living with the dead in the Middle Ages* (Ithaca, NY, 1994).

—, *Phantoms of Remembrance: memory and oblivion at the end of the first Millennium* (Princeton, 1994).

Gilbert, J.T., *A history of the city of Dublin* (3 vols, Dublin, 1854–9; reprinted with index, 1861; reprinted Dublin, 1903.)

Gilchrist, Roberta & Morris, Robert, 'Monasteries as settlements: religion, society, and economy, AD 600–1050', *In search of cult: investigations in honour of Philip Rahtz*, ed. M.O. Carver (Woodbridge, 1993), pp 113–16.

Gillespie, R., 'Funerals & society in early 17th century Ireland', *JRSAI*, CXV (1985), pp 86–91.

Gittings, Clare, *Death, burial & the individual in early modern England* (London & Sydney, 1984).

Gosling, P., 'From Dún Delca to Dundalk: the topography and archaeology of a medieval frontier town AD c.1187–1700', Co. *Louth Arch. Jnl* (1991), pp 225–353.

Grabowski, K.C., 'The interaction of politics, settlement and the church in medieval Ireland: Uí Maine as a case study', unpublished PhD thesis, Cambridge University, 1989.

—, and D.N. Dumville, *Chronicles and annals of medieval Ireland and Wales* (Woodbridge, 1984].

Graves, Robert, *The white goddess* (London, 1948).

Greenhill, F.A., *Incised effigial slabs: a study of engraved stone memirals in Latin Christendom* c.*1100* to c.*1700* (London, 1976).

Gresham, Colin A., *Medieval stone carving in North Wales* (Cardiff, 1968).

Gwynn, Aubrey, 'A breviary from St Mary's Abbey, Trim', *Ríocht na Midhe*, III (1964), pp 290–328.

—, 'The Black Death in Ireland', *Studies*, XXIV (1935), pp 25–42.

—, 'Brian in Armagh', *Seanchas Ardmacha*, IX (1978), pp 35–50.

—, 'Documents relating to the medieval diocese of Armagh', *Archivum Hibernicum*, XXIII (1947), pp 1–26.

— and D.F. Gleeson, *A history of the diocese of Killaloe*, I (Dublin, 1962).

— and R. Neville Hadcock, *Medieval religious houses: Ireland* (London, 1970).

—, 'Provincial and diocesan decrees of the diocese of Dublin during the Anglo–Norman period', *Archivum Hibernicum*, XI (1944), pp 31–117.

— and Purton, W.J., 'The monastery of Tallaght', *PRIA*, XXIX (C) (1911), pp 152–79.

—, *The twelfth century reform* (Dublin & Sydney, 1968).

—, 'Were the Annals of Inisfallen written at Killaloe?', *North Munster Antiquaries Journal*, VIII (1958–61), pp 20–33.

Gyug, R.F., 'Consecration of cemeteries', *Dictionary of the Middle Ages*, III, ed. J.R. Strayer (New York, 1982), p. 541.

Hallam, Elizabeth M., 'The Eleanor crosses and royal burial customs', *Eleanor of Castile 1290–1990: essays to commemorate the 700th anniversary of her death* (Stamford, 1991), pp 9–22.

Hamlin, Ann, 'The archaeology of the early Irish Church', *Peritia*, IV (1985), pp 261–78.

—, 'The early Irish church: problems of identification', *The early Church in Wales & the West*, eds N. Edwards & A. Lane (Oxford, 1992), pp 138–44.

— and Foley, Claire. 'A woman's graveyard at Carrickmore, Co. Tyrone and the separate burial of women', *UJA*, XLVI (1983), pp 41–6.

Harbison, Peter, *Guide to the National Monuments of Ireland* (Dublin 1970).

—, *Irish art and architecture* (London, 1978).

—, 'Some medieval sculpture in Kerry', *Kerry Archaeog. Society Jnl*, VI (1973), pp 8–22.

—, 'Some medieval Thomond tomb-sculpture: lost, found, and imaginary.' *North Munster Antiquaries Journal*, XIV (1971), pp 29–36.

Harding, Vanessa, 'Burial choice and burial location in later medieval London', *Death in towns: urban responses the dying and the dead 1000–1600*, ed. Stephen Bassett (Leicester, 1992), pp 119–35.

Healy, Revd Dr, 'Two royal abbeys, Cong and Inismaine', *JRSAI*, XXXV (1905), pp 1–20.

Heist, William L., 'Irish saints lives, romance, and cultural history', *Medievalia et Humanistica: medieval hagiography & romance*, New Series, VI, ed. P. Clogan (London, 1975), pp 25–40.

Henry, Françoise & G. Marsh-Micheli, 'Manuscripts and illuminations: 1169–1603', *New history of Ireland*, ed. A. Cosgrove (Oxford, 1993), pp 780–801.

Henry, P.L. 'The land of Cokaygne: cultures in contact in medieval Ireland', *Studia Hibernica*, VII (1972), pp 120–41.

Herbert, Máire, *Iona, Kells and Derry* (Oxford, 1988; reprint Dublin, 1996).

Herity, Michael, 'The hermitage in Ardoilean', *JRSAI*, CXX (1990), pp 65–101.

Hickey, E., 'Medieval stone at St John's cemetery, Kells', *Ríocht na Midhe*, IV (1974), p. 104.

Higgins, J.G., 'Some early Christian and medieval sculpture from Coolsashin, Co. Kilkenny', *Old Kilkenny Review*, IV, 1 (1989), pp 599–610.

Hirst, Susan, 'Some aspects of the analysis and publication of an inhumation cemetery,' *Anglo-Saxon Cemeteries 1979*, BAR British Series 82 (Oxford, 1980), pp 239–54.

Hughes, Kathleen, *The Church in early Irish society* (London, 1966).

—, 'The distribution of Irish scriptoria and centres of learning from 730–1111', *Church and society in Ireland*, ed. D.N. Dumville (London, 1987).

—, *Early Christian Ireland: introduction to the sources* (London, 1972).

—, 'An Irish litany of pilgrim saints, compiled c.800', *Analecta Bollandiana*, LXXVII (1959), pp 305–32.

—, 'The office of S. Finnian of Clonard & S. Cíanán of Duleek', *Analecta Bollandiana*, LXXIII (1955), pp 342–56

—, *The sources of history: studies in the uses of historical evidence* (Cambridge 1977; reprint, 1979).

Hunt, John, *Irish medieval figure sculpture, 1200–1600* (2 vols, Dublin and London, 1974).

—, 'Rory O'Tunney and the Ossory tomb sculptures', *JRSAI*, LXXX (1950), pp 22–8.

Hurley, Maurice F., 'The early Church in the southwest of Ireland: settlement and organisation', *Early Church in Wales and the West* , eds N. Edwards & A. Lane, Oxbow Monograph XVI (Oxford, 1992), pp 53–65.

—, 'Excavations at an early ecclesiastical enclosure at Kilkieran, Co. Kilkenny', *JRSAI*, CXVIII (1988), pp 124–33.

Ivens, R.J., 'The early Christian monastic enclosure at Tullylish, Co. Down', *UJA*, I (1987), pp 55–121.

James, Heather, 'The cult of St David in the Middle Ages', *In search of cult*, ed. M.O.H. Carver (Woodbridge [England], 1993), pp 105–10.

—, 'Early medieval cemeteries in Wales', *The early Church in Wales and the West*, eds N. Edwards & A. Lane (Oxford, 1992), pp 90–103.

Jankuhn, Herbert, 'The interdisciplinary approach to the study of the early history of medieval towns', *Comparative history of urban origins in non-Roman Europe*, eds H.B. Clarke & A. Simms, BAR Int'l Series, CCLV (2 vols, Oxford, 1985), pp 15–44.

Jaski, Bart, 'Marriage laws in Ireland and on the Continent in the early Middle Ages', *The fragility of her sex: medieval Irish women in their European context*, eds C.E. Meek & M.K. Simms (Dublin, 1996).

'J.C.', 'Burial without coffins', *Journal of the Waterford and southeast archaeological society*, XV (1912), pp 197–8.

Johnson, Mark, 'The Saxon monastery at Whiby: past, present, future', *In search of Cult*, ed. M.O. Carver (Woodbridge, [England], pp 85–89.

Joyce, Patrick W., *Irish names of places* (3 vols, Dublin [no date]).

—, *A social history of ancient Ireland* (2 vols, Dublin & Belfast, 1903).

Kehnel, Annette, 'S. Ciarán's church and his lands: a study of the history and development of Clonmacnois', unpublished PhD thesis, University of Dublin (Trinity College), 1994.

Kelly, Fergus, *A guide to early Irish law* (Dublin, 1988).

Kelly, Richard J., 'St Jarlath of Tuam', *Journal of the Galway Archaeological & Historical Society*, I (1900–1901), pp 90–108.

Kendrick, T.D., 'Gallen Priory excavations 1934–5', *JRSAI*, IX (1939), pp 1–20.

Kenney, James F., *The sources for the early history of Ireland: ecclesiastical* (Dublin, 1929; reprint Dublin, 1997).

Kenny, Colum, *Kilmainham: The history of a settlement older than Dublin* (Dublin, 1995).

King, H.A., 'A thirteenth-century civilian effigy at Christ Church, Cork', *Journal of the Cork Historical and Archaeological Society*, XLII (1987), pp 47–9.

—, 'The carved stone collection in Kildare,' *Journal of the County Kildare Archaeological Society*, XVII (1987–91), pp 59–95.

Kjølbye-Biddle, Birthe, 'Disperal or concentration: the disposal of the Winchester dead over 2000 years', *Death in towns*, ed. Steven Bassett (Leicester, 1992), pp 210–39.

Klemperer, D., 'Study of burials at Hulton Abbey', *Medieval Europe: death and burial*: pre-printed papers, Society for Medieval Archaeology, York Archaeological Trust, University of York, IV (Oxford, 1992). pp 85–9.

Knox, H.F., 'The De Burgo Clans of Galway', *Journal of the Galway Archaeological & Historical Society*, I (1900), pp 124–30.

Kolsrud, Oluf, 'The Celtic bishops in the Ilse of Man, the Hebrides and Orkneys', *Zeitschrift fur celtische philologie*, 9 (1913), pp 357–79.

Laing, Lloyd, 'The Romanisation of Ireland', *Peritia*, IV (1985), pp 261–78.

Lang, J.J., 'The Castledermot hogback', *JRSAI*, CIV (1984), pp 154–8.

Lamont, W.D., *Ancient and medieval sculptured stones of Islay* (Edinburgh, 1968).

Leask, H.G., 'A cenotaph of "Strongbow's Daughter" ' at New Ross, Co. Wexford', *JRSAI*, LXXVIII, pt. 1 (1948), pp 65–7.

—, *Irish churches and monastic buildings* (3 vols, Dundalk, 1955–60).

—, 'Tullylease, Co. Cork: its church and monuments', *Journal of the Cork Historical & Archaeological Society*, 2nd Ser., part I, XLII (1938), pp 101–8.

Le Braz, Anatole, *La légende de la mort chez les Bretons Armoricains* (Paris 1928; reprint, 1990).

Le Goff, J., *Medieval civilization: 400–1500* (Oxford, 1988).

Leslie, J.B., 'Old Records of Co. Louth', *Journal County Louth Archaeological and Historical Society*, VII (1930), pp 278–9.

Lionard, Pádraig, 'Early Irish graveslabs', *PRIA*, LXI (C) (1961), pp 95–169.

Lewis, Samuel, *Topographical dictionary of Ireland* (3 vols, London, 1837).

Livingston, P., *The Fermanagh story* (Enniskillen, 1969).

Litten, Julian, *The English way of death* (London, 1991).

Liversage, G.D., 'Excavations at Dalkey Island, Co. Dublin, 1956–1959', *PRIA*, LXVI (C) (1968), pp 53–234.

Lydon, James F., *Ireland in the later middle ages* (Dublin, 1973).

—, 'The middle nation', *The English in medieval Ireland*, ed. J.F. Lydon (Dublin, 1984), pp 1–26.

Lyons, F.S.L., 'The burden of our history', *Interpreting Irish history: the debate on historical revisionism, 1938–1994*, Ciaran Brady, ed. (Dublin, 1994).

Lyne, G.J., 'Journal of a visit to Kerry in July 1788', *Journal of the Kerry Archaeological & Historical Society*, XXI (1988), pp 133–9.

Lynn, C.J., 'Excavation in the Franciscan friary church, Armagh', *UJA*, 38 (1975), pp 61–80.

Macalister, Robert A., 'An ancient cemetery, Mooretown, Ardee', *Journal of the County Louth Archaeological and Historical Society*, IV (1916), p. 61.

—, *Clonmacnoise memorial slabs* (Dublin, 1909).

—, *Corpus inscriptionum insularum Celticarum* (2 vols, Dublin, 1949).

—, 'The history and antiquities of Inis Cealtra', *PRIA*, XXXIIII (1916–17), pp 93–174.

McCone, Kim, 'Brigit in the 7th century: a saint with three lives?', *Peritia*, I (1982), pp 107–45.

McCormick, Finbar, ' A new light on burial practice', *Archaeology Ireland*, VIII (Autumn 1994), pp 27–8.

McCullough, N., *Dublin: an urban history* (Dublin, 1989).

McGovern, Alan (Ailbhe Mac Shamhráin), 'Church and polity in pre-Norman Ireland: the case of Glendalough', unpublished PhD dissertation, University of Dublin (Trinity College), 1994.

MacLysaght, E., *Irish Families* (Dublin, 1991).

McManners, J., 'Death and the French historians', *Mirrors of mortality: studies in the social history of death*, ed. J. Whaley (London, 1981), pp 106–30.

McNamara, L.F., 'An examination of the medieval Irish text *Caithréim Thoirdhealbhaigh*: the historical value', *North Munster Antiquaries Journal*, VIII (1958–61), pp 182–92.

MacNeill, Eoin, *Phrases of Irish history* (Dublin, 1919; reprint, 1968).

Mac Niocaill, Gearóid, *The medieval Irish annals*, Medieval Irish History Series, iii (Dublin, 1975).

Mallory, J.P., *In Search of the Indo-Europeans* (London 1989).

—, 'The world of Cú Chulainn: the archaeology of the Táin Bó Cúailnge', *Aspects of the Táin*, ed. J.P. Mallory (Belfast, 1992).

Manning, Conleth, 'Archaeological excavations at two church sites on Inismore, Aran Islands', *JRSAI*, CXV (1985), pp 96–120.

—, 'Excavation at Kilteel Church, Co. Kildare', *Journal of the Kildare Archaeological Society*, XVI (1981–2), pp 173–229.

—, 'The excavation of the early Christian enclosure of Killederdadrum in Lackenavorna, Co. Tipperary', *PRIA*, LXXXIV (C) (1984), pp 237–68.

—, 'St Buite, Mellifont and Toberboice', *Peritia*, III (1984), pp 324–5.

—, 'Toureen Peakaun: three new inscribed slabs', *Journal of the County Tipperary Historical Society* (1991), pp 209–14.

Marsden, J. *The tombs of the kings* (Felinfach 1994).

Marstrander, Carl, 'A new version of the battle of Mag Rath', *Ériu*, V (1911), pp 226–47.

Martin, Francis X., *No hero in the house: Diarmait Mac Murchada and the coming of the Normans to Ireland* (Dublin, 1976).

Maxwell, Sir Herbert, *A History of the House of Douglas from the earliest times down to the legislative union with England and France* (London, 1902).

Metcalf, P. & Huntington, R., *Celebrations of death: the anthropology of mortuary ritual* (Cambridge, 1991).

Mills, J., 'Sixteenth century notices of the chapels and crypts of the church of the Holy Trinity, Dublin', *JRSAI*, VI (C) (1900), pp 195–203.

Moncrieffe of that Ilk, Sir Iain, *The Highland clans*, revised edition (New York, 1982).

Mooney, Canice, 'Franciscan architecture in pre-reformation Ireland', *JRSAI*, LXXXV (C) (1955), pp 133–73; LXXXVI (1956), pp 125–69; LXXXVII (C) (1957), pp 1–38; 103–24.

Moore, Ellen W., *The fairs of medieval England* (Toronto, 1985).

Moore, M J , *Archaeological inventory of County Meath* (Dublin, 1987).

Morris, Henry, 'The battle of Faughart', *Journal of the County Louth Archaeological and Historical Society*, I (1903–7), pp 77–91.

Morris, H., 'Some Ulster proverbs', *Journal of the County Louth Archaeological and Historical Society*, IV (1918), pp 258–72.

Murphy, D., 'The distribution of early Christian monastic sites and its implications for contemporary secular settlemet in Co. Louth', *Journal of the County Louth Archaeological and Historical Society* (1992), pp 364–86.

Murphy, Margaret, 'The high cost of dying: an analysis of *pro anima* bequests in medieval Dublin', in *The Church and wealth*, eds W.J. Shiels and Diana Wood (*Studies in Church history*, XXIV, Oxford, 1987), pp 111–22.

—, 'Ecclesiastical censures: an aspect of their use in thirteenth century Dublin', *Archivum Hibernicum*, XLIV (1989), pp 89–97.

Murphy, Seán, *Bully's Acre and the Royal Hospital Kilmainham graveyards: history and inscriptions* (Dublin, 1989).

Mytum, H.C., *The origins of early Christian Ireland* (London, 1992).

Nicholls, K.W., *Gaelic and gaelicised Ireland in the middle ages* (Dublin, 1972).

Ní Dhonnchada, M., 'The lex innocentium: Adamnán's law for women, clerics and youth', *Chattel, servant and citizen*, eds M. O'Dowd & S. Wickert (Belfast, 1995), pp 58–69.

O'Brien, Elizabeth, 'Late prehistoric – early historic Ireland: the burial evidence reviewed', unpublished MPhil thesis, National University Ireland (University College Dublin), Department of Irish Studies, 1984.

—, 'A re-assessment of the "great sepulchral mound" containing a Viking burial at Donnybrook, Dublin', *Medieval Archaeology*, XXXVI (1992), pp 170–3.

Ó Corráin, Donncha, 'Topographical Notes – II', *Ériu*, XXI (1971), pp 97–9.

—, *Ireland before the Normans* (Dublin and London, 1972).

—, 'Foreign connections and domestic politics: Killaloe and the Uí Briain in twelfth century hagiography', *Ireland in early medieval Europe* , eds D. Whitelock, R. McKitterick & D.M. Dumville (Cambridge, 1982), pp 213–31.

O'Curry, Eugene, *On the manners and customs of the ancient Irish* (3 vols, London and Dublin, 1873).

Ó Dálaigh, Brian, 'History of an O'Brien stronghold: Clonroad, *c.*1210–1626', *North Munster Antiquaries Journal*, XXIX (1987), pp 16–31.

O Daly, Máirín, 'Lánellach Tigi Rích 7 Ruirech', *Ériu*, XIX (1962), pp 81–6.

O Donnabháin (O'Donovan), John, 'A study of the human remains from Tintern Abbey, Co. Wexford', unpublished MA thesis, University College, Cork 1985.

Ó Duilearga, Seámus, 'Scéalta agus seanchus Sheán Í Shé Ó Íbh Ráthach', *Béaloideas*, XXIX (1961), pp 1–153.

O'Dwyer, B., 'The annals of Connacht and Loch Cé and the monasteries of Boyle and Holy Trinity', *PRIA*, LXXII (C) (1972), pp 83–101.

Ó Fiannachta, Pádraig, 'The debate between Pádraig and Oisín', *The heroic process*, eds B. Almquist, S. Ó Catháin, P. Ó Héalaí (Dun Laoghaire, 1987), pp 183–206.

O'Gorman, T., 'On the site of the battle of Clontarf', *Journal of the Royal historical and archival association*, 4th ser., V, pp 169–78; VI, pp 444–55.

O'Hanlon, John, *Lives of the Irish saints* (10 vols, Dublin and London, 1904).

O'Keeffe, J.G., 'Colman MacDuach and Guaire', *Ériu*, II (1904), pp 43–7.

O'Keeffe, Tadhg, 'Omey and the sands of time', *Archaeology Ireland*, VIII (Summer 1994), pp 14–17.

O'Kelly, M.J., 'Church Island near Valencia, Co. Kerry,' *PRIA*, LIX (C) (1958), pp 57–136.

O'Laverty, James, 'Notes on pagan monuments in the immediate vicinity of ancient churches in the diocese of Down, and on peculiar forms of Christian interments observed in some of the ancient graveyards', *Journal of the Royal Historical and Archaeological Association of Ireland*, V, pt 1 (1879).

Olmstead, Garret S., 'Irish hilltop enclosures', *Études Celtiques* (1979), pp 171–85.

O Lochlainn, Colm, 'Roadways in ancient Ireland', *Féil-sgríbhinn Eóin mhic Néill*, eds J. Ryan & E. McNeill (Dublin, 1938; reprint Dublin, 1995), pp 465–74.

O'Rahilly, T., *Early Irish history and mythology* (Dublin, 1946).

—, 'The history of the Stowe missal', *Ériu*, X (1926–28), pp 95–109.

Ó Riain, P., 'Boundary association in early Irish society', *Studia Celtica*, VII (1972), pp 12–29.

—, 'Pagan example and Christian practice: a reconsideration', *Cultural identity and cultural intergration: Ireland & Europe in the early Middle Ages*, ed. Doris Edel (Dublin, 1995), pp 144–56.

—, 'The Tallaght martyrologies redated', *Cambridge medieval Celtic studies*, XX (Winter 1990), pp 25, 37–8.

Orpen, G.H., *Ireland under the Normans, 1169–1333* (4 vols, Oxford, 1968).

—, *Song of Dermot and the earl*, ed. G.H. Orpen (Oxford, 1892).

Ó Súilleabhán, Seán, 'Adhlacadh leanbhaí', *JRSAI*, lxix (1939), pp 143–51.

—, *A handbook of Irish folklore* (Dublin, 1942).

—, *Irish wake amusements* (Cork, 1967).

Otway-Ruthven, A.J., *A history of medieval Ireland* (London, 1968; 2nd edition, 1980).

Palmer, R.C., *The county courts of medieval England: 1150–1350* (Princeton, 1982).

Panofsky, Erwin, *Tomb sculpture* (London, 1964).

Parsons, David, 'Stone', *English medieval industries*, eds J. Blair & N. Ramsay (London, 1991), pp 1–28.

Pearce, S.M., Radford. C.R., eds, *Early Church in western Britain and Ireland*, BAR Ser. CII (Oxford, 1982.)

Plummer, Charles, 'Notes on some passages in the Brehon Laws III', *Ériu*, IX (1921), pp 109–17.

Podhradsky, G., *New dictionary of the Liturgy* (London, 1967).

Powell, D., 'St Patrick's Confession and the Book of Armagh', *Analecta Bollandiana*, XCIX (1972), pp 371–85.

Power, Catryn, 'Glenbane: excavation of medieval church and graveyard', *Journal Tipperary Historical Society* (1989), pp 137–45.

—, 'Human Skeletal Remains', *Late Viking Age and Medieval Waterford: Excavations 1986–1992*, eds M.F. Hurley & O. Scully (Waterford).

Prendergast, E, 'Burial at Rossmakay, Co. Louth', *Journal County Louth Archaeological and Historical Society*, XIV (1957), pp 38–9.

Prestwich, M., *Edward I* (London, 1988).

Puckle, Bertram, *Funeral customs: their origin and development* (London, 1926).

Rae, E.C., 'Irish sepulchral monuments of the later middle ages', *JRSAI*, C (1970), pp 1–318, 101, CI (1971), pp 1–39.

— 'The Rice monument in Waterford cathedral', *PRIA*, LXIX (C)(1970), pp 1–15.

—, 'Architecture and sculpture: 1169–1603', *New history of Ireland*, ed. A. Cosgrove (1993), pp 737–78.

Rahtz, Philip, 'Irish settlement in Somerset', *PRIA*, LXXVI (C)(1977), pp 223–9.

Ramsay, Nigel, 'Alabaster', *English medieval industries*, eds J. Blair & N. Ramsay (London, 1991), pp 29–40.

Reynolds, Roger. E., 'Death and burial in Europe', *Dictionary of the Middle Ages*, ed. J.R. Strayer (New York, 1983), III, p. 118–22.

Richardson, H.G. and Sayles, G.O., *The administration of Ireland, 1172–1377* (Dublin, 1963).

Roe, Helen, 'A carved stone at Castledermot, Co. Kildare', *JRSAI*, XCVII (1967), pp 179–80.

Rollason, David, *Saints and relics in Anglo-Saxon England* (Oxford, 1989).

Rudolf, Conrad, *Things of greater importance: Bernard of Clairvaux's 'Apologia' & the medieval attitude toward art* (Philadelphia, 1990).

Rutherford, R., *The death of a Christian* (New York, 1980).

Rynne, Étienne, 'Ancient Burials at Ballinlough, Co. Laois', *Journal of the County Kildare Archaeological Society*, XV (1962), pp 430–3.

—, 'Meiler de Bermingham's tombstone,' *Journal of the Galway Archaeological Society*, XLI (1987–8), pp 144–7.

Sawyer, P.H., 'Early medieval English settlement', *Medieval settlement: continuity and change*, ed. P. Sawyer (London, 1976), pp 1–10

Sellevold, B.J., 'Burials in medieval Norwegian monasteries', *Medieval Europe: death & burial*: pre-printed papers, IV (York, 1992).

Sharpe, Richard, *Medieval Irish saints' lives* (Oxford, 1991).

Simms, Katharine, 'Bardic poetry as a historical source', *The writer as witness: literature as historical evidence*, Tom Dunne, ed., *Historical Studies*, XVI (Cork, 1987), pp 58–75.

—, 'Bards and Barons: the Anglo-Irish aristocracy and the native culture', *Medieval frontier societies*, eds R. Bartlett & A. Mackay (Oxford, 1989), pp 177–97.

—, 'The Battle of Dysert O'Dea and the Gaelic resurgence in Thomond', *Dal gCais*, V (1979), pp 59–66.

—, 'The Norman invasion and the Gaelic recovery', *The Oxford illustrated history of Ireland*, ed. Roy F. Foster (Oxford, 1989), pp 53–102.

—, 'The O'Reillys and the kingdom of East Breifne', *Breifne*, V (1979), pp 305–19.

—, 'Propaganda use of the *Táin* in the later middle ages', *Celtica*, XV (1983) pp 142–9.

Simpson, Linzi, *The excavations at Isolde's Tower, Dublin* (Dublin, 1994).

Smyth, A.P., *Celtic Leinster: towards a historical geography of early Irish civilisations, AD 500–1600* (Dublin, 1982).

—, 'The earliest Irish annals: their first contemporary entries,' *PRIA*, LXXIV (C) (1972), pp 1–48.

Stalley, R., *Architecture and sculpture in Ireland, 1150–1350* (Dublin, 1971).

—, 'Corcomroe abbey: some observations on its architectural history', *JRSAI*, CV (1985), pp 21–46.

—, 'The medieval sculpture of Christ Church cathedral, Dublin', *Archaeologia*, CVI (1979), pp 107–22.

—, 'Mellifont abbey: some observations on its architectural history', *Studies*, LXIV (1975), pp 107–22.

Steer, K.A. & Bannerman, J.W.M., *Late medieval monumental sculpture in the West Highlands* (Edinburgh, 1977).

Swan, Leo, 'Excavations at Kilpatrick churchyard Killucan, Co. Westmeath', *Ríocht na Midhe*, VI (1976), pp 89–96.

Sweetman, P.D., 'Archaeological excavations at Abbeyknockmoy, Co. Galway', *PRIA*, LXXXVII(C) (1987), pp 1–12.

—, 'Archaeological excavations at Ferns castle, Co. Wexford', *PRIA*, LXXIX (C)(1979), pp 217–45.

—, 'Archaeological excavations at St John's Priory, Newtown Trim, Co Meath.' *Ríocht na Midhe*, VIII, *Journal of the County Louth Archaeological and Historical Society* (1990), pp 88–104.

— 'Archaeological excavations at Trim castle, Co. Meath, 1971–74', *PRIA*, LXXVIII (C) (1978), pp 127–98.

Tempest, H.G., 'Graves discovered at Dundalk in 1881', *Journal of the County Louth Archaeological and Historical Society*, XII (1952), pp 251–2.

Thackeray, William Makepeace, *The Irish sketch book* (Belfast, 1985).

Thomas, Charles, *The early Christian archaeology of north Britain: the Hunter Marshall lectures* (Oxford, 1971).

—, 'The early church in Wales and the West', *The early Church in Wales and the West*, eds N. Edwards & A. Lane (Oxford, 1992), pp 145–9.

Tohall, P., 'The Dobhar-Chú tombstone of Glenade, Co. Leitrim', *JRSAI*, LXXVIII (1948), pp 127–9.

Urquhart, J.J., 'Lollards', *Catholic Encyclopedia*, XV (New York, 1910), pp 333–5.

van de Noort, Robert, 'Early medieval barrows in Western Europe' M*edieval Europe: death & burial*, pre-printed papers, IV (York, 1992), pp 29–34.

Viking settlement in medieval Dublin, T. Crooks, co-ordinator, Curriculum development unit; (Dublin, 1978).

Waddell, J. & Holland, P., 'The Peakaun site: Duignan's 1944 investigations', *Journal of the Tipperary Historical Society*(1990), 165–81.

Wakeman, W.F., 'The antiquities of Inis Muiredaich', *Royal Irish Historical & Archaeological Society*, VII (1885), pp 184–329.

Walsh, Paul, *Irish men of learning*, ed. Colm O Lochlainn (Dublin, 1947).

—, 'The monastic settlement on Rathlin O'Byrne Island, Co. Donegal', *JRSAI*, CXIII (1983), pp 53–66.

Ward, Jennifer C., 'The English noblewoman and her family in the later Middles Ages', *'The fragility of her sex'?*, eds C.E.Meek & M.K. Simms (Dublin, 1996).

Waterman D.M., 'An early Christian mortuary house at Saul, Co. Down' *UJA*, XXIII (1960), pp 82–8.

—, 'Banagher Church, Co. Derry', *UJA*, XXXIX (1976), pp 25–39.

Watt, J.A., 'Approaches to the history of fourteenth-century Ireland', *New history of Ireland*, A. Cosgrove, ed. (Oxford, 1994), pp 303–12.

—, 'The church and the two nations in late medieval Armagh', *The churches, Ireland, and the Irish*, eds W.J. Shiels and Diana Wood, Studies in Church history, XXV (Oxford, 1989), pp 37–45.

—, *The Church in medieval Ireland* (Dublin, 1972).

—, 'Ecclesia inter Anglicos et inter Hibernicos: confrontation and coexistence in the medieval diocese and province of Armagh', *The English in medieval Ireland*, ed. J. Lydon (Dublin, 1984).

—, 'English law and the Irish church: the reign of Edward I', *Medieval studies presented to A. Gwynn* (1961), pp 133–67.

Webb, J.J., *The guilds of Dublin* (Dublin, 1929).

Westropp, T.J.,. 'The Augustinian houses of the Co. Clare: Clare, Killone and Inchicronan', *JRSAI*, VI (1900), pp 11–35.

—, 'Ennis Abbey and the O'Brien tombs', *JRSAI*, XXV (1895), pp 135–54.

—, 'Paintings in Adare Abbey, County Limerick,' *JRSAI*, XLV (1915), pp 151–2.

—, 'St Mochulla of Tulla, Co. Clare', *JRSAI*, XLI (1911), pp 5–19.

Williams, Bernadette, 'The late Franciscan Anglo–Irish annals of Medieval Ireland', unpublished PhD thesis, University of Dublin (Trinity College), Dept of Med. Hist. (1992).

Wilson, John, *The English martyrology* (1602; reprint London, 1975.)

Witoszek, N. & Sheeran, P., *The Irish funerary tradition* (Galway, 1990).

Yates, M.J., 'Preliminary Excavations at Movilla (sic) Abbey, Co. Down, 1980', *UJA*, XLVI (1983), pp 53–89.

Yorke, B., 'Anglo-Saxon royal burial: the documentary evidence', *Medieval Europe: death & burial*, pre-printed papers, IV (York, 1992), pp 41–6.

WORKS OF REFERENCE

AA Road Atlas of Ireland

Archaeological survey of Northern Ireland (Belfast, 1966)

The complete Peerage of England, Scotland, Ireland and Great Britain under the United Kingdom, eds G.E. Cokayne, et al. (London, 1916 forward)

Contributions to a dictionary of the Irish language (RIA Dict.), eds M. Joynt, E. Knott, E.G. Quin, C.J. Marstrander, M. O Daly & A. O'Sullivan (Dublin, 1913–76).

Councils and Synods, eds M. Brett, C.N.L. Brooke, D. Whitelock (2 vols, Oxford, 1981).

Councils & Synods: 1205–1265, eds F.M. Powicke & C.R. Cheney (Oxford, 1964).

Dineen's dictionary of the Irish language, eds Patrick S. Dineen (Dublin, 1904).

Dublin c.840–c.1540: the medieval town in the modern city (map produced by Ordnance Survey of Ireland, Dublin, 1978).

Handbook of British chronology, eds E.B. Fryde, D.E. Greenway, S. Porter & I. Roy (Royal Historical Society, 3rd edition, London, 1986).

Index to the townlands and towns, parishes and baronies of Ireland, based on the census of 1851, ed. W. Donnelly (London, 1861; reprint Baltimore, 1984).

Map of medieval Dublin: c.840–1540, prepared by H. Clarke (OPW, Dublin, 1978).

Mediae latinitatis lexicon minus, ed. E.J. Brill (Leiden, 1984).

Monastic map of Ireland (2nd edn), prepared by R.N. Hadcock, Ordnance Survey Office (Dublin, 1979).

Onomasticon Goedelicum locorum et tribuum Hiberniae et Scotiae, ed. Edmund Hogan (Dublin, 1910; reprint Dublin, 1993)

Ordnance survey road map of Ireland (Dublin, 1993).

The Oxford dictionary of saints, ed. D.H. Farmer (2nd edn., Oxford, 1987).

Oxford dictionary of the Christian church, ed. F.L. Cross (London, 1957).

Oxford English dictionary, eds J.A. Simpson & E.S.C. Weiner (2nd edn, Oxford, 1989).

Revised medieval Latin word-list, ed. R.E. Latham (London, 1965).

Shorter Oxford English dictionary, ed. C.T. Onions (Oxford, 1959).

Sloinnte Gaedheal is Gall (Irish names and surnames), ed. Patrick Woulfe (Dublin, 1923).

Index

UNIVERSITY OF PLYMOUTH
LIBRARY SERVICES (PLYMOUTH)

DEVON LIBRAT